# Lecture Notes in Computer Science 7059

Commenced Publication in 1973
Founding and Former Series Editors:
Gerhard Goos, Juris Hartmanis, and Jan va

Andreas Harth   Nora Koch (Eds.)

# Current Trends
# in Web Engineering

Workshops, Doctoral Symposium, and Tutorials
Held at ICWE 2011
Paphos, Cyprus, June 20-21, 2011
Revised Selected Papers

 Springer

Volume Editors

Andreas Harth
Karlsruher Institut für Technologie (KIT)
Institut AIFB
Englerstraße 11
76128 Karlsruhe, Germany
E-mail: harth@kit.edu

Nora Koch
Ludwig-Maximilians-Universität
Oettingenstraße 67
80538 München, Germany
E-mail: kochn@pst.ifi.lmu.de

ISSN 0302-9743                         e-ISSN 1611-3349
ISBN 978-3-642-27996-6                 e-ISBN 978-3-642-27997-3
DOI 10.1007/978-3-642-27997-3
Springer Heidelberg Dordrecht London New York

Library of Congress Control Number: 2011945290

CR Subject Classification (1998): H.5, H.4, H.3, K.6, D.2, C.2, H.3.5, H.5.3

LNCS Sublibrary: SL 3 – Information Systems and Application, incl. Internet/Web
and HCI

*Typesetting:* Camera-ready by author, data conversion by Scientific Publishing Services, Chennai, India

Printed on acid-free paper

Springer is part of Springer Science+Business Media (www.springer.com)

# Foreword

The series of the International Conference on Web Engineering (ICWE) promotes scientific and practical excellence on Web Engineering, and brings together researchers and practitioners working with technologies, methodologies, tools, and techniques used to develop and maintain Web-based applications.

The 11th edition of ICWE extended its conference program with workshops, a doctoral symposium and tutorials providing a complementary overview on current research issues. The main topics covered all aspects of enabling and improving the dissemination and use of content and services through the Web: Web application engineering, Web service engineering, and Web data engineering. In particular, the workshops offered Web engineering researchers and practitioners highly interactive sessions including in-depth presentations on focused topics and a discussion forum on emerging challenges. Within the scope of the doctoral symposium, PhD students presented their approaches and preliminary results to obtain constructive feedback from experts. Tutorials held by senior Web engineering researchers provided a wide overview on their particular research activities.

The ICWE 2011 conference and its satellite events took place in Paphos (Cyprus) during June 20–24, 2011. It followed editions of the conference in Vienna (Austria), San Sebastián (Spain), Yorktown Heights NY (USA), Como (Italy), Palo Alto CA (USA), Sydney (Australia), Munich (Germany), Oviedo (Spain), Santa Fé (Argentina) and Cáceres (Spain).

This volume contains the papers presented at the workshops and the doctoral symposium, as well as the tutorial summaries. The workshop Program Committee selected seven proposals from ten submissions; due to few submissions one was canceled and the following six workshops were held during June 20–21, 2011.

- Third International Workshop on Lightweight Composition on the Web (ComposableWeb)
- First International Workshop on Search, Exploration and Navigation of Web Data Sources (ExploreWeb)
- Second International Workshop on Enterprise Crowdsourcing (EC)
- 7th Model-Driven Web Engineering Workshop (MDWE)
- Second International Workshop on Quality in Web Engineering (QWE)
- Second Workshop on the Web and Requirements Engineering (WeRE)

The doctoral symposium and four tutorials complemented the conference and workshop program. The doctoral symposium in particular provided helpful feedback to the PhD students and special motivation for their work in the Web engineering field. The tutorials accepted were two full-day presentations: "Multi-Dimensional Context-Aware Adaptation for Web Applications" and "Automating the Use of Web APIs Through Lightweight Semantics," and two half-day presentations: "Context-Aware Adaptation for Web Applications" and "Improving Quality in Use of Web Applications in a Systematic Way."

We thank the ICWE 2011 conference General Chair, George Papadopoulos, and the Program Chairs, Oscar Diaz and Sören Auer, for their constant support in our work. We would like to thank the members of the Program Committee for selecting high-quality workshops, and the organizers of the workshops for providing a world-class program and leading fruitful discussions during the workshop days. Our gratitude goes to the Doctoral Symposium and Tutorial Chairs. Finally, a special thanks to all researchers and students who contributed with their work, presentation and participation to the success of the ICWE 2011 satellite events: workshops, doctoral consortium and tutorials.

September 2011                                           Andreas Harth
                                                          Nora Koch

# Organization

## Workshop Program Committee

| | |
|---|---|
| Andreas Abecker | FZI Forschungszentrum Informatik, Germany |
| Fabio Casati | University of Trento, Italy |
| Federico Facca | Create Net, Italy |
| Athula Ginige | University of Western Sydney, Australia |
| Alexander Knapp | Universität Augsburg, Germany |
| Maristella Matera | Politecnico Milano, Italy |
| Martin Nussbaumer | Karlsruhe Institute of Technology, Germany |
| Luis Olsina | Universidad Nacional de La Pampa, Argentina |
| Oscar Pastor | Universidad de Valencia, Spain |
| Gustavo Rossi | Universidad Nacional de La Plata, Argentina |
| Marco Winkler | University Paul Sabatier, Toulouse, France |

# Preface

The preface of this volume presents the prefaces of the workshop proceedings of the individual workshops, the PhD symposium and the tutorials. The papers of the workshops and the PhD symposium as well as the summaries on the tutorials are grouped by event and can be found in the body of the volume.

## Third International Workshop on Lightweight Composition on the Web (ComposableWeb 2011)

**Organizers:** Florian Daniel, Sven Casteleyn, and Geert-Jan Houben

The third edition of ComposableWeb was again held in conjunction with the International Conference on Web Engineering (ICWE), which took place this year in Paphos, Cyprus. As such, ComposableWeb has become part of this conference and of its workshop program, a result we are particularly glad of.

The workshop focuses on research, practical experiences, and novel ideas in the context of component-based development of Web applications, lightweight composition on the Web, Web 2.0, and mashups. The goal of the workshop is to provide a discussion forum bringing together researchers and practitioners working in these areas, in order to jointly advance current state-of-the-art solutions. The topics of the workshop typically attract enthusiastic people that like to play with novel technologies and that try to make application development accessible also to less skilled developers or – as envisioned by many – even to end-users. Submissions typically range from mature works to position or vision papers.

The scientific program of the 2011 edition of the workshop consisted of nine papers, spanning a variety of topics. All submissions went through a rigorous blind review process by our Program Committee, and only submissions with positive feedback were selected for publication. Among accepted papers, the reader will find a survey on mashup tools, a semantics-based approach to mashup development, a recommendation approach of mashup components, telco mashups, a W3C widget extension for inter-widget communication, cross-domain communications, linking-based protocols for RESTful interactions, transaction support for RESTful services, and security support for mashups.

We intended to re-use last year's successful workshop format, with a whole day of paper presentations and a final demonstration and discussion session, in which also participants without an accepted paper could showcase their ideas and results. For organizational reasons, however, this year we hosted three papers of the Second International Workshop on Enterprise Crowdsourcing in the last session of the day, which focused on crowd-adapted Web applications, human computation, and crowd-assisted IT management (all contributions can be found in this proceedings volume). This unexpected merge yielded a dense and interesting program with unexpected interaction points among the two workshops and good opportunities for cross-fertilization.

We would like to thank all the authors who contributed to the workshop with their papers and presentations, our Program Committee for the constructive and competent feedback, and the audience for actively participating in the discussions. We thank Maja Vuković and Claudio Bartolini, the organizers of the Enterprise Crowdsourcing Workshop, for contributing to ComposableWeb 2011. Finally, we thank the ICWE Organizers and Workshop Chairs for hosting the workshop and providing a nice, relaxed, and constructive environment.

July 2011                                                      Florian Daniel
                                                              Sven Casteleyn
                                                            Geert-Jan Houben

# Organization

## Program Committee

| Luciano Baresi | Politecnico di Milano, Italy |
| Boualem Benatallah | University of New South Wales, Australia |
| Fabio Casati | University of Trento, Italy |
| Francisco Curbera | IBM Research, USA |
| Olga De Troyer | Vrije Universiteit Brussel, Belgium |
| Schahram Dustdar | Technical University of Vienna, Austria |
| Peep Kúngas | University of Tartu, Estonia |
| Maristella Matera | Politecnico di Milano, Italy |
| John Musser | ProgrammableWeb.com, USA |
| Tobias Nestler | SAP, Germany |
| Moira Norrie | ETH Zurich, Switzerland |
| Cesare Pautasso | University of Lugano, Switzerland |
| Florian Rosenberg | IBM Research, USA |
| Gustavo Rossi | Universidad Nacional de La Plata, Argentina |
| Takehiro Tokuda | Tokyo Institute of Technology, Japan |

## External Reviewers

| Benjamin Satzger | Technical University of Vienna, Austria |
| Stefano Soi | University of Trento, Italy |
| Carlos Rodriguez | University of Trento, Italy |

# Search, Exploration and Navigation of Web Data Sources (exploreWeb 2011)

**Organizers:** Marco Brambilla, Piero Fraternali, and Daniel Schwabe

The First International Workshop on Search, Exploration and Navigation of Web Data Sources (exploreWeb 2011) was held on June 20, 2011 in Paphos, Cyprus.

The motivation for this initiative stands in the exponential growth of data sources available on the Web and in the need of devising efficient information exploration options to the users. Web data providers offer a plethora of different ways of accessing their data sources, spanning from APIs (e.g., Google APIs, location-based APIs, and so on) to proprietary query languages (such as Yahoo! Query Language, YQL) to endpoints accessible through standard query languages (e.g., SPARQL). This trend is associated with the increased tendency toward labeling, tagging, and linking data semantically, as pushed also by social networking applications (e.g., social bookmarking, user networks, and so on).

These data sources expose their content as semi-structured information (e.g., JSON, XML, ...) and more and more enrich it in the form of the so-called linked data cloud, with uri-based references between the resources. This is a major change of paradigm with respect to traditional Web publishing. On the one hand, it enormously facilitates access and querying of information with respect to the old-fashioned page-based Web paradigm. On the other hand, however, this challenges the current approaches to Web navigation and information collection by end users. With the growth of the available open and linked data, the need arises for effective mechanisms targeted to human users for searching, exploring, and consuming such data.

Cross-fertilization between different disciplines is mandatory for this purpose: exploratory search approaches should be merged with usability and cognitive science to identify the best interaction paradigms over such new data sources; Web engineering approaches should be extended with data integration and Semantic Web /linked data-based practices (such as knowledge exploration tools) to connect linked and non-linked data, and to provide proper navigational applications to the end users.

The initiative was very successful: the workshop got 12 submissions, of which 7 were accepted for presentation. The program also included an extremely interesting invited talk by Sóren Auer on "Exploration and Other Stages of the Linked Data Life Cycle." Such a life cycle comprises the following phases: extraction, storage and querying, authoring, linking, evolution, exploration, and visualization. The keynote raised a lively discussion that continued throughout the day after each paper had been presented.

The workshop was organized into four sessions: the first one was dedicated to the keynote talk; the second one was on linked data exploration; the third one was on tag clouds and NLP; and the fourth one dealt with Web data navigation and exploration.

The first paper of the linked data exploration session was written by Alessandro Bozzon, Marco Brambilla, Emanuele Della Valle and Chiara Pasini (from Politecnico di Milano) and presented a "Conceptual Framework for Linked Data Exploration Based on the Search Computing Infrastructure." Then Marcelo Cohen and Daniel Schwabe (from PUC-Rio) presented their paper dealing with "Support for Reusable Explorations of Linked Data in the Semantic Web."

In the tag clouds and NLP session the presented paper included: "Generation of Semantic Clouds Based on Linked Data for Efficient Multimedia Semantic Annotations," by Han-Gyu Ko and In-Young Ko from Korea Advanced Institute of Science and Technology; "Segmentation of Geo-Referenced Queries," presented by Mamoun Abu Helou, from Politecnico di Milano; and "SimSpectrum: A Similarity-Based Spectral Clustering Approach to Generate a Tag Cloud," written by Frederico Durao, Peter Dolog, Martin Leginus and Ricardo Lage from Aalborg University.

Finally, the Web data navigation and exploration session included the presentations of the following works: "Graph Access Pattern Diagrams (GAP-D): Towards a Unified Approach for Modeling Navigation over Hierarchical, Linear and Networked Structures," written by Matthias Keller and Martin Nussbaumer (from Karlsruhe Institute of Technology, KIT); and "Data-Driven and User-Driven Multidimensional Data Visualization" written by Rober Morales-Chaparro, Juan Carlos Preciado and Fernando Sanchez-Figueroa (from University of Extremadura).

The resources related to the workshop (including the presentation used by the speakers) are available online on the exploreWeb website at:
http://exploreweb.search-computing.org .

We wish to thank the ICWE 2011 Organizing Committee, the ExploreWeb Program Committee that did a great job in reviewing the submitted papers, and the Search Computing project (http://www.search-computing.org) that sponsored the event.


June 2011                                          Marco Brambilla
                                                    Piero Fraternali
                                                    Daniel Schwabe

# Organization

## Program Committee

| | |
|---|---|
| Alessandro Bozzon | Politecnico di Milano, Italy |
| Marco Brambilla | Politecnico di Milano, Italy |
| Sven Casteleyn | Universidad Politécnica de Valencia, Spain |
| Mathieu D'Aquin | The Open University, UK |
| Florian Daniel | University of Trento, Italy |
| Tommaso Di Noia | Politecnico di Bari, Italy |
| Oscar Diaz | University of the Basque Country, Spain |
| Alan Dix | Talis, UK |
| Peter Dolog | Aalborg University, Denmark |
| Federico Facca | Create-Net, Italy |
| Piero Fraternali | Politecnico di Milano, Italy |
| Michael Grossniklaus | Portland State University, USA |
| Nora Koch | Ludwig-Maximilians-Universität München, Germany |
| Maristella Matera | Politecnico di Milano, Italy |
| Santiago Meliá | University of Alicante, Spain |
| Gabriella Pasi | Università degli Studi di Milano Bicocca, Italy |
| Oscar Pastor | University of Valencia, Spain |
| Cesare Pautasso | University of Lugano, Switzerland |
| Fernando Sanchez Figueroa | Universidad de Extremadura, Spain |
| Daniel Schwabe | PUC-Rio, Brazil |
| Giovanni Tummarello | DERI, National University of Ireland Galway, Ireland |

# Second International Workshop on Enterprise Crowdsourcing (EC 2011)

**Organizers:** Maja Vuković and Claudio Bartolini

Web 2.0 provides the technological foundations upon which the crowdsourcing paradigm evolves and operates, enabling networked experts to work collaboratively or competitively to complete a specific task. Crowdsourcing has the potential to significantly transform Web-enabled business processes by incorporating the knowledge and skills of globally distributed experts to drive business objectives at shorter cycles and lower cost. Many interesting and successful examples exist, such as TopCoder and Amazon Mechanical Turk. Global enterprises are increasingly adopting crowdsourcing given the ease of access to a scalable workforce online. In this context, crowdsourcing takes many different shapes and forms, from mass data collection to enabling end-user driven customer support services. However, to fully adopt this mechanism in enterprises and benefit from appealing value propositions in terms of reducing the time-to-value, a set of challenges remain to be solved.

Based on the increasing number of applications, and platforms that provide crowdsourcing capabilities, this workshop seeks to identify novel enterprise crowdsourcing applications and use them to derive requirements for common protocols and reusable Web service components, leading to a set of standardized interfaces for supporting them.

The first paper paper written by Nebeling and Norrie highlighted an interesting application of crowdsourcing to enable context-aware and adaptive Web interfaces. With the ever-increasing range and diversity of Web browser properties, crowdsourcing provides a low-cost alternative to enabling a wider range of use contexts to which Web applications can adapt. Nebeling positioned this application of crowdsourcing within the most recent crowdsourcing taxonomy by Quinn and Benderson. The key challenge in this work is how to design a suitable ranking model when crowd workers supply multiple adaptations.

In his presentation Lukas Biewald of CrowdFlower discussed opportunities for new business models on top of existing crowdsourcing marketplaces, providing quality assurance capabilities. For example, quality-controlled human intelligence is being employed to weed through business listings and company information to ensure the correctness of data for CrowdFlower clients. Beyond business-driven tasks, CrowdFlower also enables volunteering-type tasks through their GiveWork iPhone application, developed jointly with Samasource, allowing people in developing countries to complete short tasks that are used for training purposes.

Tata Consultancy Services introduced the use of crowdsourcing internally within the enterprise, with a resulting improvement of the efficiency of their software engineering processes. Untapped talent, such as new trainees, and experts not practicing fully their technical skills are being exposed to challenging tasks, introducing the disruptive resource allocation model. The proposed system enables a reputation model, as means of motivating the participation of in-house experts. Vuković presented how crowdsourcing mechanisms can be applied within large IT organizations to drive end-to-end on-cloud migration processes. Different crowds of experts, such as application owners, system administrators, business analysts, are harnessed to gather the knowledge that is critical to identifying migration candidates, evaluating the feasibility and impact of this transformation to existing business processes. The key challenge is how to design sustainable incentives, as the crowd may be engaged multiple times during the process.

As crowdsourcing examples abound in enterprise, in scientific and public domains, open questions remain. How can we carry over human relationships arising from the social context to the online work marketplaces? The question of setting effective incentives remains, both for attracting high performers, but also for rewarding and retaining top contributors.

July 2011

Maja Vuković
Claudio Bartolini

# Organization

## Program Committee

| | |
|---|---|
| Daren Brabham | University of Utah, USA |
| Fabio Casati | University of Trento, Italy |
| Schahram Dustdar | Technical University of Vienna, Austria |
| Yaniv Corem | IBM Research, Israel |
| Vassilis Kostakos | University of Madeira, Portugal |
| Osamuyimen Stewart | IBM Research, USA |

# 7th Model-Driven Web Engineering Workshop (MDWE 2011)

**Organizers:** Gustavo Rossi, Geert-Jan Houben, Marco Brambilla, and Santiago Meliá

The International Workshop on Model-Driven Web Engineering (MDWE 2011) was held in conjunction with the 11th International Conference on Web Engineering (ICWE 2011) in Paphos (Cyprus) on July 21, 2011. MDWE promotes a trend with growing importance in Web application development, which is currently moving from ad-hoc implementations mainly focused on the application of innovative technologies and methods to a more systematic development principally oriented to model-driven, automatic generation, maintenance and modernization of Web systems. In the Web Engineering field, elements such as models, meta-models, model transformations and tools, which are all essential in model-driven approaches, are gaining more and more relevance possibly due to the increasing number of scenarios in which they have successfully proven to be useful.

In this year's edition of the workshop, the five accepted papers addressed a wide set of topics and proposed several approaches for automating the development process of Web applications. The topics covered the whole spectrum of current Web applications from the client or user interface (using traditional Web applications or rich Internet applications) to the server (generating service-oriented architectures, SOAs). Moreover, the proposals introduced the most recent techniques in the field of model-driven engineering (e.g., architecture-centric MDA, aspect-oriented development or modernization) to improve the current Web development processes.

In particular, the first paper, "Aspect-Oriented Modeling of Web Applications with HiLA," by Gefei Zhang and Matthias Hölzl, presented an aspect-oriented, model-driven approach aiming to avoid potential interferences between Web engineering concerns and also to specify feature combinations. Regarding the service-oriented architecture topic, Achilleas Achilleos, Georgia Kapitsaki and George Papadopoulos presented their work, "A Model-Driven Framework for Developing Web-Oriented Applications," which specifies multi-platform mobile applications with a client-side DSL model using a PML and an SOA server with WSDL. The third paper titled "Developing Enterprise Web Applications Using the Story-Driven Modeling Approach" (by Christoph Eickhoff, Nina Geiger, Marcel Hahn and Albert Zündorf) introduces an adaptation of the Fujaba Process to support the generation of enterprise Web applications (also called RIAs), implemented using the Google Web Toolkit framework.

Eban Escott, Paul Strooper, Paul King and Ian J. Hayes, in their paper "Model-Driven Web Form Validation with UML and OCL," employed architecture-centric MDA (AC-MDA) techniques that, starting from an analysis of implementation of a set of target Web forms, derive a collection of models and transformations capable of representing and generating them, respectively. Finally, "Modernization of Legacy Web Applications into Rich Internet Applications" (by Roberto Rodriguez-Echeverria, Jose Maria Conejero, Pedro J. Clemente, Juan Carlos Preciado and Fernando Sanchez-Figueroa) was the last paper of the workshop. In this paper, the authors implemented a process of Web reengineering, based on techniques of architecture-driven modernization, whose final goal was to implement a reengineering process from a traditional Web 1.0 application to a rich Internet application.

The most significant contribution of MDWE is to provide an open discussion forum with renowned experts in this field and to combine works with a solid theoretical basis with experiences in the use of model-driven approaches in real-life scenarios. This year's discussion was centered on the manner in which the different MDWE approaches respond to the new challenges of Web 2.0. In this regard, the majority of the accepted papers were aligned with relevant Web 2.0 topics, such as service-oriented architectures or rich Internet applications. Another interesting discussion topic was the diffusion of MDWE approaches in real business scenarios: how to improve the adoption of MDWE approaches in the software development market and which would be the optimal mechanisms to maximize the dissemination of the research in different universities and companies.

Last but not least, we would like to express our sincere gratitude to all the authors and workshop attendees for their active participation and contribution to the discussions. We would also like to thank all the members of the Program Committee and the external reviewers for the high quality of their reviews, which provided excellent feedback to the authors. We extend these thanks to the ICWE 2011 Organizing Committee and Workshop Chairs for their support. For more information, please visit the website of MDWE 2011: http://mdwe2011.pst.ifi.lmu.de/

July 2011

Gustavo Rossi
Geert-Jan Houben
Marco Brambilla
Santiago Meliá

# Organization

## Program Committee

| | |
|---|---|
| Luciano Baresi | DEI - Politecnico di Milano, Italy |
| Jordi Cabot | INRIA - École des Mines de Nantes, France |
| María Valeria De Castro | Universidad Rey Juan Carlos, Spain |
| Olga De Troyer | Vrije Universiteit Brussel, Belgium |
| Piero Fraternali | Politecnico di Milano, Italy |
| Heinrich Hussmann | LMU Munich, Germany |
| Alexander Knapp | Universität Augsburg, Germany |
| Maristella Matera | Politecnico di Milano, Italy |
| Vicente Pelechano | Universidad Politcnica de Valencia, Spain |
| Alfonso Pierantonio | University of L'Aquila, Italy |
| Juan Carlos Preciado | University of Extremadura, Spain |
| Fernando Sanchez-Figueroa | University of Extremadura, Spain |
| Antonio Vallecillo | University of Malaga, Spain |
| Marco Winckler | LIIHS-IRIT, University Paul Sabatier, France |

## Additional Reviewers

| | |
|---|---|
| Manuel Wimmer | TU Wien, Austria |

# Second International Workshop on Quality in Web Engineering (QWE 2011)

**Organizers:** Cinzia Cappiello, Cristina Cachero, Maristella Matera, and
Silvia Abrahão

The production of Web applications has been among the fastest growing segments of the software industry for several years. In fact, they are an interesting opportunity for companies to deliver services and products at distance. The effectiveness of such applications is dependent on their capability to satisfy the customer needs; thus the quality of Web applications, responsible for the related transactions, has become a crucial factor. However, some recent studies suggest that more than 50% of the delivered Web applications are of poor quality.

The quality of any class of Web products (e.g., a data-intensive application, a Web service, a community portal), should be addressed at different levels: in Web processes, Web artifacts, Web products (applications, services) and in Web content. Also, any quality-oriented approach needs the specification of quality models defining the set of relevant quality attributes to be assessed. Otherwise, quality assessment is left to the intuition or the responsibility of people who are in charge of the process. This need to reflect and advance on methods and techniques that help improve the quality of delivered Web applications led us to organize the second edition of the International Workshop on Quality in Web Engineering (QWE 2011) that was held in conjunction with the 11th International Conference on Web Engineering (ICWE 2011).

The main purpose of the workshop was to discuss and get to know the most innovative and advanced experiences for guaranteeing the quality of Web applications, and the role that Web Engineering methods can play in this respect. In particular this year's edition of the workshop encouraged a discussion on the emergent issues related to the quality of Web 2.0 applications. These applications foster a great user involvement in the production of content, annotations and evaluations, never experienced before in the Web. Traditional quality criteria no longer suffice: a central role is played by the huge amount of user-generated content that is now populating the Web and that is considered as an invaluable source of opinions in several contexts, especially in the enterprise context. The discussions during the workshop thus highlighted the need for new quality models, privileging aspects such as the quality of user-created content (e.g., its trustworthiness and credibility), the user participation in the content creation process and the content authors' reputation.

The discussion of the previous issues was facilitated by the presented papers, which focused on Web 2.0 applications and highlighted the need for new quality models and, in some cases, the inapplicability of traditional dimensions.

We would like to thank the authors for submitting their papers to the workshop and contributing to the interesting discussion during the workshop. We are also grateful to the members of the Program Committee for their efforts in the reviewing process, and to the ICWE organizers for their support and assistance in the production of these proceedings. More details on the workshop are available at http://gplsi.dlsi.ua.es/congresos/qwe11/.


July 2011

Cinzia Cappiello
Cristina Cachero
Maristella Matera
Silvia Abrahão


# Organization


## Program Committee

| | |
|---|---|
| Shadi Abou-Zahra | World Wide Web Consortium (W3C) |
| Carlo Batini | Universitá degli Studi di Milano-Bicocca, Italy |
| Giorgio Brajnik | University of Udine, Italy |
| Ismael Caballero | University of Castilla-la-Mancha, Spain |
| Coral Calero | University of Castilla-la-Mancha, Spain |
| Tiziana Catarci | University of Rome, Italy |
| Sven Casteleyn | Universidad Politécnica de Valencia, Spain |
| Maria Francesca Constabile | Universitá degli Studi di Bari, Italy |
| Florian Daniel | Politecnico di Milano, Italy |
| Adrian Fernandez Martinez | University of Valencia, Spain |
| Bernd Heinrich | Innsbruck University School of Management, Austria |
| Emilio Insfran | Universidad Politécnica de Valencia, Spain |
| Nora Koch | Ludwig-Maximilians-Universität München, Germany |
| Sergio Lujan | University of Alicante, Spain |
| Vicente Luque Centeno | University Carlos III, Spain |
| Luis Olsina | Universidad Nacional de La Pampa, Argentina |
| Barbara Pernici | Politecnico di Milano, Italy |
| Geert Poels | University of Ghent, Belgium |
| Gustavo Rossi | LIFIA, UNLP, Argentina |
| Carmen Santoro | ISTI-CNR, Italy |
| Monica Scannapieco | University of Rome, Italy |
| Wieland Schwinger | Johannes Kepler University, Austria |
| Marco Winckler | University Paul Sabatier, France |

# Second Workshop on the Web and Requirements Engineering (WeRE 2011)

**Organizers:** Irene Garrigós, Jose-Norberto Mazón, Nora Koch, and
Maria Jose Escalona

The Second International Workshop on the Web and Requirements Engineering (WeRE) was held in conjunction with the 11th International Conference on Web Engineering (ICWE 2011) in Paphos (Cyprus) on July 21, 2011. WeRE provides an international forum for exchanging ideas on both using Web technologies as a platform in the requirements engineering field, and applying requirements engineering in the development and use of websites. Papers presented at WeRE focused on new domains and new experiences with the connection between requirements engineering and the Web. For more information, please visit the website of WeRE 2011: http://gplsi.dlsi.ua.es/congresos/were11.

In the last decade, the number and complexity of Web-based software systems and the amount of information they offer has been continuously growing. In the context of software engineering, design methods and methodologies were introduced to provide mechanisms to develop these complex Web applications and rich Internet applications (RIAs) in a systematic way. Most of these methodologies focus on implementation and neglect other tasks such as requirement analysis and quality management. However, in the development of traditional (non-Web) applications, both practitioners and process experts regard requirements engineering as a phase of crucial relevance in the development process.

It is well-known that the most common and time-consuming errors, as well as the most expensive ones to repair, are those that arise from inadequate engineering of requirements. Therefore, although the relevance of requirements engineering is well known these techniques should be studied more widely in the Web Engineering community due to the complexity of Web Engineering problems. This complexity is caused by the size and changing nature of the community of stakeholders involved, as well as the diversity of requirements, including navigation requirements, self-adaptivity requirements, as well as usability and the user experience.

On the other hand, requirements engineering is a complex activity whose success depends on stakeholder participation. Therefore, the techniques proposed in the requirements engineering field need a more participative environment to support effective collaboration among stakeholders. In this context, the Web (especially Web 2.0 applications) provides a convenient platform that supports active participation by stakeholders in the requirements engineering process.

For this edition two papers were selected for presentation. The first one focuses on "Detecting Conflicts and Inconsistencies in Web Application Requirements." The second one discusses "Streamlining Complexity: Conceptual Page

Re-modeling for Rich Internet Applications." The workshop included a discussion slot were participants were very active. The discussion finally focused on the Web 2.0 and requirements engineering that is a hot and challenge topic, which brought some controversy.

Finally, we would like to thank the authors and presenters for their contribution, and the workshop participants for the lively discussion. We also would like to thank the Program Committee for the review of the papers and the ICWE 2011 Organizing Committee for their support. In addition, we would like to gratefully acknowledge the support of our sponsors Sadiel (http://www.sadiel.es), Everis (http://www.everis.com) and Novasoft (http://www.novasoft.es), as well as the financial support of the University Institute for Computing Research (IUII) at the University of Alicante and the MANTRA research project (GRE09-17) from the University of Alicante (Spain) and from the Valencia Government (GV/2011/035).

June 2011

Irene Garrigós
Jose-Norberto Mazón
Nora Koch
María José Escalona

# Organization

## Program Committee

| | |
|---|---|
| Silvia Abrahao | Universidad Politécnica de Valencia, Spain |
| Jose Alfonso Aguilar | Universidad Autónoma de Sinaloa, Mexico |
| Joao Araujo | Universidade Nova de Lisboa, Portugal |
| Davide Bolchini | Indiana University, USA |
| Marco Brambilla | Politecnico di Milano, Italy |
| Travis Breaux | North Carolina State University, USA |
| Jordi Cabot | École des Mines de Nantes, France |
| Fabio Casati | University of Trento, Italy |
| Sven Casteleyn | Universidad Politécnica de Valencia, Spain |
| Jean Louis Cavarero | University of Nice, France |
| Florian Daniel | University of Trento, Italy |
| Xavi Franch | Universitat Politécnica de Catalunya, Spain |
| Piero Fraternalli | Politecnico di Milano, Italy |
| Martin Gaedke | Chemnitz University of Technology, Germany |
| Athula Ginige | University of Western Sydney, Australia |
| Paolo Giorgini | University of Trento, Italy |
| Geert-Jan Houben | Delft University of Technology, The Netherlands |
| Emilio Insfran | Universidad Politécnica de Valencia, Spain |
| Ivan Jureta | University of Namur, Belgium |
| David Lowe | University of Technology, Sydney, Australia |
| Manuel Mejías | University of Seville, Spain |
| Maria Ángeles Moraga | University of Castilla La Mancha, Spain |
| Ana Moreira | Universidade Nova de Lisboa, Portugal |
| Óscar Pastor | Universitat Politécnica de Valencia, Spain |
| Vicente Pelechano | Universitat Politécnica de Valencia, Spain |
| Gustavo Rossi | University of La Plata, Argentina |
| Norbert Seyff | City University London, UK |
| Ambrosio Toval | University of Murcia, Spain |
| Roel Wieringa | University of Twente, The Netherlands |
| Marco Winckler | Université Toulouse, France |
| Eric Yu | University of Toronto, Canada |

# Doctoral Symposium 2011

**Doctoral Symposium Chairs:** Peter Dolog, and Bernhard Haslhofer

The ICWE 2011 Doctoral Symposium aimed at providing PhD students with an opportunity to discuss their Web engineering research in an international forum with well-known experts in the field. It helped students to develop and sharpen their research questions, to find methodologies to answer the questions and to exchange ideas with other students and experienced researchers.

Besides the traditional ICWE themes such as *Web Application Development* and *Web Service Engineering*, this year's Doctoral Symposium featured the special theme *Web Data Engineering*. With this theme, the main aim was to address the developments in the Semantic Web and linked data community: creating a Web of data on top of the existing Web architecture. This is interesting for Web Engineering because these developments lift data management to the Web level and pose novel challenges for Web application design and Web service engineering in general. Vice versa, the experiences gained in Web engineering research can be valuable input for the further development of the Web of data. The research ideas presented and further developed in the ICWE 2011 Doctoral Symposium can benefit from these synergies and lead to novel and exciting research directions.

These proceedings collect the papers presented at the ICWE 2011 Doctoral Consortium. All the submissions were peer-reviewed by at least two independent reviewers from the Web Engineering and/or Semantic Web community. In total, we received 17 submissions and selected 10 based on the reviewers' comments. This gives an acceptance rate of 59%. The topics range from a traditional focus on development methods, such as product lines, domain-specific languages, interface specification, application architecture design, end-user programming and Web mashups through information and relation extraction, data modeling, XML document management, and linked data.

We would like to thank the authors for submitting their manuscripts to the Doctoral Symposium and contributing to an interesting program. Also, we would like to thank the members of the Program Committee for reviewing the papers and giving their feedback. Finally, we thank the General Chairs for supporting us in organizing and setting up this Doctoral Symposium.

May 2011

Peter Dolog
Bernhard Haslhofer

# Organization

## Program Committee

| | |
|---|---|
| Sören Auer | Universität Leipzig, Germany |
| Peter Dolog | Aalborg University, Denmark |
| Piero Fraternali | Politecnico di Milano, Italy |
| Martin Gaedke | Chemnitz University of Technology, Germany |
| Bernhard Haslhofer | Cornell University, USA |
| Michael Hausenblas | DERI Galway, Irleand |
| Geert-Jan Houben | Delft University of Technology, The Netherlands |
| Antoine Isaac | VU Amsterdam, The Netherlands |
| Gerti Kappel | Technical University of Vienna, Austria |
| Christoph Lange | Jacobs University Bremen, Germany |
| Óscar Pastor Lopez | University of Valencia, Spain |
| Thomas Risse | L3S Research Center, Germany |
| Gustavo Rossi | Universidad Nacional de La Plata, Argentina |
| Harald Sack | Hasso Plattner Institute, Germany |
| Fernando Sanchez-Figueroa | University of Extremadura, Spain |
| Raphael Troncy | Eurecom, France |
| Vassilis Tzouvaras | National Technical University of Athens, Greece |
| Wolfram Wöß | Johannes Kepler University Linz, Austria |

# ICWE 2011 Tutorials

**Tutorial Chairs:** Steffen Lohmann, and Cesare Pautasso

Following its tradition, the 2011 edition of the International Conference on Web Engineering (ICWE 2011) complemented its main program with a rich tutorial program. It took place jointly with the workshops and PhD symposium on the first two days of the conference. The tutorials provided conference attendees with an opportunity to gain new knowledge, insights, skills and abilities on key Web engineering topics, tools and techniques.

We had space for four tutorials this year that were selected from a number of high-quality submissions following an open call. They all covered areas that are of high relevance to the Web Engineering community. On the first day (June 20), Vivian Genaro Motti and Jean Vanderdonckt talked about "Multi-Dimensional Context-Aware Adaptation for Web Applications" and Fabian Abel and Geert-Jan Houben about "Engineering the Personal Social Semantic Web." The program of the second day (June 21) also consisted of two tutorials: Maria Maleshkova, Dong Liu, and Carlos Pedrinaci lectured on "Automating the Use of Web APIs Through Lightweight Semantics" and Philip Lew and Luis Olsina on "Improving Quality in Use of Web Applications in a Systematic Way." Summaries of the tutorials are included in this volume—for the first time in the history of the ICWE conference series.

We would like to thank the Conference Chair George Angelos Papadopoulos, the Program Chairs Sören Auer and Oscar Diaz, and the Workshop Chairs and editors of this volume Andreas Harth and Nora Koch for giving us the opportunity to publish the summaries of the tutorials. We believe this is a good way to document, give additional visibility and archive the tutorials. It also offers tutorial attendees and other conference participants as well as the wider public a possibility to look up the tutorial contents and discover interesting aspects and pointers of relevance to their own work. In addition, most summaries include links to Web resources that contain further material.

Last but not least, we would like to thank the tutorial speakers for sharing their knowledge and expertise and the numerous tutorial attendees for their active participation. They helped to make ICWE 2011 a successful event.

July 2011

Steffen Lohmann
Cesare Pautasso

# Table of Contents

## Third International Workshop on Lightweight Composition on the Web (ComposableWeb 2011)

An Evaluation of Mashup Tools Based on Support for Heterogeneous
Mashup Components . . . . . . . . . . . . . . . . . . . . . . . . . . . . . . . . . . . . . . . . . . . . . . 1
 *Saeed Aghaee and Cesare Pautasso*

An Approach to Construct Dynamic Service Mashups Using
Lightweight Semantics . . . . . . . . . . . . . . . . . . . . . . . . . . . . . . . . . . . . . . . . . . . 13
 *Dong Liu, Ning Li, Carlos Pedrinaci, Jacek Kopecký,*
 *Maria Maleshkova, and John Domingue*

Task-Based Recommendation of Mashup Components . . . . . . . . . . . . . . . . 25
 *Vincent Tietz, Gregor Blichmann, Stefan Pietschmann, and*
 *Klaus Meißner*

Integration of Telco Services into Enterprise Mashup Applications . . . . . . 37
 *Olexiy Chudnovskyy, Frank Weinhold, Hendrik Gebhardt, and*
 *Martin Gaedke*

Orchestrated User Interface Mashups Using W3C Widgets . . . . . . . . . . . . 49
 *Scott Wilson, Florian Daniel, Uwe Jugel, and Stefano Soi*

Cross-Domain Embedding for Vaadin Applications . . . . . . . . . . . . . . . . . . . 62
 *Janne Lautamäki and Tommi Mikkonen*

Web Linking-Based Protocols for Guiding RESTful M2M Interaction . . . 74
 *Jesus Bellido, Rosa Alarcon, and Cristian Sepulveda*

Batched Transactions for RESTful Web Services . . . . . . . . . . . . . . . . . . . . . 86
 *Sebastian Kochman, Paweł T. Wojciechowski, and Miłosz Kmieciak*

Secure Mashup-Providing Platforms - Implementing Encrypted
Wiring . . . . . . . . . . . . . . . . . . . . . . . . . . . . . . . . . . . . . . . . . . . . . . . . . . . . . . . . . 99
 *Matthias Herbert, Tobias Thieme, Jan Zibuschka, and*
 *Heiko Roßnagel*

## First International Workshop on Search, Exploration and Navigation of Web Data Sources (ExploreWeb 2011)

A Conceptual Framework for Linked Data Exploration . . . . . . . . . . . . . . . 109
 *Alessandro Bozzon, Marco Brambilla, Emanuele Della Valle,*
 *Piero Fraternali, and Chiara Pasini*

Support for Reusable Explorations of Linked Data in the Semantic
Web . . . . . . . . . . . . . . . . . . . . . . . . . . . . . . . . . . . . . . . . . . . . . . . . . . . . . . . . . . . .   119
    *Marcelo Cohen and Daniel Schwabe*

Generation of Semantic Clouds Based on Linked Data for Efficient
Multimedia Semantic Annotation . . . . . . . . . . . . . . . . . . . . . . . . . . . . . . . . .   127
    *Han-Gyu Ko and In-Young Ko*

Ontology Based Segmentation of Geo-Referenced Queries . . . . . . . . . . . . .   135
    *Mamoun Abu Helou*

SimSpectrum: A Similarity Based Spectral Clustering Approach to
Generate a Tag Cloud . . . . . . . . . . . . . . . . . . . . . . . . . . . . . . . . . . . . . . . . . . . .   145
    *Frederico Durao, Peter Dolog, Martin Leginus, and Ricardo Lage*

Graph Access Pattern Diagrams (GAP-D): Towards a Unified Approach
for Modeling Navigation over Hierarchical, Linear and Networked
Structures . . . . . . . . . . . . . . . . . . . . . . . . . . . . . . . . . . . . . . . . . . . . . . . . . . . . . . .   155
    *Matthias Keller and Martin Nussbaumer*

Data-Driven and User-Driven Multidimensional Data Visualization . . . . .   159
    *Rober Morales-Chaparro, Juan C. Preciado, and
    Fernando Sánchez-Figueroa*

## Second International Workshop on Enterprise Crowdsourcing (EC 2011)

Context-Aware and Adaptive Web Interfaces: A Crowdsourcing
Approach . . . . . . . . . . . . . . . . . . . . . . . . . . . . . . . . . . . . . . . . . . . . . . . . . . . . . . . .   167
    *Michael Nebeling and Moira C. Norrie*

Massive Multiplayer Human Computation for Fun, Money, and
Survival . . . . . . . . . . . . . . . . . . . . . . . . . . . . . . . . . . . . . . . . . . . . . . . . . . . . . . . . .   171
    *Lukas Biewald*

Enterprise Crowdsourcing Solution for Software Development in an
Outsourcing Organization . . . . . . . . . . . . . . . . . . . . . . . . . . . . . . . . . . . . . . . . .   177
    *Ranganathan Jayakanthan and Deepak Sundararajan*

## Seventh Model-Driven Web Engineering Workshop (MDWE 2011)

A Model-Driven Framework for Developing Web Service Oriented
Applications . . . . . . . . . . . . . . . . . . . . . . . . . . . . . . . . . . . . . . . . . . . . . . . . . . . . . .   181
    *Achilleas Achilleos, Georgia M. Kapitsaki, and
    George A. Papadopoulos*

Developing Enterprise Web Applications Using the Story Driven
Modeling Approach . . . . . . . . . . . . . . . . . . . . . . . . . . . . . . . . . . . . . . . . . . . . . . 196
    *Christoph Eickhoff, Nina Geiger, Marcel Hahn, and Albert Zündorf*

Aspect-Oriented Modeling of Web Applications with HiLA . . . . . . . . . . . . 211
    *Gefei Zhang and Matthias Hölzl*

Model-Driven Web Form Validation with UML and OCL . . . . . . . . . . . . . 223
    *Eban Escott, Paul Strooper, Paul King, and Ian J. Hayes*

Modernization of Legacy Web Applications into Rich Internet
Applications. . . . . . . . . . . . . . . . . . . . . . . . . . . . . . . . . . . . . . . . . . . . . . . . . . . . . . . 236
    *Roberto Rodríguez-Echeverría, José María Conejero,*
    *Pedro J. Clemente, Juan C. Preciado, and*
    *Fernando Sánchez-Figueroa*

## Second International Workshop on Quality in Web Engineering (QWE 2011)

Quality Models for Web [2.0] Sites: A Methodological Approach and a
Proposal . . . . . . . . . . . . . . . . . . . . . . . . . . . . . . . . . . . . . . . . . . . . . . . . . . . . . . . . . . 251
    *Roberto Polillo*

Exploring the Quality in Use of Web 2.0 Applications: The Case of
Mind Mapping Services . . . . . . . . . . . . . . . . . . . . . . . . . . . . . . . . . . . . . . . . . . . . 266
    *Tihomir Orehovački, Andrina Granić, and Dragutin Kermek*

## Second Workshop on the Web and Requirements Engineering (WeRE 2011)

Detecting Conflicts and Inconsistencies in Web Application
Requirements. . . . . . . . . . . . . . . . . . . . . . . . . . . . . . . . . . . . . . . . . . . . . . . . . . . . . . 278
    *Matias Urbieta, Maria Jose Escalona, Esteban Robles Luna, and*
    *Gustavo Rossi*

Streamlining Complexity: Conceptual Page Re-modeling for Rich
Internet Applications . . . . . . . . . . . . . . . . . . . . . . . . . . . . . . . . . . . . . . . . . . . . . . 289
    *Andrea Pandurino, Davide Bolchini, Luca Mainetti, and*
    *Roberto Paiano*

## Doctoral Symposium 2011

A Flexible Graph-Based Data Model Supporting Incremental Schema
Design and Evolution. . . . . . . . . . . . . . . . . . . . . . . . . . . . . . . . . . . . . . . . . . . . . . . 302
    *Katrin Braunschweig, Maik Thiele, and Wolfgang Lehner*

ProLD: Propagate Linked Data . . . . . . . . . . . . . . . . . . . . . . . . . . . . . . . . . . . . 307
    *Peter Kalchgruber*

Causal Relation Detection for Activities from Heterogeneous Sources ...    312
  *Philipp Katz and Alexander Schill*

XML Document Versioning, Revalidation and Constraints ............    317
  *Jakub Malý and Martin Nečaský*

A Reuse-Oriented Product-Line Method for Enterprise Web
Applications ......................................................    322
  *Neil Mather and Samia Oussena*

A Flexible Architecture for Client-Side Adaptation ..................    327
  *Sergio Firmenich, Gustavo Rossi, Silvia Gordillo, and
  Marco Winckler*

Applications of Mobile Application Interface Description Language
MAIDL ...........................................................    332
  *Prach Chaisatien, Korawit Prutsachainimmit, and Takehiro Tokuda*

A Domain-Specific Language for Do-It-Yourself Analytical Mashups ....    337
  *Julian Eberius, Maik Thiele, and Wolfgang Lehner*

Information Extraction from Web Pages Based on Their Visual
Representation ....................................................    342
  *Ruslan R. Fayzrakhmanov*

End-User Programming for Web Mashups: Open Research
Challenges .......................................................    347
  *Saeed Aghaee and Cesare Pautasso*

## ICWE 2011 Tutorials

Multi-dimensional Context-Aware Adaptation for Web Applications ....    352
  *Vivian Genaro Motti and Jean Vanderdonckt*

Engineering the Personal Social Semantic Web ......................    355
  *Fabian Abel and Geert-Jan Houben*

Automating the Use of Web APIs through Lightweight Semantics ......    357
  *Maria Maleshkova, Carlos Pedrinaci, Dong Liu, and
  Guillermo Alvaro*

Improving Quality in Use of Web Applications in a Systematic Way ....    359
  *Philip Lew and Luis Olsina*

**Author Index** ................................................    361

# An Evaluation of Mashup Tools Based on Support for Heterogeneous Mashup Components

Saeed Aghaee and Cesare Pautasso

Faculty of Informatics, University of Lugano, Switzerland
first.last@usi.ch
http://www.pautasso.info/

**Abstract.** Mashups are built by combining building blocks, which are commonly referred to as mashup components. These components are characterized by a high level of heterogeneity in terms of technologies, access methods, and the behavior they may exhibit within a mashup. Abstracting away this heterogeneity is the mission of the so-called mashup tools aiming at automating or semi-automating mashup development to serve non-programmers. The challenge is to ensure this abstraction mechanism does not limit the support for heterogeneous mashup components. In this paper, we propose a novel evaluation framework that can be applied to assess the degree to which a given mashup tool addresses this challenge. The evaluation framework can serve as a benchmark for future improved design of mashup tools with respect to heterogeneous mashup components support. In order to demonstrate the applicability of the framework, we also apply it to evaluate some existing tools.

**Keywords:** Mashup Components, Evaluation Framework, Component Model, Expressive Power.

## 1 Introduction

Mashups are Web applications built by reusing and combining mashup components. These components are not only programming and data abstraction but also can deliver Web contents that are not syndicated or made accessible via a public interface [1]. In other words, mashup components can be defined as any kind of reusable elements on the Web that can contribute to developing composite Web application. Thereby, mashup components often possess very heterogeneous characteristics in terms of the access methods through which they are published (e.g., protocols) as well the way they behave inside a mashup (e.g., synchronous and asynchronous interactions).

The heterogeneity of mashup components poses serious challenges on designing mashup tools aiming at lowering the barriers of mashup development through increasing the level of automation. It is due to the fact that one of the most important steps in automating mashup development is to abstract away this heterogeneity to enable seamless composition. Such an abstraction is defined as a component model that describes the characteristics of mashup components as well as the way they can be composed together [2].

A. Harth and N. Koch (Eds.): ICWE 2011 Workshops, LNCS 7059, pp. 1–12, 2012.

A component model for mashups should be able to equally take two aspects into consideration. The first is indeed the level of abstraction that indicates the amount of technical skill required form a user to interact with the underlying mashup components. The higher the abstraction level is, the lower barriers are imposed on the end-users side. The second aspect is the expressive power in terms of how many and how heterogeneous types of mashup components come under its umbrella. The increased level of expressive power results in a more powerful tool. On the other hand, there is a trade-off between obtaining a higher level of abstraction and having more expressive power that should be considered while designing a mashup tool. This, however, requires a formal definition of the expressive power for mashup component models which is currently missing in literature.

The goal of this paper is thus to propose such a definition in the form of a framework. The framework can serve as a benchmark for evaluating mashup tools in this regard. Such an evaluation can then contribute to advancing the state-of-the-art mashup tools by identifying their weaknesses and strengths. The framework enables a white-box evaluation process and comprises six dimensions underlying the level of support for discovery, input/output data types, access methods, recursion, output types, and runtime behavior. To show how the framework can be utilized, we also apply it to evaluate some existing mashup tools.

The rest of this paper is structured as follows. In the next section we present our proposed framework. Section 3 is dedicated to evaluate some selected mashup tools based on the framework. The discussion, including the evaluation summary, will be given in section 4. An overview of the related work will be provided in Section 5. We conclude this paper in Section 6.

## 2   Evaluation Framework

To define the expressive power of a mashup component model, we need to understand what are required to be expressed by a user that concern the component model. In our proposed framework, these are referred to as dimensions which, in turn, are refined into a set of characteristics. To extract these dimensions, we consider a scenario in which a mashup is developed by a user using a tool. Initially, the user searches for relevant components depending on the goal of the mashup she intends to develop (discovery dimension). If the required components are not found in the library, they need to be newly wrapped by the user (recursion, access method, and output dimensions). Once the required components are ready, the user proceeds with the design process by composing the components to form a new mashup. During the design-time the user determines how the components are supposed to exchange data and control with each other (input/output data type and behavior dimension).

### 2.1   Discovery

Mashup component discovery is the whole process of retrieving appropriate components with regards to the needs of a developer [3]. Hence, a component model should provide adequate support to facilitate this step. Mashup tools supporting component discovery usually offer a local library storing reusable components. In order to support component discovery, a mashup tool can choose among three approaches outlined below:

– **Semantical Discovery.** Applying this approach requires a model that allows to add semantic descriptions of components (e.g., input/output parameters and functionality). In this approach, a component is discovered based on the information contained in its semantic description.

– **Syntactic Discovery.** In this approach component discovery is guided based on the component syntax exposed in its model (e.g., input/output data types).

– **Keyword Discovery** This approach is based on matching query keywords with tags and textual descriptions contained within the component model.

### 2.2 Input/Output Data Type

A mashup component interacts with others through its input and output parameters. In order to make use of a component inside a tool, the data types of its parameters should be defined in the tool component model. In general, these data types can be categorized into two main groups as follows.

– **Primitive.** This groups is equivalent to standard variable types of a programming language (e.g., string, int, boolean, etc.).

– **Multipurpose Internet Mail Extensions (MIME).** MIME types can be any standard data formats or media types found on the Web including (but not limited to) XML, JSON, RSS, and JPG.

### 2.3 Access Method

This dimension is concerned with the way in which a mashup component is made accessible for composition inside a mashup. The access method utilized by various mashup components are highly heterogeneous and can be categorized as follows.

– **Language-dependent.** This method forces the use of a specific programming, scripting or markup language. For instance, JavaScript APIs, HTML IFrame widgets, Plain Old Object Java Objects (POJOs), Enterprise Java Beans (EJB) can be all considered within this category. Though some of these methods are considered outdated (POJO and EJB), they are still being used within enterprise. Moreover, Google Maps [4] which is the most popular mashup components [5] is accessible via JavaScript APIs.

– **Protocol-based.** Using standard protocols for accessing a mashup component eliminates the requirements for a specific language. Popular protocols for mashup components are Web services (e.g., RESTful, HTTP, and SOAP) and Web feeds (e.g., RSS and Atom). According to the ProgrammableWeb [5], the dominant portion of Web APIs currently constitutes REST Web services.

– **Database.** Within a mashup, a database can be considered a component that act as either a read-only or a read/write data source. A database not only can deliver data and functionality (i.e., query and update features) but also can become a permanent storage for writing user-related data (e.g., username and password).

– **Non-Standard.** There are many Websites that do not officially allow any reuse of their content or backend functionality. These mostly follow the Web 1.0 paradigm, in which the content is merely assumed to be readable by humans. Extracting the content and functionality of such websites as mashup components might still be considered valuable, depending on the goal of the target mashup. These kind of mashup components are made accessible through two major non-standard techniques: Web scraping [6], which is the act of converting human-readable data to machine-readable formats, and Web clipping [7], by which only a portion of a Webpage is extracted.

## 2.4   Recursion

A mashup can be incorporated into another mashup as a component. This process can be called *recursion* whose concept is analogous to service composition [8]. In this sense, mashup components provided by third-party vendors are similar to atomic services. Likewise, a mashup is a user-defined component created through the composition of other mashups and different atomic components (like a composite service). What concerns a component model in this regard is the ability of reengineering a mashup that can reduce the required effort for mashup development through reuse and reconfiguration.

## 2.5   Output

There are three types of output a mashup component can generate in the final mashup composition: functional, data, and visual. The development of a mashup can span one or all of the integration levels including process integration level, data integration level, and UI integration level, depending on the output types of its building components [9]. It is also of note that, a single component may have multiple output types (e.g., a Web Widget).

– **Functional.** Mashup Components with functional output are delivered as services that contribute to the business logic layer of a mashup. Such components are usually orchestrated together in a workflow to deliver a capability [10].

– **Data.** Components generating data act as external data sources, which deliver data to a mashup either as continuous data streams with real-time properties or as snapshots of a remote or local dataset. Most Web data sources are read-only, but in some cases they may also support updates. Within the mashup, they are likely to be converted, transformed, filtered, or combined with other data sources [11].

– **Visual.** Visual output is generated by UI components [12] or widgets [13]. These components provide some kind of graphical user interaction mechanism which can be reused at the mashup UI level. The visual part of a component is incorporated in the mashup UI independently from other UI elements and component.

## 2.6  Behavior

At the runtime, the control flow of a mashup determines the sequence of component invocation. Nevertheless, the internal execution mechanism of a mashup component may also affect its parent mashup control flow. This is referred to as the runtime behavior of a mashup component that can be either task-based or event-based.

– **Task-based.** A component with a task-based behavior represents a single invocation of a local or remote operation, which may provide an output given an input. It resembles traditional functions or methods, which execute and transmit responses only when called. In the context of the overall mashup, such components are passive (they are executed only when control reaches them).

– **Event-based.** When a component has an event-based behavior, it is triggered and produces an output only when a specific action (independent from the composition) has been taken (e.g., user interactions or an asynchronous message is received from a remote service). An event-based component is, therefore, an active part of a mashup, which may trigger the execution of a sequence of tasks.

## 3  Evaluation

In this section, we give an overview of the selected existing mashup tools and evaluate their corresponding component models based on the framework mentioned in Section 2 (Table 1). Considering the fact that our goal is not to evaluate all existing mashup tools but rather to demonstrate how the framework can be applied, we selected a sample group of mashup tools (Yahoo Pipes [14], Presto Cloud [15], Serena Mashup Composer [16], JOpera [17], and Husky [18]) based on two criteria. The first criterion was to ensure the diversity of End-User Programming techniques [19] utilized by the selected tools. These techniques for the selected tools include visual language (Yahoo Pipes, JOpera, Presto Cloud, Serena Mashup Composer), domain specific language (Presto Cloud), and spreadsheet-based programming (Husky). The second one takes into account the availability of the tools which otherwise can hinder the evaluation process.

In order to make the process of evaluation more concrete as well as to motivate and exemplify the need for a more powerful component model, we also benchmark the ability of the selected tools to develop an existing manually developed mashup called TwBe [20]. TwBe is a mashup developed using PHP and JavaScript without utilizing any mashup tools. The goal of TwBe is to provide a stream of YouTube videos as they are retrieved from a user's Twitter stream. Its main components include YouTube player[1], YouTube data API, Twitter API[2], Twitter OAuth library[3], and a local MySQL database (Figure 1). In order to authenticate with the twitter, TwBe uses the Twitter PHP library for OAuth (there are also libraries for other languages such as JavaScript). The Twitter

---

[1] http://code.google.com/apis/youtube/overview.html
[2] http://apiwiki.twitter.com/w/page/22554648/FrontPage
[3] https://github.com/abraham/twitteroauth

**Table 1.** Evaluation of Mashup Tools

| | | Yahoo Pipese | Presto Cloud | Serena Mashup Composer | JOpera | Husky |
|---|---|---|---|---|---|---|
| Discovery | Semantic | - | - | - | - | - |
| | Syntactic | - | - | - | - | - |
| | Keyword | X | X | - | X | - |
| Data Formats | Primitive | X | X | X | X | X |
| | MIME | XML, RSS, ATOM, JSON | XML, RSS, ATOM | XML, JSON | XML, HTML | - |
| Access Method | Language-dependent | - | JS, HTML | JS, HTML | JS, HTML, POJO | - |
| | Protocol-based | REST, RSS | HTTP, SOAP, REST | SOAP, REST | HTTP, SOAP, REST | SOAP |
| | Database | - | SQL | - | SQL, JDBC | - |
| | Non-standard | Scraping | - | - | Scraping | - |
| Recursion | | X | X | - | X | - |
| Output | Data | X | X | X | X | X |
| | Functionality | X | X | X | X | X |
| | Visual | - | X | X | X | - |
| Behavior | Task-based | X | X | X | X | X |
| | Event-based | - | X | - | X | - |

API is then invoked to retrieve tweets of a current user and periodically check for new ones. After the new tweets are available, those that do not contain link to a YouTube videos are filtered out. The videos that are going to be played by YouTube player are fetched from YouTube data API. Finally, the database is used to cache video tweets belonging to the current user in order to accelerate further access.

### 3.1   Yahoo Pipes

Yahoo Pipes is a popular tool for creating mashups by integrating data coming from various sources on the Web. It utilizes visual programming technique to hide the complexity of mashup development. The visual language is based on

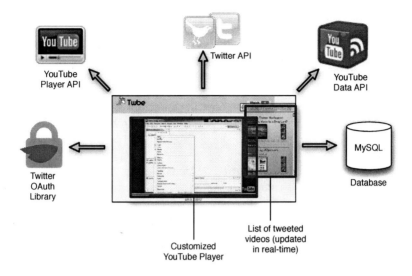

**Fig. 1.** TwBe Main Components

the wiring paradigm in which data sources, blocks, operators, and other tools are represented as parametrizable boxes which connect to each other. The result of connecting these boxes forms a pipe through which data flows and will be eventually visualized or syndicated to the user.

– **Discovery.** Yahoo Pipes supports component discovery, however, it only allows the discovery of mashups published in its local library. The discovery is based on matching keywords in user queries with the tags provided by the publishers.

– **Input/Output Data Format.** Primitive data types such as string and numerical values as well as frequently used MIME types like XML, RSS, Atom, and JSON are all defined in Yahoo Pipes. These are also the data types negotiated by the TwBe components.

– **Access Method.** The supported access methods include RSS/Atom feeds and HTTP. Thereby, YouTube videos and tweets can be easily retrieved as they are accessible via HTTP protocol. However, Twitter OAuth library and Youtube Player, which both use language dependent access method, as well as MySQL database cannot be utilized inside Yahoo Pipes.

– **Recursion.** Recursion is fully supported by Yahoo pipes. Mashups that are published in the tool library can be discovered and reused within a new mashup.

– **Output.** Components generating data and functionality are only supported by this tool. As a result it does not allow insertion of UI components such as YouTube Player.

– **Behavior.** This tool only supports task-based behavior of components and therefore, an event-based component cannot trigger a flow of control.

Overall, Yahoo Pipes can not be solely employed to develop TwBe as it does not support Twitter OAuth library, YouTube Player, and MySQL database.

## 3.2   Presto Cloud

Presto Cloud includes both a visual language and a powerful XML-based domain specific language called the Enterprise mashup Markup Language (EMML). It enables users to switch between the textual (EMML) [21] and visual mode depending upon their interests and background knowledge. Presto Cloud offers similar features as Yahoo Pipes for creating mashups integrating various data sources. It also adds support for integrating and designing mashup UI.

– **Discovery.** Component discovery is enabled and supported via keyword-oriented search.

– **Input/Output Data Format.** Components can declare both primitive and MIME (XML, RSS, Atom) types.

– **Access Method.** The two supported language-dependent techniques (HTML and JavaScript) can be used to create *APPs*. APPs are similar to widgets that visualize data and can be recursively created through integration of other existing APPs. For instance, both the Twitter OAuth JavaScript library and the YouTube player that build the TwBe mashup can be wrapped as APPs. Moreover, all the frequently used protocol-based access methods (HTTP, SOAP, REST) are support by Presto Cloud.

– **Recursion.** Recursion can happen both in the back-end (data and functionality integration) and the UI (APPs)

– **Output.** Components with visual output are called APPs. *Blocks* abstract components with data and functional output.

– **Behavior.** Both task-based and event-based behavior of mashup components are handled by Presto Cloud. APPs can publish topics (events) to which other APPs can subscribe.

Presto Cloud can be used to create TwBe.

## 3.3   Serena Mashup Composer

Serena Mashup Composer is part of the Serena Mashup Suite. It decomposes mashups into orchestration, which defines the execution order of Web services, and application, which specifies the front-end of the mashup.

– **Discovery.** *Mashup Central* is a library containing templates and mashups shared by other users. However, it does not appear to support discovery of mashup components.

– **Input/Output Data Format.** Other than primitive data types, components can negotiate JSON and XML.

– **Access Method.** It supports protocol-based (REST, SOAP) and language-dependent (JavaScript, HTML) access methods. In the latter case, JavaScript and HTML is used to embed widgets. This can also be used to incorporate the Twitter JavaScript library for OAuth.

This tool does not support the use of databases, and therefore can not be used to create TwBe.

### 3.4   JOpera

JOpera is a rapid visual service composition tool. Service composition using JOpera is based on drawing a control flow graph that determines the sequence of service execution and one or more data flow graphs that indicate the flow of data between the services. JOpera allows abstraction of services of different types by concealing their internal mechanism (i.e., access method, input/output data types, etc.) behind a unified interface [22].

– **Discovery.** JOpera library stores both atomic and composite services and allows their discovery based on keyword-oriented search.

– **Input/Output Data Format.** JOpera data flow parameters can contain any data type.

– **Access Method.** It supports language-dependent (JavaScript, POJO, and HTML), protocol-based (HTTP, SOAP, REST), database (SQL, JDBC), and non-standard access methods (Web scraping) which cover all the access methods utilized by the TwBe components.

– **Recursion.** Recursion is supported by JOpera through the subprocess construct.

– **Output.** It handles all the three possible output of a mashup component (functional, data, visual).

– **Behavior.** JOpera not only supports task-based behavior of components but also allows handling exception events. Other types of event-based behavior such as data stream updates and UI events are not supported.

A very similar version of TwBe (in terms of UI), thanks to the high expressive power of JOpera in UI design (i.e., using *Echo* adapter that outputs DHTML code to browser), can be developed using JOpera.

### 3.5   Husky

Husky is a spreadsheet-based tool for service composition. Each cell of a Husky spreadsheet encapsulates a service. The sequence of service invocation is defined by placing service invocation events into adjacent cells.

– **Input/Output Data Format.** It only supports primitive data types.

– **Access Method.** The only supported access method is WSDL/SOAP Web services, which is not relevant in the case of TwBe example.

– **Output.** Since it only supports Web services, the only output types are functional and data.

This tool can not make any contribution to developing TwBe (none of TwBe components use SOAP Web service as their method of access).

## 4   Discussion

As the evaluation suggests, many of the selected tools do not provide adequate support for language-dependent mashup components. These are mostly exemplified by widgets accessible through JavaScript APIs (e.g., Google Maps). Tools like JOpera, Presto Cloud, and Serena Mashup Composer offer a JavaScript and HTML container to wrap such widgets. However, language-dependent components are not limited to JavaScript APIs and HTML, they may also be PHP libraries (for instance Twitter PHP library for OAuth).

A common limitation among the tools was the lack of support for event-based behavior of mashup components, which is usually the case in widgets. Even though JOpera and Serena Mashup Composer provide support for embedding widgets, they are unable to handle events fired by them through user interactions. The only tool of our selection that can manage UI events is indeed Presto Cloud. Furthermore, event-based behavior does not merely involve widgets, but also mashup components which generate data output can be used to subscribe to a source of streaming data. This also results in firing an event that should be handled by the mashup, e.g., when a new tweet containing a link to a YouTube video appears.

Interestingly, none of the tools thoroughly support component discovery. As a matter of fact, component discovery is one of the most important steps in the mashup development process. The majority of the selected tools (Yahoo Pipes, Presto Cloud, Serena Mashup Composer), except for JOpera, do not include atomic components in their library but only mashups that have been published by users. Moreover, the only discovery technique utilized by all of these tools was based on keyword-oriented search. Even though semantic discovery is not yet matured, its state-of-the-art [23] not only can contribute to streamlining mashup discovery but also can enable a higher degree of automation in mashup development.

Regarding the output types, the majority of the tools do not handle components maintaining their own UIs (i.e., visual output). Moreover, a tool that supports components with visual output may not necessarily support UI integration. JOpera is an example of this case, where the majority of UI components and widgets are supported, though the required means of carrying on UI integration such as handling the communication of UI events [12] are not supported.

The level of support for recursion and input/output data types were satisfactory. In the latter case, however, the only supported MIME types were XML, HTML, RSS, and JSON. Though these are the most common media types for mashup components, they still need to broaden their support range to also cover less frequently used types such as YAML [24].

In general, supporting all types of mashup components is a challenging task. It gets even more challenging to keep the usability of a tool in a satisfactory level while increasing the expressive power of its component model. This can also be generalized to other aspects of mashup development such as composition and evolution. This is an important tradeoff that confronts the design of mashup tools, and thus needs to be addressed in future research.

## 5  Related Work

Previous efforts on proposing evaluation frameworks for mashup tools have been conducted along two directions. The first concerns the usability of mashup tools.

For instance, the evaluation frameworks presented in [25,26] can both be considered towards this direction.

The second direction, within which this paper is to be considered, focuses on evaluating the expressive power of mashup tools. Previous evaluation frameworks target various aspects of mashup development that need to be expressed to end-users. For instance, [27] presents a benchmark for assessing mashup tools with respect to their data integration capabilities. The framework presented in [28] is also another example that classifies mashup tools and evaluates their expressive power concerning their support for process integration. We consider this paper as a complement to all the previous work done in this direction, the expressive power of component modeling for mashups.

## 6  Conclusion

The purpose of mashup tools is to lower the barriers of mashup development to the degree that even non-programmers can develop mashups. Even though the usability and ease-of-use are important factors for mashup tools, these should not compromise the expressive power offered by such tools and vise versa. One aspect of mashup development that determines this expressive power is the level of support for composing heterogeneous mashups components. In this paper, we have presented an evaluation framework that measures mashup tools based on to which extent they deal with the heterogeneity and diversity of mashup components. We defined the framework in terms of multiple dimensions and used it as the basis for undertaking an evaluation of a small group of mashup tools.

We believe the proposed evaluation framework can provide a roadmap towards an improved design for the next generation of mashup tools. To do so, heterogeneity can be addressed within a component model by means of adaptation and standardization. Adaptation is feasible in the short term and entails transforming heterogeneous mashup components into a common existing technology so that they conform with each other [2]. This method is harnessed by Mashape [29] by providing a programmable platform for converting various services and APIs into REST Web services. Standardization will require a more concerted effort and can provide a better solution in the long term, assuming that the resulting standard for mashup components become widely adopted. The Open Mashup Alliance (OMP) is now actively working on standardizing mashups, for example with EMML.

## References

1. Ogrinz, M.: Mashup Patterns: Designs and Examples for the Modern Enterprise. Addison-Wesley (2009)
2. Assmann, U.: Invasive Software Composition. Springer, Heidelberg (2003)
3. Zhao, Q., Huang, G., Huang, J., Liu, X., Mei, H.: A web-based mashup environment for on-the-fly service composition. In: Proc. of SOSE (2008)

4. Google Maps API,
   http://code.google.com/apis/maps/documentation/javascript/)
5. ProgrammableWeb, http://www.programmableweb.com/
6. Schrenk, M.: Webbots, Spiders, and Screen Scrapers. No Starch Press (2007)
7. Smith, I.: Doing web clippings in under ten minutes. Technical report, Intranet Journal (2001)
8. Milanovic, N., Malek, M.: Current solutions for web service composition. IEEE Internet Computing 8, 51–59 (2004)
9. Maximilien, E.M., Wilkinson, H., Desai, N., Tai, S.: A Domain-Specific Language for Web APIs and Services Mashups. In: Krämer, B.J., Lin, K.-J., Narasimhan, P. (eds.) ICSOC 2007. LNCS, vol. 4749, pp. 13–26. Springer, Heidelberg (2007)
10. de Vrieze, P., Xu, L., Bouguettaya, A., Yang, J., Chen, J.: Process-oriented enterprise mashups. In: Proc. of GPC 2009 (2009)
11. Maximilien, E.M., Ranabahu, A., Gomadam, K.: An online platform for web apis and service mashups. IEEE Internet Computing 12, 32–43 (2008)
12. Daniel, F., Yu, J., Benatallah, B., Casati, F., Matera, M., Saint-Paul, R.: Understanding ui integration: A survey of problems, technologies, and opportunities. IEEE Internet Computing 11, 59–66 (2007)
13. Hoyer, V., Fischer, M.: Market Overview of Enterprise Mashup Tools. In: Bouguettaya, A., Krueger, I., Margaria, T. (eds.) ICSOC 2008. LNCS, vol. 5364, pp. 708–721. Springer, Heidelberg (2008)
14. Yahoo Pipes, http://pipes.yahoo.com/pipes/
15. Presto Cloud, http://www.jackbe.com/enterprise-mashup/
16. Serena Mashup Composer,
    http://www2.serena.com/pages/mashups/campaigns/
    composer-download/index.html
17. JOpera, http://www.jopera.org/
18. Husky, http://www.husky.fer.hr/
19. Myers, B.A., Ko, A.J., Burnett, M.M.: Invited Research Overview: End-User Programming. In: Proc. of CHI 2006 (2006)
20. TwBe, http://arc.inf.unisi.ch/twbe/twitter/
21. EMML, http://www.openmashup.org/
22. Pautasso, C., Alonso, G.: From Web Service Composition to Megaprogramming. In: Shan, M.-C., Dayal, U., Hsu, M. (eds.) TES 2004. LNCS, vol. 3324, pp. 39–53. Springer, Heidelberg (2005)
23. Mohebbi, K., Ibrahim, S., Khezrian, M., Munusamy, K., Tabatabaei, S.G.H.: A comparative evaluation of semantic web service discovery approaches. In: Proc. of iiWAS 2010 (2010)
24. Yaml, http://www.yaml.org/
25. Grammel, L., Storey, M.A.: An end user perspective on mashup makers. Technical Report DCS-324-IR, University of Victoria (2008)
26. Grammel, L., Storey, M.-A.: A Survey of Mashup Development Environments. In: Chignell, M., Cordy, J., Ng, J., Yesha, Y. (eds.) The Smart Internet. LNCS, vol. 6400, pp. 137–151. Springer, Heidelberg (2010)
27. Di Lorenzo, G., Hacid, H., Paik, H.-y., Benatallah, B.: Data integration in mashups. SIGMOD Rec. 38, 59–66 (2009)
28. Daniel, F., Koschmider, A., Nestler, T., Roy, M., Namoun, A.: Toward process mashups: key ingredients and open research challenges. In: Proc. of Mashups 2010 (2010)
29. Mashape, http://www.mashape.com/

# An Approach to Construct Dynamic Service Mashups Using Lightweight Semantics

Dong Liu, Ning Li, Carlos Pedrinaci, Jacek Kopecký, Maria Maleshkova, and John Domingue

Knowledge Media Institute, The Open University
Walton Hall, Milton Keynes, MK7 6AA, UK
{d.liu,n.li,c.pedrinaci,j.kopecky,
m.maleshkova,j.b.domingue}@open.ac.uk

**Abstract.** Thousands of Web services have been available online, and mashups built upon them have been creating added value. However, mashups are mostly developed with a predefined set of services and components. The extensions to them always involve programming work. Furthermore, when a service is unavailable, it is challenging for mashups to smoothly switch to an alternative that offers similar functionalities. To address these problems, this paper presents a novel approach to enable mashups to select and invoke semantic Web services on the fly. To extend a mashup with new semantic services, developers are only required to register and publish them as Linked Data. By refining the strategies of service selection, mashups can behave more adaptively and offer higher fault-tolerance.

**Keywords:** Mashup, Semantic Web Services, Service Selection, Service Invocation.

## 1   Introduction

More and more companies and organisations expose their core functionalities as SOAP or RESTful services on the Web, so that third-party developers can create new Web applications atop of these services in a more agile way. Repositories and marketplaces such as ProgrammableWeb[1], Seekda[2] and Mashape[3], have been established to collect and publish descriptions of Web services. On the other hand, mashups integrate data, services and contents available online into a coherent application that creates new value [20]. Tools such as Yahoo Pipes[4] and IBM Mashup Center[5], have been available for assisting the development of mashups.

---

[1] http://www.programmableweb.com
[2] http://webservices.seekda.com
[3] http://www.mashape.com
[4] http://pipes.yahoo.com/
[5] http://www.ibm.com/software/info/mashup-center/

A. Harth and N. Koch (Eds.): ICWE 2011 Workshops, LNCS 7059, pp. 13–24, 2012.
© Springer-Verlag Berlin Heidelberg 2012

However, the mashups built with these tools are essentially static, i.e. depending upon a predefined set of APIs and components. This has an impact on the extendibility and fault-tolerance. Developers of a mashup have to work on the programming code, even if they just want to extend it with services or APIs offering similar functionalities. For instance, there are a few companies now offering local business searching services, e.g. Scoot API[6], Yahoo Local Search API[7], Yelp[8] and CityGrid[9]. New local business searching services might also come to the market at some point. Combining new business searching services to an existing mashup requires both hard coding and re-deployment.

Online services might be unaccessible for reasons such as expiration of API keys, connection failures, request timeout, etc. End-users will suffer from the long response time of the mashups built with these unaccessible services. One possible way to overcome this issue is to switch the mashups to other alternative services. For example, although most of the local business services cover different regions of the world, they (e.g. Yelp and Yahoo Local Search) may have some overlaps with each other. When one of them is off-line, the mashups can use the other one instead.

To address these issues, we propose a novel approach to build dynamic mashups using Web services with lightweight semantics. The UI components interact with unified interfaces of each kind of services, rather than invoking those services directly. iServe, together with its extensions, performs service selection and invocation behind those interfaces. The services to be invoked by the mashups through iServe are controllable and determined at runtime. Therefore, mashups built following our approach are more flexible and robust.

The rest of the paper is organised as follows: Section 2 discuss principles related to semantic services and mashups. Section 3 details the proposed approach to build dynamic service mashups. Section 4 summaries related work. Finally, Section 5 concludes this paper and highlights our future work.

## 2   Services, Mashups and Semantics

A Web service is a set of operations on resources, which are accessible online. Accordingly, there have emerged two types of Web services: operation-oriented services (e.g. SOAP services) and resource-oriented services (e.g. RESTful services). Both SOAP and RESTful services can be exploited as reusable building blocks for new applications. Efforts made to integrate Web services are regarded as service composition [15]. Service composition is usually performed on the business logic layer, and results in executable workflows or plans that fulfil certain requirements of the new Web application. Mashup is an innovative way to develop Web applications by syndicating contents, data and functionalities from distributed sources on the Web. Different from service composition, mashup can

---

[6] http://www.scoot.co.uk/about-us/add-scoot/reference.html

[7] http://developer.yahoo.com/search/local/V3/localSearch.html

[8] http://www.yelp.com/developers/documentation/v2/search_api

[9] http://docs.citygridmedia.com/display/citygridv2/Places+API

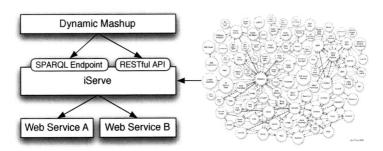

**Fig. 1.** Mashup model

be carried out on layers ranging from data to presentation. Rather than enacting a predefined workflow, components of a mashup are more loose-coupled, and can interact with end-users. In this paper, we focus on service mashups that are aim to bring them together mashups with easy-to-accomplish end-user service compositions [3].

Semantic technologies have been adopted to automate service annotation, discovery, composition and invocation [1]. Ontological models such as OWL-S [10] and WSMO [16] provide formal languages for semantically describing Web services, whereas annotation-based approaches (e.g. SAWSDL [19], hRESTS [7]) enable the creation of lightweight semantic Web services. We employ Minimal Service Model (MSM)[10] to capture the semantics of SOAP and RESTful services, which are essential for selection and invocation of hybrid services. In MSM, a `Service` is defined as a set of operations plus links to functional classifications and non-functional properties. An `Operation` is an atomic unit to be invoked, having properties like input messages, output messages, addresses, faults, etc. Instances of `MessageContent` are containers of the input and output messages exchanged during the invocation of services. A `MessageContent` may comprise a hierarchy of `MessagePart`. Additionally, `modelReference` borrowed from SAWSDL enables the linking of service elements to semantic models via URIs, while `liftingSchemaMapping` and `loweringSchemaMapping` are used to specify data transformations from a syntactic representation to its semantic counterpart and vice versa.

From all above, dynamic mashup is defined as a Web application implemented by selecting and invoking Web services described using MSM. Figure 1 shows the conceptual model of dynamic mashup. By querying against iServe's SPARQL endpoint, a dynamic mashup selects some relevant APIs, and then quests iServe to invoke them. Service invocation through iServe is always in a RESTful way, and some of the inputs might be from the Web of Data. Some of the key features of dynamic mashups are outlined as follows:

- **Dynamics** Mashups can determine which services to invoke on the fly.

---

[10] http://cms-wg.sti2.org/ns/minimal-service-model

- **Transparency** The technical details of service selection and invocation are transparent for the UI components of a mashup.
- **Configurability** Maintainers can easily control the behaviours of a mashup just by revising the strategy of service selection, yet without programming work.
- **Extendibility** To integrate more services offering similar functionalities, developers only need to formally describe those services, and publish them on the Web.
- **Robustness** When a service is temporarily unavailable, a dynamic mashup can smoothly switch to the alternatives.

## 3   Building Dynamic Mashups

In our previous work [13], we have presented iServe, a public registry for semantic services. It can import service descriptions conforming to heterogeneous schemas, and publish them as Linked Data on the Web. iServe exposes a set of Web APIs for manipulating the published service descriptions[11], as well as for service discovery on higher level of abstraction [12].

The proposed approach to build dynamic mashups centres upon iServe and its extensions for service invocation [8]. This section elaborates how to construct dynamic mashups by taking advantage of iServe's capabilities of service discovery and invocation, and also by following the steps listed below.

- **Semantic Services Authoring** This step includes 1) annotating service descriptions with concepts of the MSM and domain ontologies; 2) publishing them as Linked Data via iServe.
- **Specifying Strategies of Service Selection** This step can be done by either exploiting iServe's built-in service discovery mechanisms, or writing SPARQL queries to be executed against the RDF dataset of iServe.
- **Defining Lowering and Lifting Schema Mappings** This step outcomes XSPARQL [2] queries for translating RDF triples into parameters used to invoke services, and also for rewriting the invocation results as RDF statements.
- **Merging Service Invocation Results** This step deals with issues regarding to put together invocation results from different sources, e.g. eradicating any duplicated items, sorting by specific properties, etc.

In order to demonstrate the workflow of building a dynamic mashup, an example is given in this section, which visualises the local business search results on a map (see Figure 2). Besides the Web APIs for local business searching mentioned previously, the mashup also makes use of Google map API[13] and Google Web Toolkit[14].

---

[11] http://iserve.kmi.open.ac.uk/wiki/index.php/IServe_RESTful_API

[12] http://iserve.kmi.open.ac.uk/wiki/index.php/
IServe_Higher_Level_Discovery_API

[13] http://code.google.com/apis/maps/

[14] http://code.google.com/webtoolkit/

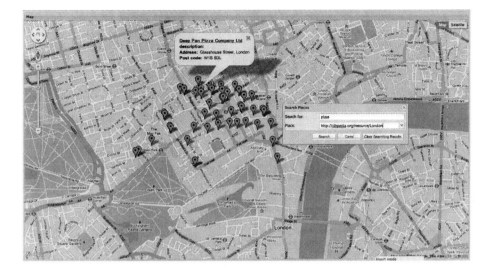

**Fig. 2.** Screenshot of the example of dynamic mashup

### 3.1   Semantic Services Authoring

Essentially, semantic services authoring is to add annotations to the original documents of service descriptions, so as to make them more understandable for machines. Tools such as SWEET and SOWER [9], have been developed to facilitate annotating both HTML and WSDL files. Although authors can arbitrarily annotate services descriptions, we argue that semantic services will be easier to be discovered and invoked, if being annotated following principles and patterns shown below.

- Service categories should be attached to services rather than operations or messages. This can simplify service discovery based on functional classifications.
- The addresses and types of HTTP methods, e.g. GET, POST, PUT, etc., should be declared, otherwise operations will not be able to be invoked.
- Information related to groundings of input messages should be provided.
- Lowering schema mappings must be associated with input messages. When an input message has a hierarchical structure, lowering schemas are usually utilised to annotated message parts on the lowest level. Section 3.3 shows how this can help in the preparation for service invocation.
- In principal, lifting schema mappings are for output messages only.
- In many cases, messages are annotated with concepts of domain ontologies, while their sub-parts are annotated with properties of such concepts. This can ensure the alignment of formal semantics of input/output messages and the ontological knowledge. In addition, it also gives hints on writing and understanding the lifting and lowering schema mappings.

For instance, Listing 1 shows the aforementioned Scoot API described in RDF, using the vocabulary of MSM and several domain ontologies such as DBpedia ontology[15], Service Categories ontology[16] and W3C WGS84 vocabulary[17].

```
service:Scoot a msm:Service;
    msm:hasOperation operations:search;
    sawsdl:modelReference finder:InternetSearch .
operations:search a msm:Operation;
    msm:hasInput inputs:query , inputs:place ;
    msm:hasOutput outputs:result ;
    hrests:hasMethod "GET" ;
    hrests:hasAddress "http://www.scoot.co.uk/api/find.php?format=xml&what={p1
        }&lat={p2}&long={p3}" .
inputs:query a msm:MessageContent;
    sawsdl:modelReference rdf:Literal ;
    hrests:isGroundedIn "p1" .
inputs:place a msm:MessageContent;
    sawsdl:modelReference dbp-ont:Place ;
    msm:hasPart types:lat , types:lng .
outputs:result a msm:MessageContent;
    msm:hasPart types:result-item .
types:lat a msm:MessagePart;
    sawsdl:modelReference geo-pos:lat ;
    sawsdl:loweringSchemaMapping lowerings:lat ;
    hrests:isGroundedIn "p2" .
types:lng  a msm:MessagePart;
    sawsdl:modelReference geo-pos:long ;
    sawsdl:loweringSchemaMapping lowerings:lng ;
    hrests:isGroundedIn "p3" .
types:result-item a msm:MessagePart;
    sawsdl:modelReference dbp-ont:Place ;
    sawsdl:liftingSchemaMapping liftings:result-item .
```

**Listing 1.** Description of Scoot API in RDF

As depicted by Listing 1, Scoot API is assigned to the category of Internet Search. It has one operation called "search", which takes keywords and an instance of `dbp-ont:Place` as inputs, and returns a list of relevant local businesses also as instances of `dbp-ont:Place`. Note that the input message `inputs:place` has one model reference `dbp-ont:Place` and two sub-parts `types:lat` and `types:lng`. And, the model references of `types:lat` and `types:lng` are respectively `geo-pos:lat` and `geo-pos:long`, which are two properties of the concept `dbp-ont:Place`.

## 3.2   Service Selection

This sub-section focuses on SPARQL-based service selection, which enables the on-the-fly refinement of the selection strategies. Listing 2 gives an example seeking for the services used to implement the mashup mentioned before, i.e. those under the category of "Internet Search", taking a `rdf:Literal` value and an instance of `dbp-ont:Place` as inputs, and returning instances of `dbp-ont:Place` as outputs.

---

[15] http://wiki.dbpedia.org/Ontology
[16] http://www.service-finder.eu/ontologies/ServiceCategories
[17] http://www.w3.org/2003/01/geo/wgs84_pos

```
SELECT DISTINCT ?s WHERE {
    ?s rdf:type msm:Service .    ?s sawsdl:modelReference ?c .
    ?c rdfs:subClassOf finder:InternetSearch .
    ?s msm:hasOperation ?o .     ?o msm:hasInput ?in1 .
    ?in1 sawsdl:modelReference rdf:Literal .
    ?o msm:hasInput ?in2 .   ?in2 sawsdl:modelReference ?in2mr .
    dbp-ont:Place rdfs:subClassOf ?in2mr .
    ?o msm:hasOutput ?out . ?out msm:hasPart ?outpart .
    ?outpart sawsdl:modelReference ?outmr .
    ?outmr rdfs:subClassOf dbp-ont:Place .
}
```

**Listing 2.** SPARQL query for service selection

By means of rewriting the SPARQL query above, the mashup can behave more adaptively, namely, dynamically choose the services to invoke. Three examples for the typical usage are listed as follows. Mashup developers can create more complex queries to satisfy their own requirements.

FILTER (?s != service:Scoot)
> When the Scoot service is now unavailable, this filter can avoid the attempts to invoke it. In this way, it also can meet the requirement for smoothly switching between services at runtime.

?o hrests:hasAddress ?addr FILTER regex(str(?addr), ".uk") .
> This clause with the regular expression can select services having addresses that contains ".uk", i.e. services provided by companies registered in the UK.

LIMIT 3
> The solution sequence modifier LIMIT can restrict the number of services to invoke, so as to reduce the response time of the mashup.

### 3.3   Service Invocation

The overall process of service invocation includes dereferencing, lowering, grounding, invoking and lifting. When identifiers of resources on the Web of Data are used as parameters for invoking services, iServe will first attempt to retrieve RDF triples describing those resources, i.e. dereferencing the resources. After that, RDF statements are lowered to literal values by executing XSPARQL queries. Those values are then used to instantiate requests to be sent to the service endpoints. Grounding refers the instantiation of service requests, which is the last step of the preparation for the actual invocation of services. After receiving the results in the format of XML, another set of XSPARQL queries will be executed to transform them into RDF.

As stated in the beginning of Sectionn 3, iServe provides RESTful APIs for publishing and removing the descriptions of semantic services. And, all the services stored in iServe are to be invoked as RESTful APIs. Therefore, an action resource [6], named "invoke", has been added to each operation of the services. In other words, the template of the addresses to invoke services stored in iServe is:

http://.../services/service-id/operations/operation-id/invoke?
 parameter1=$V_1$&parameter=$V_2$&...

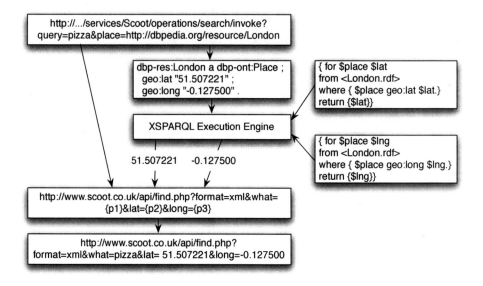

**Fig. 3.** An example for preparing the service request

Figure 3 illustrates the preparation for calling of the search operation of the Scoot service. iServe first found a dereferenceable URI, `http://dbpedia.org/resource/London` in the original request, and got a piece of RDF by sending there an HTTP `GET` with header `Accept: application/rdf+xml`. Then, the XSPARQL query engine loaded that piece of RDF as well as the lowering schema mappings shown on the right hand side of Figure 3, and extracted the latitude and longitude of London. Finally, variables in the URI template were replaced with the query keywords and the values of latitude and longitude. Part of the raw XML file returned by Scoot API is shown in the upper left of Figure 4, while the XSPARQL query guided the lifting of service invocation results is in the upper right. And, some of the generated RDF triples are shown in the lower part of Figure 4.

### 3.4   Extensions to Existing Mashups

As stated in Section 1, one of the key features of dynamic mashups is the extendibility. Developers can integrate new semantic services to built-up mashups without efforts on the modification of the source codes. Taking as an example CityGrid[18], another local business searching service, the following things have to be done to ensure being found by executing the SPARQL query in Section 3.2: firstly, put it into the category of Internet Search by adding a model reference to the service; secondly, use the DBpedia ontology and W3C WGS84 vocabulary to annotate the service description. Moreover, to make it invocable, developers have

---

[18] `http://docs.citygridmedia.com/display/citygridv2/Places+API`

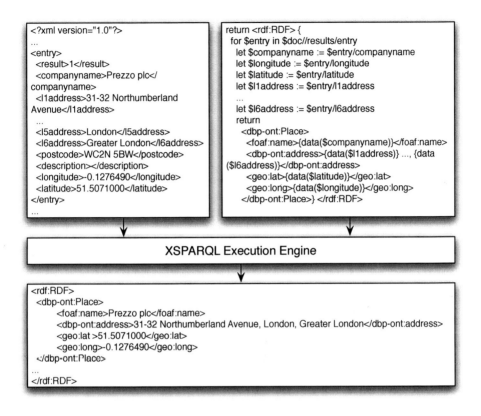

**Fig. 4.** An Example for Lifting

to specify the lowering and lifting schema mappings for the CityGrid service. The lowering schema for Scoot API is particularly reusable in this case. Therefore, the developers only need to write the XSPARQL query (see Listing 3) for data lifting on the basis of analysis on the sample results of invoking the CityGrid service.

```
return < rdf : RDF > {
 for $entry in $doc//locations/location
  let $name := $entry/name
  let $address := $entry/address
  let $street := $address/street
  let $city := $address/city
  let $state := $address/state
  let $postal_code := $address/postal_code
  let $longitude := $entry/longitude
  let $latitude := $entry/latitude
  return < dbp-ont : Place >
    < foaf : name >{data($name)}</ foaf : name >
    < dbp-ont : address >{data($street)}, {data($city)}, {data($state)}, {data(
        $postal_code)}</ dbp-ont : address >
    < geo : lat >{data($latitude)}</ geo : lat >
    < geo : long >{data($longitude)}</ geo : long >
 </ dbp-ont : Place >}  </ rdf : RDF >
```

**Listing 3.** XSPARQL query for lifting CityGrid invocation results

All the results of service invocation are transformed into RDF through data lifting, and they conform to the same ontology. Thus, developers can easily merge them together by adding them to a common RDF model before serialising and sending them to the client side.

# 4   Related Work

Several platforms have been established to facilitate the design and development of mashups. For instance, IBM *Sharable Code* is an online platform to support the whole life-cycle of Web APIs and service mashups [11]. Mashup developers are required to use Domain Specific Language (DSL) to specify data mediation, process mediation and UI customisation. A lightweight framework, Mashlight, is proposed in [5], which is composed of four components: *Block Builder*, *Block Library*, *Mashup Builder* and *Run-time Engine*. Developers can use the Block Builder to encapsulate functionalities as Mashlight Blocks, and save them into the Block Library. Mashup Builder is a visual tool for defining the workflow, and the Run-time Engine is the execution environment to enact the mashups. The overall architecture of Mashlight is similar to our work, but lack of explicit semantics and effective discovery and selection mechanisms.

MatchUp built on top of the IBM Mashup Center provides a solution to the mashup autocompletion [4]. The proposed autocompletion algorithm can recommend relevant components and the connections between them to help users building mashups in a more convenient and intuitive way. Comparing with MatchUp, our approach intends to enable mashups to automatically select and invoke services at runtime, rather than design time.

In the context of Web services, RESTful service composition is another related topic to our work. Bite, a lightweight and executable language for RESTful service composition, is proposed in [17]. Bite offers a basic set of language constructs for specifying the business logics of Web-scale workflows, and inherits concepts from scripting languages such as dynamic data types. Bite has four runtimes to satisfy different requirements. In contrast to introducing a new language, minor extensions are made to BPEL for the composition of RESTful services [12]. Efforts also have been made to automate the process of RESTful service composition [21].

The work stated above adopts little semantic technology. SA-REST, an annotation-based approach to add semantics to RESTful services, is briefly described in [18]. Mashups created using SA-REST, denoted with *smashup* (semantic mashup), are to be hosted at a proxy server together with domain ontologies. Similar to our approach, the data mediation is carried out through lowering and lifting, but implemented with XSLT. To my best knowledge, SA-REST does not address the issues of service modelling, registry and discovery.

Apart form SA-REST, *Semantic Web Pipes* (SWP) proposed in [14] is a rapid prototype method of semantic mashups on the data layer. SWP provides a set of operators for merging, splitting and transforming RDF triples in the cloud of Linked Data. It extends SPARQL with workflows, and implements dynamic transformations of RDF data using XQuery and XSPARQL. Our approach also follows the principles of Linked Data and applies SPARQL, XSPARQL for data mediation.

## 5  Conclusions and Future Work

In this paper, we present a novel method of building mashups using Web services with lightweight semantics, which is implemented based on iServe and its extensions for service invocation. By applying our approach, mashups gain the ability of selecting and invoking semantic services. Moreover, developers can easily extend a mashup without programming work, as well as switch it to the alternatives with a service is unaccessible. In short, our approach is effective for building mashups more flexible, robust and extendible.

Our future work will involve realising the caching mechanisms for service selection, and filtering services by QoS parameters, e.g. availability, response time, throughput, etc. In addition, we will also focus on the context-awareness of mashups, i.e. automatically change the strategies of service selection according the running state of the involving services. For example, when a service is down, mashups can be aware of it and automatically switch to alternative ones with high semantic similarity.

**Acknowledgements.** This work is partly funded by the EU project SOA4All (FP7-215219) and NoTube (FP7-231761). The authors would like to thank the European Commission for their support.

## References

1. Agarwal, S., Handschuh, S., Staab, S.: Annotation, composition and invocation of semantic web services. Web Semantics 2(1), 31–48 (2004)
2. Akhtar, W., Kopecký, J., Krennwallner, T., Polleres, A.: XSPARQL: Traveling Between the XML and RDF Worlds – and Avoiding the XSLT Pilgrimage. In: Bechhofer, S., Hauswirth, M., Hoffmann, J., Koubarakis, M. (eds.) ESWC 2008. LNCS, vol. 5021, pp. 432–447. Springer, Heidelberg (2008)
3. Benslimane, D., Dustdar, S., Sheth, A.: Services Mashups: The New Generation of Web Applications. IEEE Internet Computing 12(5), 13–15 (2008)
4. Greenshpan, O., Milo, T., Polyzotis, N.: Autocompletion for Mashups. Proceedings of the VLDB Endowment 2(1), 538–549 (2009)
5. Guinea, S., Baresi, L., Albinola, M., Carcano, M.: Mashlight: a Lightweight Mashup Framework for Everyone. In: Proceedings of 2nd Workshop on Mashups, Enterprise Mashups and Lightweight Composition on the Web (MEM 2009) at WWW 2009 (2009)
6. Hadley, M., Pericas-Geertsen, S., Sandoz, P.: Exploring Hypermedia Support in Jersey. In: Proceedings of the First International Workshop on RESTful Design, WS-REST 2010, pp. 10–14. ACM, New York (2010)
7. Kopecký, J., Gomadam, K., Vitvar, T.: hRESTS: an HTML Microformat for Describing RESTful Web Services. In: The 2008 IEEE/WIC/ACM International Conference on Web Intelligence (WI 2008). IEEE CS Press (2008)

8. Li, N., Pedrinaci, C., Kopecký, J., Maleshkova, M., Liu, D., Domingue, J.: Towards Automated Invocation of Web APIs. In: Poster at the 8th Extended Semantic Web Conference, ESWC 2011 (to appear, 2011)
9. Maleshkova, M., Pedrinaci, C., Domingue, J.: Supporting the Creation of Semantic RESTful Service Descriptions. In: Workshop: Service Matchmaking and Resource Retrieval in the Semantic Web (SMR2) at 8th International Semantic Web Conference (2009)
10. Martin, D., Paolucci, M., McIlraith, S.A., Burstein, M., McDermott, D., McGuinness, D.L., Parsia, B., Payne, T.R., Sabou, M., Solanki, M., Srinivasan, N., Sycara, K.: Bringing Semantics to Web Services: The OWL-S Approach. In: Cardoso, J., Sheth, A.P. (eds.) SWSWPC 2004. LNCS, vol. 3387, pp. 26–42. Springer, Heidelberg (2005)
11. Maximilien, E.M., Ranabahu, A., Gomadam, K.: An Online Platform for Web APIs and Service Mashups. IEEE Internet Computing 12(5), 32–43 (2008)
12. Pautasso, C.: RESTful Web Service Composition with BPEL for REST. Data and Knowledge Engineering 68(9), 851–866 (2009)
13. Pedrinaci, C., Liu, D., Maleshkova, M., Lambert, D., Kopecký, J., Domingue, J.: iServe: a Linked Services Publishing Platform. In: Proceedings of Ontology Repositories and Editors for the Semantic Web at 7th ESWC (2010)
14. Phuoc, D.L., Polleres, A., Tummarello, G., Morbidoni, C., Hauswirth, M.: Rapid Semantic Web Mashup Development through Semantic Web Pipes. In: Proceedings of the 18th World Wide Web Conference (WWW 2009), Madrid, Spain, pp. 581–590 (2009)
15. Rao, J., Su, X.: A Survey of Automated Web Service Composition Methods. In: Cardoso, J., Sheth, A.P. (eds.) SWSWPC 2004. LNCS, vol. 3387, pp. 43–54. Springer, Heidelberg (2005)
16. Roman, D., Keller, U., Lausen, H., de Bruijn, J., Lara, R., Stollberg, M., Polleres, A., Feier, C., Bussler, C., Fensel, D.: Web Service Modeling Ontology. Applied Ontology 1(1), 77–106 (2005)
17. Rosenberg, F., Curbera, F., Duftler, M.J., Khalaf, R.: Composing RESTful Services and Collaborative Workflows: A Lightweight Approach. IEEE Internet Computing 12(5), 24–31 (2008)
18. Sheth, A.P., Gomadam, K., Lathem, J.: SA-REST: Semantically Interoperable and Easier-to-Use Services and Mashups. IEEE Internet Computing 11(6), 91–94 (2007)
19. W3C: Semantic Annotations for WSDL and XMLSchema (2007), http://www.w3.org/TR/sawsdl/
20. Yu, J., Benatallah, B., Casati, F., Daniel, F.: Understanding Mashup Development. IEEE Internet Computing 12(5), 44–52 (2008)
21. Zhao, H., Doshi, P.: Towards Automated RESTful Web Service Composition. In: Proceedings of 7th IEEE International Conference on Web Services(ICWS 2009), pp. 189–196. IEEE Computer Society (2009)

# Task-Based Recommendation
# of Mashup Components

Vincent Tietz*, Gregor Blichmann**, Stefan Pietschmann, and Klaus Meißner

Technische Universität Dresden, Faculty of Computer Science
01062 Dresden, Germany
{vincent.tietz,gregor.blichmann,stefan.pietschmann,
klaus.meissner}@tu-dresden.de

**Abstract.** Presentation-oriented mashup applications are usually developed by manual selection and assembly of pre-existent components. The latter are either described on a very technical, functional level, or using informal descriptors, such as tags, which bear certain ambiguities. With regard to the increasing number and complexity of available components, their discovery and integration has become a challenge for non-programmers. Therefore, we present a novel concept for the task-based recommendation of mashup components, which comprises a more natural, task-driven description of user requirements and a corresponding semantic matching algorithm for universal mashup components. By its realization and integration with an composition platform, we could prove the feasibility and sufficiency of our approach.

**Keywords:** Requirements specification, task modeling, mashup component recommendation, semantics, methodology.

## 1 Introduction

Presentation-oriented *mashups* introduce the user interface (SWS) as a new integration layer for service-based applications and have become a prominent approach for the lightweight integration of distributed and decoupled web resources. Originally, mashups have been developed by manual, script-based integration of heterogeneous application programming interfaces (SWSs). Addressing non-programmers, *mashup tools* like *Yahoo! Pipes*, *JackBe Presto* or the *mashArt editor* [7] have emerged to support the visual composition of technology-independent web services, SWSs and SWS components.

Despite the simplicity of composition metaphors, the discovery of components remains difficult. The search is occasionally facilitated by recommendations based on keywords, interface descriptions and community feedback, e. g., in *programmableweb.com* and *IBM Mashup Center*. However, in the light of growing repositories and ambiguous tags, the identification of proper search criteria becomes an increasing challenge for unexperienced users.

---

* Funded by the European Social Fund (ESF), Free State Saxony (Germany) and Saxonia Systems AG (Germany, Dresden), filed under ESF-080939514.
** Funded by the ESF and Free State Saxony (Germany), filed under ESF-080951805.

A. Harth and N. Koch (Eds.): ICWE 2011 Workshops, LNCS 7059, pp. 25–36, 2012.

Instead of coping with technical details, users – typically domain experts – need to express their requirements in a more natural way. Since task analysis is considered as an intuitive way to gather user requirements for interactive systems [12], we strive for a task-based elicitation of user requirements. Thereby, user activities can be identified at design-time, avoiding low-level implementation details and using intuitive decomposition into smaller parts as well as the identification of used domain and application objects [16].

Fig. 1 shows an exemplary task description for planning a conference participation. In order to receive suggestions for routes of the public transportation services, a participant needs to input start and destination location as well as corresponding temporal constraints. In addition he or she needs information about available hotels and the weather near the conference location. Therefore, the task "Conference Participation" is decomposed into "Specify Criteria", "Calculation" and "Read Travel Information". Mashup components can be considered as self-contained entities solving these tasks. As an example, a map component could be used to specify start and destination location *(interaction task)*. Similarly, list components can display routes and hotels. In contrast, for "Search Hotels" and "Search Routes" components encapsulating web services could be employed, as these tasks are performed by the system *(system task)*.

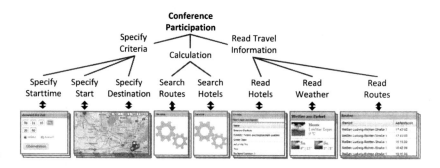

**Fig. 1.** Travel planning scenario

In this paper, we present a concept for the task-based recommendation of mashup components. It comprises a formal task model, whose instances serve as requirements descriptions, and a corresponding semantic matching algorithm that enables recommendation during design-time. The basis of our approach is the idea of universal mashup composition that we outline in Section 2. In Section 3, we summarize the related work for task modeling and task-based web service discovery. Building on that, we describe our ontology-based task model in Section 4 and our approach for task-based recommendation of mashup components in Section 5. Finally, we discuss the results in Section 6 and outline further work in Section 7.

# 2    Model-Driven Semantic Mashup Composition

As mashup components are considered as task-solving entities, a component description beyond the exposure of interface signatures is needed, representing both functional and data semantics. Therefore, our concept builds on the component model of the CRUISe project [19], as it provides a universal semantic interface to heterogeneous web resources, ranging from UI widgets to SOAP and RESTful web services. Additionally, automatic and semi-automatic encapsulation of web content and applications is gradually improved by ongoing work.

The central idea of CRUISe is the extension of the service-oriented paradigm to the presentation layer supporting *universal composition* [7]. Therein, mashups are built from uniform constituents residing on all application layers. Back-end services can be seamlessly integrated with UI components using the same principles and abstract interface descriptors. Thus, we denote a *mashup application* as a composition of uniform components encapsulating distributed web resources, i.e., services providing data, business logic, or user interface parts. With respect to this paper, all of those components represent tasks or subtasks – either involving user interaction or application logics.

CRUISe proposes a model-driven development process for building mashup applications from these components. It includes a platform-independent composition model as well as a service-oriented infrastructure for the dynamic, context-aware composition and adaptation at runtime. As our concept employs the same component models and covers the design-time phase of this process, we briefly outline the most relevant conceptual foundations for our work in the following.

## 2.1    Semantic Component Model

The universal composition of a mashup requires that all constituent parts adhere to a generic component model [20]. In the following, we highlight the semantic annotations, as they form the basis for our task-based recommendation.

In our conceptual space, every component – representing a service, application logic, or UI – is a black-box of independent software with an internal state. All components are described using three abstractions, namely *property*, *event*, and *operation*. The set of properties resembles the visible state and allows the configuration of components. Whenever the internal state changes, events are issued to inform the runtime system and other components. Finally, state changes, calculations and other arbitrary functionality of a component can be triggered by invoking their operations with the help of events. Events and operations may themselves contain *parameters*, realizing the data flow within the mashup.

The *Semantic Mashup Component Description Language (SWS)* allows the description of a component interface – comparable to WSDL for web services – and the semantic annotation of a component descriptor $C_c$ at three different levels by linking certain parts with semantic models: typing of properties and parameters (*data semantics*), the definition of *functional semantics* of components $A_c$, operations $OP_c$, and events $EV_c$, as well as *non-functional semantics*, e.g., for pricing, licensing, and other metadata $M_c$.

Listing 1.1 shows a partial description of a SWS component "RouteHotel-Comp" $(C_1)$, which facilitates the search for public transportation service routes (using start/destination location and start/destination time) and hotels in a certain area. As a result, the component displays routes and hotels using sortable lists. The semantic annotation of its interface is realized by linking it to semantic descriptors for "functionality" and data "type". The prefix "to" denotes concepts of the travel domain as part of a domain ontology $TO$, while "ao" is used for concepts of the action ontology $AO$, which currently represents actions through a combination of specializations out of *ao:Input*, *ao:Output* and *ao:Manipulate* via inheritance. Since the functionality of sortable lists is not represented by the component interface (because it is triggered only by user interaction), the corresponding semantic concept *ao:Sort* is annotated at component level (line 1). The data semantics of the parameter *location* in the operation *setStart* is related to the concept *to:Location* (line 3). The functional semantics of *setStart* (line 2), *setDest* (line 5), *setStartTime* (line 8), *setDestTime* (line 11) and *rSearched* (line 14) is equally *ao:SearchRoute*, because all this pieces are necessary to realize the search of routes. The attribute "trigger" (e.g., line 14) indicates the source of the event, which is either *system, operation*, or *interaction*.

```
 1  <mcdl ... name="RouteHotelComp" functionality="ao:Sort"> ...
 2  <operation name="setStart" functionality="ao:SearchRoute">
 3      <parameter name="location" type="to:Location"/>
 4  </operation>
 5  <operation name="setDest" functionality="ao:SearchRoute ao:SearchHotel">
 6      <parameter name="location" type="to:Location"/>
 7  </operation>
 8  <operation name="setStartTime" functionality="ao:SearchRoute">
 9      <parameter name="time" type="to:StartTime"/>
10  </operation>
11  <operation name="setDestTime" functionality="ao:SearchRoute">
12      <parameter name="time" type="to:DestinationTime"/>
13  </operation>
14  <event name="rSearched" trigger="operation" functionality="ao:SearchRoute">
15      <parameter name="result" type="to:RouteList"/>
16  </event>
17  <event name="hSearched" trigger="operation" functionality="ao:SearchHotel">
18      <parameter name="result" type="to:HotelList"/>
19  </event>
20  <event name="rSelected" trigger="interaction" functionality="ao:Input">
21      <parameter name="result" type="to:Route"/>
22  </event> ... </mcdl>
```

**Listing 1.1.** Example mashup component $C_1$ for searching routes and hotels

## 2.2   Semantic Mashup Composition

In CRUISe, a platform-independent composition model [20] specifies the components to be integrated, incorporating information from their descriptors and defining aspects like the data and control flow, the visual layout, the adaptive behavior of the overall composition. It is interpreted by a runtime environment, which further integrates all components from a repository and executes the mashup, correspondingly. This infrastructure and integration process as well as the adaptivity concepts have been realized and validated. Yet, it is important to realize the crucial role of the design-process, i.e., the authoring, in this context. They key challenge in rapid mashup development – especially with regard to *end-user development* – is the discovery and seamless integration of the right components in a certain context. Hence, the remaining paper addresses the question, how non-programmers may be able to find components and build such models. Before we get more into details, we discuss related efforts from the fields of task modeling and task-based service discovery.

# 3   Related Work

As already stated, our work envisions the recommendation of mashup components from task descriptions. Therefore, the latter must feature a formal representation with semantic references, so that actions and data of the tasks can be semantically matched with functionality and data of mashup components.

In this context, the lack in using semantic technologies and in formalism of action and domain modeling impede the use of traditional task modeling approaches (e. g., HTA [1], GOMS [5], GTA [22] and K-MAD [3]). A prominent task modeling approach is CTT [17] that is used in many model-based user interface development approaches, e. g., MARIA [18] and UsiXML [14]. However, based on the CAMELEON reference framework [4], which includes a four-stage transformation starting with a task model and ending up with the final SWS, only the manual identification of presentation items and sets is utilized.

With regard to the semantic matching of data and functional concepts, semantic web service (SWS) discovery utilizes logic-based, e. g., [6], non-logic-based, e. g., [9], or hybrid matchings [10]. While logic-based approaches use deduction to decide if concepts are equal (exact match), part of each other (subsume) and (plug-in) or distinct (fail), non-logic-based ones rely on syntactic, structural and numerical analysis, and hybrid approaches combine both. Overall, the major drawback of SWS is the use of technical service templates for discovering web services, which impedes non-expert users from expressing and satisfying their business demands [21].

Task-based recommendation usually involves the mapping of an interaction or system task to a SWS or non-SWS component, whereas also sets of tasks and components need to be considered. Corresponding task-based discovery mechanisms are supported by an extension of MARIA [11] and the SeTEF framework [21]. However, the former only supports the discovery of web services for system tasks, while the latter uses an ontology-based task description OWL-T that is transformed to SAWSDL and, therefore, is restricted to non-UI components. Furthermore, the description of tasks highly depends on knowledge about available service operations, and only one-on-one mapping between tasks and service operations are supported, which impedes the search for combinations of operations. In contrast, our approach facilitates the task-based recommendation of SWS and non-SWS mashup components during design-time by using semantic annotations in tasks and components across operations and events.

In the following, we introduce the underlying ontology-based task model and the matching algorithm employed for component recommendation.

## 4   Ontology-Based Task Model

Based on specific [15,17] and uniforming [8,13] task models, we derived a mini-
malistic task ontology – illustrated in Fig. 2 – to support user-centered analysis
and description of a specific domain problem. Since mashup components are
considered as black-boxes, we focus rather on the expression of required data
and functional semantics than on conditions and effects in order to recommend
components. Therefore, a *task* is mainly characterized by its inputs *(hasInputObject)*, outputs *(hasOutputObject)*, manipulating actions *(hasAction)* and category
*(hasCategory)*. A *composite task* consists of at least two subtasks *(hasChildTask)*,
whereas, subtasks are always a specialization of a parent task. *Grouping* enables
the temporal relations *sequence, arbitrary sequence, choice* and *parallel* between
subtasks of a composite task [2]. Both, task hierarchy and grouping facilitate
task analysis and description at different abstraction levels.

   In order to express *what* is intended to be done, *actions* can be assigned to
composite and atomic tasks. Because, *atomic tasks* comprises only one action,
we can specify exactly the data objects involved to realize the functionality represented by the action (e. g., the search of a list of hotels based nearby a certain
location). Data objects *(hasInputObject* and *hasOutputObject)* are represented
as ontology concepts or individuals from a domain ontology. Actions are formalized by the independent classification *AO* to represent the task's functionality
(e. g., *ao:Sort* and *ao:Search* in Fig. 3).

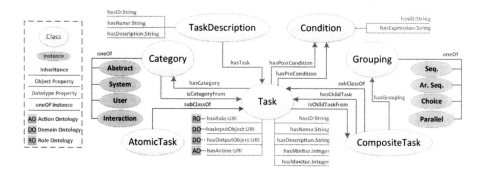

**Fig. 2.** Task ontology

   Since mashups provide SWS and non-SWS components, we follow [17] and
distinguish the *task categories*: *system, interaction, user* and *abstract*. System
tasks are exclusively performed by components. For example, "Search Routes" in
our scenario could be modeled as a system task. Whereas, *interaction* indicates
that an interaction between humans and an SWS is required, e. g., setting a
marker on a map in order to specify the start location. User tasks require no
interaction with the system, e. g., fetching a folder. An abstract task groups
heterogeneous subtasks (e. g., "Conference Participation") and is the default
task category providing all kinds of components during recommendation.

Finally, we formalize tasks as a tuple $T_t = (M_t, A_t, c_t, IN_t, OUT_t, R_t, C_t)$ defined by metadata $M_t$ like name and description, a set of actions $A_t \subseteq AO$, a category $c_t \in \{interaction, system, user, abstract\}$, a set of inputs and outputs $IN_t, OUT_t \subseteq DO$, roles $R_t$ and conditions $C_t$. Considering our scenario, an example task "Search Routes" requires a start and a destination location as well as a start time to search a list of routes. Therefore, the task $T_1$ is defined as $(\{$"Search Routes"$\}, \{ao{:}Search\}, system, \{to{:}StartLocation,$ $to{:}DestinationLocation, to{:}StartTime\}, \{to{:}RouteList\}, \emptyset, \emptyset)$. Because roles and conditions are required neither in the scenario nor to explain the recommendation algorithm, these sets are empty. However, a role could be *Administrator*, represented by a concept of a role ontology. The restriction that *to:StartLocation* needs to be a European city is a possible pre-condition.

Using semantic technologies this ontology-based task model enables the task-based recommendation of previously introduced mashup components which is presented in the following section.

## 5   Task-Based Recommendation

Our approach aims to fill the gap between a user-centered requirements specification and semantic mashup component discovery. In order to match different semantic concepts annotated in task and component descriptions, we propose the two subsumption-based functions *CoreMatch* and *SetMatch*. Further, we consider the mapping of inputs and outputs between tasks and components as well as their functional semantics. Building on that, we present our task-based recommendation algorithm.

### 5.1   Calculation of Subsumption-Based Similarity

In order to compare and rate different semantic annotations used in tasks and components, we propose a subsumption-based matching, referring to logic-based web service matchings [6].

The core matching degrees $CoreMatch(r, a)$ between the request $r$ and the advertisement $a$ are defined by *exact* ($5 \Leftrightarrow r \equiv a$), *plug-in* ($\frac{4}{s} \Leftrightarrow r \sqsubseteq a$), *subsume* ($3 \Leftrightarrow a \sqsubseteq r$) and *fail* ($0 \Leftrightarrow else$), where $s$ is the number of sibling nodes $s$ (with $s \geq 1$) at the same distance. Fig. 3 shows an example for requesting *ao:SearchRoute*. Therein, the advertisement *ao:SearchBusRoute* subsumes *ao:SearchRoute* and, therefore, the result is 3. The distance $dist(r, a)$ is defined by the number of inheritances related from the request $r$ to the advertisement $a$. In the case of a plug-in, we divide the result by $s$ in order to consider partial concepts, e. g., the advertisement of *ao:Sort* represents only one part of the requested functionality and can be potentially combined with other sub-functionalities. For example, the functionality represented by *ao:Search* is a specialization of *ao:Sort* and *ao:Calculate*. Therefore, *ao:Sort* and *ao:Calculate* are siblings at the distance 2 and $CoreMatch(ao{:}SearchRoute, ao{:}Sort) = \frac{4}{2} = 2$.

Further, we define the function $SetMatch(R, A)$ that calculates the rank of $R$ and $A$ as sets of requested and advertised ontology concepts. First, this function

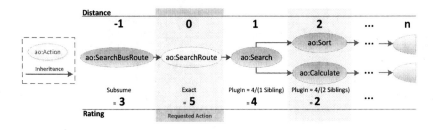

**Fig. 3.** Rating and distances related to a request of *ao:SearchRoute*

groups all best core matches of each member of $R$ and $A$ and, finally, returns the average of all best matching degrees. For example, $SetMatch(\{ao:SearchRoute,$ $ao:SearchHotel\},\{to:Search\}) = 2.0$, because $ao:SearchRoute$ builds the best assignment with $ao:Search$ as subsumption (4) and $ao:SearchHotel$ could not be further matched because $A$ has no concepts left. The final result is 2.0, the average of 4.0 and 0.0. In the following, we use $SetMatch(R, A)$ for rating different aspects (e. g. data and functional semantics) of tasks and components.

### 5.2   Mapping Data Semantics of Components with Tasks

In general, component descriptions include events representing output and operations representing input (cf. Section 2). In order to match tasks and components, a task-aligned interpretation of these descriptions is required. From the perspective of user interaction, a SWS component signalizes the input of data by triggering an event, e. g., as result of a user selecting a location on a map component. On the other hand, the output of data, e. g., its visualization on the map, is realized by an operation. Therefore, inputs of an interaction task must be mapped to the data semantics of events $IN_t \rightarrow d(EV_c)$, while its outputs must be mapped to operations of a component $OUT_t \rightarrow d(OP_c)$, accordingly.

While this applies to interaction tasks, it does not for system tasks. In this case, inputs are mapped naturally to operations $(IN_t \rightarrow d(OP_c))$, e. g., to invoke a search for hotels based on a location as parameter, and the outputs are mapped to events $(OUT_t \rightarrow d(EV_c))$. If the task category is *abstract*, it cannot be decided how to map inputs and outputs. Therefore, the mapping and rating needs to be carried out for both, whereas the maximum of both ratings is returned.

### 5.3   Task-Based Recommendation

In the following, we describe the algorithm $Match(T, C)$ that returns an ordered list of rated recommendations out of a set of components $C$ for a task instance $T$ that is compliant with the proposed task ontology. The algorithm exploits the previously mentioned matching principles in order to rate CRUISe components for each task.

**Reducing complexity.** In the first step, the complexity of the task model is reduced in order to optimize the matching performance. Therein, user tasks are omitted, because no component is required. Next, parent tasks are removed, because subtasks are an equal or more detailed representation of their parents regarding actions, inputs, and outputs. Finally, the amount of component candidates is reduced for each task based on its category. If the category is *interaction*, service and logic components are excluded, because they offer no SWS.

**Interim ratings and data structure.** In the second step, we compare each task $T_t$ with each component candidate $C_c$. The final rating $rtc_{fin}$ of a component, is the maximum of the two interim ratings $rtc_1$ and $rtc_2$. $rtc_1$ reflects the matching of the overall semantic annotation of the component and $rtc_2$ considers the semantics of operations and events (including data and functionality) of the component. In order to calculate the interim rating $rtc_2$, a data structure similar to Table 1 is created that represents a task-like interpretation of each component description. With the help of the table, the ratings of the functional semantics $m_{act}^i$ and the data semantics $m_{in}^i$ and $m_{out}^i$ of the component are determined. In the following, we describe in detail, how the table is filled and how both interim ratings are calculated. For this, we use the previously introduced task $T_1$ (cf. Section 4) and component $C_1$ (cf. Section 2).

**Table 1.** Intermediate results of the matching algorithm $Match(T_1, C_1)$

| $i$ | $d_{ti}$ | $act_i$ | $m_{act}^i$ | $D_{in}(act_i)$ | $m_{in}^i$ | $D_{out}(act_i)$ | $m_{out}^i$ | $r_i$ |
|---|---|---|---|---|---|---|---|---|
| 1 | -1 | ao:SearchRoute | 3.0 | to:Location to:Location to:StartTime to:DestinationTime | 4.33 | to:RouteList | 5.0 | 3.83 |
| 2 | -1 | ao:SearchHotel | 3.0 | to:Location | 1.67 | to:HotelList | 0.0 | 1.92 |
| 3 | $\infty$ | ao:Input | 0.0 | $\emptyset$ | 0.0 | to:Route | 0.0 | 0.0 |
| | | | | | | | $rtc_2$ | 3.83 |

**Functional semantics of components.** The first interim rating $rtc_1$ reflects the matching of the overall semantic annotation of the component $A_c$ requesting the actions of the task $A_t$. Using our example, this is $rtc_1 = SetMatch(A_t, A_c) = SetMatch(\{ao:Search\}, \{ao:Sort\}) = 2.0$ (cf. Fig. 3). Because we define that functional and data semantic are equally weighted and no data semantic is annotated at this level, $rtc_1$ is divided by 2 which results in 1.0.

**Functional semantics of operations and events.** In order to calculate the ratings of the functional semantics $m_{act}^i$, each annotated action $act_i$ of all operations and events is added to a distinct action list. If an interaction task is requested, only events with the trigger "interaction" are considered (e. g., line 20 in Listing 1.1). Then, the rating for the functional semantics $m_{act}^i$ is calculated by $SetMatch(A_t, act_i)$. This means that all actions of the task $A_t$ are requested for each functionality $act_i$ of the component. In our example, $m_{act}^1 = SetMatch(\{ao:Search\}, \{ao:SearchRoute\}) = 3.0$.

**Data semantics.** The rating of the data semantics $m_{in}^i$ and $m_{out}^i$ is based on both columns $D_{in}(act_i)$ and $D_{out}(act_i)$ as advertisements and the input $IN_t$ and output $OUT_t$ of the task as requests. According to our example, the task category equals *system*, therefore, $D_{in}(act_i)$ gets filled with the data semantics of all operations annotated by the functionality $act_i$ and $D_{out}(act_i)$ gets filled with the data semantics of all events annotated the functionality $act_i$ (cf. Section 5.2). In general, $m_{in}^i$ is calculated by $SetMatch(IN_t, D_{in}(act_i))$ and $m_{out}^i$ by $SetMatch(OUT_t, D_{out}(act_i))$.

For example, $m_{in}^1 = SetMatch(\{to:StartLocation, to:DestinationLocation, to:StartTime\}, D_{in}(act_1)) = 4.33$. Further, $m_{out}^1 = SetMatch(\{to:RouteList\}, D_{out}(act_1)) = 5.0$. Because we weight functional and data semantics equally, the rating for each row $(r_i)$ is the average of $m_{act}^i$ and the average of $m_{in}^i$ and $m_{out}^i$. For example, $r_1 = \frac{1}{2}(3.0 + \frac{1}{2}(4.33 + 5.0)) = 3.83$.

**Detecting sub-functionalities.** As mentioned in Section 5.1, it is possible to detect and merge associated sub-functionalities like *ao:Calculate* and *ao:Sort*. For this, we use the distance $d_{ti}$ between the requested $A_t$ and advertised $act_i$ and group all *subsumes* (where $0 < d < \infty$) having the same distance.

Then, we sum their functional semantics rating and build the average of their data semantic rating, to end up in one new row including all sub-functionalities. This allows us to handle functionalities across multiple operations and events. In our example, no grouping is necessary, because we get two subsuming concepts (*ao:SearchRoute, ao:SearchHotel*) and two fails (*ao:Input, ao:Output*).

**Final rating result.** As previously mentioned, $rtc_1$ considers the overall functionality of the component and $rtc_2$ represents the best match for functional and data semantics of all operations and events. Therefore, $rtc_2$ is the maximum of all $r_i$. Finally, the highest value out of $rtc_1$ and $rtc_2$ is the final result $r_{fin}$ of the matching algorithm for a task and a component. In our example $r_{fin}$ equals 3.83, because this is the maximum of $rtc_1 = 1.0$ and $rtc_2 = 3.83$. The matching is done for all tasks $\in T$ and all components $\in C$. In the end, the result tuple $RT = (T_t, \{(C_c, rtc_{fin})\})$ includes for every task $T_t$ a set of component proposals, represented by their id and rating.

## 6   Implementation and Discussion

We have successfully implemented the proposed algorithm as a part of a service-oriented and Java-based component repository of CRUISe. The repository registers, manages, matches and ranks components and offers a web service interface. The matching can be based on a SMCDL template or, as used in this case, on an instance of the task ontology. The repository and the matching algorithm use the semantic web framework Jena (http://jena.sourceforge.net/) in order to access OWL knowledge bases using plain Java.

We have tested the algorithm with a task model representing our scenario and a set of components such as generic and specific input and output components (e. g., for locations, time and routing) getting expected ranks. However, in order to get reliable results we plan to evaluate the algorithm within a broad user study utilizing more scenarios and components.

Since we address the design-time, performance is negligible to a certain degree. However, the current response time is about 1s for one task and 50 components and tends to be more than proportional with the increasing number of components and tasks. Therefore, we plan to implement caching and other optimizations.

Regarding the use of ontologies, we assume that component developers and task modelers have a common understanding of how functionalities and data are semantically represented. Currently, we use self-developed travel and action ontologies on the basis of the introduced scenario. In principle, any knowledge base can be used and matching as well as aggregating ontology concepts can be applied in future.

## 7 Conclusion and Further Work

The contribution of this work is twofold. First, we presented an ontology-based task model that allows formal and lightweight modeling of user's requirements for composite mashup applications on the basis of existing knowledge bases. This addresses our key requirements regarding the formalization and abstraction of any specific service operation or user interface component. Second, we provide a matching algorithm based on semantically annotated mashup components in order to support discovery for task-based requirements. The key feature is the proposal and rating of components realizing specific as well as partly supported functionalities across services and components during the design-time.

Regarding the discussion in Section 6, further work addresses the optimization and evaluation of the recommendation algorithm particularly by utilizing a user study. Further, we explore the opportunity of semi-automatic composition utilizing the proposed task model and recommendation of components. Currently, we work on the design and the implementation of an authoring tool in order to allow task modeling for non-programmers and to determine concepts for ontology-based modeling. Finally, this work is an important step towards a task-based development approach for composite mashup applications.

## References

1. Annett, J., Duncan, K.: Task analysis and training design. Hull Univ. (England). Dept. of Psychology (1967)
2. Betermieux, S., Bomsdorf, B.: Finalizing Dialog Models at Runtime. In: Baresi, L., Fraternali, P., Houben, G.-J. (eds.) ICWE 2007. LNCS, vol. 4607, pp. 137–151. Springer, Heidelberg (2007)
3. Caffiau, S., Scapin, D.L., Girard, P., Baron, M., Jambon, F.: Increasing the expressive power of task analysis: Systematic comparison and empirical assessment of tool-supported task models. Interacting with Computers 22(6), 569–593 (2010)
4. Calvary, G., Coutaz, J., Thevenin, D., Limbourg, Q., Bouillon, L., Vanderdonckt, J.: A Unifying Reference Framework for multi-target user interfaces. Interacting with Computers 15, 289–308 (2003)
5. Card, S., Moran, T., Newell, A.: The Psychology of Human-Computer Interaction. Lawrence Erlbaum, Hillsdale (1983)

6. Chabeb, Y., Tata, S., Ozanne, A.: YASA-M: A Semantic Web Service Matchmaker. In: 24th IEEE International Conference on Advanced Information Networking and Applications (AINA 2010), pp. 966–973 (2010)
7. Daniel, F., Casati, F., Benatallah, B., Shan, M.-C.: Hosted Universal Composition: Models, Languages and Infrastructure in mashArt. In: Laender, A.H.F., Castano, S., Dayal, U., Casati, F., de Oliveira, J.P.M. (eds.) ER 2009. LNCS, vol. 5829, pp. 428–443. Springer, Heidelberg (2009)
8. Goschnick, S., Sonenberg, L., Balbo, S.: A Composite Task Meta-Model as a Reference Model. In: Forbrig, P., Paternó, F., Mark Pejtersen, A. (eds.) HCIS 2010. IFIP Advances in Information and Communication Technology, vol. 332, pp. 26–38. Springer, Heidelberg (2010)
9. Klein, M., König-Ries, B.: Coupled Signature and Specification Matching for Automatic Service Binding. In: Zhang, L.-J., Jeckle, M. (eds.) ECOWS 2004. LNCS, vol. 3250, pp. 183–197. Springer, Heidelberg (2004)
10. Klusch, M.: Semantic web service coordination. In: CASCOM: Intelligent Service Coordination in the Semantic Web. Whitestein Series in Software Agent Tech. and Autonomic Computing, Birkhäuser, pp. 59–104 (2008)
11. Kritikos, K., Paternò, F.: Service discovery supported by task models. In: 2nd ACM SIGCHI Symp. on Engineering Interactive Computing Systems, EICS 2010 (2010)
12. Limbourg, Q., Vanderdonckt, J.: Comparing task models for user interface design. In: The Handbook of Task Analysis for Human-Computer Interaction, pp. 135–154. Lawrence Erlbaum Associates (2003)
13. Limbourg, Q., Pribeanu, C., Vanderdonckt, J.: Towards Uniformed Task Models in a Model-Based Approach. In: Johnson, C. (ed.) DSV-IS 2001. LNCS, vol. 2220, pp. 164–182. Springer, Heidelberg (2001)
14. Limbourg, Q., Vanderdonckt, J., Michotte, B., Bouillon, L., López-Jaquero, V.: USIXML: A Language Supporting Multi-Path Development of User Interfaces. In: Feige, U., Roth, J. (eds.) DSV-IS 2004 and EHCI 2004. LNCS, vol. 3425, pp. 134–135. Springer, Heidelberg (2005)
15. Mahfoudhi, A., Abid, M., Abed, M.: Towards a user interface generation approach based on object oriented design and task model. In: Proc. of the 4th Intl. Worksh. on Task Models and Diagrams, pp. 135–142. ACM (2005)
16. Mori, G., Paternò, F., Santoro, C.: CTTE: Support for developing and analyzing task models for interactive system design. IEEE Trans. Software Eng. 28(8) (2002)
17. Paternò, F., Mancini, C., Meniconi, S.: ConcurTaskTrees: A diagrammatic notation for specifying task models, pp. 362–369. Chapman & Hall (1997)
18. Paternò, F., Santoro, C., Spano, L.D.: MARIA: A universal, declarative, multiple abstraction-level language for service-oriented applications in ubiquitous environments. ACM Trans. Comput.-Hum. Interact. 16(4), 1–30 (2009)
19. Pietschmann, S.: A model-driven development process and runtime platform for adaptive composite web applications. Intl. Journal On Advances in Internet Technology (IntTech) 4(1), 277–288 (2010)
20. Pietschmann, S., Tietz, V., Reimann, J., Liebing, C., Pohle, M., Meißner, K.: A metamodel for context-aware component-based mashup applications. In: Proc. of the 12th Intl. Conf. on Information Integration and Web-Based Applications & Service (iiWAS 2010), pp. 413–420 (2010)
21. Tran, V.X., Tsuji, H.: A task-oriented framework for automatic service composition. In: Proc. of the 2009 Congress on Services - I (SERVICES 2009), pp. 615–620. IEEE (2009)
22. van Welie, M., van der Veer, G.C., Eliëns, A.: An ontology for task world models. In: 5th Int. Worksh. on Design, Specification, and Verification of Interactive Systems, DSV-IS (1998)

# Integration of Telco Services into Enterprise Mashup Applications

Olexiy Chudnovskyy, Frank Weinhold, Hendrik Gebhardt, and Martin Gaedke

Department of Computer Science, Chemnitz University of Technology
09111 Chemnitz, Germany
{olexiy.chudnovskyy,frank.weinhold,hendrik.gebhardt,
martin.gaedke}@informatik.tu-chemnitz.de

**Abstract.** In this paper we present our approach to integrate telco services into enterprise mashup applications. We show how cross-network integration and multi-user-oriented mashup concept support execution and orchestration of business processes. We identify the main classes of telco services and provide a reference architecture for telco-enabled mashup applications. Finally, we describe our approach for systematic integration process and give an outlook into our further research.

**Keywords:** Mashup, Telco Services, Enterprise, Integration.

## 1    Introduction

The availability and ubiquity of mobile devices is a matter of course nowadays. According to Gartner report of February 2011 more than 1.6 billion mobile devices were sold 2010, which is a 32% increase compared to 2009 [1]. Both operator networks and mobile devices provide sophisticated capabilities regarding voice, video and data transfer (so called telco services), which can be leveraged in business process integration and orchestration scenarios. However, the integration of these functionalities into Web applications is still challenging. We identified the following three problems: First, not all of the operator network services are exposed in ways easy to deal with for Web developers. Though the number of dedicated gateways and APIs grows with every year [2], their heterogeneity and fast evolution complicate the development of consumer applications. Second, without adequate models and tools the integration of telephony services is a time-consuming and error-prone task. And finally, the novelty of the emerging services and device capabilities requires a systematic approach and guidelines to support unskilled Web developers in the integration process.

We claim the adoption of Web mashup techniques will significantly decrease the effort to develop and maintain telco-enabled Web applications. Much work has already been done on the field of Web mashup. Many dedicated models, architectures and development tools exist [3]. All of them are characterized through the end-user oriented development paradigm and continuous reuse of already existing components

A. Harth and N. Koch (Eds.): ICWE 2011 Workshops, LNCS 7059, pp. 37–48, 2012.

and functionalities. New goal-oriented mashups can be constructed even without programming skills - leveraging the experience and building blocks produced by other developers [4].

Our goal is to extend traditional mashups towards telco-enabled ones, which would simplify the integration of telephony services and reveal new application possibilities of mashups within enterprise scenarios.

The rest of this paper is structured as follows. First, we illustrate an application possibility of telco-enriched mashups using an example scenario from the property management domain. Then we identify and describe challenges on the way towards integration of telco services into Web mashups. Afterwards, we present a reference architecture for telco mashups and the internals of a corresponding execution platform. Section 5 reviews which aspects have to be considered when developing telco mashups and how this can be done systematically. Finally, we conclude the paper by pointing out the current challenges in our research.

## 2    Example Scenario

In the following example, we show how telco mashups can support business scenarios dealing with orchestration and integration of business processes. In this example the availability of alternative communication channel, i.e. operator network and mobile devices, enable faster response and data transfer between involved parties. Especially human actors get better integrated into the decision-making processes, as decisions and required information can be provided from anywhere and to any time.

Pete's Apartments (PA) is a medium-sized apartment leasing company. PA takes care about billing and management issues, while flat maintenance is performed by partner firms. PA uses classical Web mashups for business intelligence tasks but also telco-enabled ones to coordinate different business processes and to communicate with its partners.

Lucy works as a customer advisor for PA. She uses a dedicated telco-mashup application to communicate with customers and to initiate various workflows regarding management, flat maintenance etc. One day Lucy gets a call from the renter Joe, who is having problems with his bathroom light (cf. Fig. 1). The mashup identifies Joe by his phone number and displays his customer information on Lucy's screen (1, 2). He reports the problem and Lucy captures it within a dedicated job-management-component (3). Based on the given information the map-component displays craftsmen from partner firms close to Joe's apartment. Lucy selects one or several craftsmen, who should be notified about the job details (4). She uses one of the messaging components (like instant messaging, voice-calls, SMS/MMS) to contact the craftsmen. Lucy sends an MMS to the selected craftsmen with Joe's address and problem description (5, 6).

The electrician Peter is one of the contacted craftsmen. He receives the message from Lucy while on the road and confirms the task via a SMS from his mobile phone. Usually, when in the office Peter replies by calling into the mashup application using his traditional office phone to get further information or coordinate next actions with

Lucy (7). The mashup confirms that Peter accepted the job and displays a notification message on Lucy's screen (8). Lucy accepts his confirmation and assigns him to this job (9).

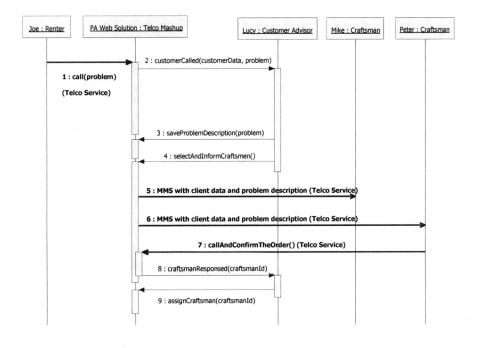

**Fig. 1.** Enterprise mashup application with integrated telco services

The example shows how two different processes (order registration and light repair) can be seamlessly integrated into a single workflow under different communication constraints (Internet, land and mobile phone lines). The integrating medium hereby is the dedicated telco mashup application, transcending technological communication constrains and thus enabling communication and data exchange between involved parties in a new way.

The presented scenario is a typical everyday scenario and limited in complexity – but its implementation is hindered through several problems we have identified during our research.

1. Telecommunication networks and mobile devices are not yet perceived as an efficient communication channel being able to perform process integration and coordination.
2. The missing models and frameworks hinder the integration of telephony services into Web- and software solutions.
3. Development of telco-enabled solutions is a time-consuming and error-prone task. Despite many existing tools and frameworks there is no rigorous and systematic

approach enabling costs-efficient development and evolution of telco-enabled Web applications.

To tackle the stated problems we derive the main research challenges discussed in the next sections:

- What types of telco services do exist and what are their key characteristics?
  It is important to classify and analyze different types of telco services. Services may operate in various networks and provide different data transfer capabilities (e.g. instant messaging, signaling, SMS/MMS etc.) Their characteristics have a crucial impact on scenarios and application possibilities for process orchestration and integration.
- How can telco services be combined with other functionalities and data sources?
  Web mashups has shown that development of new applications based on existing components and functionalities can be easy and even accessible for end users. It is necessary to devise a dedicated mashup model and architecture, which would support data transfer and process integration using telco services.
- How should a systematic approach for telco-enabled mashups development look like?
  It is necessary to devise a dedicated development process and a framework, which would reduce time and costs for the development of telco mashups. The average users should be supported in the process of creating their own mashups in a systematic and efficient way.

In the following sections, we focus on these research questions, analyze different kinds of telco services and introduce telco mashups with dedicated development process and framework.

## 3    Telco Services and Enterprise Applications

We define telco services as software services that provide communication and collaboration support. Depending on the network these services operate in, we distinguish between internet telco services, converged services and signaling services.

*Internet telco services* operate exclusively in the Internet, e.g. Voice over IP (VoIP) or instant messaging. The variety of available protocols and technologies enable these services to be used in complex data transfer and workflow execution scenarios between distributed systems. Internet telco services provide an efficient tool for asynchronous data transfer and synchronous voice/video communication. Furthermore, data transferred over services like instant messaging can be processed automatically by software and initiate further execution steps. Skype [5], Sipgate [6] or Google Voice [7] are some examples of the internet telco services providers.

*Converged services* mediate between different networks and communication protocols. A SMS message or VoIP calls from Internet to a mobile phone are examples of converged services. Converged services enable location-independent data exchange between parties, who have no access to the Internet but can communicate over other channels like operator networks. Especially processes and decision tasks, where people are involved, can benefit from capabilities of operator networks and pervasive availability of mobile devices. The data packets are usually limited in size and the mediation between networks is more expensive. However, small messages are often enough to confirm tasks or to provide required information. Monitoring and management of processes can be performed as well by notification using SMS or MMS. Tropo [8] and Twilio [9] are two wide-spread converged services providers.

*Signaling services*, which provide access to a network operator's signaling infrastructure. Examples of signaling services are notifications about incoming calls or negotiation of Quality of Service (QoS) parameters. Furthermore, signaling services can be used to establish a connection between two parties in order to initiate data transfer over alternative communication channel. Providers of signaling services are for example Developergarden [10], Comfone Signaling [11] or Orange API [12].

Finally, we define *device APIs* as services, which enable access to device capabilities such as cameras, microphone, location services etc. Device APIs provide additional data, which can be important or wishful for many enterprise scenarios. For example, location data from smartphones with GPS support can be utilized for decision making and task assignment process. As a result a better awareness of communication partners can be achieved. Furthermore device APIs enable mashup applications to be partially executed on the end devices and provide additional functions to the user.

Based on this classification, we derive a reference architecture, which enables Web mashups to integrate the presented telco services.

# 4 Integrating Telco Services into Mashups

Telco mashups represent an enhancement of classic Web mashups and leverage the capabilities of telco services. Within a mashup telco services are combined with other functionalities, which enable execution of both ad-hoc and complex cross-organizational workflows. We identified several layers of combination and aggregation possibilities regarding data, application logic and pieces of user interface:

- *Service Binding Layer* specifies data sources and services to be integrated into the mashup. Due to the variety of available standards and protocols (SOAP, REST, Atom, RSS etc.) the interface of services exposed to the upper layers should be unified and expressed within one semantically enriched description language. Policies, security considerations as well as quality of service aspects have to be defined at this point to enable cross-organizational data transfer and service invocation. Federation aspects of services should be systematically designed using dedicated modeling languages as presented in [13, 14].
- The *Data Mashup Layer* represents a step, where data coming from a number of heterogeneous sources are transformed, filtered and aggregated. The combination algorithm to be applied might be given either in form of a simple script snippet or using a dedicated mashup language, e.g. EMML [15] or DERI Pipes [16]. The underlying models may vary as well, e.g. the combination of data can be expressed

in form of pipes (the output of service A is connected with input of service B) or in terms of declarative instructions (data federation pattern). The data mashup enables integration of information coming from different organizations and departments in order to visualize workflows, execution states, relationships etc. In enterprise scenarios the aggregated data can be used to make decisions and initiate further execution steps or processes [17].

- The third layer, the *Widget Layer* specifies graphical interfaces and interaction with underlying data mashups or services. The resulting components, called widgets, can be based on various standards, e.g. W3C Widgets [18], Java Portlets [19], Google Gadgets [20] etc. Pre-defined packaging formats and well-defined interfaces to the run-time environment make widgets highly reusable and easily distributable. Widgets can be produced by different vendors and business partners, so that complete processes and workflows are implemented within one single component. To facilitate the reusability of widgets we propose to use a dedicated widget repository. The discovery of components should be enabled through an expressive semantic description language.

- The composition of widgets towards the final Web application is performed within the *Workspace Layer*. A workspace (or UI/UX-mashup) is a set of inter-connected widgets with additional services and configurations regarding inter-widget communication, layout, user interface presentation and user experience. The user of a mashup works with the workspace and consumes functions provided by the widgets. Widgets communicate with each other using a dedicated event bus and access general services implemented by the telco mashup execution platform. Incoming calls or messaging services are propagated by the platform to the workspace, so that each widget is notified about context changes or events. Inter-widget communication is a useful mechanism to transfer data between single business processes and o coordinate execution of single tasks [21].

The Telco Mashup Execution Platform represents the core component of telco-enabled mashups. The platform provides access to built-in telco services and supports the whole lifecycle of a mashup. Based on the presented architecture we derive requirements and identify main functions, which should be implemented by the platform in order to operate telco mashups (Fig. 2).

The platform should provide a bridge between the Internet and one or several operator networks. Telco mashups are executed within the platform, which is actually distributed on the *client side* (embedded into the Web browser) and *server side*. Server side provides access to embedded telco services and mashup management facilities. Upon request, new mashups are instantiated based on their configuration (stored in *mashup repository*) and *user profile settings* (security, billing and service level agreements). The execution of mashups is managed by the *life cycle manager* component, which guarantees, that charging and QoS settings, predefined availability as well as security and federation rules are respected. The *communication manager* hosted on the server side of the execution platform provides endpoints for mobile devices, manages incoming calls and routes them to corresponding mashup instances.

As such, the execution platform provides facilities to manage and operate telco-enabled mashups. Following, we analyze its application and provide guidance to take all presented aspects of the platform and telco mashups into account.

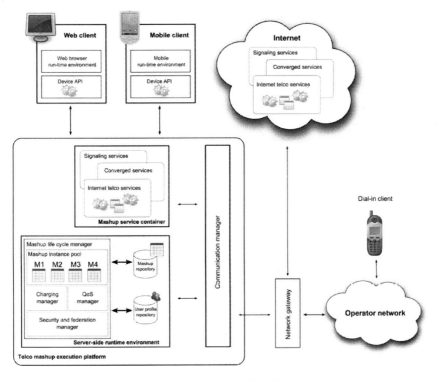

**Fig. 2.** Telco mashup execution platform

## 5    Development of Telco Mashups

The development of telco mashups differs from traditional Web applications in many aspects. First, mashups in general are based on the latest, easy-to-use Web technologies like REST, Atom, RSS etc. and serve typically a specific situational need [3]. Second, the development paradigm envisions that even end users are able to build their own mashups. Finally, the heterogeneity of mashup components, data sources and services requires a systematic evolution management and careful mashup design [22]. Following, we analyze these and telco-specific aspects, which should be considered while developing and maintaining telco mashups. We separate concerns and describe tasks to be performed in different phases of mashup lifecycle (Fig. 3).

The lifecycle of a new telco mashup application begins with its Conceptual Design, e.g. with the definition of essential mashup characteristics like title, description, category and purpose. Financial and governance rules, quality of service aspects and usage policies are specified within this stage. The definitions can be made both by end-users as well as skilled developers. The specified policies should be respected in the later design phases as well as during mashup execution. To support end-users in this process, the mashup development platform should provide discovery and recommendation facilities. Mashups built by other users can be re-used as a starting point or as a template for the newly created one.

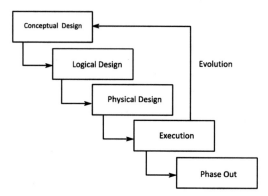

**Fig. 3.** Telco mashup lifecycle

Within the Logical Design stage one defines the abstract layout and basis components of the mashup. Developer (or end-user) assign a layout to the workspace and select components to be assembled. At this point the mashup is specified on a logical level only, i.e. using abstractions of components instead of concrete implementations. Pre-defined layouts as well as composition suggestions should be provided by the development platform to simplify these steps. The logical description of a mashup instance is an important artifact, which is used in later phases to suggest implementation possibilities or to exchange components at run-time, especially in telco-specific scenarios such as roaming. We suggest using RDF-based description languages and dedicated knowledge models to enable automatic composition and context adaption tasks [23].

The subsequent Physical Design phase can be completed either by skilled developer or automatically derived from the logical description. At this point, the system assigns concrete implementations of widgets, services and data sources to the logical representatives that have been composed as workspace. The mashup development platform should provide a repository with ready-to-use components and templates, which can be completed by mashup developers. If no component satisfies the goals, a dedicated widget editor is used to create new data mashups and wrap them using graphical interface. The look and feel of mashup is customized in compliance to corporate design and specific guidelines. Though the physical design will usually be done manually in the early beginning, the mashup development platform should provide automatic completion facilities as well. They can be used by unskilled developers, for prototyping purposes or to produce simple short-living mashup applications. The decisions made in the logical design phase, such as widget type or component requirements are used now to select concrete implementation and service bindings. For example, a map widget defined in logical design can be represented by either a Google Map or a Bing Map component. After the physical design phase executable description of mashup is available. Parts of the physical design like widget combinations or data mashup definitions are analyzed and stored by recommendation engine, which will suggest them in future if similar mashups are constructed.

The Execution phase is a step when a mashup instance is running and is used by one or several actors to perform their tasks. Telco mashups provide plenty of collaboration functionalities, which don't require the participants to act within one single network. To achieve this mashup platform implements basic telco services and gateways, takes care about network mediation, manages billing and QoS aspects of mashup applications. The application is running according to policies and governance rules defined in the conceptual phase. For example, the platform should guarantee that the maximal number of participants is respected or the operation time is not exceeded. The front-end of the mashup is rendered according to the physical design specification. Hereby the presentation may differ on desktop and mobile clients.

An important phase of each mashup instance is the Evolution stage. While the components and APIs used in the mashup evolve, obsolete widgets might be removed from the workspace or replaced by better ones, and new requirements might be met with the addition of new widgets. The dedicated repositories and recommendation engines simplify modification and extension of existing mashup instances and support their continuous evolution. Service bindings and operation rules can evolve as well, so that dynamic adaption facilities are needed to deal with the changing context. At this point, the logical definition of mashup helps to find alternative implementations of components and to suggest the best fitting ones. Governance rules from the conceptual phase define if and what components can be exchanged. For example, one can disable or restrict messaging functions of mashup while operating abroad in foreign operator networks. Mashup run-time can detect this context change and switch from Internet-based communication to SMS-based one.

Finally, the Phase Out is the last phase of a mashup instance, where the data produced during the execution is collected and archived according to the pre-defined rules and policies. Users cannot access the mashup anymore, but are able to retrieve operation statistics, log files, protocols or collect their own data etc. before the mashup is finally terminated. What information is important and how data should be dealt with after the mashup becomes unavailable is retrieved from the conceptual description of the mashup.

As we have shown, systematic development of telco-enhanced mashup applications and integration of telco services into mashup applications requires many additional considerations (and often dedicated supporting software) during the development process. The quality and effort needed to develop such kind of applications depend among others on the facilities provided by the development platform. We consider reusability as a key success factor for costs- and time-efficient development of mashup applications. Therefore, components like mashup repository and recommendations are integral parts of our proposed mashup platform and will gain more attention in future research and development.

# 6    Related Work

Much work has already been done in the field of mashups, both on the consumer mashups as well as on enterprise-oriented mashups side. The latter ones are especially related to our work as they enable integration of heterogeneous sources in different dimensions (data, services and UI/UX components) and take governance, management and security aspects into account. Following, we present and analyze some of the recent developments and show their relation to our approach.

IBM Mashup Center [24] is a popular enterprise mashup solution, which targets enterprise users with different needs and skills. The produced mashups enable integration of data, services and widgets from various (also legacy) sources. Similar to our model and architecture, mashups produced by IBM Mashup Center are assembled on both data and UI levels. Similar to our approach, a repository with mashup templates is available, which significantly simplifies the development of new applications. Though IBM Mashup Center provides much support in the mashup design, the telco-related aspects and invocation of local services like device APIs are not covered.

Another representative of mashup development platforms is JackBe Presto [25]. Its goal is to facilitate implementation of management dashboards, enterprise mashups and business intelligence applications. Same as IBM Mashup Center, the JackBe Presto platform provides a graphical editor for data mashups and visualizes them using widget-like objects called Apps. Though JackBe Presto provides a powerful platform to develop enterprise mashup applications, the integration of telco services remains challenging. Incoming voice calls and messages should be handled manually. Collaborative functions and life cycle management is also not considered within this approach.

In academia, the models and architectures of enterprise mashup applications have been thoroughly explored, e.g. in [26], [27], or [28]. Similar to our proposal, the proposed mashup models usually consist of several aggregation layers. The aggregation is performed both on data and UI - this approach covers many of the enterprise use cases and meets different needs of the end-users. Though many approaches exist, none of them addresses the telco aspects of enterprise mashups.

There are some few initiatives in European projects which research on the field of telco service and Web 2.0 integration. For example, OPUCE [29] focuses on building an infrastructure to facilitate the development and orchestration of Web services. The platform supports mashup adaptability and context awareness regarding users, operator networks and devices. Furthermore, it integrates various telco services like in- or outgoing calls, messaging services etc. However, billing and QoS management aspects are not addressed by resulting mashups. OPUCE produces single-user-applications and not multi-user-enabled ones as in our approach.

SPICE [30] is another European project, which targets particularly telco domain. The editor produced in the project enables semantic annotation of services to take non-functional telco-related aspects into account. In- and outgoing calls are supported through a media gateway (Asterisk PBX [31]) and enable also dial-in clients to communicate with mashup application. Also charging and management function are addressed through communication with other platform components over FTP or Ro interface. As with OPUCE, collaboration of several users using different devices is not addressed within SPICE mashups.

The presented approaches deal well with enterprise mashups when it comes to integration of sources available (or made available) over the Web. As we have seen above, integration of telco services is rather challenging and thus requires dedicated models, architectures and composition approaches.

## 7    Conclusions and Outlook

In this paper we have presented our 'work in progress' on the field of telco mashups. We analyzed how business scenarios benefit from the availability of several communication channels (i.e. Internet and operator network) and demonstrated it using an example scenario from property management domain. We proposed a dedicated telco mashup reference architecture and execution platform. To provide guidance in the development process, we analyzed their lifecycle and gave recommendations to each operation stage. Requirements made on the development platform will serve as basis for our future research. Currently, we are working on the specification of dedicated mashup and workspace description languages, which should cover all the aspects of presented lifecycle. Furthermore, we are going to develop first prototypes of execution and development platforms and apply them to implement the example above.

**Acknowledgements:** This work was supported by funds from the European Commission (project Omelette, contract no. 257635).

## References

1. Market Share Analysis: Mobile Devices, Worldwide, 4Q10 and 2010 (April 22, 2011), http://www.gartner.com/DisplayDocument?ref=clientFriendlyUrl &id=1542114
2. ProgrammableWeb - Mashups, APIs, and the Web as Platform (June 09, 2011), http://www.programmableweb.com/
3. Yu, J., Benatallah, B., Casati, F., Daniel, F.: Understanding Mashup Development. IEEE Internet Computing 12, 44–52 (2008)
4. Roy Chowdhury, S., Rodríguez, C., Daniel, F., Casati, F.: Wisdom-Aware Computing: On the Interactive Recommendation of Composition Knowledge. In: Maximilien, E.M., Rossi, G., Yuan, S.-T., Ludwig, H., Fantinato, M. (eds.) ICSOC 2010. LNCS, vol. 6568, pp. 144–155. Springer, Heidelberg (2011)
5. Skype (April 25, 2011), http://www.skype.com/intl/en/home
6. Sipgate (April 25, 2011), http://www.sipgate.de/basic
7. Google: Google Voice (April 25, 2011), https://www.google.com/voice
8. Tropo - Cloud API for Voice, SMS, and Instant Messaging Services (April 25, 2011), https://www.tropo.com/home.jsp
9. Twilio (April 25, 2011), http://www.twilio.com/
10. Developergarden (April 25, 2011), http://www.developergarden.com/startseite

11. Confome Signaling (April 25, 2011),
    http://www.comfone.com/index.php/services/signalling
12. Orange API (April 25, 2011), http://www.api.orange.com/
13. Meinecke, J., Gaedke, M.: Modeling Federations of Web Applications with WAM. IEEE (2005)
14. Heil, A., Gaedke, M., Meinecke, J.: Identifying Security Aspects in Web-Based Federations. IEEE (2008)
15. Viswanathan, A.: Mashups and the Enterprise Mashup Markup Language (EMML) (October 18, 2010), http://www.drdobbs.com/article/printableArticle.jhtml?articleId=224300049&dept_url=/java/
16. Phuoc, D.L., Polleres, A., Tummarello, G., Morbidoni, C.: DERI Pipes: visual tool for wiring Web data sources (2008)
17. Truong, H.-l., Dustdar, S.: Integrating Data for Business Process Management. IEEE Data Eng. Bull. 32, 48–53 (2009)
18. Widget Packaging and Configuration (June 09, 2011),
    http://www.w3.org/TR/widgets/
19. Sun Microsystems: Introduction to JSR 168—The Java Portlet Specification (June 09, 2011), http://developers.sun.com/portalserver/reference/techart/jsr168/
20. Gadgets Specification - Gadgets API - Google Code (June 09, 2011),
    http://code.google.com/intl/de-DE/apis/gadgets/docs/spec.html
21. Daniel, F., Soi, S., Tranquillini, S., Casati, F., Heng, C., Yan, L.: From people to services to UI: distributed orchestration of user interfaces, pp. 310–326 (2010)
22. Cappiello, C., Daniel, F., Matera, M., Pautasso, C.: Information Quality in Mashups. IEEE Internet Computing 14, 14–22 (2010)
23. Fortier, A., Rossi, G., Gordillo, S.E., Challiol, C.: Dealing with variability in context-aware mobile software. Journal of Systems and Software 83, 915–936 (2010)
24. IBM: IBM Mashup Center (2011),
    http://www-01.ibm.com/software/info/mashup-center/
25. JackBe: Presto (April 24, 2011), http://www.jackbe.com/
26. López, J., Bellas, F., Pan, A., Montoto, P.: A Component-Based Approach for Engineering Enterprise Mashups. In: Gaedke, M., Grossniklaus, M., Díaz, O. (eds.) ICWE 2009. LNCS, vol. 5648, pp. 30–44. Springer, Heidelberg (2009)
27. Yu, J., Benatallah, B., Saint-Paul, R., Casati, F., Daniel, F., Matera, M.: A framework for rapid integration of presentation components. In: Proceedings of the 16th International Conference on World Wide Web - WWW 2007, p. 923 (2007)
28. Gurram, R., Mo, B., Gueldemeister, R.: A Web Based Mashup Platform for Enterprise 2.0. In: Hartmann, S., Zhou, X., Kirchberg, M. (eds.) WISE 2008. LNCS, vol. 5176, pp. 144–151. Springer, Heidelberg (2008)
29. Sienel, J., Martín, A.L., Zorita, C.B., Martínez, B.C.: OPUCE: A Telco-Driven Service Mash-Up Approach. Bell Labs Technical Journal 14, 203–218 (2009)
30. Droegehorn, O., Konig, I., Le-Jeune, G., Cupillard, J., Belaunde, M., Kovacs, E.: Professional and end-user-driven service creation in the SPICE platform. In: 2008 International Symposium on a World of Wireless, Mobile and Multimedia Networks, pp. 1–8. IEEE (2008)
31. Asterisk- The Open Source Telephony Projects | Asterisk (April 24, 2011),
    http://www.asterisk.org/

# Orchestrated User Interface Mashups
# Using W3C Widgets

Scott Wilson[1], Florian Daniel[2], Uwe Jugel[3], and Stefano Soi[2]

[1] University of Bolton, United Kingdom
scott.bradley.wilson@gmail.com
[2] University of Trento, Povo (TN), Italy
{daniel,soi}@disi.unitn.it
[3] SAP AG, SAP Research Dresden, Germany
uwe.jugel@sap.com

**Abstract.** One of the key innovations introduced by web mashups into the integration landscape (basically focusing on data and application integration) is *integration at the UI layer*. Yet, despite several years of mashup research, no commonly agreed on component technology for UIs has emerged so far. We believe *W3C's widgets* are a good starting point for componentizing UIs and a good candidate for reaching such an agreement. Recognizing, however, their shortcomings in terms of inter-widget communication – a crucial ingredient in the development of interactive mashups – in this paper we (i) first discuss the *nature of UI mashups* and then (ii) propose an *extension of the widget model* that aims at supporting a variety of inter-widget communication patterns.

**Keywords:** UI Mashups, W3C widgets, Inter-widget communication.

## 1 Introduction

If we analyze the state of the art in mashups today, we recognize that basically two different approaches have reached the necessary critical mass to survive: data mashups and UI (user interface) mashups. ***Data mashups*** particularly focus on the integration and processing of data sources from the Web, e.g., in the form of RSS or Atom feeds, XML files, or other simple data formats; mashup platforms like Yahoo! Pipes (http://pipes.yahoo.com/pipes/), JackBe Presto (http://www.jackbe.com/), or IBM's Damia [1] are examples of online tools that aim at facilitating data mashup development. ***UI mashups***, instead, rather focus on the integration of pieces of user interfaces sourced from the Web, e.g., in the form of Ajax APIs or HTML markup scrapped from other web sites; Intel Mash Maker [2] or mashArt [3] both support the integration of UI components, but most of the times these mashups are still coded by hand (e.g., essentially all of the mashups on programmableweb.com are of this type).

The mashup platforms focusing on data mashups typically come with very similar features in terms of supported data sources, operators, filters, and the like. RSS, Atom, or CSV are well-known and commonly accepted data formats, and there are not many different ways to process them. Unfortunately, this is not what happens in

A. Harth and N. Koch (Eds.): ICWE 2011 Workshops, LNCS 7059, pp. 49–61, 2012.

the context of UI mashups. In fact, there are still many different ways to look at the problem and, hence, each tool or programmer uses its own way of componentizing UIs (both in JavaScript inside the browser and in other languages in the web server) and of integrating them into the overall layout of the mashup. As a consequence, UI components are not compatible among mashup tools, and we are far from common concepts and approaches when it comes to UI mashups.

Given for granted that UI components are able to encapsulate and deliver pieces of UIs that can be embedded into a mashup and operated by its users, the key ingredient for UI componentization we identify is the component's ability to **interoperate** with its surroundings, i.e., with other UI components and the hosting mashup logic. Interoperability is needed to enable components to synchronize upon state changes, e.g., in response to user interactions or internal logics. While technically this is not a huge challenge, conceptually it is not trivial to understand which communication paradigm to adopt, which distribution logic to support, or which data format to choose, maximizing at the same time the reusability of UI components across different mashup platforms, also fostering interoperability among mashups themselves.

In this paper, we approach these challenges by leveraging on a UI componentization technology that we believe will have a major impact in the near future, i.e., W3C's Widgets [4]. This choice is motivated, firstly, by the comprehensiveness of W3C's Widgets specifications family which tries to cover models and functionalities proper of the most used widget technologies existing so far, e.g., Google gadgets, Yahoo widgets and, in particular, Open Social gadgets. Moreover, the W3C consortium is a leading actor in web standards creation and its proposal already attracted important vendors that are implementing W3C's Widget compliant tools (e.g., Apache Wookie and Rave).

Specifically, in this paper, we provide the following **contributions**:

- We discuss three types of *mashup logics for widgets* and identify a set of requirements the widgets should satisfy, in order for them to be mashed up.
- We propose an *extension of the W3C widget model* expressed in terms of an API extension and set of expected behaviours.
- We report on our experience with the *implementation* of a UI mashup following one of the described mashup logics and the extended widget model.

Before going into the details of our proposal, in the next section we briefly summarize the logic of and technologies used in the implementation of W3C widgets. Then, in Section 3, we investigate the basic mashup types for widgets. In Section 4 we specifically look at one type of mashups and derive a set of requirements for widgets. In Section 5 we propose an according extension of the W3C widget model, also providing concrete implementation examples. Finally, in Section 6 we discuss related works, in order to conclude the paper in Section 7.

## 2     W3C Widgets

The World Wide Web Consortium (W3C) provides a set of specifications collectively known as the *Widget family of specifications*. A Widget is defined by W3C (http://dev.w3.org/2006/waf/widgets-land/) as "an end-user's conceptualization of an interactive single purpose application for displaying and/or updating local data or data on the Web, packaged in a way to allow a single download and installation on a user's machine or mobile device."

Widgets are made available to users by a *widget runtime* (also known as a *widget engine*). A *widget runtime* is an application that can import a widget that has been packaged according to the *W3C Widgets: Packaging and Configuration* specification [4]; the runtime may also make available at runtime any script objects required by the widget, for example the *W3C Widget Interface* [5] (the API a widget exposes to provide access to the widget's metadata and to persistently store data) or *W3C Device APIs* [6] (client-side APIs that enable the development of widgets that interact with device services like calendar, contacts, or camera). Widget runtimes are available on mobile devices, as desktop applications, or for embedding widgets in websites.

The Packaging and Configuration specification defines the metadata terms used to describe the widget (such as name, author and description) and to enable the configuration of the widget runtime. Configuration information includes the <feature> element, which can be used by the widget author to request that the widget runtime makes additional features available when the widget is running; examples of features include JavaScript APIs, libraries, and video codecs.

Within the W3C Widget family of specifications, widgets are largely conceptualized as operating independently, communicating with the widget runtime using the Widget Interface and with the client environment using standard browser features such as the Document Object Model and related JavaScript APIs.

While a widget runtime may render multiple widgets to the user simultaneously – for example, on the Home screen of a mobile device, or as part of the layout of a portal or social networking site – there are no mechanisms specified by the W3C Widget family of specifications by which the widgets communicate with each other as members of a mashup.

## 3    User Interface Mashups

Given a set of widgets that comply with the W3C Widget family of specifications, the question is therefore how a mashup of widgets could look like. Considering the state of the art in which widgets do not support inter-widget communications, we define a *basic UI mashup*, as a tuple $m = \langle L, W, VA \rangle$ with:

- $L = \langle l, V \rangle$ being the *layout* of the mashup, of which $l$ is the layout *template* (typically the template consists of an HTML page, a set of JavaScript and image files, and one or more CSS style sheets) and $V = \{v_i\}$ is the set of *viewports* inside $l$ that can be used for the rendering of the widgets (e.g., iframes or div elements);
- $W = \{w_j\}$ being the set of *widgets* in the mashup, where each widget is of type $w_j = \langle id_j, name_j, Pref_j, version_j, height_j, width_j \rangle$ with $Pref_j$ being a set of configuration *preferences* (typically, name-value pairs); and
- $VA = \{va_k | va_k \in W \times V\}$ being the set of *widget-viewport associations* needed for placing and rendering the widgets inside the mashup.

This model focuses on the layout only and is clearly not able to represent UI mashups like most of the ones that can be found on programmableweb.com. In fact, UI mashups typically are able to synchronize their widgets or UI elements upon user interactions, a feature that is missing in mashups of type $m$ above.

Assuming now that widgets are able to communicate, in the following subsections we define three UI mashup models that are able to deal with inter-widget communications and to support widget synchronization:

- *Orchestrated UI mashups*, where the interactions between the widgets in the mashup are defined using a central control logic;
- *Choreographed UI mashups*, where the interactions between the widgets in the mashup are not defined, but instead emerge in a distributed fashion from the internal capabilities of the widgets;
- *Hybrid UI mashups*, where the emerging behaviour of a choreographed UI mashup is modified by inhibiting individual behaviours, practically constraining the ad-hoc nature of choreographed UI mashups.

We define each of these mashup types in the following, while in the rest of this paper we will specifically focus on orchestrated UI mashups, which can be considered the basis also for the development of the other two types of UI mashups.

### 3.1    Orchestrated UI Mashups

We define an ***orchestrated UI mashup*** as a tuple $m^o = \langle L, W, VA, C \rangle$ with:

- $L$ being the layout as defined before;
- $W = \{w_j | w_j = \langle id_j, name_j, Pref_j, version_j, height_j, width_j, E_j, O_j \rangle\}$    being the set of widgets with $E_j = \{e_{jl} | e_{jl} = \langle name_{jl}, P_{jl} \rangle\}$ being the set of events the widget can generate, $O_j = \{o_{jm} | o_{jm} = \langle name_{jm}, P_{jm} \rangle\}$ being the set of operations supported by the widget, and $P_{jl}$ and $P_{jm}$, respectively, being the sets of output and input parameters;
- $VA = \{va_k | va_k \in W \times V\}$ being the set of widget-viewport associations; and
- $C = \{c_n | c_n \in E \times O, E = \bigcup_j E_j, O = \bigcup_j O_j\}$ being the set of direct inter-widget communications, i.e., message flows between two widgets connecting an event of the source widget with an operation of the target widget.

This definition of UI mashup implies that the mashup (and, therefore, the mashup developer) knows which events are to be mapped to which operations and that it is able to propagate the respective data items on behalf of the user of the mashup. This is common practice, e.g., in web service composition languages like BPEL, and does not require the widgets to know about each other.

The strength of this model is that mashups behave as they are expected to, that is, as specified in the mashup specification. A drawback is that this central mashup logic must be specified in advance, i.e., before runtime, which require a good knowledge of the used widgets by the mashup developer.

Note that in the above definition and in the following we intentionally do not introduce complex data mappings (e.g., requiring data transformation logics) or service components (e.g., requiring to follow web servie protocols), in order to keep the model simple and focused. We however assume each inter-widget communication $c_n$ also contains the necessary mapping of event outputs to operation inputs.

We believe UI mashups are good candidates for end user development and that data transformations or web services are not intuitive enough to them in order to profitably use them inside a mashup. Possible complex data transformations or service composition logics can always be developed by more skilled developers and plugged in in the form of dedicated widgets.

### 3.2    Choreographed UI Mashups

We define a ***choreographed UI mashup*** as a tuple $m^c = \langle L, T, W, VA \rangle$ with:

- $L$ being the layout of the mashup;
- $T = \{t_n | t_n = \langle name_n, P_n \rangle\}$ being the reference topic ontology for events and operations, i.e., the set of concepts and associated parameters $P_n$ the widgets in the mashup can consume as input or produce as output;
- $W = \{w_j | w_j = \langle id_j, name_j, Pref_j, version_j, height_j, width_j, E_j, O_j \rangle\}$ being the set of widgets with $E_j = \{e_{jl} | e_{jl} = \langle name_{jl}, Topic_{jl} \rangle\}$ being the set of events the widget can generate, $O_j = \{o_{jm} | o_{jm} = \langle name_{jm}, Topic_{jm} \rangle\}$ being the set of operations supported by the widget, and $Topic_{jl}, Topic_{jm} \subseteq T$, respectively, being the set of topics an event sends data to and an operation reacts to; and
- $VA = \{va_k | va_k \in W \times V\}$ being the of widget-viewport associations.

In contrast to orchestrated UI mashups, choreographed UI mashups do not have an explicitly defined set of mappings of operations and events. Instead, each widget is capable of sending and receiving communications and of acting on them independently. Interoperability is achieved in that each widget complies with the reference topic ontology $T$, which provides a reference terminology and semantics each widget is able to understand. The behaviour of a choreographed UI mashup, therefore, is not modelled centrally by the mashup developer and rather emerges in a distributed way by placing one widget after the other into the mashup. That is, only placing a widget into the mashup allows the developer to understand how it behaves in the mashups and which features it supports.

The strength of this approach is that there is no need for explicit design of interactions: a developer simply drops widgets into his mashup and they autonomously interact. One weakness is that the reference topic ontology must be "standardized" (or, at least, understood by all widgets), in order for any meaningful communication to occur. This may reduce the overall richness of communication possible to a small number of fairly primitive topics – for example, location, dates and unstructured text. Another weakness is that with no predefined "plan" of the mashup, there could be the risk of the emergent behaviour of the widgets being pathological – for example, self-reinforcing loops or hunting. This could be a serious problem where the mashup components have real-world consequences, such as SMS-sending widgets or similar.

### 3.3    Hybrid UI Mashups

We define a **hybrid UI mashup** as a tuple $m^h = \langle L, T, W, VA, C \rangle$ with:

- $L$ being the layout of the mashup;
- $T = \{t_n | t_n = \langle name_n, P_n \rangle\}$ being the reference topic ontology;
- $W = \{w_j | w_j = \langle id_j, name_j, Pref_j, version_j, height_j, width_j, E_j, O_j \rangle\}$    being the set of widgets with $E_j = \{e_{jl} | e_{jl} = \langle name_{jl}, Topic_{jl} \rangle\}$ being the set of events the widget can generate and $O_j = \{o_{jm} | o_{jm} = \langle name_{jm}, Topic_{jm} \rangle\}$ being the set of operations supported by the widget;
- $VA = \{va_k | va_k \in W \times V\}$ being the set of widget-viewport associations; and
- $C = \{c_n | c_n \in T \times O, O = \bigcup_j O_j\}$ being a set of constraints preventing operations from reacting to the publication of an event referring to a given topic.

In hybrid UI mashups, integration is achieved in a bottom-up fashion by the widgets themselves, while there is still the possibility for the mashup developer to control the interaction logic of the overall mashup in a top-down fashion by inhibiting interactions and, hence, application features that are not necessary for the implementation of his mashup idea.

The strength of this approach is that it brings together the benefits of both orchestrated and choreographed UI mashups, that is, simplicity of development and control of the behaviour. On the downside, the overall mashup logic is buried inside two opposite composition logics: the implicit capabilities of the widgets and the explicit constraints by the developer. This may be perceived as non-intuitive by less skilled developers or end users.

## 4    A W3C Widget Extension for Orchestrated UI Mashups

As a first step toward supporting the above UI mashup types, in this paper we aim at enabling the development of *orchestrated UI mashups*, a task that is already not possible with the W3C widget model as is. From the definition of $m^o$ above we can, in fact, derive a set of extension requirements for W3C widgets, without which the implementation of interactive UI mashups is not possible:

1. Widgets must be able to communicate internal state changes via *events* to the outside world, i.e., the mashup or other widgets in the mashup. That is, while the users interacts with the widget, the widget must implement an internal logic that tells the widget when it should raise an event, in order to allow other widgets in a same mashup to synchronize.

2. Widgets must be able to accept inputs via *operations*, in order to allow the outside world to enact widget-internal state changes. The enacting of an operation is the natural counterpart an event being raised. Typically, the operation implements the necessary logic to synchronize the state of the widget (e.g., the content rendered in the widget's viewport) with the event.

3. The *data formats* for the data exchanged among widgets should be kept as simple as possible (we propose simple name-value pairs), in order to ease

inter-widget communication. Considering that synchronizing widgets based on user interactions or internal state changes typically will require only the transfer of one or two parameters [3], e.g., an object identifier upon a selection operated by the user, this assumption seems reasonable. Remember that here we do not focus on web service orchestration or data processing.

We approach each of these requirements in the following sections and show how so extended widgets can be mashed up into UI mashups.

# 5    A Prototype Implementation

In order to better explain our ideas, in the following we adopt a by-example approach and contextualize them in our prototype implementation, finally also showing how the extended widget model can be successfully used for the implementation of orchestrated UI mashups.

## 5.1    Widget Configuration

The W3C Widgets: Packaging and Configuration specification supports the run-time loading of extensions using the <feature> element of the widget's config.xml file. This requires that the widget runtime environment can resolve the URI of the feature to an installed capability. For example, given the feature URI *http://example.org/rpc* a runtime may install an implementation specific to that runtime environment, or a generic one if the functionality is relatively simple. If the URI is not recognized, the runtime will reject the installation of the widget if the required attribute is set to "true", but will proceed (optionally warning the user) if it is set to "false".

However, it is also possible for a W3C Widget to load capabilities dynamically while running, using <script src> elements in the HTML start file or using lazy loading techniques to dynamically insert new <script> elements based on the current context. Therefore for an orchestration interface we have to make a decision as to which approach to take in loading the required capabilities. Each has its advantages and disadvantages.

An advantage of using <feature> loading is that it gives the runtime environment the option to use server-side capabilities or augmented functionality. For example, to load an API in the widget that then talks to a high-performance server-side messaging service. The disadvantage is that if the runtime does not support the feature, then the widget is either not able to be installed, or is installed without necessary functionality. The advantage of using HTML-based script loading is that it should work in any widget runtime environment; however it is not able to take advantage of any special capabilities of the runtime. A compromise solution is to use the <feature> declaration but to set the required attribute to "false", and provide a dynamic <script> tag loader as a fallback. This enables the widget to take advantage of native runtime implementations, but has a fallback option if none is provided. This can be implemented using a fairly simple script in the widget, as illustrated in Figure 1.

```
If (widget.intercom && typeof(widget.intercom)==function){
  // the runtime has provided the intercom API
} else {
  // load the fallback library - in this case PMRPC
  widget.intercom = loader.load("pmrpc.js");
}
```

**Fig. 1.** Widget-internal JavaScript logic to decide whether to load a fallback library or not

## 5.2    Widget Interface

We enable widgets to participate in orchestrated UI mashups through the specification of a so-called ***Intercom*** interface as an extension of the W3C Widget Interface. An implementation of the Intercom object must have the following three capabilities:

- It must be able to execute *operations* on the widget;
- It must be able to raise *events*; and
- It must be able to expose *metadata* about the operations and events supported by the widget.

The implementation of the Intercom interface may be made available at runtime through the use of a *<feature>* element in the widget configuration document or as a direct extension to the W3C Widget Interface specification implemented by the widget runtime.

The Intercom does not specify any orchestration configuration, but the capabilities of the orchestration participants and an interface to access the inter-widget communication features of the Intercom implementation. Therefore, we propose to introduce an attribute intercom to the W3C Widget Interface (see Figure 2).

```
[NoInterfaceObject]
interface Widget {
      readonly attribute DOMString        author;
      readonly attribute DOMString        authorEmail;
      readonly attribute DOMString        authorHref;
      readonly attribute DOMString        description;
      readonly attribute DOMString        id;
      readonly attribute DOMString        name;
      readonly attribute DOMString        shortName;
      readonly attribute Storage          preferences;
      readonly attribute DOMString        version;
      readonly attribute unsigned long height;
      readonly attribute unsigned long width;
      readonly attribute Intercom         intercom;
};
```

**Fig. 2.** Widget interface extended with intercom attribute

The Intercom interface itself is defined as described in Figure 3: Inspecting the `metadata` attribute of the Intercom interface allows the widget runtime environment to obtain the list of events and operations implemented by the widget, along with their respective output/input parameters. The two functions `raise` and `call` can then be used to generate an event and to enact an operation, respectively.

```
interface Intercom {
    void raise(in DOMString operationName, in optional DOMString param1, ... );
    void call(in DOMString operationName, in optional DOMString param1, ... );
    readonly attribute IntercomMetaData metadata;
}
interface IntercomMetaData {
    readonly attribute sequence<IntercomSignature> events;
    readonly attribute sequence<IntercomSignature> operations;
}
interface IntercomSignature {
    readonly attribute DOMString name;
    readonly attribute sequence<IntercomArgument> parameters;
}
interface IntercomArgument {
    readonly attribute DOMString name;
}
```

**Fig. 3.** A possible Intercom interface, including access functions and metadata structures

For instance, Figure 4 exemplifies how a widget can use its Intercom to raise the events "eventName", and how an external RPC module (e.g., the one used by the specific Intercom implementation) can use the widgets' intercoms to call operations.

```
//called from widget
this.intercom.raise("eventName", arg1, arg2);


//called from communication module
widget.intercom.call("operationName", arg1, arg2);
```

**Fig. 4.** Using the intercom object

With the help of the Intercom interface, an automatic composition component or a composition tool can use the `metadata` attribute of several widgets to learn about the composition capabilities that the widget supports.

To keep the Intercom interface as simple as possible, we do not support operation return types or complex parameter types.

## 5.3    Widget Implementation and Behaviour

In Figure 5 we provide a possible implementation of the Intercom interface, which makes use of the external communication infrastructure (SOMERPC) declared as required <feature> in the widget configuration.

```
var SOMERPC = {/* some rpc module required by this Intercom implementation */};

var Intercom = function( widget ) {
    var w = widget,
        rpcmodule = SOMERPC,
        operations = {},

        // reads the meta data from a config file, xml, etc.
        metadata = rpcmodule.getMetaData( w.name ),
        raise = function( eventName ){        //init public raiseEvent method
            var args = Array.prototype.splice.apply(arguments, 1,
                                                    arguments.length-1);
            rpcmodule.raiseEvent( w, eventName, args );
        },
        call = function( opName ){
            var args = Array.prototype.splice.apply(arguments, 1,
                                                    arguments.length-1);
            //call widget operation if it is in the public operations
            if(operations[opName]) {
                operations[opName].apply( w, args );
            }
        },
        i = 0;

    //setup the private operations list for faster access when 'call' is executed
    for(i = 0; i < metadata.operations.length; i += 1) {
        operations[metadata.operation[i].name] = w[metadata.operation[i]];
    }

    this.raise = raise;
    this.call = call;
    this.metadata = metadata;

    //register this intercom at the rpc module
    rpcmodule.register( this );
};
```

**Fig. 5.** A basic implementation of the Intercom interface

The Intercom of a widget should be initialized in the widget constructor to prevent modifications from the outside:

```
// called from the widget contructor
this.intercom = new Intercom( this );
```

After the intercom is set up, a widget can start raising events via its own Intercom, and all modules that have access to the widget or the widget's Intercom can call operations on the widget.

## 5.4    UI Mashup Implementation

Using the formalization introduced in Section 3, we are able to model a variety of mashups involving multiple widgets. The specification does not include any additional runtime aspects, such as message delivery time, message buffering, or similar technical aspects. Thereby, it is flexible enough to also accomodate mashups with more complex characteristics, such as mashups involving multiple windows or multiple origins, and it is agnostic as to whether communication is purely within the browser (e.g., using HTML 5 PostMessage) or also involving the server side.

Implementing a UI mashups can be achieved relatively simply through the use of publish-subscribe services propagating events from one widget to others. In orchestrated UI mashups of type $m^o = \langle L, W, VA, C \rangle$, it is the inter-widget communication logic $C$ that subscribes widgets, i.e., their operations, to events. In choreographed UI mashups of type $m^c = \langle L, T, W, VA \rangle$, each widget publishes its events to the topics in $T$ and subscribes to the topics it understands. In hybrid UI mashups $m^h = \langle L, T, W, VA, C \rangle$, the bottom-up subscriptions by the widgets can be fine-tuned via the constraints $C$. All this can implemented using a range of existing mature software technologies, for example, client-side using OpenAjax Hub[1] or server-side using solutions such as Faye[2] or ActiveMQ[3].

# 6    Related Work

In our former work [8], we developed an approach to the componentization and inter-communication of UI components. The approach is different from the one proposed in this paper, in that it aims to wrap full-fledged web applications developed with traditional, server-side web technologies. The wrapping logic requires the presence of simple event annotations inside the application's HTML markup in order to intercept events and a descriptor for the enacting of operations on the wrapped web app. Widgets, instead, are pure client-side apps.

In the context of widgets, Sire et al. [7] proposed an idea that is similar to what we propose in this paper, also advocating the use of events and event listeners (the equivalent of our operations). The widget decides whether an event is distributed in a unicast (one receiver), multicast (multiple receivers), or broadcast (all possible receivers) fashion. This design choice, however, leads to tightly coupled widgets, in that a widget must know in advance with which other and how many widgets it will communicate, a limitation we do not have in our proposal. In fact, in our case it is the mashup logic (which, for choreographed UI mashups, may be missing) that manages the inter-widget communication, and widgets are unaware of their neighbours.

The Java Portlet Specification 2.0 [9] proposes inter-widget communication for web portals. Portlets may communicate via events, but interactions occur on the server-side, a strong limitation in a UI-intensive Web 2.0 context. So far, the adoption of this technique is relatively low, also because its limitation to the Java world.

Communicating across technical boundaries, as proposed in this paper, is required in many networked computing domains. Especially for web browsers, the communi-

---

[1]  http://www.openajax.org/whitepapers/Introducing%20OpenAjax%20Hub%202.0%
20and%20Secure%20Mashups.php

[2]  http://faye.jcoglan.com/

[3]  http://activemq.apache.org/

cation across domains and across browser windows (including iframes) is an important issue. Therefore, the HTML 5 standard defines a messaging API [10], which is, for example, used by the "pmrpc" project [11]. This project provides a Javascript module that adds a *pmrpc* object to a running website *window* object. All scripts running inside this window may access *pmrpc* to register own operations, or make calls to other windows/frames [12].

Our investigation of these and similar RPC approaches showed that different projects use different interface syntax and mainly focus on cross-window communication. In comparison to that, our proposed interface extension does not specify any cross-domain/window aspects. A single *widget*, in our case, is similar to a *window* in these related approaches, but there can be many *widgets* in many *windows* that constitute a *mashup*. All widgets will use their *intercom* transparently. Cross-domain issues must be solved internally by the Intercom implementation, which may of course use, e.g., *pmrpc* internally for this aspect.

## 7    Conclusion and Future Work

In this paper, we addressed a relevant issue in UI-based mashup development, i.e., the intercommunication of W3C widgets. Mashups are typically heavily UI-based, but so far no standard for how to componentize UIs and how to get them into communication has emerged. We believe W3C widgets have the potential to represent this agreement and that they will gain importance in the near future in both desktop and mobile computing environments.

The aim of our research in this context is to come up with an inter-widget communication interface and respective widget behaviours, which – thanks to our involvement in the standardization of the widget technology – we would like to propose to the W3C for standardization. This is an effort we carry on in the context of the European project Omelette (http://www.ict-omelette.eu).

In order to obtain a first feedback from the community regarding the proposed communication interface, in this paper we focused on inter-widget communication at the level of events and operations. In the future, we also aim to identify and propose a standard format for the exchange of data among widgets, e.g., based on the OData protocol or similar initiatives.

**Acknowledgements.** This work was supported by funds from the European Commission (project OMELETTE, contract no. 257635).

## References

1. Altinel, M., Brown, P., Cline, S., Kartha, R., Louie, E., Markl, V., Mau, L., Ng, Y.-H., Simmen, D., Singh, A.: Damia: a data mashup fabric for intranet applications. In: VLDB 2007, VLDB Endowment, pp. 1370–1373 (September 2007)
2. Ennals, R., Brewer, E., Garofalakis, M., Shadle, M., Gandhi, P.: Intel Mash Maker: join the web. SIGMOD Rec. 36(4), 27–33 (2007)

3. Daniel, F., Casati, F., Benatallah, B., Shan, M.-C.: Hosted Universal Composition: Models, Languages and Infrastructure in mashArt. In: Laender, A.H.F., Castano, S., Dayal, U., Casati, F., de Oliveira, J.P.M. (eds.) ER 2009. LNCS, vol. 5829, pp. 428–443. Springer, Heidelberg (2009)
4. W3C. Widget Packaging and Configuration. W3C Working Draft (March 2011), http://www.w3.org/TR/widgets/
5. W3C. The Widget Interface. W3C Working Draft (September 2010), http://www.w3.org/TR/widgets-apis/
6. W3C. Device APIs and Policy Working Group Charter, http://www.w3.org/2009/05/DeviceAPICharter
7. Sire, S., Paquier, M., Vagner, A., Bogaerts, J.: A Messaging API for Inter-Widgets Communication. In: WWW 2009, pp. 1115–1116. ACM (April 2009)
8. Daniel, F., Matera, M.: Turning Web Applications into Mashup Components: Issues, Models, and Solutions. In: Gaedke, M., Grossniklaus, M., Díaz, O. (eds.) ICWE 2009. LNCS, vol. 5648, pp. 45–60. Springer, Heidelberg (2009)
9. Hepper, S.: Java(TM) Portlet Specification Version 2.0. Proposed Final Draft, Rev. 29, http://jcp.org/aboutJava/communityprocess/pfd/jsr286/index.html
10. WHATWG. HTML Living Standard, Communication. WHATWG specification (April 2011), http://www.whatwg.org/specs/web-apps/current-work/multipage/comms.html
11. Kovic, I., Zuzak, I.: Pmrpc, HTML5 inter-window and web workers RPC and pubsub communication library (April 2011), http://code.google.com/p/pmrpc/
12. Kovic, I., Zuzak, I.: List of system that enable inter-window or web worker communication (April 2011), http://code.google.com/p/pmrpc/wiki/IWCProjects

# Cross-Domain Embedding for Vaadin Applications

Janne Lautamäki and Tommi Mikkonen

Department of Software Systems, Tampere University of Technology,
Korkeakoulunkatu 1, FI-33720 Tampere, Finland
{janne.lautamaki,tommi.mikkonen}@tut.fi

**Abstract.** Although the design goals of the browser were originally not at running applications or at displaying a number of small widgets on a single web page, today many web pages considerably benefit from being able to host small embedded applications as components. While the web is full such applications, they cannot be easily reused because of the same origin policy restrictions that were introduced to protect web content from potentially malicious use. In this paper, we describe a generic design for cross domain embedding of web applications in a fashion that enables loading of applications from different domains as well as communication between the client and server. As the proof-of-concept implementation environment, we use web development framework Vaadin, a Google Web Toolkit based system that uses Java for application development.

**Keywords:** Vaadin, JSONP, cross-domain applications.

## 1 Introduction

Web applications – systems that resemble desktop applications in their behavior but are run inside the browser – are becoming increasingly common. The current trend is that web pages have dynamic components side by side with the traditional web content, such as static text and images. These dynamic components can be small widgets that for instance display current weather information or stock exchange data, or even full-fledged web applications that offer a service related to the theme of the web page where they are located [1].

Creating dynamic web pages is much more complex than building plain old web pages. However, since numerous applications are readily available, it would be attractive to simply reuse applications that already exist instead of building them from scratch for a particular application. This would be a step towards 'mashware' envisioned in [2], where the idea of composing complex applications is out of components readily available in different web sites. Furthermore, there are real-life examples of this happening. For instance, it has been possible to embed Google Maps (*http://maps.google.com/*) functionality as a part of any web site for some years by now. Similarly, the popularity of embedded Google Maps components verifies our assumption that application embedding is a valued feature.

A. Harth and N. Koch (Eds.): ICWE 2011 Workshops, LNCS 7059, pp. 62–73, 2012.

Unfortunately, reusing web applications that already exist in some web site is not straightforward, even if the applications could be downloaded in an uncomplicated fashion. The same origin policy inside the browser, defined to protect web pages from malicious code, prevents a document or script loaded from one web domain from getting or setting the properties of a document from another domain [3]. Furthermore, creating web pages that host such dynamic applications is much more complex than building plain old web pages to begin with, because the page must offer hosting services to the application. Consequently, implementing a service that readily provides small applications in web pages requires considerably more attention than simple reference to the service in the embedding web page.

At present, there are two obvious ways to perform application embedding. A web application can be embedded inside a <div> or an <iframe> element. Both of the approaches have been associated with consequences that deplete their potential, and hence they are not too widely deployed solutions. These properties will be discussed in more detail later on.

In this paper, we describe how to embed cross-domain web applications in a web page. While the design itself is generic and technology-independent, we demonstrate the approach with a server side web development framework called Vaadin [4]. The implementation combines strengths of <div> and <iframe> based approaches, but is not plagued by their main weaknesses. Furthermore, the implementation is kept as simple as possible for the developer who wishes to embed an application in a web page, to the extent that only a single line of HTML is needed for taking an application to use.

The rest of the paper is structured as follows. In Section 2, we give an overview to the Vaadin Framework and its particularities that are important for our implementation. In Section 3, we explain the details of the embedding we have enabled in detail, and in Section 4, we discuss some sample applications. In Section 5, we provide some directions for future work, and in Section 6 we draw some final conclusions.

## 2    The Vaadin Framework

The Vaadin Framework extensively relies on the facilities of Google Web Toolkit, GWT (*http://code.google.com/webtoolkit/*) [5]. GWT is an open source development system that allows the developer to write Ajax-based (Asynchronous JavaScript and XML) web applications using Java that can then be compiled to highly optimized JavaScript, which can be run in all browsers. In the Vaadin Framework, GWT is used for compiling web browser client-side engine and for Ajax-based communication – in essence asynchronous *XMLHttpRequest* calls – between a client and the server (Figure 1).

Consequently, from the developer perspective individual Vaadin applications can be implemented like Java Standard Edition desktop applications. The only difference to common Java applications is that the developer has to use the specific set of Vaadin UI components. For customized look and feel, the developer can use Cascading Style Sheet (CSS) files or directly modify the properties of the components in Java.

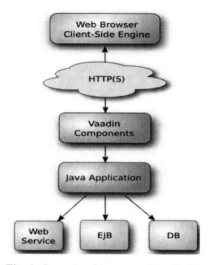

**Fig. 1.** General architecture of Vaadin [4]

In the Book of Vaadin [4], the main introductory paper documentation regarding the Vaadin Framework, two different approaches for embedding a Vaadin application as a part of a static web page are described – the Vaadin application can be embedded inside a <div> or <iframe> element. For the <div> approach, the downside is associated with the same origin policy, which makes it difficult to embed applications from other domains as a part of a website. Applications running on the same domain can be embedded, but this means that a copy of the embedded application must be available in the same domain. With the <iframe> approach, the same origin policy related problems can be overlooked, and applications can be added from any domain inside an <iframe>. However, upon enabling the download of applications, the <iframe> also traps the application inside it. Consequently, if an application running inside an <iframe> opens a dialog, the dialog stays inside original borders of the <iframe>. In contrast, with a <div> the application would appear to be a part of the web page as the new dialog could be opened anywhere on the web page.

As an example, Figure 2 shows the same Vaadin application embedded in an <iframe> and in a <div>. In <iframe> based embedding the "My Window" dialog is trapped inside the <iframe>, whereas with <div> approach the dialog can move freely around the page. By examining the <iframe> solution, it is obvious that left side of the "My Window" dialog has been cut away by the <iframe>.

Furthermore, another difficult with <iframe> approach is that communication between the page and the application inside the <iframe> is limited to using URL fragment IDs or hacks of different kind as with <div> approach the embedded application can be manipulated using the document object model (DOM) tree.

When embedding a Vaadin application in a web page, the situation gets even more complex, and being able to access an HTML file from another domain is just the beginning. We must also support communication between the client running inside the browser and the web site that runs the server part of the application. This is commonly implemented using the *XMLHttpRequest* mechanism, an integral part of Ajax, to enable data transmissions, which, even if we could download the client part of the application, would be blocked due to the same origin policy based.

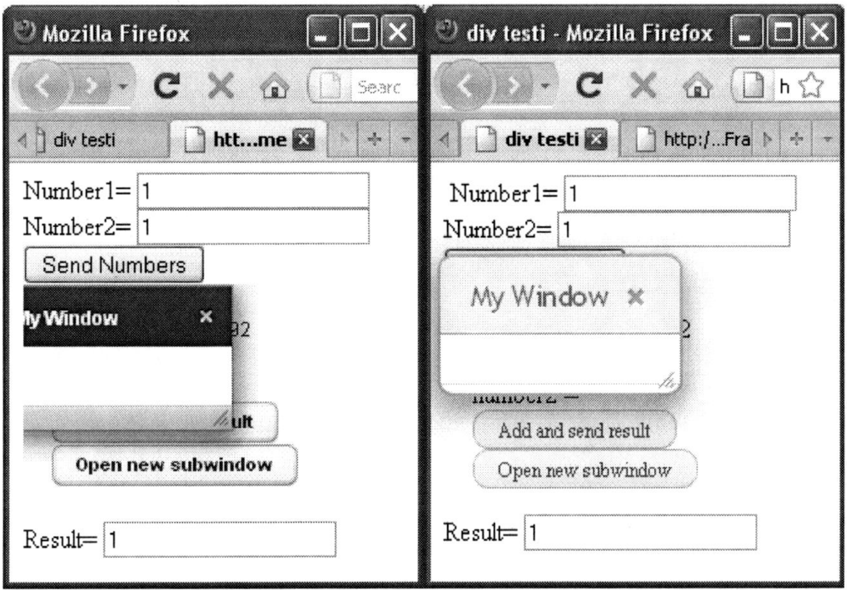

**Fig. 2.** Application in <iframe> (left) and in <div> (right)

However, there are some notable exceptions to the same origin policy. Images, scripts and style sheets downloaded from another domain are not subjected to the same origin policy. Consequently these formats can be used for circumventing the restrictions related to the policy. Next, we explain how this can be implemented for Vaadin applications.

# 3    Embedding Vaadin Applications

The traditional way to implement a web application that comprises a Vaadin component from another web site would be to use a proxy to communicate with the component. However, setting up the proxy is in some cases impossible and in any case the introduction of the proxy is an unnecessary complicating step – the setup procedure of such proxy is much more difficult than simply editing HTML source code. Therefore, we aim at a more developer-friendly solution, described in the following.

In a nutshell, to make Vaadin application embedding work on an arbitrary web page, two problems must be solved: (1) how to download the client-side part of the application, and (2) how to enable communication between the client-side engine and the server. In the following, we discuss two problems separately and explain our solutions.

## 3.1    Downloading the Client-Side Engine

Vaadin application consists of the server-side engine implemented with Java and GWT based JavaScript client-side engine. The file structure of the Vaadin client-side engine is presented in Figure 3. During the startup, the Vaadin client-side engine is

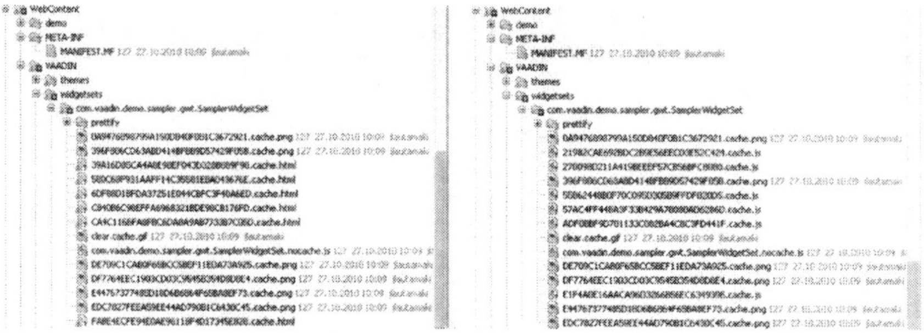

**Fig. 3.** Original (left) and modified (right) Structure of Vaadin WebContent

downloaded. Starting up the client-side engine is made in four phases listed in Table 1. Images and CSS files that are also needed for loading the client-side engine are not subjected to the same origin restriction, and therefore they are omitted from the table. At the first, browser requests an *index.html* file from the server and the file is returned. In the second phase, the <script> tag inside file *index.html* causes the download of file *vaadinWidgetset.nocache.js*. In the third phase, the *nocache.js* file recognizes the browser version and requests for the right client-side engine version. The server returns page *hashNumber.cache.html*, which contains the client-side engine. In the fourth phase, the system is initiated and user interface description is downloaded from the server.

Assuming that this approach is used for loading an embedded application to foreign web pages, the same origin policy prohibits us from loading HTML pages from other domains. Consequently phases 1 and 3 given in Table 1 will not succeed.

A brief analysis reveals that downloading *index.html* is not necessary when embedding the application. Instead, we could start by requesting the *vaadinWidgetset.nocache.js* script. However, *index.html* contains a lot of additional information, including the locations of associated CSS files, and overlooking this part would cause numerous problems for the developer. As a solution, we moved the modified content of the *index.html* file to the *index.js* file, which can easily be downloaded using <script> tag. The content of the *hashNumber.cache.html* files consist almost completely of JavaScript and just a thin HTML wrapper around them is needed. Consequently we moved JavaScript parts to JavaScript files and use *vaadinWidgetset.nocache.js* to generate the necessary HTML code. The generated HTML downloads scripts from JavaScript files using <script> tags. After this modification, everything that the client-side engine needs can be downloaded, and the engine can be initialized. The method for downloading the initial UIDL is described in more detailed in the next subsection.

After modifications (Table 2), *index.js* is first downloaded inside the <script> tag of the target page. In the second phase, *vaadinWidgetset.nocache.js* is downloaded. In the third phase, the script in *nocache.js* recognizes the browser version and requests for the right *hashNumber.cache.js* version to be downloaded. In the fourth phase, *HashNumber.cache.js* is evaluated, the system starts up, and the user interface description can be downloaded.

**Table 1.** Initialization of Client-Side Engine

| | Client-side engine | Server |
|---|---|---|
| 1 | Requests root or index.html | Returns index.html |
| 2 | Requests nocache.js startup script | Returns startup script |
| 3 | Requests the client-side engine HTML file | Returns the HTML file |
| 4 | Requests the initial UIDL | UIDL returned as JSON |
| 5 | Renders user interface and starts waiting for user initiated events | |

**Table 2.** Initialization of embedded Client-Side Engine

| | Client-side engine | Server |
|---|---|---|
| 1 | Requests index.js | Returns a JavaScript file |
| 2 | Requests nocache.js startup script | Returns startup script |
| 3 | Requests the client-side engine JavaScript file | Returns the JavaScript file |
| 4 | Requests the initial UIDL | UIDL returned as JSONP |
| 5 | Renders user interface and starts waiting for user initiated events | |

Since GWT is used to generate the file structure of the framework, we should not modify files by hand, since then changes would be lost at the first time when the framework is modified and recompiled. Fortunately, cross-domain scripting capabilities are something that is commonly needed, and Google has included support for such features in GWT. Therefore, we only added a single line to the GWT configuration file:

```
<add-linker name="xs"/>
```

and recompile the system. The old file structure and the new cross-domain capable web content are presented in Figure 3. Structures are the same apart from the filename extensions – the content of html files is moved inside js files.

*Index.js* is not generated by GWT and the system can be used and embedded without *index.js* script, but it would be much more complex for an embedding developer. Without the *index.js* script, the embedding developer would have to use paths to the actual *WidgetSet.nocache.js* script, which could be arbitrarily complex. Furthermore, the developer would also have to define the location of the CSS file, which again can be complex. Thus, in a nutshell the reason for using *index.js* is redirecting the call to the actual files and linking the system to the right style sheets.

With the above modifications, embedding the Vaadin application as simple as adding a single line of html to the body of the target document:

```
<script type="text/javascript" src="http://jlautamaki.
   virtuallypreinstalled.com/embedding/index.js">
</script>
```

## 3.2    Communication with the Server

As already discussed, after being able to download the client-side engine to the browser, we must also enable the communication with the server that runs the actual application. In Vaadin applications, the client-side engine uses the *XMLHttpRequest* mechanism for all the interactions with the server side (Table 3). There are some straightforward ways to make *XMLHttpRequest* familiar from Ajax work on cross-domain environment. The most obvious alternative is to use <iframe> tags, as already discussed above, but it is also possible to use on <iframe> as a proxy for *XMLHttpRequests* [6]. In addition, W3C has proposed a method for Cross-Origin Resource sharing [7], implemented already in Firefox 3.5, using an HTTP header: *Access-Control-Allow-Origin: * [8]. Finally, in some old Safari versions there was a security leak that permitted cross-domain *XMLHttpRequests* to work, but this has now been fixed [9].

Despite the possibilities provided by individual browser features and hacks, using them as the basis for long-lasting, generic web services is not feasible. Therefore, we decided to rely on another communication technology, JSONP (JSON with padding) [10], which is commonly used for making cross-domain calls. Furthermore, JSONP works in all modern browsers.

Our JSONP based design gains advantage of the open policy for the <script> tag and uses scripts as a communication channel. A new script can be downloaded when needed, and after the download, the scripts are evaluated and later removed. An injected <script> tag has attribute src. This attribute points to the Vaadin application and downloads the script from there. Messages from the client to the server can be sent as an attribute of the URI:

```
<script type="text/javascript"
  src="http://URL/getjson?jsonp=parseResponse&
  secondAttribute=hello">
</script>
```

Vaadin application gets called the same way as with *XMLHttpRequest* based communication. By default, Vaadin applications use JSON for communication, and consequently the only thing we must add is the padding. With this approach, the browser gets the following message:

```
parseResponse({"Name": "Cheeso", "Rank": 7});
```

In this response, the padding is *"parseResponse()"* and JSON is *{"Name": "Cheeso", "Rank": 7}*. Return value will invoke the *parseResponse* function in the client side engine. The actual message is handled similarly to previously discussed *XMLHttpRequest* messages.

The communication process is summarized in Table 4. First, the user interacts with the UI, for example pushes a button. As a consequence, (second phase) the client-side engine adds a new <script> tag to the web page and sets the appropriate URI for the source of the script. The message passed to the server side is added to the URI as an attribute. As a result the URI for the new script could be for example: *http://url/?okButton=pressed*. The server gets called and it uses *request.getAttribute* to get information that the button has been pressed. Once the server has processed the actions associated with the button, it returns the response to client-side engine, again using JSON with padding. The JSONP message is loaded inside the <script> tag we previously created and is evaluated (the third phase). The evaluation leads to calling the padding function with JSON as a parameter and results are made visible for the user.

**Table 3.** Original communication

| | Client | Server |
|---|---|---|
| 1 | User interaction | |
| 2 | POSTS XMLHTTPRequest with requestData | Gets message and returns JSON |
| 3 | RequestCallback function gets JSON message | |

**Table 4.** Modified communication

| | Client | Server |
|---|---|---|
| 1 | User interaction | |
| 2 | New script tag is added, src is url+parameters: "http://url/parameters" | Gets message and returns JSONP |
| 3 | JSONP message is evaluated | |

In comparison to *XMLHttpRequest*, JSONP has a number of weaknesses. Perhaps the biggest problem is that by allowing cross-domain accesses, the use of JSONP also introduces vulnerabilities. When a JSONP call is made, there has to be absolute trust to the other participant, since JavaScript programs are downloaded as data, and consequently the loaded code can do anything. This has not been considered as a problem in the usual case of Vaadin applications, where everything comes from the same origin. However when embedding and mashupping applications, the problem is that JavaScript loaded from the other domain inevitably gets full access to the content loaded from another domain. In case of the malicious application developers, anything can happen. In our case, we have decided that integrator of the html page just trusts all the widget developers and their services and services have no critical security aspects.

In addition, when using the *XMLHttpRequest* mechanism, there are certain methods for handling errors that take place in communication. In contrast, with JSONP there is no automatic error handling, and any actions to this end should be included in the application. There are certain libraries to simplify this, but in general error checking features are still missing.

Finally, there are a lot of minor implementation-level issues that have been encountered. In particular, in Vaadin applications, messages were already padded using *for(;;);* as a safety mechanism and for making cross site scripting more difficult. This is of course something we had to remove in our implementation, and the obvious consequence is less secure communication.

## 4    Examples

For demonstrating and explaining the value of our embedding facility, we have created a web page to *http://www.cs.tut.fi/* domain and used it for embedding two different web applications running on the *http://jlautamaki.virtuallypreinstalled.com/* domain. Our sample web page is based on Wikipedia's Body Mass Index (BMI) entry. BMI is a heuristic proxy for human body fat based on an individual's weight and height. BMI is defined as the individual's body weight divided by the square of his or her height. If BMI index falls between 18.5 and 25 then the person is a normal

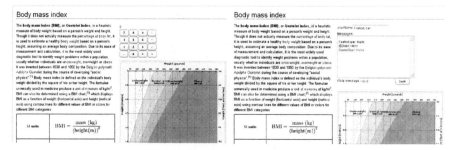

**Fig. 4.** Embedded Calculator (left) and Chat (right) applications

weighted. Most of the web page development systems can be used to create a simple page like this. The page is just plain text and a couple of pictures and tables. However, for our examples we have spiced up this simple page with two different Vaadin applications.

Consider a user who visits the body mass index page. If the BMI is a new concept for user, the first thing to do is obvious – the user wants to calculate his own BMI and needs a calculator. Of course it would be possible to use a calculator from a mobile phone or a separate desktop calculator application, but it would also be nice to have a calculator embedded directly in the BMI page. The calculator is a web application and is not easily implemented by every web developer. However, given a ready-made calculator, it can be easily embedded in a web page by using our system. This is visualized in Figure 4, and the actual web page is available at available for testing purposes at the address: *http://www.cs.tut.fi/~delga/vaadin/calc.html*. Furthermore, it is also possible to try out the embedding of the calculator application. Only things needed are a web page that can be edited and some trust that we are not trying to do anything hostile. To get the calculator embedded on the web page, only the following script has to be added to the body of the html page:

```
<script type="text/javascript" src="http://jlautamaki.
  virtuallypreinstalled.com/embedding/calc.js">
</script>
```

Our second example, shown in Figure 4 and available at *http://www.cs.tut.fi/~delga/vaadin/chat.html*, is providing a chat widget for the BMI page. The goal of the widget is to enable the user to chat with other users of the page and in this case for example send weight and height as a chat message and other users can then comment on those values and give feedback. It would be possible to create a channel for each page in which chat component has been embedded and then the visitors of the page could communicate with each other. In our example, it is just one channel chat. In the sense of the implementation, this application is considerably more complex since it requires communication between users. Consequently it cannot be implemented with plain client side JavaScript since the server must mediate messages between users. The sequence diagram is presented in Figure 5. In the diagram, we have cheated a little bit for sake clearness. In reality chat clients poll the server once in 2 seconds, but in Figure 5 we have presented communication like messages could be pushed directly from server to client. Similarly to the calculator, the chat application can be embedded by adding the following script to the body of the html page:

```
<script type="text/javascript" src="http://jlautamaki.
  virtuallypreinstalled.com/embedding/chat.js">
</script>
```

## 5    Future Work

We still have some considerations and refinement to do with respect to the security aspects. At present, we are not fully aware what kinds of new attacks are possible against the embedded version, which would not be enabled for the original Vaadin applications. However, we do acknowledge that the embedding might introduce some properties that cannot be made as safe as without embedding, no matter how much we try.

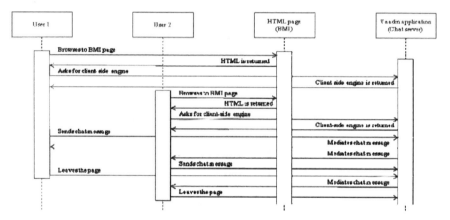

**Fig. 5.** Sequence diagram with two users chatting

In order to consider the wider use of embedding, an obvious target is to try out our system in real world examples. At present, the whole system is available for testing at *http://vaadin.com/directory#addon/vaadin-xs* and the next step would be to use the system in real use cases with real customers to gain feedback from actual users.

The long-term goal of this work is to create a library of Vaadin applications that could be used by anybody. Assuming that we can figure out the remaining technological details addressed above, there will also be research challenges associated with numerous business related issues. We are in the middle of considering how to set up an ecosystem of widgets, where they could be deployed in embedded mode. On one hand, we should be able to serve web developers who are interested in embedding web applications but do want to implement them, and at the same time we must provide support for developers creating new widgets for others to embed. So far, we have not introduced any business logic that would define how parties hosting embedded applications would get their income, so this is an obvious direction for future work.

Finally, there are some possible advantages that can be gained with other web technologies. In particular, instead of JSONP we could use CORS (Cross-Origin Resource Sharing), a browser technology specification for scripts originating from different domains [7]. Using CORS would introduce some potential benefits, mainly because while JSONP only supports the GET request method, CORS also support the other types of requests. Furthermore, CORS also has better error handling mechanisms than JSONP. As a drawback, CORS is only supported by limited set of modern browsers.

## 6     Conclusion

In this paper, we presented a way to compose embedded web applications in a fashion that combines the best properties of commonly used approaches without their major downsides. The implementation is composed using the Vaadin Framework, where any completed application consists of the client-side engine. The client-side engine acts as the front end for a Java application running on the server side. The approach was demonstrated with two applications (or widgets) that can be tried out. Furthermore, these applications embedded to any web site by just adding one <script> tag to the body of the HTML document hosting the applications.

As a part of this work, we modified the Vaadin Framework. The modifications have been contributed to the Vaadin community, and are available through Vaadin directory (*http://vaadin.com/directory#addon/vaadin-xs*) for all Vaadin developers.

The most attractive direction for future work – apart from polishing the technology itself – is the creation of an ecosystem where embeddable Vaadin applications could be hosted as a service. In the long run, the vision is to establish a full library of different kinds of web applications, available for embedding to different web pages around the world. This in turn will introduce numerous technical and business challenges for researches as well as for practitioners.

## References

[1]  O'Reilly, T.: What is Web 2.0: Design Patterns and Business models for the Next Generation of Software. Communications & Strategies (1), 17 (2007)
[2]  Mikkonen, T., Taivalsaari, A.: The Mashware Challenge: Bridging the Gap Between Web Development and Software Engineering. In: Proceedings of the FSE/SDP Workshop on the Future of Software Engineering Research (FoSER 2010), Santa Fe, New Mexico, USA, November 7-8 (2010)
[3]  Same origin policy, World Wide Web Consortium (W3C),
     http://www.w3.org/Security/wiki/Same_Origin_Policy
[4]  Grönroos, M.: Book of Vaadin (2009) (uniprint)
[5]  Perry, B.W.: Google Web Toolkit for Ajax. O'Reilly Short Cuts, pp. 1–5. O'Reilly (2007)
[6]  How to make XMLHttpRequest calls to another server in your domain, Ajaxian,
     http://ajaxian.com/archives/how-to-make-xmlhttprequest-calls-to-another-server-in-your-domain

[7]  Cross-Origin Resourced Sharing, World Wide Web Consortium (W3C),
     http://www.w3.org/TR/cors/
[8]  HTTP access control, Mozilla Foundation,
     https://developer.mozilla.org/En/HTTP_Access_Control
[9]  Safari same origin hole, The Spanner, JavaScript and general security blog,
     http://www.thespanner.co.uk/2007/06/29/
     safari-same-origin-hole/
[10] Remote JSON – JSONP (December 5, 2005),
     http://bob.pythonmac.org/archives/2005/12/05/
     remote-json-jsonp/

# Web Linking-Based Protocols for Guiding RESTful M2M Interaction

Jesus Bellido, Rosa Alarcon, and Cristian Sepulveda

Computer Science Department
Pontificia Universidad Catolica de Chile
jbellido@uc.cl, ralarcon@ing.puc.cl, cmsepul@uc.cl

**Abstract.** The *Representational State Transfer (REST)* style has become a popular approach for lightweight implementation of Web services, mainly because of relevant benefits such as massive scalability, high evolvability, and low coupling. It was designed considering the human-user as the one who drives service invocation and discovery. Attempts to provide machine-clients a similar autonomy have been proposed and recently, interesting discussion evaluate explicit semantics in the form of well-defined media types but introducing higher levels of coupling. We explore Web linking as a lightweight mechanism for representing *link* semantics and guiding machine-clients in the execution of well-defined choreographies and illustrate our approach with the OAuth and OpenId protocols exploring asynchrony and machine expectations as the interaction moves forward.

## 1 Introduction

The web has become a platform not only for the delivery of content, but also for the provision of services. Diverse functionality is made available to massive amount of users, and new services are built on top of others offering aggregated value. Popular service interfaces are generally classified into WSDL-based or REST based services, although other variants such as XML-RPC, Atom, JSON-RPC, etc. are also available[1]. In addition, the reuse of services into compounds (service composition) is highly desirable not only because it reduces costs and provides aggregated value, but also because it allows the creation of enriched applications, leveraging the Web as a services platform.

A REST service is a web of interconnected *resources* identified with *URIs*, that can be manipulated through a *uniform interface* (e.g. HTTP operations), whose *state* is served through *representations* (e.g. an HTML page) embedding *links* and *controls* (e.g. a `form` indicating a `POST` operation), which define the underlying hypermedia model that determines not only the relationships among resources but also the possible net of resource state transitions. REST consumers discover and decide which links/controls to follow/execute at *run-time*. This constraint is known as HATEOAS (Hypermedia As The Engine Of Application

---

[1] see http://www.programmableweb.com/apis/directory

A. Harth and N. Koch (Eds.): ICWE 2011 Workshops, LNCS 7059, pp. 74–85, 2012.
© Springer-Verlag Berlin Heidelberg 2012

State). A composition of REST services can be seen not only as the availability of new resources but also of new navigation paths (links/controls) that allow clients to traverse the hypermedia model corresponding to various independent REST services.

Providing support for automatic composition is also desirable since it may reduce development time and costs, but is far from trivial since REST services lack a standard machine-readable description, so that REST service providers describe their APIs in natural language (e.g. HTML pages) forcing machine-client developers to interpret the intended way of use of the API, to identify any change manually and to program the clients accordingly; most often, old APIs version are not supported. REST suppose humans as its principal consumer and they are expected to drive resource discovery and state transition by understanding the representation's content semantics, i.e. the links/controls embedded in representations such as HTML pages. The lack of explicit domain-level semantics in current media-types (e.g. HTML), makes harder for machine-clients to select, among the available links and controls, those they must follow in order to accomplish a specific navigation path or to engage in a predetermined way with various resources, as is the case for instance, of business processes, choreographies or authentication protocols. Some [1], propose the definition of domain specific media-types that portray the resource's state and the related hyperlinks. A machine-client that is aware of such custom media-types could then understand such representations and proceed accordingly. However, this requires that both client and servers agree on the media-types meaning, which introduces a strong coupling.

We are interested in exploring Web Linking [2] as a mechanism for specifying application-domain semantics for complex interaction such as business processes. In this paper we analyze the OAuth [3] and OpenID [4] protocols as case studies that implement Web choreographies, including control flow, asynchronous calls, out-of-band interactions and various media-types. The proposal allows a machine-client to understand resources' representation and to dynamically determine a navigation path, enacting the expected choreography. The paper is organized as follows, section 2 discuss related work, section 3 presents our approach, and finally section 4 present our conclusions.

## 2   Related Work

A few languages have been proposed to create machine readable RESTful services description. The Web Application Description Language (WADL) [5] describes RESTful services as *resources* identified by URI patterns, media types and the schemas of the expected *request* and *response* as well as *representations*. The latter supports *parameters* that can contain links to another resources. WADL, however, does not support link discovery or link generation for new resources, the resulting model is operation-centric and introduces additional complexity with unclear benefits for both human and machine-clients.

In [6], we proposed ReLL (*Resource Linking Language*), a hypermedia-centric REST service description. A ReLL description considers not only resources and representations, but fundamentally links and the mechanisms for identifying changes in the described REST service (e.g. changes in the URIs). ReLL allows machine-clients to retrieve, on run-time, links and state information embedded in representations so that a simple Web machine-client (a crawler) is able to traverse and discover the interlinked resources of a REST service. A ReLL description requires to annotate described resources and links/controls with *types*, serving as the basis for generating a semantic model. This approach made possible to semantically integrate independent REST services and execute queries that traverse the integrated web [7,8]. ReLL was used also as the basis for building machine-clients that traverse the Web enacting a predetermined workflow defined by a Petri Net[9]. The latter approach delegates on the Petri Net the responsibility of determining, at design time, the navigation path a machine-client must follow, resources, however, are dynamically bound. One of the main drawbacks of this approach is that, even though separation of concerns facilitates the design of workflows, it introduces coupling between the ReLL and Petri layers (horizontal interfaces [10]), so that changes on the ReLL description would make clients fail since the Petri Net is unaware of such changes.

Other approaches [1], avoid the need of a description by defining domain specific media-types (e.g. an XML schema for a company's bills) that portray the resource's state and the related hyperlinks. Authors define a *Domain Application Protocol (DAP)* as a collection of media types, URI entry points, HTTP idioms and the link relations portrayed in the representations. The DAP determines the set of legal interactions between a consumer and a set of resources involved in a business process and is also an implicit contract between the disparate parties in the composition, it is not clear though, how a machine-client may understand how to comply the DAP, unless both client and servers agree on the media-types meaning, which introduces a strong coupling.

In [11], Steiner and Algermissen acknowledge the limitations of relying on media-types to portray both content for human-consumption (that may require human-friendly formats such as HTML) and semantics directed to machine-clients (that may require RDF) and they propose content-negotiation (HTTP Options) to dynamically find out the appropriate media type. They propose also an extension of the RDF HTTP Vocabulary in order to become the media-type intended for machine-clients as well as the usage of links served as HTTP Headers annotated according to the Web linking standard [2].

The standard specifies *relation types* for Web links, defines a registry for them, and regulates its usage in HTTP headers (Link headers). A *link* is a typed connection between two resources, that involves a context URI (the origin resource URI), a link relation type, a target IRI, and optionally, target attributes. No restrictions are placed on cardinality or relative ordering of the links. Target *attributes* are key/value pairs that further describe the link or its target (e.g. `media="text"`). A *link relation type* identifies the semantics of a link (e.g. `rel="copyright"`) and there are two kind of relation types, registered and extension. The former are well-defined, registered tokens; while extension relation types are URIs that uniquely identify the relation type. Steiner [11] relies on registered tokens and media-types that lack domain-level semantics which introduces less coupling but makes impossible for a machine-client to make sense of the presented information and decide which link to follow and which information may be relevant for such decision. In addition the proposed media-type do not allow to dynamically discover links and controls to related resources.

# 3   REST Services Composition and Interaction Protocols

We are interested in the development of machine-clients that enable service composition involving REST services. Statelessness is a key REST constraint that dictates not to store the state of the interaction between clients and servers on the server side. This constraint has two consequences, stateless servers are much less complex than stateful ones, providing massive levels of scalability and fault tolerance (e.g. hardware replicas); but this also requires that each request to the server must contain all the information needed to provide a response. Service composition has traditionally focused on stateful approaches where a central component orchestrates the dialogue between the parties and store all the necessary information to move forward the interaction.

A stateless, RESTful scenario where there is no such orchestrator but a cooperation of the involved resources, that is a choreography, requires that the representations served to each other mediate the interaction. The HATEOAS constraint is fundamental in this scenario, provided that machine-clients can understand the semantics of the links and controls served in the representations, and they have the required semantics to move forward the interaction.

We could argue that at a very general level, Web linking registered relation types such as start, previous, next, first, last [2], could be used to embed instructions within the served representations and add basic semantics to guide resources interaction. However, interaction have explicit semantics in particular domains that can be exploited for servers to steer machine-clients. For instance, let's consider the REST APIs implementing the OAuth and OpenId protocols; callbacks and redirection are part of the interaction; they implement an interrupted, asynchronous conversation where third parties (out-of-band) later affect resources' state and dynamically generate pieces of information that are expected to be carried out at various steps of the interaction.

## 3.1   Security Domain: OAuth 2.0 and OpenId

Modeling non functional aspects of services have captured the attention of researchers as a medium for enriching and constraining automatic compositions and one of these aspects is security. In [12], a survey determines that most Web APIs use one of five authentication mechanisms, namely, they use credentials (API key or username and password) to restrict access to a service, Web authentication protocols (HTTP Basic Authentication, HTTP Digest Authentication and OAuth), or even ad-hoc authentication mechanisms (parts of the HTTP request). OAuth accounts for a mere 6% of the APIs surveyed, however recent adoption of stronger security capabilities such as OAuth and HTTPS for mayor players in the industry (e.g. Facebook, Twitter) will have an influence on applications developed on top of these platforms.

**OAuth 2.0.** The OAuth 2.0 authorization protocol allows to grant third-party applications limited access to an HTTP service on behalf of a user, by orchestrating an approval interaction protocol between the user and the HTTP service. OAuth defines four grant types: authorization code, implicit, resource owner password credentials, and client credentials, and provides an extension mechanism for defining additional grant types. Each grant type defines an authorization interaction flow between four parties, the *client*, the *resource owner*, the *authorization server* and the *resource server*.

The authorization code grant type flow is illustrated in Figure 1. The client obtain some credentials (1, 2) and requests authorization from the resource owner directly, or preferably through an authorization server (A). The server authenticates the resource owner through a user-agent (e.g. a form displayed in a Web browser). This communication occurs out-of-band between the Resource Owner (e.g. LinkedIn) and the user. Once the resource owner grants access to the required resources, the authorization server redirects the user-agent to the callback and includes an authorization code provided to the client (C). The authorization code is used to request an access token (D) from the authentication server, once the token is granted (E), the client application can use it to access resources stored in the resource server (F, G).

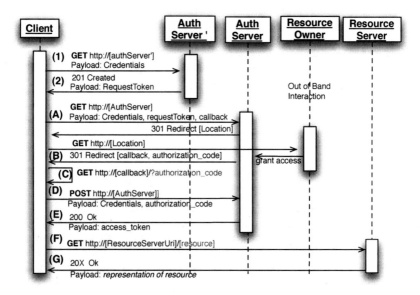

**Fig. 1.** OAuth 2.0 Abstract protocol sequence diagram

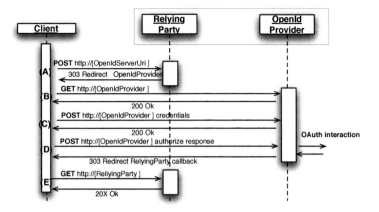

**Fig. 2.** OpenID abstract protocol sequence diagram

**OpenID.** The OpenID protocol allows consumers to present, to a service, claims about their identity that have been authenticated by an identity provider trusted by that service. OpenID allows a service to delegate the responsability for storing consumer credentials to one or more OpenID providers. The providers are responsible for checking a consumers credentials and informing a service if an identity claim is valid.

Figure 2 shows the protocol for a client to register an OpenID URI that they claim to own to a Relying Party (e.g. LiveJournal). In an Initiation step (A), the Party redirects the client to the proper OpenId Provider (e.g. Blogger) (B) that requires the user to provide both, credentials (user, password) and optionally to choose a preferred authentication server (C). With that information, the OpenID provider validates user credentials and if necessary may redirect the client to the appropriate OpenId provider (e.g. Google, PayPal, Yahoo, etc.), this in turn verifies the consumer credentials and confirms the registry of the user OpenID, otherwise, it redirects the consumer to the OAuth server in order to grant access to identity information (e.g. Google, Facebook, etc.).

### 3.2   Linking Requirements: Modeling Stateless Choreographies

In order to design stateless interaction, state (client-server interaction) must be explicitly modeled either as a different resource [10], as cookies, or be embedded in the representations so that clients can build later the subsequent requests properly. As seen in Figure 3, the latter approach can be accomplished without requiring extensive changes in the representations by exploiting Web Linking. The text in italics (red) shows our proposal for Link Headers, the URI part represents the URI of the resource to be retrieved. The semantics of the link are explicitly presented by the `rel` parameter as an extension relation type (an abbreviated URI in our case) that refers to a particular realm, process or application domain, a target attribute identify the *expected* state that can be achieved

**(0)** *Link:  <https://api.linkedin.com/uas/oauth/requestToken>; rel="oauth:start";*
           *state="[oauth:started | oauth:denied]"; method="GET"*

**(1)** GET https://api.linkedin.com/uas/oauth/requestToken
        Authorization=OAuth
        oauth_consumer_key= ...,
        oauth_nonce="180098101",
        oauth_timestamp="1284497324",
        oauth_signature=...,
        oauth_callback="oob",
        oauth_signature_method="HMAC-SHA1",
        oauth_version="1.0"

**(2)** HTTP/1.1 201 Created
        Content-Length=236, null=HTTP/1.1 201 Created, Date=Tue, 14 Sep 2010 20:52:18 GMT,
        Content-Type=text/plain, Server=Apache-Coyote/1.1
        *Link:  <https://api.linkedin.com/uas/oauth/authorize>; rel="oauth:grant";*
               *state="[oauth:granted | oauth:denied]"; method="GET";*
        Params:
        oauth_token=142e1172-aca0-40e8-9a3f-163f52969cda
        oauth_token_secret=b795c3ae-bf72-4451-baaf-eb31b6b024e1
        oauth_callback_confirmed=true
        oauth_request_auth_url=https://api.linkedin.com/uas/oauth/authorize
        oauth_expires_in=599

**(A)** GET https://api.linkedin.com/uas/oauth/authorize?oauth_token=142e1172-
        aca0-40e8-9a3f-163f52969cda

**(C)** HTTP/1.1 200 OK
        *Link:  <https://api.linkedin.com/uas/oauth/accessToken>; rel="oauth:accessToken";*
               *state="[oauth:authorized | oauth:unauthorized]"; method="POST";*
        https://www.linkedin.com/uas/oauth/authorize/oob?
        oauth_token=4be35e7e-9d5b-4cb9-82fa-3dfd6b694fdc

**(D)** POST https://api.linkedin.com/uas/oauth/accessToken
        Authorization=OAuth
        Params:
        oauth_consumer_key="..."
        oauth_nonce="-46807422"
        oauth_timestamp="1284754819"
        oauth_signature="UCgAG4ueyGRcSZluUwz8dhOYCOk%3D"
        oauth_verifier="92577"
        oauth_callback="oob"
        oauth_signature_method="HMAC-SHA1"
        oauth_token="ae98a651-36a0-41c8-ab24-e2a2e1672bcb"
        oauth_version="1.0"

**Fig. 3.** Messages exchanged during OAuth 2.0 protocol, for a LinkedIn implementation

by the machine-client if the link is followed, as well as the method to be performed. Control flow operators that are common in service composition such
as conditional invocation, selection of the best result, parallel execution, etc.
[13], should be also considered. We model such controls as XPath expressions
(operators) that are evaluated at run-time with the assistance of a ReLL description. For the OAuth case, the choreography starts with a first link (Figure
3.0). For a more general case, such as a business process, this will indicate that a
process initiates a subtask at a particular entry-point (which can be dynamically
discovered). The request (1) to the URI changes the state of the oauth:start
resource. The new served response (2) is processed by the machine-client using
ReLL as a means to derive some hints from the content.

For instance, it verifies that the URI matches clients' expectancy (no changes in the URI); it retrieves the representation expecting to be encoded as *text/plain*, and verifies whether a regular expression is contained. In such case, it determines wether the expected state `oauth:started` (a 201 HTTP code indicates, in the LinkedIn implementation, that a new Request Token was *created*) was achieved and prepares to discover the next step of the orchestration. The link `request grant` is followed in order to obtain an `oauth:grant` resource, the link is retrieved from the representation by executing a `select` expression that can be encoded as a regular expression or as an XPath expression depending on the content media type. Since Web Linking determines rules to transform links to XML, we decided to transform the link to XML and use XPath expressions for illustrating the dependance on the media-type. The method can be also retrieved from the content. Once the link is followed (A), the new served response includes instructions to force a redirection on the machine-client which will lose control of the interaction, and could either wait for an asynchronous message to regain control, look for an answer later, or stop its execution and trust that the next message will contain the necessary information for resuming the interaction without losing information. We implemented the latter alternative in the machine-client by sending all which is necessary to continue the interaction, since the OAuth protocol allows for an `extra` parameter for such kind of purposes. Eventually, the interaction is resumed by a message received through a callback (`http://darwin.ing.puc.cl` ...). Figure 4 presents a snippet of a ReLL description for an Linkedin OAuth implementation shown in figure 3.

```
<resource xml:id="oauth:start">
   <uri match="https://api.linkedin.com/uas/oauth/requestToken" type="regex"/>
   <representation xml:id="requestToken-text" type="iana:text/plain">
      <name>oauth_token request parameters</name>
      <state name="oauth:started" select="HTTPV1\.1\ 201" type="regex"/>
      <link type="request_grant" target="oauth:grant" minOccurs="0" maxOccurs="1">
         <selector name="href"   select="//Link/@href" type="xpath"/>
         <selector name="state" select="//Link/@state" type="xpath"/>
         <protocol type="http">
            <request>
               <selector name="method" select="//Link/@method" type="xpath"/>
            </request>
            <response media="iana:text/plain"/>
         </protocol>
      </link>
   </representation>
</resource>
<resource xml:id="oauth:grant">
   <uri match="http://darwin.ing.puc.cl\?oauth_token=[a-zA-Z0-9\-]*" type="regex"/>
   ...
</resource>
```

**Fig. 4.** ReLL snippet describing the RequestToken resource according to LinkedIn implementation (step 1 in Figure 2)

On run-time and starting from a seed, a machine-client retrieves a resource (e.g. an HTML form indicating that the user must authenticate by clicking a button), such page (e.g. `https://api.linkedin.com/uas/oauth/requestToken`) is described as an `oauth:start` resource, and the corresponding ReLL declarations are applied; that is, the XPath expressions or selectors, retrieve both state variables (`state`), and `links`. Since a control flow operator is omitted, the `request_grant` link determines that the next link to be retrieved corresponds to the `oauth:grant` category (`target`). State variables are carried along and stored by the machine-client.

It is also possible to dynamically generate new Links from the state variables and (part of ReLL dynamic late binding characteristics) add cardinality constraints for links. In Figure 2, step D indicates a REST composition of both OpenId service (e.g. Blogger's OpenId) and OAuth service (e.g. LinkedIn's OAuth). Again, this interaction is triggered by the OpenId Provider sending a GET message to LinkedIn in order to access a resource. The message is directed to the resource URI and a state variable (security_token) is sent in the body of the message. If valid, LinkedIn will confirm user authorization, if not, the user will follow OAuth from step 1.

### 3.3   Coupling Facets in Our Approach

One of the risks of supporting REST services descriptions is the increasing of coupling between clients and servers. Coupling has been described as a multidimensional property [10], where dimensions or facets include relevant design aspects that determine the degree of coupling in a system. In our approach ReLL serves as an abstraction layer between RESTful services and a machine-client. According to the defined coupling facets, ReLL will not increase the coupling degree between RESTful Web services and machine-clients as detailed below:

- *Discovery.* RESTful web services can be discovered by decentralized referrals exchanging hyperlinks. Services are not registered in any standardized way (e.g. UDDI). ReLL allows a machine client to discover resources by following the links encountered in resource representations. ReLL's `select` expression allows the machine client to retrieve embedded links, and `generate-uri` allows to dynamically mint new URIs from expressions embedded in a resource representation. The latter feature allows a designer to compensate the lack of hypermedia on current RESTful APIs.
- *Identification.* A URI globally identifies RESTful web services, URIs however are not constrained only to the `http` scheme. URIs identify services in different contexts and services are free to use different identifications schemes. ReLL allows a machine-client to follow a link that leads to discover another URI under any scheme (i.e. any protocol).
- *Binding.* Dynamic binding resolves at run-time the URI to be invoked, the binding is established only when it becomes necessary. ReLL allows a machine client to follow and resolve, at run-time, the URI of the link encountered in a representation obtained as a result of an invocation.

- *Platform.* Platform independency requires that services built using different and heterogeneous platforms can interact with each other without a bridge. ReLL describes resources using XML in a platform independent way. XPath expressions are also well known and standard.
- *Interaction.* Asynchronous interaction allows two services to interact without being available at the same time. HTTP is a synchronous communication protocol, and ReLL supports both synchronous scenarios and asynchronous scenarios which, in the Web context, requires to perform callbacks to a URI. This is not trivial, since servers (instead of clients) redirect user-agents to the callback URI which causes machine-clients a loss of context of the previous interaction. For the case of REST, this is solved by carrying out context information along the interchanged messages, hence, no state of the interaction is stored on the served side (session). ReLL supports this feature by injecting links and context information (through the `generate-uri` expression) that restores the interaction sequence obtained from the resource representations only when it is required.
- *Interface Orientation.* Vertical interfaces rely on using protocols for allowing components to directly communicate between them, horizontal interfaces or layered architectural styles introduce a stronger dependency among the layers which makes the architecture more coupled. ReLL relies on protocols to allow client machines to interact with services, protocols are described in terms of methods to be invoked and the media-types to be expected when a link is followed. Our previous version, used a Petri Net layer that introduced a stronger coupling between the ReLL description and the Petri Net making it hard to support server evolution without breaking the machine-client.
- *Model.* Self describing messages do not require to share a model for marshaling and unmarshaling messages. ReLL do not require any particular message format (i.e. a canonical media-type), instead it allows a client machine to recover information from representations by using XPath or regular expressions. However, if the server changes the representations, the machine-client will fail to retrieve information embedded in the content and proceed with its intended interaction. By using Web Linking however, servers can change arbitrarily the URLs of the resources involved in the choreography without causing machine-clients to break.
- *State.* Stateless services keep the state in the messages that are passed between cooperating services instead of storing the client-server interaction on the server side. ReLL discovers a cooperating service URI and its parameters from the served resource representation, and then, it generates the link to be invoked as well as the protocol and method. That is, it assumes that the message contains the state information, and it is even capable of extracting part of the message and mint context and links.
- *Generated Code.* A service description can be used to generate code, automatically (stub), that represents the service facade, either on the server or the client side. It introduces a strong contract between clients and servers and hence strong coupling. Code generation only works if the communications requirements are completely specified in a machine-readable form. It is not

possible to generate code from a ReLL service description, because it does not have a full detail of the URIs (i.e. do not register all the available URIs, nor a URI pattern), nor a full detail of the representations (i.e. it annotates the expected media-type and expected patterns in the representations, but not the content itself). A ReLL document is a partial, arbitrary (since it represents a particular client view of the service) description of a REST service. Such description expresses the expectations of a generic machine-client when interacting with a REST service but do not force servers to comply with the description, allowing then servers to freely evolve.

– *Conversation.* A reflective inspection mechanism enables clients to interact with the service by inquiring it about the possible future steps of the interaction. In our proposal, servers have full control of the links and representation served and can change them at any time, ReLL descriptions represent the expectancies of a machine-client but do not constraint in any way the server actions, instead, it contains the mechanisms (select expressions) to discover on run-time the hyperlinks. By enriching the links with Web Linking features (`rel` and target expressions such as `state`), the server explicitly indicates to its clients what state could be achieved when following a link.

## 4   Conclusions

A set of media-types determined a priori (e.g. XML) allow machine-clients to make sense of the contents and proceed accordingly, however, application-domain media types evolve continuously, sometimes media-types with no support for links or structure (e.g. binary) are required, and furthermore, they require an agreement between clients and servers, introducing stronger coupling and limiting service evolvability. By relying in well formed REST representations that fully support the HATEOAS constraint, it is possible for a machine-client to pursue a series of operations that transform the resource state.

Service descriptions (e.g. ReLL), increase coupling between clients and servers but in less degree. ReLL allows machine-client designers to encode rules and assumptions for the understanding and processing of the resources without limiting service evolvability. It facilitates to detect whether some assumptions have changed (e.g. more links than expected are served, the URIs have changed, the protocol have changed etc.), and take a proper action. Web Linking relations can be formally described as vocabularies with well-defined semantics so that machine-clients can make complex assumptions and derive plans dynamically. As for future work, we are interested in the definition of business processes enabled by lightweight infrastructures that steer a machine-client dynamically through the underlying hypermedia, so a vocabulary for Web Linking that extends relation types for Business Processes will be our next endeavor. This goal is quite challenging because it requires also to deal with conversation state [10], but also with user interaction, events, complex control flow and complex information transformation. OAuth and OpenId features such as asynchronous communication, callbacks, and state handling shed some lights for facing events and user interaction as out-of-band communication, delegating control on third parties and resuming later the navigation provided that state can be carried along the interaction.

**Acknowledgment.** Research supported by the Center for Research on Educational Policy and Practice (CONICYT), Grant 11080143.

# References

1. Webber, J., Parastatidis, S., Robinson, I.: REST in Practice: Hypermedia and Systems Architecture. O'Reilly & Associates, Sebastopol (2010)
2. Nottingham, M.: Web linking. Internet RFC 5988 (October 2010)
3. Barnes, R., Lepinski, M.: The oauth security model for delegated authorization. Internet Draft draft-barnes-oauth-model-01 (2009)
4. Recordon, D., Reed, D.: Openid 2.0: a platform for user-centric identity management. In: Juels, A., Winslett, M., Goto, A. (eds.) Digital Identity Management, pp. 11–16. ACM (2006)
5. Hadley, M.: Web application description language. World Wide Web Consortium, Member Submission SUBM-wadl-20090831 (August 2009)
6. Alarcón, R., Wilde, E.: Restler: Crawling restful services. In: Rappa, M., Jones, P., Freire, J., Chakrabarti, S. (eds.) 19th International World Wide Web Conference, pp. 1051–1052. ACM Press, Raleigh (2010)
7. Alarcon, R., Wilde, E.: Linking data from restful services. In: Third Workshop on Linked Data on the Web, Raleigh, North Carolina (April 2010)
8. Alarcón, R., Wilde, E.: From restful services to rdf: Connecting the web and the semantic web. School of Information, UC Berkeley, Berkeley, California, Tech. Rep. 2010-041 (June 2010)
9. Alarcón, R., Wilde, E., Bellido, J.: Hypermedia-driven restful service composition. In: Feuerlicht, G., Lamersdorf, W., Ortiz, G., Zirpins, C. (eds.) 6th Workshop on Engineering Service-Oriented Applications (WESOA 2010), San Francisco, California (December 2010)
10. Pautasso, C., Wilde, E.: Why is the web loosely coupled?: a multi-faceted metric for service design. In: Proceedings of the 18th International Conference on World Wide Web, WWW 2009, pp. 911–920. ACM, New York (2009), http://doi.acm.org/10.1145/1526709.1526832
11. Steiner, T., Algermissen, J.: Fulfilling the hypermedia constraint via http options, the http vocabulary in rdf, and link headers. In: Pautasso, C., Wilde, E., Alarcón, R. (eds.) Second International Workshop on RESTful Design (WS-REST 2011), pp. 11–14 (March 2011)
12. Maleshkova, M., Pedrinaci, C., Domingue, J., Alvaro, G., Martinez, I.: Using Semantics for Automating the Authentication of Web APIs. In: Patel-Schneider, P.F., Pan, Y., Hitzler, P., Mika, P., Zhang, L., Pan, J.Z., Horrocks, I., Glimm, B. (eds.) ISWC 2010, Part I. LNCS, vol. 6496, pp. 534–549. Springer, Heidelberg (2010)
13. Hamadi, R., Benatallah, B.: A petri net-based model for web service composition. In: Schewe, K.-D., Zhou, X. (eds.) Fourteenth Australasian Database Conference (ADC 2003), CRPIT, vol. 17, pp. 191–200. ACS, Adelaide (2003), http://crpit.com/confpapers/CRPITV17Hamadi.pdf

# Batched Transactions for RESTful Web Services

Sebastian Kochman, Paweł T. Wojciechowski, and Miłosz Kmieciak

Poznań University of Technology

**Abstract.** In this paper, we propose a new transaction processing system for RESTful Web services; we describe a system architecture and algorithms. Contrary to other approaches, Web services do not require any changes to be used with our system. The system is transparent to non-transactional clients. We achieve that by introducing an overlay network of mediators and proxy servers, and restricting transactions to be a batched set of REST/HTTP operations (or requests) on Web resources addressed by URIs. To be able to use existing Web hosts that normally do not support versioning of Web resources, transaction resources are currently modified in-place, with a simple compensation mechanism. Concurrent execution of transactions guarantees isolation.

## 1  Introduction

The *REpresentational State Transfer (REST)* [5] is an architecture style for Web-based applications. It has gained, and is still gaining, enormous popularity due to its simplicity, scalability and, interoperability – thanks to wide acceptance of the Hypertext Transfer Protocol (HTTP)[1]. REST offers simplicity at the expense of lacking some standards well supported in other styles. For example, SOAP-based Web Services have a WS-AtomicTransaction [12] standard for transaction processing, while REST currently lacks a similar standard (see also [13]).

Transaction processing is a broad and complex issue. We may consider transactions on different levels of abstraction and supporting different properties. Transactions usually model operations that have to be executed atomically, i.e., they should either be executed completely and successfully or not at all. Alternative approaches are, e.g. Sagas [16] that do not guarantee atomicity. Transactions are a very useful abstraction of the real world business operations. That's why transaction processing could be a valuable extension to REST.

Although there are many interesting proposals of introducing transactions to REST, no one has gained wide acceptance among the community. In most cases such systems or patterns arguably break some of the REST style principles. For example, the client-server communication is constrained by no client context being stored on the server between requests. This *statelessness* constraint – a key requirement in relation to RESTful Web services – is often a subject of discussions about interpretation. Developers of systems (including some transaction systems described later) often worked around the issue of statelessness constraint by giving the session state a resource identifier on the server side. An

---

[1] In this paper, we focus on REST over HTTP and URI.

A. Harth and N. Koch (Eds.): ICWE 2011 Workshops, LNCS 7059, pp. 86–98, 2012.

interpretation proposed in [3] disallows it and claims that such a design cannot be called RESTful. But it might be REST with some exceptions, and this "with exceptions" approach is probably right for most enterprise architectures.

In this paper, we introduce *Atomic REST* – a new, lightweight transaction system. We restrict transactions to be a batched set of REST/HTTP operations (or requests) on Web resources addressed by URIs. While other proposals of transactions in REST are mostly software design patterns or libraries to be used by the client/server implementers, our approach is different: most of the transaction processing work is done by separate services – proxies and mediators – communicating using an overlay network. In particular, Web services do not require any changes to be used with our system. Moreover, the system is transparent to the clients that do not require transactions. These features enable easy integration of Atomic REST with existing RESTful Web services.

To be able to use existing Web hosts that usually do not support versioning of Web resources, transaction resources are currently modified in-place, with a (best-effort) compensation mechanism that is based on the symmetry of HTTP operations. Concurrent execution of transactions guarantees isolation. In the paper, we describe the Atomic REST's design and algorithms. To demonstrate the main concept, we develop a prototype implementation of Atomic REST; more information is available on the project page [7].

The paper has the following structure. First, we discuss related work. Then, the main idea of our transaction system is presented in Section 3. In Section 4 we describe the algorithms that we designed for Atomic REST, followed by the discussion of their properties and proofs of isolation in Section 5. Next, we briefly describe an example validation test of our experimental implementation in Section 6. Finally, we conclude.

## 2   Related Work

*Pessimistic Transactions* One of the first proposals of atomic transactions in REST is described by JBoss [10]. It is an extension of JAX RS – a popular Java API for RESTful Web services, with atomic transactions based on exclusive locks represented as resources on the server side. Contrary to their approach, we have adopted a different architecture, introducing separate services (mediators) that are responsible for the execution of transactions, and using server proxies that allow the services to remain unaware of transaction processing.

A similar approach to [10] is represented by RETRO [8] – a transaction model that defines many fine-grained resources for transaction processing, with a choice of exclusive and shared locks. We are not aware of any RETRO implementation announced yet. Some authors [15] pointed out drawbacks of this model: cluttering the business representations with transactional entities and the complexity that makes programming cumbersome.

*Optimistic Transactions.* Optimistic concurrency control [2] fits REST better than pessimistic transactions because it increases availability of a Web service by decreasing resource blocking. Below we characterize example approaches.

The most common solution for providing atomic transactions to REST is using the POST method to execute a batched set of operations. The concurrency control is optimistic since the data is cached by a client, and the consistency of the cache is checked during commit-time. The main advantage of the overloaded POST-based solution is its simplicity. On the other hand it is often criticized because it does not respect the semantics of uniform interface methods [5]: POST should create a resource, not execute any operations. Moreover, the mechanism is quite limited, e.g. contrary to Atomic REST, it does not allow transactions spanning many services.

Overloading the POST method is used, among other systems, in the cloud computing environments, such as Microsoft Windows Azure [6]. It offers structured storage in the form of tables with a REST-compliant API, enabling to perform a transaction across entities stored within the same table and partition. An application can atomically perform multiple Create/Update/Delete operations across multiple entities in a single batch request to the storage system, as long as the entities in the batch operation have the same partition key value and are in the same table [9]. Thus, the high scalability and accessibility of the service is achieved by introducing the limitation on the set of resources that may be included in one transaction.

A simple design pattern that provides transactions in REST is described in [14]. A new transaction is created by sending a POST to a factory resource. Once the transaction is created successfully, we can access it as a "gateway" to the main service, sending all possible HTTP requests to a variety of resources. The pattern is simple and seems to be effective, but is it RESTful? In the same book, the authors emphasize the difference between application state and resource state. The user transaction is, in fact, the application state, therefore it should not be maintained by the server. Exposing it as resources does not change anything. In fact, the authors admit that their proposal is not "the official RESTful or resource-oriented way to handle transactions" – it is just "the best one they could think up". On the other hand, even if the pattern breaks the statelessness constraint of REST, it is a clean concept that can work successfully for a variety of services.

*Compensation.* An alternative (or complementary) approach to atomic transactions is the transaction compensation mechanism, which can be well suited for some applications. Operations are executed normally, and in case of a failure, the compensation procedure is called in order to revert the transaction's changes. Let's consider an example of a holiday trip. One would like to reserve an airline ticket, a hotel room and a bus trip to a national park. One wants only all or nothing. How can we provide such transaction semantics over several autonomous systems? This problem is solved frequently with compensation, even though it does not guarantee atomicity. However, it may provide an acceptable contract: a high probability of success and acceptable side effects in case of failure (e.g. a cancellation fee at one of the services).

A model of compensating RESTful transactions, called *jfdi*, has been made available by JBoss [11]. To our best knowledge, the model has not been implemented yet. In terms of the interface, it is similar to JBoss's lock-based transactions that we described earlier. Although it does not provide any locks, the compensation logic is held on the server side – the transaction objects and compensation controllers (called *compensators*) are exposed as resources. It is very comfortable for the client that does not need to know how to compensate each operation on that particular service. However, similarly to pessimistic transactions, this design decision invalidates the statelessness constraint.

A popular compensation pattern known as Saga (described, e.g. in [16]) differs from jfdi in many respects. Saga is not intended to be a product, it is just a software pattern. In Saga, the whole compensation logic is held on the client's side. An advantage is that services do not have to be prepared anyhow. However, a given client is specific for a certain case, and so it can be hard to extend the client's code to work with other services. On the other hand, jfdi is more service-centric; it can only support services that use jfdi, but clients can be much simpler, generic and, more reusable.

This section shows that the existing transaction processing patterns are either too limited or do not produce generic, reusable clients. On the other hand, service-centric products often break the REST statelessness constraint. When designing our system, we have used the best ideas from the work described above but at the same time we tried to develop a fresh approach. In the following section we describe our system.

## 3    Basic Definitions

We explain the main idea of our system using two examples of interaction patterns in Figures 1 and 2. We can identify four components (ignore the arrows for a while):

- *Server* – provides a user-defined RESTful Web service, executing client requests and returning results, without knowledge of Atomic REST;
- *Client* – a user-defined client, with or without knowledge of Atomic REST;
- *Mediator* (or *Transaction Manager*) – a Web service managing transaction execution on behalf of the client;

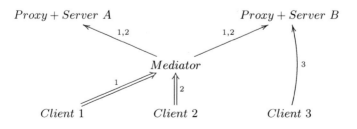

**Fig. 1.** An example interaction pattern of Atomic REST (single mediator)

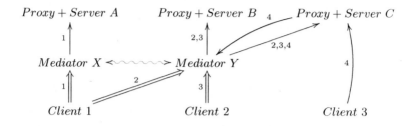

**Fig. 2.** An example interaction pattern of Atomic REST (many mediators)

- *Proxy* – a server's *façade*, intercepting messages addressed to the server and handling Atomic REST-specific requests; the proxy enables a RESTful Web service to support transactions without any changes in its code.

A *distributed transaction* in our system (or a *transaction*, in short) is a batch of REST operations (or requests) to be applied to different resources maintained by servers. Thus, from a client view-point a transactional request does not differ much from an ordinary HTTP request. This means that clients are able to cache transaction responses, which fulfills one of the REST architectural constraints, i.e. *cacheable responses*. Execution of concurrent transactions satisfies the isolation property and a weak form of atomicity, described in Section 5.

Batching of transaction operations restricts transactions to be rather short and non-interactive (similarly to, e.g. Sinfonia [1]). Hence the time when resources are blocked by a client is reduced to a minimum. This means that our system could be deployed on the Web and platforms, such as those provided for cloud computing, in which dependencies between network nodes should be avoided and the request processing time has to be short.

A client can submit several requests to be executed by many servers, as a single transaction. For example, in Figure 1 there is a single mediator and two clients who submit their transactions 1 and 2 to the mediator for execution. The transactions request some resources on servers $A$ and $B$. The mediator executes transactions sequentially, first 1, then 2. Thus, isolation is satisfied. At the same time, client 3 submits a non-transactional request to server $B$ that does not conflict with the transactions and is handled by server $B$ normally.

In Figure 2, there is an example with many mediators. Introducing many mediators supports privacy and load balancing. Each server gets transactions only from its trusted (single) mediator, e.g. server $A$ trusts only mediator $X$. Each mediator can handle many servers. Mediators could be replicated for fault-tolerance if required. Client 1 executes transactions 1 and 2 using, respectively mediator $X$ and $Y$, while client 2 uses only $Y$. At the same time client 3 submits a non-transactional request to server $C$. Since the request conflicts with the transactions, it is forwarded to $B$'s mediator $Y$ as a transaction containing only a single request. At the end, all results will be returned to the clients. In order to agree upon the order of transaction execution, mediators communicate using a coordination protocol described below.

# 4    The Atomic REST Algorithm

Below we describe the algorithms that are executed by mediators, proxies and clients. For clarity, we omitted some details. The symbols used in pseudocode are as follows:

| | |
|---|---|
| $P$ | a proxy or an URI of the proxy/server, depending on the context |
| $t_k$ | a transaction's unique identifier |
| $op$ | a $t_k$'s single HTTP operation (or request) to be executed |
| $resource$ | a resource (defined by an URI) on which to execute the operation |
| $\langle xml \rangle$ | an operation (or request) payload |
| $M_{t_k}$ | a set of mediators coordinating the execution of a transaction $t_{t_k}$ |
| $m_{t_k}$ | a leader mediator of a transaction $t_k$ |
| $O_{t_k}$ | a set of $t_k$'s HTTP operations (or requests), of the form $\langle op\ P/resource\ \langle xml \rangle \rangle$ |
| $O_{t_k}^m$ | a set of $t_k$'s HTTP operations (or requests), to be submitted for execution by mediator $m$ |
| $R_{t_k}^m$ | a set of $t_k$'s resources whose servers trust mediator $m$ (we omit $m$ when the mediator is known from the context) |
| $R_P$ | a set of resources to be marked as "transactional" at proxy $P$ |
| $r$ | a fine-grained resource controlled by the Read/Write or Intention--to-{Read\|Write} locks |
| $res$ | a result of operation (or request) execution |

## 4.1    The Single Mediator's algorithm

Algorithm 1 defines the mediator's behaviour, assuming only one mediator in the system (this corresponds to our current implementation of Atomic REST). Later, we extend this algorithm to support many mediators.

When a mediator $m_{t_k}$ receives a transaction $t_k$ from a client, it first extracts all $t_k$'s resources $R_{t_k}$ whose servers trust this mediator (lines 1-5). Then, it tries to grab fine-grained locks on these resources atomically (lines 23-26). We describe the locking mechanism used in Atomic REST below. If succeeded, the mediator requests all proxies required to execute transaction $t_k$, to set all their resources required by $t_k$ into the "transactional" mode (lines 27-30). Otherwise, it enqueues $t_k$ into $m_{t_k}$'s First-In-First-Out queue of transactions $Q$ (lines 32-33).

Next, mediator $m_{t_k}$ synchronously sends the transaction $t_k$'s HTTP requests (or operations) $\langle op_i\ P_i/resource_i\ \langle xml \rangle_i \rangle$ to a corresponding proxy/server $P_i$ for execution, and collects the results (lines 7-8).

If some operation failed, e.g. due to the "503 Service Unavailable" error, all $t_k$'s operations executed so far must be withdrawn. Since, our system is intended to be used with existing RESTful Web services that normally do not support multiversioning of resources, all transaction operations modify resources in-place. Thus, the only way to withdraw the operations that have already been executed by a transaction is to compensate them (lines 9-19); below we explain it.

Finally, the locks on resources are released, non-conflicting transactions are dequeued (line 20) and the composite result is returned to the client (line 21).

**Algorithm 1.** A single mediator $m_{t_k}$'s code.

1: **receive** $\langle$PUT $m_{t_k}/transaction/t_k$ $\langle\{m_{t_k}\}\,O_{t_k}\rangle\rangle$: // a transaction from a client
2: **return** execute-transaction$(t_k, m_{t_k}, O_{t_k})$
3:
4: **function** execute-transaction$(t_k, m_{t_k}, O_{t_k})$:
5:   $R_{t_k} \leftarrow$ resources-of$(O_{t_k}, m_{t_k})$ // get resources whose servers trust this mediator
6:   lock-resources$(t_k, m_{t_k}, O_{t_k}, R_{t_k})$
7:   **for all** $\langle op_i\ P_i/resource_i\ \langle xml\rangle_i\rangle \in O_{t_k}$, where $i = 1..n$ and $n = |O_{t_k}|$ **do**
8:     $res_i \leftarrow \langle op_i\ P_i/resource_i\ \langle xml\rangle_i\rangle$
9:     **if** $res_i =$ error **then**
10:       // $op_i$ failed - depending on the error, compensate $op_i$ or not
11:       **for all** $j = 1..i - 1$ **do**
12:         $res_j \leftarrow$ compensate $\langle op_j\ P_j/resource_j\ \langle xml\rangle_j\rangle$,
13:           where $res_j \in \{$compensation-ok, compensation-failed$\}$
14:       **end for**
15:       **for all** $j = i + 1..n$ **do**
16:         $res_j \leftarrow$ compensation-ok // since $op_j$ $(j > i)$ not executed yet
17:       **end for**
18:     **end if**
19:   **end for**
20:   unlock-resources$(R_{t_k})$
21:   **return** $\{(1, res_1), ..., (n, res_n)\}$
22:
23: **function** lock-resources$(t_k, m_{t_k}, O_{t_k}, R_{t_k})$:
24:   // try to lock $t_k$'s resources $R_{t_k}$; for clarity of pseudocode, semaphores are used
25:   // but our implementation uses Read/Write and Intention-to-{Read|Write} locks
26:   **if** atomically $\forall r_j \in R_{t_k}$ semaphore$_j$.P$(r_j)$ succeeded **then**
27:     **for all** $R_{P_i} \in R_{t_k}$, where $i = 1..w$ **do**
28:       // set "transactional" mode for $t_k$'s resources $R_{P_i}$ at proxy $P_i$
29:       $\langle$PUT $P_i/atomicrest/R_{P_i}\ 1\rangle$
30:     **end for**
31:   **else**
32:     Q.enqueue$(t_k, m_{t_k}, O_{t_k})$ // enqueque $t_k$ and wait till $t_k$ dequeued
33:     lock-resources$(t_k, m_{t_k}, O_{t_k}, R_{t_k})$
34:   **end if**
35:
36: **function** unlock-resources$(R_{t_k})$:
37:   **for all** $R_{P_i} \in R_{t_k}$, where $i = 1..w$ **do**
38:     // unset "transactional" mode for $t_k$'s resources $R_{P_i}$ at proxy $P_i$
39:     $\langle$PUT $P_i/atomicrest/R_{P_i}\ 0\rangle$
40:   **end for**
41:   **for all** $r_j \in R_{t_k}$ **do**
42:     semaphore$_j$.V$(r_j)$ // unlock $t_k$'s resource $r_j$
43:   **end for**
44:   dequeue-trans() // dequeue non-conflicting transactions in a queue $Q$
45:
46: **function** dequeue-trans(), where $Q = (t_1, m_{t_1}, O_{t_1}); ...; (t_n, m_{t_n}, O_{t_n}), n = |Q|$:
47:   **for all** $i = 1..l$ $(l \leq n)$ **do**
48:     Q.dequeue$(t_i, m_{t_i}, O_{t_i})$, where
49:       $\forall a, b \in \{1, ..., l\}$ resources-of$(O_{t_a}, m_{t_a}) \cap$ resources-of$(O_{t_b}, m_{t_b}) = \emptyset$
50:   **end for**

---

**Algorithm 2.** Proxy $P_i$'s code.

---

1: **receive** $\langle op\ P_i/resource\ \langle xml\rangle\rangle$, where $op \in \{\text{POST, PUT, GET, DELETE}\}$:
2: **if** transactional-mode($resource$) = 0 **or** (optionally) $op = \text{GET}$ **then**
3:     // $resource$ not in a "transactional" mode or uncommitted read allowed
4:     $res \leftarrow \langle op\ P_i/resource\ \langle xml\rangle\rangle$ // execute $op$ by a server normally
5: **else**
6:     // some transaction locked $resource$, pass $op$ as a transaction to $P_i$'s mediator
7:     $(1, res) \leftarrow \langle \text{PUT}\ m/transaction/\ \langle\{m\}\ \{\langle op\ P_i/resource\ \langle xml\rangle\rangle\}\rangle\rangle$
8: **end if**
9: **return** $res$

---

*Resource locking.* To simplify the pseudocode, we have used fine-grained semaphores to block access to resources. However, in our implementation, we use multigranularity locks [2] of four types: Read, Intention-to-Read, Write and Intention-to-Write. The former two are used for GET and HEAD operations, while the latter two for PUT, POST, and DELETE.

The Intention-to-{Read|Write} locks are acquired on "ancestor" resources of the locked resources. For instance, consider a transaction containing an operation GET http://www.service.org/books/medicine?author=foo. In this case, the Intention-to-Read lock should be acquired both on http://www.service.org/ and http://www.service.org/books/ before the Read lock will be acquired on http://www.service.org/books/medicine.

Since all locks of a subtransaction are taken by each mediator locally as a single atomic operation, no deadlock can occur due to the locking order.

*Compensation.* To *compensate* an operation on some resource means to execute a complementary operation on this resource. Transaction compensation could be provided by a user or done automatically whenever possible. For the latter, the following table presents REST/HTTP and complementary operations that are used by Atomic REST for compensation (details omitted due to lack of space):

| Request | Compensating request |
|---|---|
| GET | no compensation needed |
| PUT (modification) | PUT |
| PUT (creation) | DELETE |
| POST (creation) | DELETE |
| DELETE | PUT |

## 4.2   The Proxy's Algorithm

The $P_i$ proxy (see Algorithm 2) simply receives HTTP requests, executes them, and returns results. If any resource required by an operation $op$ is in a "transactional" mode, i.e. there exists some transaction that can access this resource exclusively and $op \neq \text{GET}$, the operation cannot be directly executed by the server at $P_i$. In such a case, the operation is forwarded to $P_i$'s trusted mediator

---

**Algorithm 3.** Client's transactional code.

---

1: // get a set $M_{t_k}$ of all mediators required to execute $O_{tk}$ as a transaction
2: $M_{t_k} \leftarrow \emptyset$
3: **for all** $P_i \in$ servers-of($O_{t_k}$) **do**
4:     $m \leftarrow \langle \text{GET } P_i/atomicrest/mediator \rangle$
5:     $M_{t_k} \leftarrow M_{t_k} \cup \{m\}$
6: **end for**
7: // get the transaction's unique ID $t_k$ and use any mediator $m \in M_{t_k}$ to execute $t_k$

8: $t_k \leftarrow \langle \text{POST } m/transaction \rangle$, where $m \in M_{t_k}$
9: $result \leftarrow \langle \text{PUT } m/transaction/t_k \ \langle M_{t_k} \ O_{t_k} \rangle \rangle$

---

**Algorithm 4.** Mediator $m_i$'s code (many mediators possible).

---

1: **receive** $\langle \text{PUT } m_i/transaction/t_k \ \langle M_{t_k} \ O_{t_k} \rangle \rangle$:
2: // $m_{t_k} \leftarrow m_i$, send transaction $t_k$ to all mediators using a total order broadcast
3: atomic-bcast($t_k, M_{t_k}, O_{t_k}$) to all mediators in $M_{t_k}$
4: // collect transaction $t_k$'s partial results from all mediators and return to a client
5: **while** $\exists m \in M_{t_k} \ result_{t_k}[m] = \emptyset$ **do**
6:     ()
7: **end while**
8: **return** $result_{t_k}$
9:
10: **receive** atomic-bcast($t_k, M_{t_k}, O_{t_k}$) from $t_k$'s leader mediator $m_{t_k}$:
11: // get transaction's part that can be executed by this mediator
12: $O_{t_k}^{m_i} \leftarrow$ get-my-part($m_i, O_{t_k}$)
13: $res \leftarrow$ execute-transaction($t_k, m_i, O_{t_k}^{m_i}$)
14: send-result($t_k, res$) to $m_{t_k}$
15:
16: **receive** send-result($t_k, res$) from $m$ // executed if $m_i$ is a leader (i.e. $m_i = m_{t_k}$)
17: $result_{t_k}[m] \leftarrow res$

---

$m$ that will execute it as a single-operation transaction (line 7). Otherwise, the operation can be executed by the server as a normal HTTP request (line 4). For efficiency, we allow uncommitted reads by non-transactional clients. If this behaviour is not acceptable, the "**or** $op =$ GET" must be removed (line 2).

### 4.3 The Client's Algorithm

To execute a transaction (see Algorithm 3), the client first obtains a list of mediators (lines 2-6) and then chooses one of them to get a transaction's unique ID and to pass the transaction to it for execution (lines 9-10).

### 4.4 The Many Mediators' Algorithm

Algorithm 4 extends Algorithm 1 to support many mediators. Upon delivery of a transaction $t_k$ from a client a mediator becomes a leader and broadcasts $t_k$ to all mediators that are required to execute it (including itself). For this, a total order broadcast (also known as atomic broadcast) [4] is used. After getting $t_k$, each mediator extracts the part of $t_k$ that refers to resources accessible by the mediator, and executes it (lines 10-14); we call each such a part a *subtransaction*. The leader collects results and returns them to the client (lines 5-8, 16-17).

## 5    Properties

Below we discuss the isolation and atomicity properties that are guaranteed by the Atomic REST algorithm (their definitions follow the ACID properties [2]).

### 5.1    Isolation

Below we prove that our algorithm satisfies isolation. In case of fatal failures (defined in Section 5.2), the property can be guaranteed *up to* the fatal failure.

**Lemma 1.** *All subtransactions executed by each mediator are isolated.*

*Proof.* Each subtransaction is described by a set of resources. Since locks on the resources are taken atomically and released after a subtransaction is finished, no subtransactions sharing resources can be executed concurrently. This means that they are executed sequentially, so they are isolated. Subtransactions that do not share resources may be executed concurrently but they are isolated trivially. From this we get that all subtransactions are isolated.                    □

**Theorem 1.** *The Atomic REST algorithm guarantees transaction isolation.*

*Proof.* Proof by contradiction. Let us assume that two transactions $t$ and $t'$ are not isolated. From Lemma 1, we get that for every mediator $m_i$ ($m_i \in M$) all subtransactions of $t$ and $t'$ executed by $m_i$ (if any) are isolated. Thus, if $t$ and $t'$ are not isolated, then there must exist two mediators $m_1$ and $m_2$, such that $m_1$ first executes a subtransaction $subt_{m_1}$ of transaction $t$, then a subtransaction $subt'_{m_1}$ of transaction $t'$, while $m_2$ executes its subtransactions of transactions $t'$ and $t$ in the opposite order. But this is not possible since by atomic broadcast semantics, all mediators receive transactions in the same global order. Thus, if $m_1$ executes $subt_t^{m_1}$ followed by $subt_{t'}^{m_1}$, then $m_2$ must execute $subt_t^{m_2}$ followed by $subt_{t'}^{m_2}$. Moreover, non-transactional requests cannot modify resources processed by a transaction since they are guarded by a "transactional" mode that is kept during transaction execution. Hence by Lemma 1, it is possible to serialize all transactions, which satisfies isolation.                    □

### 5.2    Atomicity

If there are no errors, transactions are executed atomically. If there are errors, transaction atomicity is currently provided by the compensation mechanism. Since automatic compensation of transaction operations is not always possible

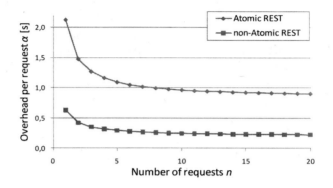

**Fig. 3.** Overhead induced by Atomic REST

(either due to HTTP-bound issues or application semantics), our system cannot guarantee atomicity in all cases. This is acceptable since Atomic REST is no more tolerant to failures than an average Web service that can fail at any time. Therefore, in case of some failures, some transaction operations may or may not have been executed or compensated; we call such failures *fatal*. Thus, the client should always check the results returned by the system, and in case of some error messages, execute a suitable action. For example, the client could repeat transaction operations. For instance, the PUT, DELETE and GET methods are *idempotent* methods, and so they can be repeated many times.

Implementing stronger semantics of atomicity would require significant changes to the code of Web services, such as resource multiversioning and the 2PC (or 3PC) protocol for the mediator-server communication. Multiversioning would allow transaction operations to be executed on shadow copies of resources, made public on transaction commit and rejected on transaction abort. However, we think that supporting existing Web services by Atomic REST compensates the drawback of a weaker atomicity semantics. Moreover, we intend our transactions to be a mechanism to increase expressiveness in Web programming, rather than for implementing fault-tolerant Web services.

## 6 Validation

We define *overhead value* per an individual REST/HTTP request (or operation), imposed by our transaction system, as $\alpha = \frac{\Delta - \Delta_{min}}{n}$ (in seconds), where $n$ is the number of requests executed by a transaction, $\Delta$ is the elapsed time between sending the first transaction request and receiving response to the last request, and $\Delta_{min}$ is the lower bound of transaction's total processing time, computed as $\Delta_{min} = n * \delta$ (in seconds), where $\delta$ is the time of processing every request by the server (in our tests we choose it to be a constant value of the sleeping time before a server can accept another client request).

In Figure 3 we show the result of an example validation test[1]. We can see that while $n$ is increasing the overhead time per request asymptotically reaches a constant value. Thus, the total overhead time per transaction is linearly dependant on the number $n$ of transaction requests. We have used a least squares method to compute the linear regression slope value, and obtained that the overhead of Atomic REST is between 3.4 and 4 times larger than the overhead of non-transactional client-server processing of the same REST/HTTP requests (denoted as non-Atomic REST in Figure 3), when compared to a purely local processing of these requests by the Web server.

## 7   Conclusion

The algorithms that we designed in this paper enabled us to develop a distributed lightweight transaction system for REST that enjoys clean design, conformance to REST constraints, support of existing Web services and transparency for non-transactional clients. Moreover, validation results of our experimental single-mediator implementation show that the overhead is acceptable.

*Acknowledgments.* This work has been partially supported by the Polish Ministry of Science and Higher Education within the European Regional Development Fund, Grant No. POIG.01.03.01-00-008/08.

## References

1. Aguilera, M.K., Merchant, A., Shah, M., Veitch, A., Karamanolis, C.: Sinfonia: A new paradigm for building scalable distributed systems. In: Proc. SOSP 2007 (2007)
2. Bernstein, P.A., Newcomer, E.: Principles of Transaction Processing. Morgan Kaufmann (2009)
3. Carlyle, B.: The REST statelessness constraint (June 2009), http://soundadvice.id.au/blog/2009/06/13/#stateless
4. Défago, X., Schiper, A., Urbán, P.: Total order broadcast and multicast algorithms: Taxonomy and survey. ACM Computing Surveys 36(4), 372–421 (2004)
5. Fielding, R.T.: Architectural Styles and the Design of Network-based Software Architectures. PhD thesis, University of California, Irvine (2000)
6. Haridas, J., Nilakantan, N., Calder, B.: Windows Azure Table. Microsoft (2009)
7. IT-SOA. Atomic REST (2011), http://www.it-soa.eu/atomicrest
8. Marinos, A., Razavi, A., Moschoyiannis, S., Krause, P.: RETRO: A consistent and recoverable RESTful transaction model. In: Proc. ICWS 2009 (July 2009)
9. Microsoft. Windows Azure - Team Blog, http://blogs.msdn.com/windowsazure
10. Musgrove, M.: (February 2009), http://community.jboss.org/wiki/TransactionalsupportforJAXRSbasedapplications

---

[1] Configuration: Intel Xeon QuadCore X3230 @2.66GHz with 4MB cache and 4GB RAM. Operating system: *openSUSE 10.3* with *Sun's JRE 1.6.0*

11. Musgrove, M.: Compensating RESTful Transactions (June 2009),
    http://community.jboss.org/wiki/CompensatingRESTfulTransactions
12. OASIS. Web Services Atomic Transaction, Version 1.2 (February 2009)
13. Pautasso, C., Zimmermann, O., Leymann, F.: RESTful Web Services vs. "Big"
    Web Services: Making the Right Architectural Decision. In: Proc. WWW 2008
    (2008)
14. Richardson, L., Ruby, S.: RESTful Web Services. O'Reilly (2007)
15. Rotem-Gal-Oz, A.: Transactions are bad for REST (June 2009),
    http://www.rgoarchitects.com/nblog/
    2009/06/15/TransactionsAreBadForREST.aspx
16. Rotem-Gal-Oz, A., Bruno, E., Dahan, U.: Saga. In: SOA Patterns, ch. 5.4. Manning
    Publications Co. (June 2007)

# Secure Mashup-Providing Platforms - Implementing Encrypted Wiring

Matthias Herbert, Tobias Thieme, Jan Zibuschka, and Heiko Roßnagel

Fraunhofer IAO,
Nobelstrasse 12,
70569 Stuttgart, Germany
{matthias.herbert,tobias.thieme,jan.zibuschka,heiko.rossnagel}
@iao.fraunhofer.de

**Abstract.** Mashups were not designed with security in mind. Their main selling point is the flexible and easy to use development approach. The fact that mashups enable users to compose services to create a piece of software with new functionalities, integrating inputs from various sources, implies a security risk. However, in many scenarios where mashups add business value, e.g. enterprise mashups, security and privacy are important requirements. A secure environment for the handling of potentially sensitive end user information is needed, unless the user fully trusts the mashup-providing-platform (MPP), which is unlikely for hosted enterprise mashups. In this paper we present a proof-of-concept implementation which enables the secure usage of a mashup-providing platform and protects sensitive data against malicious widgets and platform operators.

**Keywords:** Secure mashups, security, mashup, enterprise mashups.

## 1 Introduction

Mashup technology has a clear benefit for both users and providers. The good usability and flexibility of the mashup development process enables users to build new services without requiring professional programming skills. They just have to choose and wire up different services and widgets with the help of the mashup platform. To fully leverage this advantage, especially small and medium enterprises (SMEs) need to have their platforms hosted by a platform provider to avoid additional system administration upkeep. However, both a hosted mashup platform (Mashup-providing platform, MPP) and widgets within such a platform could intercept sensitive user data. This lack of confidentiality is a barrier to the entrance of the mashup technology in the enterprise environment.

We implemented a proof-of-concept demonstrator of a secure mashup platform based on the approach described by Zibuschka et al. [1]. The authors propose an architecture which secures the mashup's users against a malicious platform or widgets. The main benefit of this approach is that it requires neither a trusted third party, nor substantial modifications of the mashup composition process. It also suggests a way to have a client-side key generation in JavaScript without the steep performance penalties associated with approaches such as [2].

A. Harth and N. Koch (Eds.): ICWE 2011 Workshops, LNCS 7059, pp. 99–108, 2012.

The rest of this paper is structured as follows. We first present related work on mashup-security in section 2. Based on this work we present our approach in section 3 and provide the implementation details in section 4. We discuss the benefits and applications of our solution scenarios in section 5 and discuss our results in section 6 before we conclude our findings.

## 2    Related Work

To make our work more readable and readily comparable, we use the definitions from Hoyer and Fischer [3], who define mashup as: a web-based resource that combines existing resources be it content, data or application functionality, from more than one resource by empowering the actual end-users to create and adapt individual information centric and situational applications. They also define widgets as the visual representations of aforementioned Web-based resources that are combined into a mashup. Wiring is defined as communication between widgets within the platform, and piping as the transfer of external resources into the platform via backend service.

Security in mashups has been investigated by several previous works. Hasan et al [4] present a component controlling data flow within a mashup, using a 'Permit Grant Service' that acts on behalf of the mashup platform. Crites et al [5] introduce a modified browser security model addressing some of the security shortcomings of specifically mashups, while Jackson and Wang [6] describe a solution using the existing browser origin policies. However, none of the systems offer protection versus the platform itself. In the same vein, Keukelaere et al [7] propose a secure channel communication model. We extend on their work, adding encryption to protect confidentiality of the users' information versus the MPP. Zarandioon et al [2] [8] offer the most comprehensive approach to date, offering both a client-side identity management providing data flow control as well as a single sign-on (SSO) solution. However, it requires that each user administers a specific identity-providing server outside the MPP, and understands a set of (non-trivial) mediating components. It also requires that inter-widget (which are referred to as 'mashlets') communication is executed using specialized widgets, which is a counterintuitive modification of mashup programming practices, threatening mashups' main selling point, namely their ease of modification by non-experts [1]. HTML 5 will offer cross-document messaging, which potentially addresses integrity and confidentiality of communication between components [7]. However, this requires browser support, and will not be realistic in the next years [7], especially in enterprise scenarios, where older browsers, especially Internet Explorer 6, are still widely used [9].

## 3    Concept

Our paper is based on Zibuschka et al. [1], who propose reversed identity based encryption within a public-key-infrastructure to realize a secure MPP. Specifically, to avoid the need of a Trusted-Third-Party inherent in identity based encryption, the authors propose to let the users themselves act as the private key generators for communication between widgets. The originally proposed system is based on WebIBC [10], with a security model based on nested iFrames [7]. Widgets use the generated private keys to communicate, sending encrypted messages through the MPP. This idea reduces the amount of parties the user hast to trust, satisfying both the business requirements stated in the introduction of this paper, as well as strong security requirements in the vein of privacy-enhancing identity management [11]. However, Zibuschka et al. [1] only describe the theoretic concept in detail, and do not give details of a proof-of-concept implementation. Our contribution aims to fill this gap.

In contrast to their approach, we decentralize key generation by having each widget in a mashup create its own set of keys within the user's browser. This offers several advantages over their solution. First, a key distribution from key generator to the widgets, which in general offers a point of attack, is not necessary, as everybody generates their own keys. Second, the individual keys are protected against unauthorized access within each widget by the Same Origin Policy (SOP). The nested iFrame model assures that each widget is loaded within its own domain, yet is still able to communicate with the MPP and other widgets. This solution allows key generation without any browser plug-ins [2] [3]. However, this approach requires a high-performance JavaScript-implementation for the key generation.

We also use hybrid encryption instead of Combined-Public-Key-cryptography, as we were unable to find a working implementation of CPK in JavaScript. We use RSA [12] encryption to exchange the symmetric AES [13] session keys. A key exchange takes place for each wiring the user defines in the wiring tool. Wiring is unidirectional, meaning that if bidirectional communication between two widgets is desired, two wirings have to be established. This enables the user to define services that are only able to receive messages and not to send them.

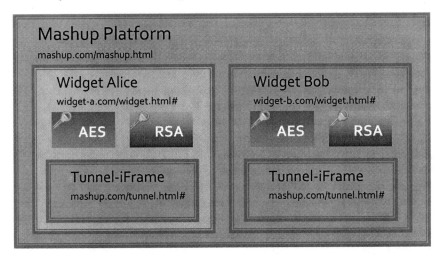

**Fig. 1.** Architecture of the mashup providing platform (MPP)

Figure 1 shows the aspects of our architecture relevant to security. Alice and Bob each generate their own set of keys. The public RSA keys are published to the MPP. When Alice wants to send Bob a message, she uses his public RSA-key to encrypt her

AES-key. Only Bob can decrypt Alice's AES key, which will be used for the actual communication.

We want the user to be able to use the mashup in a very intuitive way. Because of this requirement we fully automated key generation within the widgets and bound the key distribution to the wiring paths. During the initiation process of the mashup every participating widget generates its own keys, with a public and a private RSA key for the key exchange of symmetric AES session keys. The widgets send their public keys to the MPP, which forwards them to every wired widget. All unwired widgets are not able to read or manipulate the communication because of the SOP.

# 4    Implementation

For the proof-of-concept-implementation of our secure mashup platform we rely on existing open source software and libraries. We use the Dreamface [14] mashup platform as our MPP, which provides most common mashup functionalities, including a wiring tool, user management and a drag and drop interface for the arrangement of widgets.

Our approach requires reliable implementations of both asymmetric and symmetric ciphers in JavaScript. A quick survey showed that there are a number of libraries that implement symmetric algorithms, but only very few that implement asymmetric ones. The complicated key generation procedures of ciphers such as RSA make asymmetric schemes difficult to implement efficiently in an interpreted script language like JavaScript.

The implementation of CPK presented in [10] turned out to be incomplete. PidCrypt [15] provides a strong implementation of RSA in JavaScript, but also requires a browser plug-in, which we want to avoid. The developers of Clipperzlib [16] are working on an implementation of a public key cryptography system based on elliptic curve cryptography, but describe their implementation as "still slow and incomplete". Therefore, we decided to use the JavaScript Cryptography Toolkit [17], which provides several well-known algorithms. Among them is an implementation of RSA that will not freeze the user's browser during the time-consuming key generation. The key generation is performed in a time frame ranging from a couple dozen milliseconds to a few seconds, depending on the browser.

We use the standardized and efficient AES algorithm to encrypt the actual messaging within the mashup. We chose the implementation of AES provided by the Crypto-JS library [19] as it offers a compact interface, has a low performance overhead, and only requires a single JavaScript file to be included.

For the implementation of our prototype we chose an incremental approach. We began with the functions necessary to read from and write to the fragment identifier of an iFrame and implemented the structure of three nested iFrames that forms the basis for our secure mashup. Next, we integrated this structure into the Dreamface framework. As Dreamface itself uses no frames that could be used as a point of reference during communication, we had to assure that each message sent by a widget was properly identified by the mashup. Communication from any widget to the mashup platform is handled by a tunnel-page provided by the mashup platform. The Widgets load this page on demand in an iFrame and include their message in the fragment identifier of the page's URL. The tunnel iFrame passes the message on to the mashup platform. The mashup platform has no way of knowing which widget sent the message, as all widgets use the same tunnel iFrame. Dreamface assures that all widgets within a mashup have a unique name, even if they are instances of the same widget class. Thus, we included the name of the widget with the message from the widget to the mashup platform so the mashup platform knows which widget sent the message and can handle it properly. This technique allows an impersonation attack if a widget supplies the name of another widget in the mashup instead of its own. However this attack can be thwarted by also including a random seed with each message that only the mashup platform and the original widget know. An overview of the mechanics of message transmission is given in figure 2. Upon clicking the "Send message" link in the widget-iFrame, a test message is sent to the tunnel-iFrame and displayed in an alert window. After the window is closed, the test message is forwarded to the parent frame (representing the MPP) and displayed again.

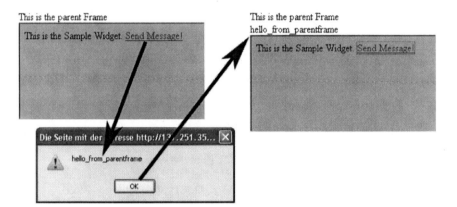

**Fig. 2.** Message transmission in test UI

As vital elements of our architecture are located at the widgets, we implemented an example widget class called "Alice" that was used to realize an "Alice & Bob"-type communication scenario within a mashup. A widget consists of two parts: The actual widget that is loaded within an iFrame and is located on the widget server, and a few JavaScript functions that need to be implemented within the mashup platform to display the widget (in our case this function loads the iFrame containing the actual widget) and handle the messaging. The latter part is a concession we had to make due to the architecture of Dreamface that assumes widgets are realized in JavaScript and provided by the mashup platform. It is not part of our architecture and can be neglected when a similar architecture is implemented within another mashup platform.

Messages in plaintext can now be exchanged between two instances of our "Alice"-widget class. In the next step, we integrated the cryptographic components into our prototype, beginning with RSA to properly exchange the symmetric AES key. As the key exchange within the mashup is done using the same messaging mechanism also used for regular messages, we defined a protocol for these messages, stating message type, message source and target, whether the message is encrypted and of course the message itself. Figure 3 shows a screenshot of the simple communication scenario. On top are the widgets "Alice" and "Bob" and below is a test widget that visualizes the messages transmitted over the MPP is displayed.

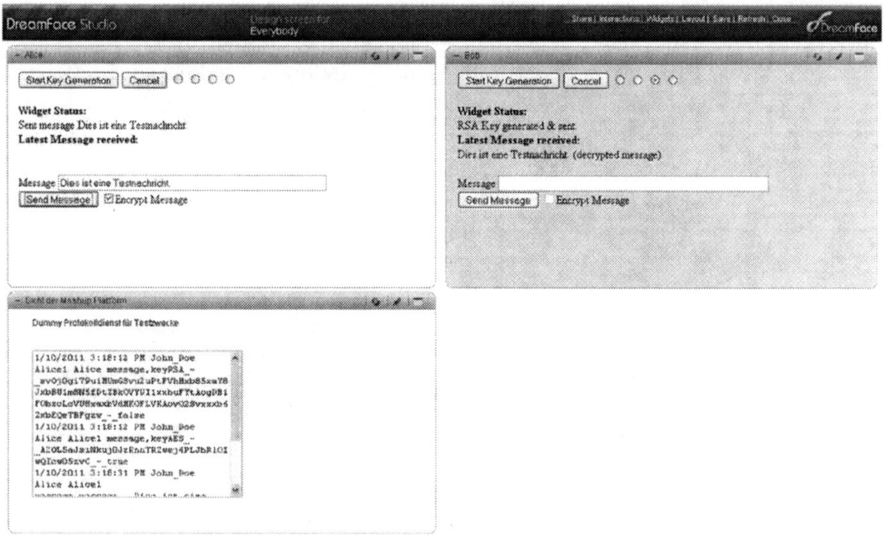

**Fig. 3.** Test Widgets within Dreamface

The implementation of AES provided by the Crypto-JS library offers a compact, easy to use interface. AES accepts any string as key, thus time-consuming key-generation procedures aren't necessary. In our prototype, we use the name of the widget the key belongs to as identifier. An implementation using entirely random generated keys will be included in a future version of our prototype. Usage of a password-based key derivation function like PBKDF#2 is also a possibility.

We made several changes to the mashup platform to automate the key exchange. All communication is encrypted with the AES key of the sending widget, which needs to be distributed to all widgets acting as receiver. Thus, this key needs to be encrypted with the public RSA key of any receiving widget during key distribution. This requires a reversal of message flow, as usually messages are only sent from sender to receiver, but not the other way round – if bilateral communication between two widgets is required, two communication channels need to be defined; in both channels the AES key created by the widget defined as sender will be used for encryption. We implemented several functions to achieve reversal of message flow during key exchange. Whenever a widget publishes its public RSA key, these functions iterate over the communication channels the user defined via the wiring tool. If the widget is defined as the receiver in at least one of those relations, the mashup platform forwards the key to the widget defined as sender. This widget uses the key to encrypt its own AES key and sends it to the widget that sent the RSA key. The key handler functions forward each AES key only to the widget that created the RSA key, that is used to encrypt the AES key. As a widget can be defined as the sending party in several communication channels, this relation can't be evaluated from the wiring. Correct delivery of all keys is guaranteed as each message contains the name of the widget sending it. When sending an encrypted AES key, the message just has to be forwarded to the widget that sent the RSA key used.

## 5    Scenarios

We implemented two example scenarios to illustrate the functionality of our prototype. These are the aforementioned simple communication scenario and a micropayment scenario, which is shown in figure 4. In both scenarios users can either use encrypted or non-encrypted communication. A special widget visualizes the message flow as the mashup platform sees it.

**Fig. 4.** Micropayment scenario

The micropayment scenario shown in figure 4 further demonstrates the possibility for MPPs to provide altogether new services to the customers that would be impossible without secure mashup technology. With secure and encrypted communication the MPPs are able to realize new products like the 'money account - widget' shown in the second scenario. Service and widget providers could provide payable services with a lot of functionalities and use these money widgets as a central and secure way of payment. This offers the advantage that the user can use the same widget as an interface to pay for multiple different services by various providers. Neither does he need to enter his payment information with each widget separately, as is the case with current payment solutions, nor does he have to trust forwarding mechanisms that, for example, direct him from the online shop to his credit card or micropayment provider and back again.

## 6    Discussion

We implemented a secure mashup-providing platform by combining existing open source software and libraries. Our implementation uses a hybrid encryption model to secure message exchange within the mashup. It offers the same usability as older, insecure platforms. Key generation, key exchange and all encryption and decryption procedures are automated and run in the background. There is no significant difference in performance to existing MPPs. The user is not impeded in his use of the mashup in any way, which is a clear advantage over other solutions. She does not need to enter a master passphrase. The wiring process is the same as in similar, insecure frameworks. Our secure MPP can be used on any current browser without having to install plug-ins or additional software. Furthermore, it does not rely on a trusted-third-party to ensure security and the users don't have to register to additional services to use the mashup.

As mentioned above we have chosen the open-source platform Dreamface as the MPP for our proof-of-concept implementation, but our approach can be generalized. In contrast to other work, our implementation is portable to other MPPs, like IBM Mashup Center [18] or JackBe [19]. Nearly every MPP is able to integrate this widget-based client-side encryption to provide a secure and privacy-friendly mashup environment. The integration is manageable without difficult changes and has potential to enable several new uses cases that require security for MPP's increasing their service spectrum and appeal.

One possible business scenario is implementing web applications offering chargeable services to users, e.g. in the context of telecommunication providers. These services can also be made available in form of widgets. The user entrusts such a mashup with potentially sensible personal information, e.g. location or payment details, the confidentiality of which needs to be ensured.

Another important use case is the enterprise environment, where companies could expand their software with mashup technology. Especially in this case the sensitive business data has to be protected. Our implementation of a secure mashup platform allows the move towards pay-per-use and enterprise mashups while maintaining security. It proves that mashup technology can be transferred to more security sensitive business fields.

Our work has several limitations. The most prominent one is the potential of a man in the middle attack that can be executed by the MPP. This is a clear disadvantage in comparison to the solution proposed in [1], which mitigates this problem using CPK. However, as to our knowledge no working JavaScript implementation of CPK exists, such a solution is not feasible at the moment, but might be possible in the near future. In the meantime several steps could be undertaken to mitigate this problem. One possible solution would be to use certification schemes to ensure the authenticity and integrity of the exchange keys. However this would also require the presence of trusted third parties, which was one of the things we wanted to avoid to sustain the paradigm of easy service composition. An alternative approach could be to visualize the fingerprints of the exchanged public keys in each of the widgets. This would enable users to spot a man in the middle attack due to inconsistencies in the fingerprints. However, this approach does require users that are at least partially familiar with the basic functionality of asymmetric encryption. According to [18], this might be too much to expect. Even if both of these approaches are not feasible there is still some hope that such an attack would be spotted in an open source environment.

# 7    Conclusion

We presented a proof-of-concept implementation enabling the secure usage of a mashup-providing platform, protecting sensitive data against malicious widgets and platform operators. We gave the design rationale, implementation details, and discussion of merits and limitations including possible application scenarios. Benchmarking of several possible approaches against each other is in process, but the first results from the proof-of-concept presented here are very encouraging.

**Acknowledgments.** This work was supported by the German Federal Ministry of Education and Research (BMBF) under Grant Number 01BS0824 (COCKTAIL).

# References

1. Zibuschka, J., Herbert, M., Roßnagel, H.: Towards Privacy-Enhancing Identity Management in Mashup-Providing Platforms. In: Foresti, S., Jajodia, S. (eds.) Data and Applications Security and Privacy XXIV. LNCS, vol. 6166, pp. 273–286. Springer, Heidelberg (2010)
2. Zarandioon, S., Yao, D., Ganapathy, V.: OMOS: A Framework for Secure Communication in Mashup Applications. In: Proceedings of the 2008 Annual Computer Security Applications Conference, pp. 355–364. IEEE Computer Society (2008)
3. Hoyer, V., Fischer, M.: Market Overview of Enterprise Mashup Tools. In: Bouguettaya, A., Krueger, I., Margaria, T. (eds.) ICSOC 2008. LNCS, vol. 5364, pp. 708–721. Springer, Heidelberg (2008)
4. Hasan, R., Winslett, M., Conlan, R., Slesinsky, B., Ramani, N.: Please Permit Me: Stateless Delegated Authorization in Mashups. In: Proceedings of the 2008 Annual Computer Security Applications Conference, pp. 173–182. IEEE Computer Society (2008)
5. Crites, S., Hsu, F., Chen, H.: OMash: enabling secure web mashups via object abstractions. In: Proceedings of the 15th ACM Conference on Computer and Communications Security, pp. 99–108. ACM, Alexandria (2008)
6. Jackson, C., Wang, H.J.: Subspace: secure cross-domain communication for web mashups. In: Proceedings of the 16th International Conference on World Wide Web, pp. 611–620. ACM, Banff (2007)
7. Keukelaere, F.D., Bhola, S., Steiner, M., Chari, S., Yoshihama, S.: SMash: secure component model for cross-domain mashups on unmodified browsers. In: Proceeding of the 17th International Conference on World Wide Web, pp. 535–544. ACM, Beijing (2008)

8. Zarandioon, S., Yao, D., Ganapathy, V.: Privacy-aware identity management for client-side mashup applications. In: Proceedings of the 5th ACM Workshop on Digital Identity Management, pp. 21–30. ACM, Chicago (2009)
9. Leyden, J.: One in five workers still clinging to IE6 - The Register, http://www.theregister.co.uk/2010/08/19/zscaler_web_security study/
10. Guan, Z., Cao, Z., Zhao, X., Chen, R., Chen, Z., Nan, X.: WebIBC: Identity Based Cryptography for Client Side Security in Web Applications. In: International Conference on Distributed Computing Systems, pp. 689–696. IEEE Computer Society, Los Alamitos (2008)
11. Hansen, M., Berlich, P., Camenisch, J., Clauß, S., Pfitzmann, A., Waidner, M.: Privacy-enhancing identity management. Information Security Technical Report 9, 35–44 (2004)
12. Rivest, R.L., Shamir, A., Adleman, L.: A method for obtaining digital signatures and public-key cryptosystems. Commun. ACM 21, 120–126 (1978)
13. Rijmen, V., Daemen, J.: The Design of Rijndael: AES. In: The Advanced Encryption Standard. Springer, Berlin (2002)
14. Dreamface: DreamFace Interactive, http://www.dreamface-interactive.com/
15. Versaneo GmbH: pidCrypt - pidder's JavaScript crypto library, https://www.pidder.com/pidcrypt/
16. Solario, G.C., Barulli, M.: Clipperzlib Javascript Crypto Library, http://sourceforge.net/projects/clipperzlib/
17. Oka, A.: JavaScript Cryptography Toolkit, http://ats.oka.nu/titaniumcore/js/crypto/
18. IBM: IBM Mashup Center, http://www-142.ibm.com/software/products/de/de/mashupcenter/
19. JackBe: JackBe Mashup Editor and Composer, http://www.jackbe.com/products/composers.php,

# A Conceptual Framework for Linked Data Exploration

Alessandro Bozzon, Marco Brambilla, Emanuele Della Valle,
Piero Fraternali, and Chiara Pasini

Politecnico di Milano, Dipartimento di Elettronica e Informazione
P.za L. Da Vinci, 32. I-20133 Milano - Italy
{name.surname}@polimi.it

**Abstract.** An increasing number of open data sets is becoming available on the Web as Linked Data (LD), many efforts has been devoted to show the potential of LD applications from the technical point of view. However, less attention has been paid to the analysis of the information seeking requirements from the user point of view. In this paper we examine the Information Seeking Process and we propose a general framework that address all its requirements in the context of LD-based applications. We support seamless integration of both Linked and non-Linked data sources and we allow designers to define complex, rank-aware result construction and exploration rules based on rank aggregation and multiple many-to-many data navigation.

## 1 Introduction

An increasing number of data sets is becoming available on the Web. In this trend, Linked Data (LD) plays a central role thanks to initiatives such as the W3C Linked Open Data (LOD) community project[1] that are fostering LD best practice adoption.

With the growth of the available corpus of Web data, the need arises for effective mechanisms targeted to human users for searching, exploring, and consuming such data. The Semantic Web Community has largely investigated this need from a technical point of view, but limited effort was devoted to considering the full set of requirements of an *Information Seeking Process* (ISP)[15,14], which classifies the activities performed by search users into a well defined set of information seeking stages, i.e. initialization, selection, exploration, formulation, collection, and presentation. Indeed, whilst LD is intrinsically well shaped for coping with information exploration and navigation, no existing works try to apply the full extent of the ISP requirements to the LD domain.

In this paper, we propose a conceptual framework that covers all the stages and requirements of the ISP in the LD setting. The approach is general enough to cover exploration of any kind of source, including deep web sources, search engines, LD sources, and proprietary repositories.

---

[1] http://esw.w3.org/SweoIG/TaskForces/CommunityProjects/LinkingOpenData/

A. Harth and N. Koch (Eds.): ICWE 2011 Workshops, LNCS 7059, pp. 109–118, 2012.
© Springer-Verlag Berlin Heidelberg 2012

Our approach introduces three additional innovative contributions with respect to the existing solutions: 1) Seamless integration of *both Linked and non-Linked data sources*. Exploration paths upon data sources can be defined using both exact matching on IRIs within LD boundaries, and exact or approximate matching on literals within LD boundaries and on generic data types outside the LD cloud; 2) *Multiple many-to-many navigation* of data. Results can be built in a structured way by combining several concepts and allowing navigation of multiple many-to-many associations at a time; 3) Support of complex *rank-aware result construction and exploration*. Composite results can take into account ranking and/or ordering of result parts coming from different sources, by supporting aggregated ranking functions.

The rest of the paper is organized as follows: Section 2 compares our work to other proposals; Section 3 presents a running example; Section 4 describes our general-purpose approach; Section 4.3 discusses the two application scenarios of free data exploration and vertical application in the context of the running example; Section 5 describes our implementation experience; and Section 6 concludes.

## 2    Related Work

In the past decades, several works proposed model for the characterization of the information seeking process [15,14]. In [14] the ISP model is characterized by 6 information seeking stages: 1) *Initialization* recognizes the information need and marks introduction of a problem; 2) *Selection* aims at identifying the general area for investigation; 3) *Exploration* is about extending the user understanding of the field and to relate it with what is already known; 4) *Formulation* makes a focused perspective on the topic emerge; 5) *Collection* gathers information and allows one to select interesting findings and to export them; and 6) *Presentation* appropriately renders the collected information.

In the context of Linked Data, we can identify three classes of applications: *data exploration, concept exploration* and *vertical applications*. Applications for *Data Exploration* typically leverage the graph representation of data to allow schema-free navigation of the existing information, and they typically apply link-traversing strategies, with no support for search, filtering, data re-shaping or alternative visualizations. Known example of *Data Exploration* are Linked Data browsers like Tabulator [3] and Marble [2].

*Concept Exploration* applications aim at allowing users to explore a dataset through concepts, their properties, and their relationships, by means of SPARQL endpoints and rich visual interfaces. They also provide data analytics, aggregation functionalities, basic visualization, filtering, faceted search, and pivoting. Parallax [12] and gFacet [11] are excellent solutions that cover formulation, collection and presentation processes of ISP. Parallax also provides support for expansion with related topics, where the available relationships are the ones pre-defined in the underlying collection. The selection and formulation stages are well covered by tools like Sig.ma [17], which provides end-users with search tools for Linked Data. A key distinguish feature of Sig.ma is the incremental display of data while relevant sources are discovered, which enhances the user experience by highlight data provenance. Explorator [8] provides extensive functionalities for the visually-aided composition of queries, and result filtering. Other noteworthy examples of visual exploration of linked data are DERI Pipes [16], RKB Explorer [9] and VisiNav [10].

Other solutions, like Microsoft Pivot [1], have been adapted to Linked Data browsing too [18], thus letting the user explore results by zooming, panning, or pivoting. Our proposal is located in the same application space as the above mentioned tools, sharing several key features such as native support for incremental exploration, data visualization, data relationships highlighting and navigation. However, only RKB Explorer provides support for the initialization and selection steps, whereby only Explorator, Pivot, VisiNav support pivoting.

A richer support to ISP is available in *vertical* LD-based applications, which exploit a well-defined and constrained set of classes and relationships in a schema to provide a predefined data exploration and rich interaction experience that usually comprises: customized interaction features, integration with non LD, and simultaneous visualization of result sets produced by several queries, along with their relationships. The BBC's Semantic Music Project [13][2] is an example of *domain specific* LD based application. Although this kind of LD-based applications are targeted to a specific domain of interest, their development would have benefited from a general purpose approach like the one proposed in this paper.

## 3   Running Example

To provide a better understanding of our approach, the rest of the paper will be discussed upon a running example targeted to the exploration of scientific publications. This is a non trivial domain where multiple class of applications can be built on the same data — e.g., recruiting of researchers, assessment of the quality level of a scientific venue, search for bibliographic references on a topic, etc. The required information is not available in a single repository, thus requiring the integration of different data sources. Some of these sources expose LD, while others expose semi-structured information. A sub-set of authors, papers and conferences are available, for instance, on DBLP (and thus amenable for queries through SPARQL end-points). Papers' citations and conferences' impact factors can be retrieved through page scraping[3] from a Web application like CiteSeer. Data about European research projects are available in Cordis database which is exposed as a SPARQL end-point.

---

[2] http://www.bbc.co.uk/music/artists
[3] We exploit YQL (Yahoo Query Language - http://developer.yahoo.com/yql/ ) as a middleware infrastructure for page scraping.

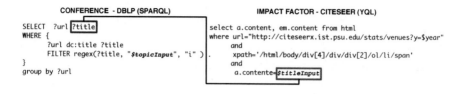

**Fig. 1.** An example of SPARQL and YQL queries involved in a *pipe* join

# 4 Our Approach

Our framework consists of a two-phase application life-cycle, comprising *configuration*, which is oriented to the application specification, and *consumption*, which is oriented toward the actual exploration of data sources within the boundaries of the existing data relationships and/or within the navigation paths defined at configuration time, possibly using the defined data visualization paradigms and interaction mechanisms.

## 4.1 Application Configuration

In the configuration phase, a domain expert (or a technical stakeholder of the application), knowledgeable about the information need and the relevant data sources, defines some aspects of the application behavior.

In the most general case, the configuration phase requires the definition of a comprehensive *exploration template*, an abstract application model that defines the set of *data sources* consumed by the application, the set of *exploration targets*, each one representing a distinct concept in the data sources (either defined intensionally —in terms of constraints on properties — or extensionally, through enumeration of concepts), a set of *input, output* and *ranking properties* for each *exploration target* ( where *rankings* denote the function that impose an order on the retrieved data), and the set of *relationships* on pairs of exploration targets, based on predicates upon *input and output properties*; such predicates can traverse existing relationships among concepts, or be applied on value-based property matching (e.g., exact matching, string similarity, spatial approximate matching, temporal approximate matching, and so on). Custom relationships are calculated at run-time by means of orchestration of queries over distributed (Linked and not-Linked) data sources. The actual sequence of queries depends on the exploration pattern, on the access restrictions imposed by the data sources, on the input-output parameters dependencies existing between the involved exploration targets (some output parameters of the second exploration target are matched to some input parameters of the first one), and on the join selectivity statistics that can be extracted from the actual joined data. The orchestration may comprise two join operators over the results of queries: *parallel* join and *pipe* join.

Figure 1 shows an example of *pipe* join that involves a Linked and a not-Linked data source, to associate all the *conferences* about topic given as input with their impact factor: the *?title* output value of each instance result from the leftmost query is provided as input to the rightmost query (*$titleInput*).

To enable advanced visualization and interaction features, the template can provide the *domain and range* values for the output properties to visualize, and the list of advanced *interaction mechanisms* allowed for the application; for instance *grouping* and *clustering* criteria that can be applied on the extracted result set to help users exploring the retrieved data.

We stress that all the above configurations can be manually or automatically defined. Our approach makes no assumption on the actual origin of the application configurations. In case of manual configuration, the configuration phase requires higher domain and technical expertise than the consumption phase (because the user must be aware of the data sources, the meaning of the exploration options, and the presentation options). However, we point out that the configuration step can be performed in a declarative, visually-aided way.

In general, orchestration and query generation exploit parametric query templates in the native query language supported by the data source. In case of non linked data, the query template must be specified by the registrar when declaring the data source in the repository.

## 4.2    Application Consumption

The *application consumption phase* is based on the approach presented in [5], which proposes a conceptualization of exploration primitives for addressing "search as a process".

Upon query submission, the system invokes the involved data sources, producing a result set of joined results (ranked according to a given function) which defines the initial user concepts space, shown to the user according to her data visualization choices (e.g., tabular representation, geographic map, charts, etc.). The result set conforms to an evolving result schema, which specifies projected attributes, ranking attributes, and allowed relationships. A set of interaction primitives enable manipulation, exploration and expansion of search results, thus allowing for continuous evolution of the query and of the result set itself. For instance, the system presents a first batch of results, and users browse them; if users are not satisfied, a *more* operation calculates additional results (within the currently defined concepts) by fetching new data and combining them, also with the previous results. The *re-rank* operation re-orders the result set according to a different ranking function; *filtering*, *grouping* and *clustering* allow the user to re-shape the current information space to better suite its view point on the retrieved data. At this point, the user can select the most relevant result instances and continue with the exploration by executing an *Expand* operation that traverse one of the available *relationships* of the selected results

After that, the user submits another object query, possibly by providing additional selection criteria; the system will then retrieve connected object instances and form a "combination" with the objects retrieved at the preceding steps. At any stage, users can "move forward" in the exploration, by adding a new class to the query, or "move backward" (backtrack), by excluding one of the classes

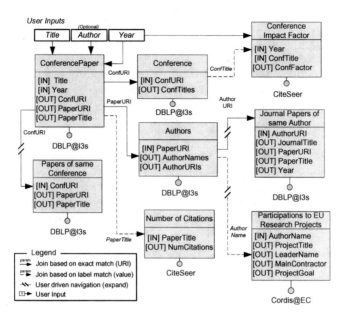

**Fig. 2.** Visual representation of the exploration template for a *vertical* running example application

from the query, or by "unchecking" some of their previous manual selections of relevant object instances.

### 4.3    Our Approach at Work on the Running Example

To make our approach more concrete, we describe its application in the context of the running example presented in Section 3.

We design a *vertical* application, where the user may submit a (part of a) conference paper title, the year of publication, and possibly one or more authors; as a response, the systems extracts for him the list of matching papers, the corresponding authors and conferences, the number of citations of each paper, and the impact factor of the conference, ordered according to the importance of the paper, expressed as function of the number of citations and of the conference relevance. To get a better overlook on the scientific relevance of the retrieved publication, the user may then decide to extend the results by navigating toward other papers published in the same conference, the journal papers of each author, and the European research projects the authors have been responsible for. Some of the information required by the application, i.e. the conference impact factor, is not available on the original LD sources, and it therefore needs to be extracted directly from the Web.

Figure 2 depicts an explanatory visual representation of the exploration template for such an application. In the example we assume that the initial results comprise information about *combinations* of: *Conference Paper, Conference, Authors, Conference Impact Factor*, and *Number Of Citations*. Custom

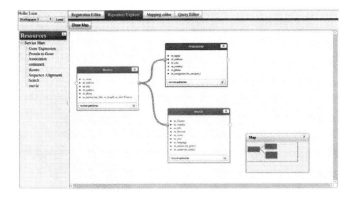

**Fig. 3.** Overview of the toolsuite for application configuration

relationships include *Participation To EU Projects*, *Papers Of Same Conference*, and *Journal Papers Of Same Author*. Some of these concepts are joined based on the navigation of IRI-based relationships, while others are joined based on literal comparison according to a predicate (e.g., string similarity, spatial distance, or others, based on the attribute type). The result is a set of concept combinations, ordered by the combination ranking function, which, in this case, rewards highly cited papers published in relevant conferences.

Indeed, the *Initialization* and *Selection* stages of the ISP process are extremely important for such an application, as the initial problem requires the definition of an exploration starting point that comprises a ranked combinations of concepts. The selection can be performed by means of appropriate visual aid tools, like the ones depicted in Figure 3.

The *Exploration* stage is also stressed, as the application includes several navigation steps to expand the retrieved information space. Likewise, the *Formulation* stage is enabled by the availability of filtering and clustering conditions.

Finally, the *Presentation* stage can be enabled by alternative visualizations of the same result set, which can stress the visual properties of the rendered outputs according to the targeted purposes. objects that constitute it are highlighted.

## 5   Implementation Experience

This section describes the software prototype that implements our framework for LD exploration applications. That showcases our approach by enabling the execution of (1) queries over selected data sources, (2) joins between queries results, and (3) data manipulation primitives for content ranking, visualization and exploration. The prototype is built upon a three-tier, distributed Web architecture (Figure 5), and it features rich and fluid user interactions (as described in Section 4.2) by means of asynchronous server communications and client-side data storage, processing and manipulation. Beside improving the user experience, a rich-client architecture provides, as additional benefit, the implementation of a

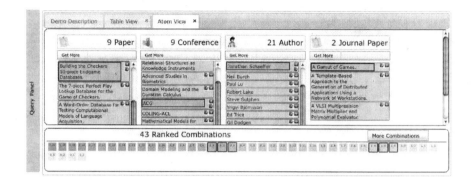

**Fig. 4.** User Interface prototype: set of concept tables (Paper, Conference, and Author tables) and ranked list of combinations (numbered list at the bottom of the screenshot)

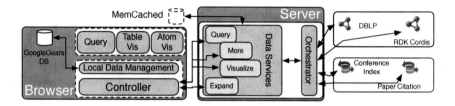

**Fig. 5.** System architecture overview

light-weight scalable REST server architecture, which naturally supports node distribution and replication.

The user interface (Figure 4) is an HTML5 application written according to the Model-View-Controller design pattern and exploiting the libraries *jQuery* and *JavascriptMVC*. The UI has been designed to be dynamically instantiated at run-time, based on the application configuration files.

The server-side is designed as a pluggable orchestration system featuring four kinds of executable nodes: *query nodes*, for query execution, *split* nodes, to trigger the parallel execution of queries, *join* nodes, to perform join operations over query results, and *data transformation* nodes, devoted to the manipulation of (joined) query results. Query and data transformation nodes provide standard interfaces for configuration management, invocation and result manipulation; the definition of the business logic required to interact with custom data sources is therefore left to the application configuration, while the framework is responsible to grant its correct execution. To reduce latency time, we adopted a distributed memory object caching system (*MemCached*) to store information about user interactions and to hold the results of query and join executions.

The server-side supports query formulation, evolution and storage. Each query is uniquely identified in the orchestrator and can be re-executed at any moment. Each result set produced by a query execution is also identifiable and retrievable. A prototype and a video based on the running example are published at: http://www.search-computing.org/demo/ui. The system is now undergoing a major implementation effort, and alternative application scenario has been recently demonstrated [6,4].

## 6   Conclusions

In this paper we presented a conceptual framework for the exploration of Linked (and non-Linked) Data that cover all the phases of the ISP process. The proposed join-based approach for the creation of custom relationships saves the user several exploratory link navigations between concepts and our tunable global ranking function provides a customizable ranking of combinations of objects. Furthermore, in our work exploration is not confined to data aggregated in one repository, but, thanks to value-based joins, can span linked data and arbitrary data sources wrapped as Web services.

**Acknowledgements.** This research is part of the Search Computing (SeCo) project[7], funded by the ERC IDEAS program (www.search-computing.org).

## References

1. Microsoft pivot: `http://getpivot.com/`
2. Becker, C., Bizer, C.: Workshop about Linked Data on the Web (LDOW2008). A location-enabled linked data browser. In: Procedings of the 1st Workshop about Linked Data on the Web, LDOW 2008 (2008)
3. Berners-lee, T., Chen, Y., Chilton, L., Connolly, D., Dhanaraj, R., Hollenbach, J., Lerer, A., Sheets, D.: Tabulator: Exploring and analyzing linked data on the semantic web. In: 3rd Int.l Semantic Web User Interaction Ws, SWUI 2006 (2006)
4. Bozzon, A., Braga, D., Brambilla, M., Ceri, S., Corcoglioniti, F., Fraternali, P., Vadacca, S.: Search computing: multi-domain search on ranked data. In: SIGMOD Conference, pp. 1267–1270 (2011)
5. Bozzon, A., Brambilla, M., Ceri, S., Fraternali, P.: Liquid Query: Multi-domain Exploratory Search on the Web. In: WWW 2010: 19th International Conference on World Wide Web, pp. 161–170. ACM Press, New York (2010)
6. Bozzon, A., Brambilla, M., Ceri, S., Fraternali, P., Vadacca, S.: Exploratory search in multi-domain information spaces with liquid query. In: WWW (Companion Volume), pp. 189–192 (2011)
7. Ceri, S., Brambilla, M. (eds.): Search Computing. LNCS, vol. 5950. Springer, Heidelberg (2010)
8. de Araújo, S.F.C., Schwabe, D.: Explorator: a tool for exploring rdf data through direct manipulation. In: LDOW (2009)
9. Glaser, H., Millard, I., Jaffri, A.: RKBExplorer.com: A Knowledge Driven Infrastructure for Linked Data Providers. In: Bechhofer, S., Hauswirth, M., Hoffmann, J., Koubarakis, M. (eds.) ESWC 2008. LNCS, vol. 5021, pp. 797–801. Springer, Heidelberg (2008)
10. Harth, A.: VisiNav: Visual Web Data Search and Navigation. In: Bhowmick, S.S., Küng, J., Wagner, R. (eds.) DEXA 2009. LNCS, vol. 5690, pp. 214–228. Springer, Heidelberg (2009)

11. Heim, P., Ertl, T., Ziegler, J.: Facet Graphs: Complex Semantic Querying Made Easy. In: Aroyo, L., Antoniou, G., Hyvönen, E., ten Teije, A., Stuckenschmidt, H., Cabral, L., Tudorache, T. (eds.) ESWC 2010, Part I. LNCS, vol. 6088, pp. 288–302. Springer, Heidelberg (2010)
12. Huynh, D.F., Karger, D.R.: Parallax and companion: Set-based browsing for the data web. Technical report, Metaweb Technologies Inc. (2009)
13. Kobilarov, G., Scott, T., Raimond, Y., Oliver, S., Sizemore, C., Smethurst, M., Bizer, C., Lee, R.: Media Meets Semantic Web – How the BBC Uses DBpedia and Linked Data to Make Connections. In: Aroyo, L., Traverso, P., Ciravegna, F., Cimiano, P., Heath, T., Hyvönen, E., Mizoguchi, R., Oren, E., Sabou, M., Simperl, E. (eds.) ESWC 2009. LNCS, vol. 5554, pp. 723–737. Springer, Heidelberg (2009)
14. Kuhlthau, C.C.: Inside the search process: Information seeking from the user's perspective. Journal of the American Society for Information Science 42(5)(5), 361–371 (1991)
15. Marchionini, G.: Exploratory search: from finding to understanding. Commun. ACM 49(4), 41–46 (2006)
16. Phuoc, D.L., Polleres, A., Hauswirth, M., Tummarello, G., Morbidoni, C.: Rapid prototyping of semantic mash-ups through semantic web pipes. In: WWW, pp. 581–590 (2009)
17. Tummarello, G., Cyganiak, R., Catasta, M., Danielczyk, S., Delbru, R., Decker, S.: Sig.ma: live views on the web of data. In: WWW 2010: 19th International Conference on World Wide Web, pp. 1301–1304. ACM, New York (2010)
18. Workbench, I.: http://iwb.fluidops.com/pivot

# Support for Reusable Explorations of Linked Data in the Semantic Web

Marcelo Cohen and Daniel Schwabe

Pontifical Catholic University of Rio de Janeiro
R. M. S. Vicente 225
Gávea, Rio de Janeiro, RJ, Brazil
`mcohen21@gmail.com, dschwabe@inf.puc-rio.br`

**Abstract.** The Linked Data cloud growth is changing current Web application development. One of the first steps is to determine whether there is information already available that can be immediately reused. We provide an environment which allows non-technically savvy users, but who understand the problem domain, to accomplish these tasks. They employ a combination of search, query and faceted navigation in a direct manipulation, query-by-example style interface. In this process, users can reuse solutions previously found by other users, which may accomplish sub-tasks of the problem at hand. It is also possible to create an end-user friendly interface to allow them to access the information. Once a solution has been found, it can be generalized, and optionally made available for reuse by other users.

**Keywords:** RDF, exploratory search, exploration, ontology, semantic web, reuse, interface, set-based navigation.

## 1 Introduction

The availability of Linked Open Data in the WWW has increased tremendously[1]. Currently, when building a new application, it is becoming increasingly common to first explore available data that can be leveraged to enhance and complete one's own data to provide the desired functionality. The BBC Music website[2] is one visible example of this approach, combining MusicBrainz and DBPedia with their own data.

Even though it is engineered to be processed by programs, it is still common that human beings need to explore these datasets, especially when they are previously unknown. In such cases, experts typically explore the repository to make sense out of the available data, to eventually be able to formulate queries that will support their tasks. Existing interfaces range from basic RDF browsers such as Tabulator[3] , Zitgist

---

[1] http://linkeddata.org
[2] http://www.bbc.co.uk/music
[3] http://www.tabulator.org/

A. Harth and N. Koch (Eds.): ICWE 2011 Workshops, LNCS 7059, pp. 119–126, 2012.

data viewer [4], Marbles[5], ObjectViewer[6] and Openlink RDF Browser[7], to query generators such as NITELIGHT [9] and iSPARQL[8], to faceted browsers [8][3] and set-based interfaces [4].

In previous work [2], we presented Explorator, a model for representing information processing by users in exploratory tasks, and its associated tool, which provides a browser interface supporting this model. Explorator is based on the metaphor of direct manipulation of information in the interface, with immediate feedback of user actions.

Our experience with Explorator [1] has shown that to be effectively used, it is necessary for users to understand the RDF model. Even for these users, once a solution was found, it was not possible to generalize it, and to save it for reuse later. These two mechanisms are essential to enable a community of users around datasets of interest, so that more experienced users can find and share solutions with less experienced ones. Furthermore, it is desirable to provide an end-user facing interface that hides the underlying data and operations, and has the look-and-feel of a traditional web application.

In this paper we present REexplorator[9], a significant extension of Explorator that allows

1. Parameterized interlinked operations, forming a graph of operations;
2. Saving these graphs for reuse;
3. The user to define new operators;
4. The user to define end-user friendly interfaces.

In the remainder of this paper, section 2 provides a running example, section 3 describes REexplorator, section 4 discusses evaluation, and section 5 draws some conclusions.

## 2    Summary of Explorator and a Running Example

### 2.1    Summary of Explorator

Explorator is an environment that allows users to explore a set of RDF repositories by direct manipulation of its contents, following a set-based metaphor. The user starts by either executing a full-text search, or by executing pre-defined queries (e.g., "All RDF Classes" or "All RDF Properties"). It is also possible to simply take a URI and de-reference it. In all cases, the results are always sets of triples.

The user explores the repositories by executing operations that take as operands sets of resources, and return new sets. The usual set operations, union, intersection and difference are available. In addition, there is the SPO operator, which corresponds to a match operation over <s, p, and o> triple patterns (e.g., $<s, *, *>$, $<s, p, *>$, for given $s$ and $p$ values, which are URIs). This match is executed against all enabled RDF triple repositories. Thus, $<s, *, *>$ corresponds to the SPARQL query

```
SELECT ?s ?p ?o WHERE  { ?s ?p ?o. Filter (?s = s )} .
```

---

[4]  http://dataviewer.zitgist.com/
[5]  http://beckr.org/marbles
[6]  http://objectviewer.semwebcentral.org/
[7]  http://demo.openlinksw.com/rdfbrowser/index.html
[8]  iSparql can be accessed at http://demo.openlinksw.com/isparql/
[9]  Available at http://www.tecweb.inf.puc-rio.br/rexplorator

In reality, the SPO operator has been defined to operate on sets of resources instead of individual ones, by taking the union of the triples resulting from individual match operations as described above.

Since each new operation takes its parameter from existing sets, the end result is a graph of inter-related operations, where the inputs of one are outputs of others. This is analogous to an Excel spreadsheet, where each cell has formulas that reference the value of other cells, forming a graph of interdependent formulas.

## 2.2    A Running Example

Consider the simple task of finding all publications of a given author. to be carried out over the "Dogfood" data server[10], containing collected publication information for several conferences related to the Semantic Web. We assume the user has no prior knowledge about the contents of this repository. The user has to

1. Find a class that represents persons
2. Find the desired person, "a".
3. Find a property "p" that relates a person to publications,
4. Find all triples of the form <a p ?pub> and collect all objects from these triples.

**Fig. 1.** All Persons, Details of a selected Person, and Publications of selected Person, in RExplorator.

---

[10] http://data.semanticweb.org

In Explorator, this is achieved by first clicking on "Menu"-> All RDF Classes", noticing class Person, mousing over it to click on "All Instances", which reveals a set of all Persons. Double-clicking on a Person (e.g. "Steffen Staab"), a new box appears with all details for this resource (i.e., all triples with this resource as subject). Looking at the details, one notices the property "made", which relates Person to Publications.

To get all publications by a Person, one may click on the "Selected Person Details" box, then click on the "S" operand position at the top; click on the "made" box and click on the "P" operand position at the top, and finally click on the "=" ("compute") operator at the top. Figure 1 shows the results after these steps.

# 3     RExplorator

RExplorator extends Explorator by
1. Allowing operations to be parameterized;
2. Allowing the results of a query to be fed as input of another query, thus forming graphs of interconnected operations;
3. Allowing to keep such graphs as separate workbenches, while enabling interconnection of graphs across workbenches;
4. Allowing the designer to import previously defined query graphs into the current workbench;
5. Allowing the designer to define additional operators beyond the builtin set and query operations provided;
6. Allowing the designer to define interfaces oriented towards end users, hiding details and customizing the look-and-feel.

RExplorator's metamodel is shown in Figure 2, which supports the implementation of these features. Some of its aspects will be elaborated as we explain these added functionalities in the coming sub-sections.

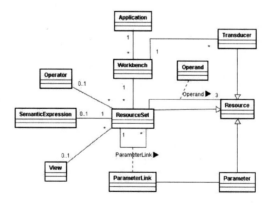

**Fig. 2.** RExplorator's meta-model

### 3.1    Parameterized Queries

The original Explorator metaphor lets users compose operations incrementally, seeing the results at each composition step. Each new query takes its operands from existing query results. In the end, one may regard this set of inter-related operations as a graph, similar to an Excel spreadsheet. However, the operations are all grounded, which would be akin to not having any variables in the formulas of the analogous spreadsheet. Thus, the first generalization made was to allow operations to have their operands parameterized, and to propagate values through the graph of operations when the value of the parameter is changed. This is equivalent to introducing variables in the expression that denotes the operation.

Consider step 4 in the example. In Explorator, this is achieved by selecting an instance of Person (e.g., "Steffen Staab in box "All Persons") in Figure 1, setting it as the subject parameter, selecting the relation "make" as the property parameter, and clicking on the "=" operator to find all triples of the form <<url for Steffen Staab> made ?o>. Clicking on the 🖉 icon in each box, as shown in Figure 3 reveals the actual operations and their dependencies.

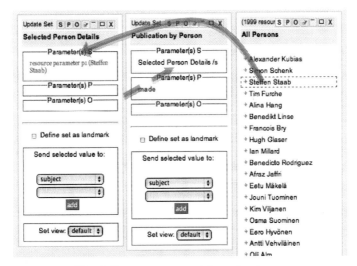

**Fig. 3.** Query structure and dependencies

The first box, **Selected Person Details**, represents the query that finds out all triples with a given Person as subject. Notice that the first position, "S", has been parameterized, and the current parameter value is (the URI for) **Stefen Staab**. If we drag any person from the rightmost box (**All Persons**) onto the "S" position in the **Selected Person Details** box, the value is replaced and the query re-evaluated.

The **Publication by Person** query (middle box) is defined as taking its "subject" parameter from the "subject" position of the **Selected Person Details** query. Therefore, if a new value is plugged into the "S" position in the **Selected Person Details** query, it is automatically propagated to this query, triggering its reevaluation.

## 3.2    Workspace Organization

RExplorator organizes the workspace into workbenches. The idea is that each workbench represents a task, or a use case in traditional Software Engineering methods. A user may save workbenches for later reuse, and share it with other users as well.

In RExplorator a workspace contains several workbenches, similar to the way an Excel a workspace contains several worksheets, where there may be cross-references between operations within separate workbenches. For example, workbench Co Workers by Person contains the Co Workers query, which can be interconnected to the "Publication by Person" query in the similarly named workbench.

## 3.3    End-user Interfaces

The development interface of RExplorator is best suited to allow users to explore RDF repositories, and requires understanding the RDF model. For non-technical end users, RExplorator allows expert users to provide end-user friendly interfaces – called the Application Interface - to solutions found while exploring datasets. For reasons of space, we refer the reader to http://www.tecweb.inf.puc-rio.br/rexplorator to visualize the Application interface.

Views make full use of CSS, which is also defined in a separate view that can be customized to change the look-and-feel of the generated interface.

## 3.4    User-Defined Operators

The original Explorator tool provides built-in set operators to manipulate the resource (triple) sets, besides the SPO query operator. Besides this, RExplorator provides a mechanism for the designer to define new operators.

Since operators work on sets of triples, a natural kind of function is the "list", "iterator" or "map" function commonly found in functional languages such as Lisp, Python, and Ruby, among others. In RExplorator, operators take two sets of triples as input and produce a set of triples as output.

As an example, one may want to filter a result set that contains datatype properties (e.g., rdf:label) according to a string value passed as a parameter. The Ruby code snippet below shows the definition of an operator that takes a resource set and a string as input parameters, and selects those triples whose object position matches the string.

```
param_a.select  {  |triple|  triple[2].to_s.strip.downcase  ==
param_b[0].to_s.strip.downcase }
```

# 4    Evaluation

We conducted a small qualitative study to have a preliminary evaluation of RExplorator. We asked 5 persons with basic RDF knowledge to build simple applications using a repository describing cellular phone models. The tasks consisted of

1. Exhibiting all available models
2. Showing models that support MP3
3. Showing models grouped by supported band

First they were shown a short video with RExplorator's basic functionalities. Then they were allowed to experiment with RExplorator for a short time and have basic questions about its functioning answered, after which they were given one hour to accomplish the tasks.

Of the five people, three were able to successfully accomplish the tasks in less the allotted time; one completed the tasks but with a slightly incorrect solution; and one could not accomplish the task.

We consider these results to be positive, showing that the tool can be effective. The test subjects were given minimal instructions, and yet most were able to accomplish the tasks. It is clear that this interface is not for beginners, but once the developer has become familiar with it, it is quite effective.

Nevertheless, the experiments indicate that the authoring interface should be improved, for example using graphics to better represent the dependencies between sets.

## 5    Conclusions

The environment that has the closest functionality to RExplorator is DERI Pipes [3], which allows the definition of mash-ups by creating networks of interconnected operators, with strings, XML or RDF data flowing through them. The desired result is obtained by the composition of the operators.

By analogy, RExplorator can be seen as a network of interconnected operators, which can be queries, set operations or customized functions. The data that flows in this network are sets of triples. Thus, the major difference is that it is oriented towards mash-up development, and as such its operators work at a lower abstraction level. In addition. DERI Pipes does not provide an interface layer, and is not meant to be used together with an exploration environment.

One of the major focuses for future work is providing a graphical authoring interface that makes it easier to visually identify the inter-dependence of the various operations. We are also investigating the reuse of solutions within communities that share solutions over a specific set of repositories.

**Acknowledgment.** Daniel Schwabe was partially supported by a grant from CNPq.

## References

1. Araújo, F.C.S., Schwabe, D., Barbosa, D.J.S.: Experimenting with Explorator: a Direct Manipulation Generic RDF Browser and Querying Tool. In: Visual Interfaces to the Social and the Semantic Web, VISSW 2009, Sanibel Island, Florida (February 2009), http://www.smart-ui.org/events/vissw2009/index.html
2. Araújo F. C. S., Schwabe D.: Explorator A tool for exploring RDF data through direct manipulation. In: Proceedings of the Linked Data on the Web Workshop (LDOW 2009), Madrid, Spain, April 20. CEUR Workshop Proceedings, pp. 1613–1673 (2009), http://CEUR-WS.org/Vol-538/ldow2009_paper2.pdf ISSN 1613-0073
3. Hildebrand, M., Ossenbruggen, J.v., Hardman, L.: /facet: A Browser for Heterogeneous Semantic Web Repositories. In: The 5th International Semantic Web Conference (ISWC), Athens, GA, USA (2005)

4.  Huynh, D., Karger, D.: Parallax and companion: Set- based browsing for the data web, http://davidhuynh.net/media/papers/2009/www2009-parallax.pdf
5.  Le Phuoc, D., Polleres, A., Morbidoni, C., Manfred Hauswirth, M., Tummarello, G.: Rapid semantic web mashup development through semantic web pipes. In: Proceedings of the 18th World Wide Web Conference (WWW 2009), Madrid, Spain (April 2009)
6.  Luna, A.M., Schwabe, D.: Ontology Driven Dynamic Web Interface Generation. In: Proceedings of the 8th International Workshop on Web Oriented Technologies (IWWOST 2009), San Sebastian, Spain. CEUR, vol. 493, pp. 16–27 (2009), http://ceur-ws.org/Vol-493/iwwost2009-luna.pdf ISSN 1613-0073
7.  Moura, S.S., Schwabe, D.: Interface Development for Hypermedia Applications in the Semantic Web. In: Proc. of LA Web 2004, pp. 106–113. IEEE CS Pres, Ribeirão Preto (2004) ISBN 0-7695-2237-8
8.  Oren, E., Delbru, R., Decker, S.: Extending Faceted Navigation for RDF Data. In: Cruz, I., Decker, S., Allemang, D., Preist, C., Schwabe, D., Mika, P., Uschold, M., Aroyo, L.M. (eds.) ISWC 2006. LNCS, vol. 4273, pp. 559–572. Springer, Heidelberg (2006)
9.  Russell, A., Smart, P.R., Braines, D., Shadbolt, N.R.: NITELIGHT: A Graphical Tool for Semantic Query Construction. In: Semantic Web User Interaction Workshop (SWUI 2008), Florence, Italy (April 5, 2008)

# Generation of Semantic Clouds Based on Linked Data for Efficient Multimedia Semantic Annotation

Han-Gyu Ko and In-Young Ko

Department of Computer Science, Korea Advanced Institute of Science and Technology,
335 Gwahangno, Yuseong-gu, Daejeon, 305-701, Republic of Korea
{kohangyu,iko}@kaist.ac.kr

**Abstract.** The major drawback of existing semantic annotation methods is that they are not intuitive enough for users to easily resolve semantic ambiguities while associating semantic meaning to a chosen keyword. We have developed a semantic-cloud-based annotation scheme in which users can use semantic clouds as the primary interface for semantic annotation, and choose the most appropriate concept among the candidate semantic clouds. The most critical element of this semantic-cloud-based annotation scheme is the method of generating efficient semantic clouds that make users intuitively recognize candidate concepts to be annotated without having any semantic ambiguity. We propose a semantic cloud generation approach that locates essential points to start searching for relevant concepts in Linked Data and then iteratively analyze potential merges of different semantic data. We focus on reducing the complexity of handling a large amount of Linked Data by providing context sensitive traversal of such data. We demonstrate the quality of semantic clouds generated by the proposed approach with a case study.

**Keywords:** Semantic Web, Semantic Annotation, Linked Data, Semantic Cloud Generation.

## 1 Introduction

As users become the center of content creation and dissemination in the current Web environment, they are playing a more significant role in metadata generation. For instance, users may create tags that can be used to enhance content search results. However, the attempts to improve content searching by merely considering tags as plain text, have led to the problem of semantic ambiguity [5, 6]. Nevertheless, the Semantic Web research community has been utilizing the semantic annotation of contents as a way to overcome these limitations.

However, these previous efforts on semantic annotation of Web contents fail to fulfill the requirements of scalability and usability [5, 6]. Most existing semantic annotation tools use terms from ontologies created by domain experts. These ontologies do not, however, provide sufficient options to cover various kinds of semantics. That is, only domain specific terms are available. In addition, these ontologies do not necessarily reflect newly created knowledge in an up-to-date manner.

A. Harth and N. Koch (Eds.): ICWE 2011 Workshops, LNCS 7059, pp. 127–134, 2012.

In this paper, we propose a semantic-cloud-based annotation scheme that makes it easier to add semantic annotations to multimedia contents in resource-constrained environments, such as IPTV (Internet Protocol Television), since an interesting application area of semantic annotation is the increasing market of businesses that use multimedia contents on the Web [7]. The proposed approach uses semantic clouds as the primary interface for semantic annotation. In order to generate the semantic clouds, we first locate essential points to start searching for relevant concepts in Linked Data [1] and then iteratively analyze potential merges of different semantic data. Users can easily resolve semantic ambiguity and choose the most appropriate semantic cloud among a set of candidates.

## 2     Multimedia Semantic Annotation Scheme

In this section, we describe the proposed semantic annotation scheme. As the following figure shows, the semantic cloud generated from the Linked Data is used as the primary interface for semantic annotation.

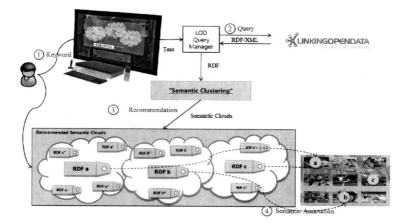

**Fig. 1.** Overview of the semantic annotation scheme applied to multimedia contents

When a user inputs a keyword while watching a multimedia content, the Linked Data query manager makes a query and obtains the relevant RDF nodes from the Linked Data. The proposed scheme generates recommended semantic clouds and the user then annotates the contents by choosing the most appropriate concept from them.

In this annotation scenario, there are three technical issues to resolve: accessing and processing large-scale Semantic Web data, generating relevant semantic clouds and providing an efficient user interface that allows intuitive interactions. In this paper, we focus on the issue of semantic cloud generation from the large-scale Semantic Web data. In order to achieve this goal, we identify the requirements for well-organized semantic clouds as follows:

1) **Small number of clouds**: The number of options should be four at most [8]
2) **Balance of contents in the cloud**: Semantically relevant terms should also be included in the same cloud
3) **No ambiguity among clouds**: Semantic ambiguity among generated semantic clouds should be minimized so as to facilitate awareness of semantic differences

The proposed semantic cloud generation approach that satisfies these requirements will be introduced in the following section.

## 3    The Proposed Semantic Cloud Generation Approach

According to the statistics [13], Linked Data contains more than 28 billion RDF triples from 203 different datasets that are domain independent. Hence, Linked Data is a large-scale and heterogeneous Semantic Web data store. In order to generate semantic clouds from the Linked Data, we need to make our semantic cloud generation process incremental and iterative.

There are three steps in the cloud generation process. First, *spotting points* for the clustering should be located. This entails finding representative RDF nodes that cover the concepts related to an input keyword.

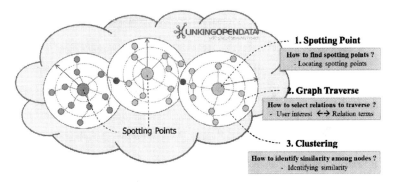

**Fig. 2.** Overall process of the semantic cloud generation

After locating the spotting points, the proposed approach selectively visits the neighboring nodes connected via relation terms interlinked with user context. This reduces the complexity of handling a large amount of Linked Data and also ensures the quality of semantic coherence of the generated semantic clouds by filtering out the less relevant relationships and the corresponding nodes.

In order to decide whether to include a visited RDF node in a cloud, it is necessary to measure the semantic similarity between the spotting point and the visited RDF node. Basically, the number of overlapping concepts could be the standard to measure the semantic similarity. The distance between a spotting point and the visited RDF node, which is measured by counting the number of hops from the spotting point to the RDF node, can be also considered to measure the semantic similarity.

## 3.1    Locating Spotting Points

The first step of finding and locating spotting points in the Linked Data is the most important process to generate high quality semantic clouds that satisfy the requirements discussed in the previous section. This is because the spotting points decide the representative semantics of the user keyword and the generated semantic clouds are dependent on the spotting points.

Locating spotting points starts with querying Linked Data to obtain the relevant RDF nodes. There exists two ways to make queries to Linked Data: via SPARQL or via Semantic Web search engines such as Swoogle [9], Falcons [10], or Sindice [11]. We chose the second method because we can obtain the relevant RDF nodes by simply adopting and using one of their Web services.

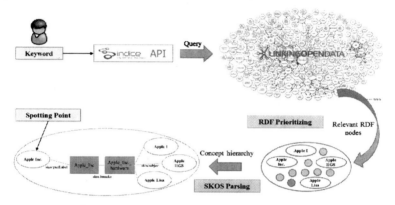

**Fig. 3.** Finding spotting points in the Linked Data

When we make a query about the keyword 'apple' via the Sindice API, it returns more than 400,000 RDF nodes. Rather than taking all the nodes, choosing some representative nodes could reduce the complexity of semantic cloud generation. Because Sindice ranks the resulting nodes by applying the principles of the PageRank algorithm as well as term frequency [12], taking the top $n$ number of query results replaces RDF prioritizing.

We finally choose the most general concepts of RDF nodes as the spotting points by comparing their relative concept hierarchies because it ensures semantic unambiguity among the spotting points, thus supporting the requirement of no ambiguity among generated semantic clouds. The SKOS (Simple Knowledge Organization System) is a common data model for sharing and linking knowledge organization system. It provides useful relationship terms such as skos:broader and skos:narrower that can be exploited to find the relative concept hierarchies to group the RDF nodes, then choose the most general RDF node as the spotting point.

Figure 3 shows an example of finding a spotting point by parsing SKOS relationships. Some RDF nodes are extracted with the keyword 'apple' such as 'Apple Inc.', 'Apple I', 'Apple IIGS', and 'Apple Lisa'. By parsing their SKOS relationships, we can recognize the most general concept of the RDF nodes; in this case 'Apple Inc.'.

### 3.2    Selecting Relations to Traverse

The second step of the proposed approach is to select relations that link the relevant RDF nodes. We can thereby reduce the complexity for the semantic cloud generation by setting traversal bounds. The ideal method to select semantically relevant relations is to automatically associate the relation terms with user contexts such as interests and preferences.

We assume that user interests are interlinked with relation terms and they are defined by each user before semantic cloud generation. For example, in the case where 'movie' is a user interest, relation terms such as 'actor', 'director', 'rating', 'background music', and 'story' become the relations to traverse.

In addition, W3C recommends that Linked Data publishers use well-defined and popular terms such as FOAF, DC, SIOC, and SKOS in order to ensure interoperability among the Linked Data datasets. The proposed approach firstly traverses the relations and then takes into account the relations selected by users with consideration of their contexts. This facilitates visiting relevant nodes while reducing the complexity for clustering these nodes.

### 3.3    Identifying Similarity and Clustering

In the third step of the proposed approach, the semantic similarity between the RDF nodes is measured in order to decide whether to include the visited RDF nodes in the same cloud.

Similar to the term frequency in information retrieval, the number of query responses from the Semantic Web search engine is also used to measure the similarity between nodes. In the following equations, $l_1$ and $l_2$ are the labels of RDF nodes, $n(l)$ denotes the number of query responses for the RDF node $l$, and $h$ is the number of hops to traverse.

$$TermFreq(l_1, l_2) = n(l_1, l_2) / n(l_1) + n(l_1, l_2) / n(l_2). \tag{1}$$

$$SemSim(l_1, l_2) = TermFreq(l_1, l_2) / w^h. \tag{2}$$

As the number of hops from a spotting point becomes larger, the value of semantic similarity exponentially decreases. For this reason the second equation that represents the semantic similarity between two RDF nodes take the inverse of the weight value $w$ powered by $h$.

We need to carefully decide the threshold value $h$ for clustering as well as the weight value $w$ such that it includes semantically related concepts toward the keyword. Deciding each value is beyond the research scope of this paper, however.

## 4    A Case Study

There are three methods of semantic cloud generation. The first approach clusters RDF nodes according to their rdf:type. However, this method does not ensure high quality semantic cloud generation. For instance, 'Apple Inc.' whose `rdf:type` is 'company' is separated from the groups 'Apple I', 'Apple IIGS', etc., whose `rdf:type` is 'Personal Computer', despite that there clearly is semantic relevance.

The next approach is using SKOS relationships. This method is useful to understand the relative concept hierarchy among RDF nodes. However, the obtained results fail to satisfy balance of content in each cloud.

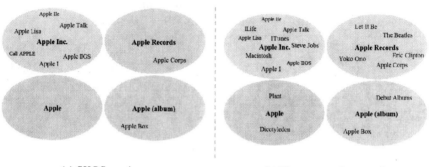

      (a) SKOS parsing                      (b) The proposed approach

**Fig. 4.** The result of Linked Data clustering toward the keyword 'apple'

As can be seen the above figure, the semantic clouds from the proposed approach provide better results, since the proposed approach also includes relevant RDF nodes which don't contain the keyword 'apple' via relation traversal.

**Fig. 5.** Implementation of the semantic annotation method for a Web-based IPTV environment

The proposed approach was also applied to a Web-based IPTV environment. The proposed approach allows users to put annotations on multimedia contents by choosing the semantic options from the semantic clouds generated from Linked Data. The annotation results are used to provide semantic search capability, which enriches the search results for multimedia contents.

# 5     Related Work

In order to overcome the limitations such as semantic ambiguity of using tags as plain text, a semantic annotation scheme has been defined and proposed. Its definition is tagging ontology class instance data and mapping it into ontology classes [5]. The major benefit of semantic annotation is enhanced information retrieval, because it exploits ontologies to infer about data from heterogeneous resources, thereby resolving ambiguities such as 'Niger' the country and 'Niger' the river.

There are three semantic annotation methods, differentiated according to the level of automation: manual, semi-automatic, and automatic annotation. Because human annotators are often fraught with errors and this form of annotation is very costly, manual semantic annotation may cause knowledge acquisition bottleneck [2]. In addition, it is impossible to provide fully automatic creation of semantic annotations. In response, semi-automatic annotation approaches have been explored. The main issues to be resolved are difficulties in choosing appropriate indexing terms for annotating and dealing with unbalanced content arising from the different conventions used in indexing by different users [3]. Also, as the basic prerequisite for representation, most works uses an ontology defining the entity classes as a knowledge base [4].

The proposed approach generates a few semantic clouds as the primary interface for semantic annotation from Linked Data, enabling users to intuitively recognize semantic options. Users can easily resolve semantic ambiguity and choose the most appropriate node among the candidate semantic clouds even in resource constrained environments.

# 6     Conclusion and Future Work

In this paper, we propose a semantic clustering approach that locates spotting points to start searching relevant concepts in Linked Data and then iteratively analyze potential merges of different semantic data. Using this approach, we attempt to reduce the complexity of handling a large amount of Linked Data by providing context sensitive traversal of Linked Data.

Through a case study, we showed that the proposed semantic cloud generation approach ensures high quality semantic clouds in terms of optimal number of choices, balance of contents, and no ambiguity among generated semantic clouds. Because it allows users put annotations on multimedia contents by simply using keywords and choosing the most appropriate concept among the generated semantic clouds, it can also be applied in resource constrained environments such as the small screen of smart phones and IPTV environments where it is difficult to use text input interfaces of remote controllers.

In future research we will carry out user studies to measure and prove the usability of the proposed semantic annotation approach as well as empirical studies to answer questions such as how many RDF nodes need to be considered at the phase of locating spotting point, how many hops need to be traversed to generate semantic clouds efficiently, and what is the most appropriate threshold value to decide whether a RDF node be included in the same cloud.

**Acknowledgments.** This research was partially supported by WCU (World Class University) program under the National Research Foundation of Korea and funded by the Ministry of Education, Science and Technology of Korea (Project No: R31-30007). This research was also supported by the KCC (Korea Communications Commission), Korea, under the R&D program supervised by the KCA (Korea Communications Agency) (KCA-2011-11913-05005).

# References

1. Christian, B., Tom, H., Berners-Lee, T.: Linked Data – The Story So Far. International Journal on Semantic Web and Information Systems 5(3), 1–22 (2009)
2. Bayerl, P.S., Lungen, H., Gut, U., Paul, K.I.: Methodology for reliable schema development and evaluation of manual annotations. In: Knowledge Markup and Semantic Annotation at the International Conference on Knowledge Capture 2003 (2003)
3. Vehvilaiinen, A., Hyvonen, E., Alm, O.: A Semi-Automatic Semantic Annotation and Authoring Tool for a Library Help Desk Service. In: Proceedings of the 1st Semantic Authoring and Annotation Conference 2006 (2006)
4. Kiryakov, A., Popov, B., Ognyanoff, D., Manov D., Kirilov A., Goranov M.: Semantic Annotation, Indexing, and Retrieval. ELSEVIER Journal of Web Semantics 2004 (2004)
5. Reeve, L., Han, H.: Survey of Semantic Annotation Platforms. In: ACM Symposium on Applied Computing (2005)
6. Uren, V., Cimiano, P., Iria, J., Handschuh, S., Vargas-Vera, M., Motta, E., Ciravegna, F.: Semantic annotation for knowledge management: Requirements and a survey of the state of the art. ELSEVIER Journal of Web Semantics (2005)
7. Ko, I.-Y., Choi, S.-H., Ko, H.-G.: A Blog-Centered IPTV Environment for Enhancing Contents Provision, Consumption, and Evolution. In: Benatallah, B., Casati, F., Kappel, G., Rossi, G. (eds.) ICWE 2010. LNCS, vol. 6189, pp. 522–526. Springer, Heidelberg (2010)
8. Lord, F.M.: Optimal Number of Choices per Item – A Comparison of Four Approaches. Journal of Educational Measurement 14(1), 33–38 (1977)
9. Ding, L., Finin, T., Joshi, A., Pank, R., Cost, S.R., Peng, Y., Reddivari, P., Doshi, V., Sachs, J.: Swoogle: a search and metadata eigine for the semantic web. In: Proceedings of the CIMK 2004 (2004)
10. Cheng, G., Ge, W., Qu, Y.: Falcons: Searching and Browsing Entities on the Semantic Web. In: Proceedings of the 17th International World Wide Web Conference, Beijing, China, April 21-25 (2008)
11. Tummarello, G., Delbru, R., Oren, E.: Sindice.com: Weaving the Open Linked Data. In: Aberer, K., Choi, K.-S., Noy, N., Allemang, D., Lee, K.-I., Nixon, L.J.B., Golbeck, J., Mika, P., Maynard, D., Mizoguchi, R., Schreiber, G., Cudré-Mauroux, P. (eds.) ASWC 2007 and ISWC 2007. LNCS, vol. 4825, pp. 552–565. Springer, Heidelberg (2007)
12. Delbru, R., Rakhmawati, N.A., Tummarello, G.: Sindice at SemSearch 2010. In: Proceedings of the 19th International World Wide Web Conference, Raleigh, North Carolina, USA, April 26-30 (2010)
13. W3C SWEO Community Project Linking Open Data,
   http://www.w3.org/wiki/SweoIG/TaskForces/
   CommunityProjects/LinkingOpenData

# Ontology Based Segmentation of Geo-Referenced Queries

Mamoun Abu Helou

Politecnico di Milano, Dipartimento di Elettronica ed Informazione,
V. Ponzio 34/5, 20133 Milano, Italy
abuhelou@elet.polimi.it

**Abstract.** The last generation of search engines is confronted with complex queries, whose expression goes beyond the capability of the Bag of Word model and requires the systems which understand query sentences. Among these queries, huge importance is taken by geo-referenced queries, i.e. queries whose understanding requires localizing objects of interest, where the user location is the most important parameter. In this paper, we focus on geo-referenced queries and show how natural language analysis can be used to decompose queries into sub-queries and associating them to suitable real-world objects. In this paper we propose a syntactic and semantic approach, which uses syntactic query segmentation techniques and the ontological notion of geographic concepts to produce good query interpretations; an analysis of the method shows its practical viability.

**Keywords:** Query Segmentation, Query Understanding, Geo-Referenced Query, Multi-Domain Query.

## 1 Introduction

Search engines perform poorly on complex queries [3]. When a query involves multiple domains and their interconnections, i.e., queries over multiple semantic fields of interest, search engines fail in understanding the query's meaning, also because they try to use all the query information in order to locate one page containing all the results. In this paper, we propose an approach to complex query understanding which focuses on the sub-problem of query segmentation. Such step is essential for decomposing a complex query into sub-queries, and then answering each sub-query independently, as contemplated by Search Computing (SeCo)[2].

However, understanding a natural language (*NL*) query requires the application of syntactical, semantic and conceptual knowledge to resolve the ambiguity that abounds in *NL*. The output desired from a query understanding process must include the objects, properties of objects and relationships among the query objects. In this paper, we focus upon geo-referenced queries, e.g. queries which ask about properties of objects which are placed at specific positions. These queries are very much used in practice, and are the majority of queries which are asked from mobile devices.

This paper is structured as follows. Section 2 presents the background and the preliminaries. Section 3 presents the related work. Section 4 describes the design and implementation. Section 5 presents the experimental results. Finally, we conclude and present some plans for future development.

A. Harth and N. Koch (Eds.): ICWE 2011 Workshops, LNCS 7059, pp. 135–144, 2012.
© Springer-Verlag Berlin Heidelberg 2012

## 2     Preliminaries

SeCo aims at the construction of a platform for multi-domain queries across search services. The project is addressing many research problems, including search service engineering and registration, efficient join methods for search services, and flexible query execution engines. SeCo uses the Semantic Resource Framework (SRF) [2] which is a multi-level (conceptual, logical, and physical level) description of data sources for *SeCo* applications. The higher layers provide an abstract semantic description of the services, building on the notions of *Service Marts* and *Connection Patterns*. The lower layers (*service interfaces* and *access patterns*) are concerned with the physical properties of the services. Ideally, every service conceptually belongs to a Service Mart. A Service Mart is structurally defined by means of attributes. Two Service Marts can be connected by a *Connection Pattern*. At the logical level, each Service Mart is associated with one or more access patterns representing the signatures of the service calls. *Access patterns* contain a subset of the attributes of the Service Mart, which are tagged with either I (input), or O (output). Attributes can also be tagged as R (ranking), to denote attributes that are used for ordering result instances. Ranking is particularly important in SeCo, because it allows mastering the combinatory explosion of multi-domain queries typical in Search Computing. For example, a query such as *"Find me a theater in San Francisco showing a romantic movie near Hilton hotel"* requires the user to manually extract and combine the answers from various queries, and this is an intricate and tedious job.

Syntax trees are widely used to preserve the original information conveyed by the query, a syntax tree is an (ordered, rooted) tree that represents the syntactic structure of a string according to some formal grammar. Figure 1 illustrates part of the Stanford Syntactic pares tree [6] of the example query. The parse tree is entire structure, starting from the *ROOT* and ending in the leaf nodes (*find, ..., hotel*). The following abbreviations given by the syntax tree help understanding the part of speech used for

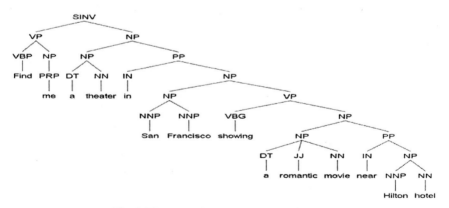

**Fig. 1.** The syntactic tree of the example query

the query words : *NP* is a noun phrase *(e.g. a theater)*, *NN (e.g. theater)* and *NNP (e.g. Hilton)* are used for nouns and proper nouns, respectively. *VP (e.g. find me)*, and *PP (e.g. near Hilton hotel)* are used for verb, and proposition phrases, respectively. *JJ (e.g. romantic)* is used for adjectives, and *IN (e.g. in)* is used for preposition or subordinating conjunction.

YAGO [5] is a large semantic *KB* which has been automatically built from Wikipedia, GeoNames[1], and WordNet[2], and contains nearly 10 million entities and events, as well as 80 million facts representing general world knowledge. In YAGO, knowledge is represented in the RDFS model. This model can be seen as a directed labeled multi-graph, in which nodes represent entities and edges represent relationships between the entities as illustrated in Figure 2. Furthermore, both the instances (such as *San Francisco*) and concepts, i.e., groups of similar instances (such as *city*), are nodes in the RDF graph. An instance is linked to its concept by the relation *type*. A concept is linked to a more general concept by the relation *subclassOf*. Instance of a sub-concept automatically inherits from super-concept, and can also be generalized as super-concept. Every concept's relation will apply automatically to all its instances (sub-classes) that exist somewhere down in the hierarchy.

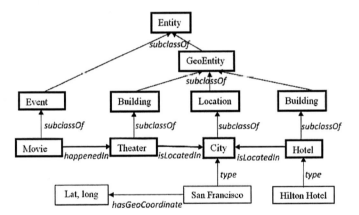

**Fig. 2.** RDF Model representing the example query based on YAGO

# 3    Related Work

The research work on Query Segmentation *(QS)* is focused on how to decompose a query into sub-queries. In [4], authors have shown that query segmentation has a positive impact on the retrieval performance. The segmentation process takes a user's query and automatically tries to separate the query words into segments so that each segment maps to a semantic component. Ideally, each segment should map to exactly one "concept" [8]. Recent work in *QS* [1] used a supervised learning method. However, this approach, as all supervised learning methods, requires a significant number of labeled training samples and well designed features to achieve good performance.

---

[1]  http://www.geonames.org/
[2]  http://wordnet.princeton.edu/

This makes it hard to adapt in real applications. As an alternative, [8] suggests unsupervised method based on expectation maximization. This approach, as it happens with most unsupervised learning methods, heavily relies on corpus statistics. In some cases, highly frequent patterns with incomplete semantic meaning may be produced. These segmentation algorithms take into account the sequential ordering of words, and do not study non-adjacent terms, therefore these approaches just deal with keyword-based short queries but hardly adapt to long *NL* queries, including complex queries. Also, they do not try to identify named entities or to assign class labels. *NL* Interface (*NLI*) systems to structured data use an underlying ontology to drive the meaning to the queries expressed by a user. [7] utilized pattern matching of a *NL* query to subject-property-object triples in a knowledge base (*KB*), before converting the query to one of SPARQL. [9] employed a named entity recognition engine, and supplemented it with more entity types and relation types to convert *NL* queries into SeRQL expressions. Nevertheless, the focus of *NLI* systems is on efficient porting interfaces between different domains rather on the understanding itself. Besides that, the understanding step should not be mixed up with the answering step. That is, we focus in understanding the search text queries leveraging the *KB* features although there is no matched answer to it in a *KB* of discourse.

# 4    Methodology

We propose a method with the objective to split a given query into sub-queries by combining the syntactic parsing with the knowledge encoded in a *KB* (ontology) to identify entities and their respective relations in a query. The method views a query as a sequence of entities and relations. The next issue is to determine the relations which link the entities. Valid relations between entities are actually constrained by the *KB*. Therefore, transformation of the *NL* query into a set of ontology concepts (i.e. classes, instances, properties) which is based on the assignment of a proper ontology concept to the query words is carried out first. Then the relations between the extracted entities are identified using the ontology. This is explained below in this section. Therefore, the main focus is to correctly recognize entities and determine their relations as expressed by the query.

Thus, the proposed method can be broken into two phases: *Query Analysis (QA)*, where the key *concepts/"Web objects"* will be extracted from the given query. , Here, the Web objects are a new way of abstraction to reinterpret concept organization in the Web, and go beyond the unstructured organization of Web page.    The second phase is *Query Interpretation (QI)*, where the possible object properties and entities are identified, and also the relationships among the extracted objects are discovered.

## 4.1    Query Analysis (*QA*)

The *QA* focuses on the identification of key *concepts* in the query. *QA* decomposes the user query into *concepts*, where each *concept* represents one search objective in a specific domain. The *concept* can either be a *simple concept* which consists of one word (e.g. hotel), or a *complex concept* consisting of multiple words (e.g. train station). *QA* employs two steps.

*Step 1: Morphological Analysis:* In this step we use the Stanford parser to get the syntax tree for the user's query. Shallow parsing is adopted to divide the sentences into a series of words that together compose a grammatical unit, mostly noun phrase (NP), and preposition phrase (PP), and also running a tokenizer, part-of-speech tagger.

*Step 2: Concept Identification:* This step identifies the key *concepts* in the query through a matching process, between the query words (*QW*) and the *KB's* concepts, to extract the query *concepts* "*geo concepts*" (*GC*). A *concept* is a *GC* if it is mapped to one of the *KB* geographical entities. The matching process, first checks if the query word is a *GC*, if not it checks if any synonym of the query word is a *GC*, failing to which it combines the query word with its consecutive word and checks if this composite word is *GC,* using the above 2 steps. Knowing that the geo spatial *concepts* are nouns, only the nouns among the *QW* are examined. For instance, running the *QA* over the example query the *GC* list :{ *theater, hotel*} was identified.

## 4.2    Query Interpretation (*QI*)

*QI* tries to extract any possible geo spatial information "*geoEntities*" (i.e. address, and geo spatial entity name). It also extracts the *concept* properties which could be seen as service invocation parameters and filtering criterion. Besides that, it identifies the relation among the extracted parts based on the defined relation in the *KB*. *QI* performs the following steps.

*Step 1: Concept properties extraction.* The adjectives and nouns associated with the *concepts* represent either a property of the entity or a more specific type for that entity than the type expressed by the *concepts* itself (e.g. Hilton hotel). For that, the adjectives and entities name are extracted based on the *NP* which has a *concept*. The *concept's* consecutive nouns are considered as entity name, while the adjectives are filtering criteria. Running step1 over the example query the name property "*Hilton*" was extracted for the *concept* "*hotel*".

*Step 2: GeoEntity extraction.* The *geoEntity* (*GE*), i.e. the entity with a permanent physical location on Earth can be described by geographical coordinates, consisting of latitude and longitude. Any geo-spatial entity/*concept* identified in the query should be associated with at least one component of the *address* field (street name, zip/postal code, city, country). The query may also contain the name for a *geo concept* (name of the geo-spatial entity), which would be extracted in (step1) e.g. Eiffel Tower. First candidate *GEs* are collected, we process the syntax tree for this purpose, and assume such entities are the *NPs* which are a child of a *PP*. And also the *GC* will be filtered and checked if any *concept* with its extracted entities names (step 1) would express a *GE*. Then, the *geo validation* process is performed to confirm these candidate entities and check if they are real world geo spatial entities.

The validation process is performed in two ways. Firstly, with the help of the *KB*. As mentioned above, YAGO the adopted *KB* already holds information about geographical entities (i.e. GeoNames entities) which holds the names of geographical entities e.g. cities, streets, monuments etc. Therefore, we are able to identify such entities and also provides the geo-concept under which this *GE* falls. Secondly, via

*Google GeoCoder* API[3], or similar APIs; the test succeeds if we are able to retrieve the address components of the candidate entity. Later, the extracted entities are processed to identify the address components by finding the best match between the name of the candidate entity and the *GeoCoder* results components. For this comparison we use *Levenshtein distance metrics, if* such distance is less than a certain threshold. The Levenshtein distance between two strings is the minimum number of operations needed to transform one string into the other, where an operation is an insertion, deletion, or substitution of a single character. And also the relation of the extracted *GE* components are defined based on the hierarchal representation of the address components (i.e. street is located in a city which is located in a country). Running step 2 over the example query, the chunk *"San Francisco"* was recognized and mapped to the ontology concept *"city"*.

***Step 3**: Relation identification.* To achieve the best possible query interpretation, we retrieve and analyze the potential relations between the identified *concepts* and entities, based on the defined relations in the *KB*. These relations are very important as they add descriptions to the *concept,* and define their behavior by adding rules and constraints. To resolve these relations the following steps are employed.

1. *Candidate relations extraction.* The possible relations for *concepts* will be extracted from the *KB*. Distinction is made between the relation's *Domain* and *Range* concepts. The query words, which have not been recognized in the extraction phases before (i.e. as a *concept* or *GE)* will be searched to match the extracted relation's *Domain/Range* concepts. For instance, the word *"movie"* is an instance of the *event* class which is a *Range* concept of the *happendIn* relation.

2. *Filtering the Improper relations.* The identified *concepts* and entities might have more than one possible relation. Similarly to [9], the candidate relations are filtered based on the property position in the hierarchy of concepts and properties. Initially, all possible matches between the extracted *concepts* and relation's *Domain/Range* concepts is performed, and then they are ranked based on the following factors: (i) on the sub property relation in the ontology, i.e. the property which placed at deeper levels in the property hierarchy has higher score, (ii) the position of the domain and range classes of the property, that is, a relation with more specific domain and ranges are ranked higher, and (iii) if any ambiguity raise up (i.e. the concept could be mapped to 2 or more concepts) the closet concepts will be related. For instance, *Location,* the sub-class of *GeoEntity*, is a *Range* concept of *isLocatedIn* which is a sub property of *placedIn* that has the *GeoEntity* as *Range* concept. Thus, the *isLocatedIn* is preferred instead of the *placedIn* to relate the location concepts or its sub classes (e.g. city, county).

| | Domain Concepts | Relation | Range Concepts |
|---|---|---|---|
| 1 | Person | wasBornIn, deidIn, livesIn | Location (**city**) |
| 2 | GeoEntity (**structure, location**) | placedIn (**isLocatedIn**),... | Location (**city**) |
| 3 | Event (**movie**) | **happenedIn** | GeoEntity (**structure , location**) |

**Fig. 3.** The example query potential relations

---

[3] http://code.google.com/apis/maps/

Figure 3 shows part of the possible relations and their *Domain/Range* concepts for the example query. The bold *concepts* are the one recognized in the query. The first relation will be discarded since the concept *person* was not found among the query words. The other relations are kept and resolved to {movie *happenedIn* theater, theater *isLocatedIn* San Francisco, hotel *isLocatedIn* San Francisco}.

Additionally, a spatial nearness relation which maintains the context of the geo- referenced query is handled based on existing keywords  (e.g. near, close to,...etc). Pattern matching is carried based on the patterns in Figure 4 , where $C_i$ and $N$ represent the *concept* and *nearness* keywords, respectively. Else a conjunctive (default) connection will be used by relating the closest *concepts* by walking through the syntax tree. Once step 3 is carried out, the relations among the *concepts* for the example query was defined, as follows :{ theater *near* hotel}.

Figure 5 shows the result of running the system over the example query as a directed graph, where the square nodes are the *concepts* in the user's query. The ellipses are the *GEs*, and the concept's properties which will serve as the services invocation parameter. The graph edges are the relations among these nodes that *SeCo* engine [2] will utilize as a filtering and join criteria; each concept node with its attached properties would be recognized as a sub query which will be mapped to a Web service. In SeCo each sub query ideally should be mapped to the appropriate access pattern of a Service mart by a Mapping tool (this would be a feature we looking to do in the future). The following represent an access pattern (AP) for a movie, theater, and hotel respectively.

*Movie* (Title$^O$, Director$^O$, Score$^R$, Year$^O$, Genres.Genre$^I$, Openings.City$^I$,Openings.Date$^I$, Actor.Name$^O$)
*Theatre* (Name$^O$, Address$^I$, City$^I$, Country$^I$, Address$^O$, City$^O$,Country$^O$, Distance$^R$, Movie.Title$^O$)
*Hotel* (Name$^I$, Address$^I$, City$^I$, Country$^I$, Addess$^O$, City$^O$, Country$^O$, Distance$^R$, Rating$^R$)

The Movie AP filters the movies by time (e.g., whose opening date in US is recent enough) and genre (e.g. romantic movies) and then extracting them ranked by their quality score. The theater AP offers a list of movie theatres with the related films ordered w.r.t. the distance from a given location. Theatre AP is connected to Movie AP via a connection pattern "Shows" using a join on titles attribute. Once the theatres have been decided, then we look for a near Hotel. The hotel AP offers a list of hotel ordered w.r.t the distance from a given address ( the theater address ) and filtered based on the name of the hotel (Hilton). At the end the user should have and order list w.r.t the distance between the theaters  which are showing a romantic movies and the hotels which called Hilton  in san Francisco.

# 5    Experiments

The RestQueries dataset provided by Mooney's group[4]  was used in the experiments, consisting of 251 queries about restaurants. Out of the 251 queries 13 were redundant and removed; the rest were manually annotated with the *GC* class, *GE* address

---

[4]  http://www.cs.utexas.edu/ users/ml/nldata/restquery.html

components (street, city, administrative area, country), and also the relation among the *GC* and *GE* as well as the *GE* relations and the concept properties (adjective, name) relations. The experiment is designed to measure the capability of the proposed system to extract the geo spatial concepts "*concepts*", the geo spatial entities components "*geoEntities*", the concepts *properties*, and also the *relations* among aforementioned parts, the relations are; Concept-to-Concept "*cc*", Concept-to-geoEntity "*ce*", geoEntity-to-geoEntity "*ee*", and Concept-to-Propriety "*cp*".

| Query Pattern | Concepts spatial relation |
|---|---|
| $c_1 \, N \, c_2$ | $c_1 \, N \, c_2$ |
| $c_1 \, N \, c_2$ and $c_3$ | $c_1 \, N \, c_2$ and $c_1 \, N \, c_3$ |
| $c_1$ and $c_2 \, N \, c_3$ | $c_1 \, N \, c_3$ and $c_2 \, N \, c_3$ |
| $c_1$ and $c_2 \, N$ | $c_1 \, N \, c_2$ |
| $c_1$ and $c_2$ | $c_1$ and $c_2$ |

**Fig. 4.** Spatial nearness patterns, where $C_i$ and $N$ represent the concept and spatial nearness relation, respectively

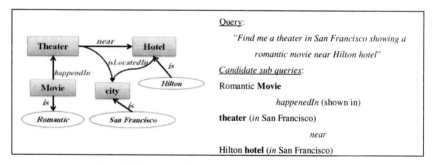

**Fig. 5.** The result of processing the example query

The correctness of the system was measured based on *Recall* and *Precision*. *Recall* is defined as the ratio between the numbers of correctly extracted parts by the system (true positive "TP") to the total number of manually tagged parts in the dataset (TP and false negative "FN" which been miss extracted). *Precision* is the ratio between the numbers of correctly extracted parts (TP) to the total number of the extracted parts using the system (TP and false positive "FP" which been extra/wrongly extracted). Figure 6 reports the results of running the system over the RestQueries. The *Precision* and the *Recall* were recorded for each extracted part. The experiment data and the result are available at ($^5$).

The system was able to extract 297 concepts, then 101 out of these concepts have been filtered in (*QI step2*), for example, "mountain view" is *GE*. Thus 100%, 196 concepts, have been all correctly extracted. 91.4% of the *GE* address components

---

$^5$ http://home.dei.polimi.it/abuhelou/data.htm

were correctly extracted. The reason behind the incorrect and the missed extraction is due to syntax tree, and also the *geo validation* process. For example, *"what are some good places for ice cream on blanding ave in alameda"*, "blanding ave" was tagged with verb phrase which cause the system to miss such entity. And the *geo validation* process was unable to recognize "fairgrounds dr", in the query *"where is a good american restaurant on fairground dr in sunyvale"*, as a street in the city "sunny-vale". 69.1% of the concepts properties was correctly extracted, again the syntax tree affect the extraction process. For instance, the adjective properties e.g. *italian*, was tagged as nouns, which caused 37 missed adjectives as well as 37 extra entity name. Furthermore, the syntax tree split some *NPs* into *NP* and *VP* which cause the system again to wrongly extract part of this name, which also will be considered as an extra extraction , for instance, the nouns "ice, and ave" were extra extracted and the name "ice cream" and the street "balnding ave" was missed as well as their relations. The overall correct extracted relations were 85%. However, the relation extraction was directly affected by the abovementioned extracted parts, the main factor was the property extraction.

An important consideration is that, the queries in this dataset mainly consist of only one geo-spatial concept. As a next step creation of a dataset consisting of more complex queries, having multiple geo-spatial concepts, attributes and relations is anticipated to test the approach more effectively.

| Extracted Parts | Over all | | | | GeoEntities | | | |
|---|---|---|---|---|---|---|---|---|
| | Concepts | GeoEntities | Properties | Relations | Street | City | Adm. A. | Country |
| TP | 196 | 290 | 291 | 545 | 46 | 167 | 56 | 0 |
| FP | 0 | 4 | 130 | 96 | 0 | 9 | 0 | 13 |
| FN | 0 | 7 | 58 | 71 | 20 | 0 | 8 | 0 |
| Precision | 100% | 98.6% | 69.1% | 85.0% | 100% | 94.9% | 100% | 0.0 |
| Recall | 100% | 97.6% | 83.4% | 88.5% | 69.7% | 100% | 87.5% | - |

| Extracted Parts | Concept classes | | | | Relations | | | Concept Properties | |
|---|---|---|---|---|---|---|---|---|---|
| | Restaurant | Café | Bakery | place | ce | ee | cp | Adjectives | Names |
| TP | 138 | 4 | 20 | 34 | 245 | 53 | 247 | 238 | 53 |
| FP | 0 | 0 | 0 | 0 | 4 | 0 | 92 | 10 | 120 |
| FN | 0 | 0 | 0 | 0 | 7 | 13 | 51 | 53 | 5 |
| Precision | 100% | 100% | 100% | 100% | 98.4% | 100% | 72.9% | 96.0% | 30.6% |
| Recall | 100% | 100% | 100% | 100% | 97.2% | 80.3% | 82.9% | 81.8% | 91.4% |

**Fig. 6.** The results of running the RestQueries dataset

# 6    Conclusions

This paper presents an approach for understanding natural language queries using geo-localizations by splitting long queries into sub-queries and understanding the role of each word in each sentence, specifically by extracting objects with their properties and identifying the geographic relationship between them. The precision and recall of the method are sufficiently high to warrant its use for geo-referenced queries. Future plans include improving and extending the method, by addressing not only geo-localized queries, but also general compound queries; we aim again at combining the syntactic method for query decomposition to other semantic methods and heuristics, using general-purpose ontological knowledge. In this way, it will be possible to understand if the method "scales" to arbitrary query decomposition, or instead its good performance descends from the extensive use of geo-localizations concepts. In future, the objective is to test the proposed approach for more complex queries. Furthermore, a stronger integration of Semantic Resource Framework with the proposed approach is anticipated to improve the results.

**Acknowledgements.** This research is part of the Search Computing (SeCo) project, funded by the European Research Council (ERC), under the 2008 Call for "IDEAS Advanced Grants", a program dedicated to the support of frontier research.

# References

1. Bergsma, S., Wang, Q.I.: Learning noun phrase query segmentation. In: EMNLP-CoNLL 2007, pp. 819–826 (2007)
2. Ceri, S., Brambilla, M. (eds.): Search Computing. LNCS, vol. 5950. Springer, Heidelberg (2010)
3. Chen, Y., Zhang, Y.-Q.: A query substitution – search result refinement approach for long query web searches. In: WI-IAT, pp. 245–251 (2009)
4. Guo, J., Xu, G., Li, H., Cheng, X.: A unified and discriminative model for query refinement. In: ACM SIGIR Conference on R&D in IR, pp. 379–386 (2008)
5. Hoffart, J., et al.: YAGO2: Exploring and Querying World Knowledge in Time, Space, Context, and Many Languages. In: WWW 2011, Hyderabad, India (2011)
6. Klein, D., Manning, C.D.: Fast exact inference with a factored model for natural language parsing. In: Becker, S., Thrun, S., Obermayer, K. (eds.) Advances in NIPS, pp. 3–10. MIT Press (2002)
7. Kaufmann, E., Bernstein, A., Fischer, L.: NLP-Reduce: A "Nave" but Domain Independent Natural Language Interface for Querying Ontologies. In: Demo-Paper at the 4th European Semantic Web Conference, pp. 1–2 (2007)
8. Tan, B., Peng, F.: Unsupervised query segmentation using generative language models and Wikipedia. In: WWW 2008, pp. 347–356. ACM (2008)
9. Tablan, V., Damljanovic, D., Bontcheva, K.: A Natural Language Query Interface to Structured Information. In: Bechhofer, S., Hauswirth, M., Hoffmann, J., Koubarakis, M. (eds.) ESWC 2008. LNCS(LNAI), vol. 5021, pp. 361–375. Springer, Heidelberg (2008)

# SimSpectrum: A Similarity Based Spectral Clustering Approach to Generate a Tag Cloud

Frederico Durao, Peter Dolog, Martin Leginus, and Ricardo Lage

IWIS — Intelligent Web and Information Systems,
Aalborg University, Computer Science Department
Selma Lagerlöfs Vej 300, DK-9220 Aalborg-East, Denmark
{fred,dolog,mlegin09,ricardol}@cs.aau.dk

**Abstract.** Tag clouds are means for navigation and exploration of information resources on the web provided by social Web sites. The most used approach to generate a tag cloud so far is based on popularity of tags among users who annotate by those tags. This approach however has several limitations, such as suppressing number of tags which are not used often but could lead to interesting resources as well as tags which have been suppressed due to the default number of tags to present in the tag cloud. In this paper we propose the *SimSpectrum:* a similarity based spectral clustering approach to generate a tag cloud which improves the current state of the art with respect to these limitations. Our approach is based on finding to which extent the tags are related by a similarity calculus. Based on the results from similarity calculation, the spectral clustering algorithm finds the clusters of tags which are strongly related and are loosely related to the other tags. By doing so, we can cover part of the tags which are discarded by traditional tag cloud generation approaches and therefore, present the user with more opportunities to find related interesting web resources. We also show that in terms of the metrics that capture the structural properties of a tag cloud such as coverage and relevance our method has significant results compared to the baseline tag cloud that relies on tag popularity. In terms of the overlap measure, our method shows improvements against the baseline approach. The proposed approach is evaluated using MedWorm medical article collection.

**Keywords:** tag, cloud, medical, information, retrieval, navigation.

## 1 Introduction

Tag clouds have been popularized as a means for navigation and exploration by social sites, such as *Flickr, Technorati* and *del.icio.us*. These sites are used by users to annotate shared resources using short textual labels, called tags. In general, tag annotation are used remembering which meaning the annotated resource had for particular readers or users of the resource and this in a collaborative manner. Aggregated set of the tags form tag clouds. Tag clouds allow users searching for certain tags and to locate resources tagged by these tags also

A. Harth and N. Koch (Eds.): ICWE 2011 Workshops, LNCS 7059, pp. 145–154, 2012.

by other users [10,15]. Tags in the cloud are hyperlinks which users can click and by following the links to see related content. The tags in the tag clouds are mostly presented alphabetically and according to their popularity, i.e. the more a tag was used in annotations of information resources on the Web, the larger the font size it has in a tag cloud. Further, the number of tags in a tag cloud is usually restricted by predefined number which results in cutting out number of tags after the number was reached following the alphabetic order.

We share the same opinion with [18] that "popularity" does not provide the most meaningful groupings to help a user to locate items of interest. For example, if we select the 20 most popular tags assigned to the results of a query "swine flu" at the *MedWorm* portal [1], there might be some articles in the query results that have not been tagged with any of the selected 20 tags and hence the article would not be reachable by the user. The issue is also that despite the popularity, the tags are not necessarily related.

Due to these limitations, we focus on the generation of tag clouds by considering the relatedness of tags. The intention is to partition all tags into disjoint groups of related tags. For instance, the tags "swine", "flu", "mexico", "2010" should be part of one sub cloud while the tags "tumor", "cancer", "blood", "biopsy" should be part of another sub cloud. The sub clouds are treated in this paper as clusters. Our hypothesis is that the organization of the entire tag cloud considering the existence of those sub clouds can better cover and represent the information it links to. Note also, that we are looking for a specific solution to group tags but in this paper, we are not studying how to effectively present those groups for which there are several options. We select only one of the possible presentations for now. The chosen presentation is close to the traditional presentation of tag clouds and only for illustration purposes. The contributions of this paper can be summarized as follows:

- We propose a method which combines *a similarity calculus with a spectral clustering algorithm to generate a tag cloud for navigation and exploration purposes*. We argue for this solution because spectral clustering performs the best in situations where computed clusters should contain strongly related members insight and are very loosely related to the members of other clusters.
- We show that the proposed approach has *promising results in terms of coverage, relevance, and overlap* especially in the context of the very sparse and low quality tagging data set such as that from a medical domain from the *MedWorm portal*. We look especially at this domain as the tag clouds can support surveillance and analysis of information relevant to some medical events such as a disease outbreak. Here the navigation and exploration aids are even more important than in general purpose tagging systems such as *del.icio.us*.

The remainder of this paper is organized as follows. In the next section we review related work on tag cloud systems. Section 3 describes our approach for

---

[1] http://www.medworm.com/rss/blogtags.php

generation of the tag cloud. Next, Section 4 describes the evaluation, based on the MedWorm dataset. Finally, we conclude the work and point out future works.

## 2   Related Work

Research on tag clouds has mostly focused on presentation and layout aspects [2,15]. For selecting tags to be displayed in a tag cloud, social information sharing sites mostly use popularity-based schemes. Recently, tag selection algorithms that try to find good and not necessarily popular tags have been developed for structured data [14]. This work relates to our approach in the sense that tag relatedness was also addressed however with less focus on the generation of the tag cloud. There has been extensive research on clustering search results [9,12]. Although not dealing with tag clouds, our work converge to those approaches since all rely on clustering techniques based on tag relatedness. There is also work on query results labeling [13] and categorizing results of SQL queries [5]. [6] adapt tag clouds to provide visual summaries of researchers' activities and use these to promote awareness within a research group. [11] show how tag clouds can be used alongside more traditional query languages and data visualization techniques as a means for browsing and querying databases by both experts and non-expert users. In the same line, Sinclair et al. [16] studied the usefulness of tag clouds versus search interfaces for different types of tasks (general versus specific searches). Similarly to our work, [16] investigate the idea that tag clouds can provide a helpful visual summary of the contents regardless tag popularity. [3] applies tag clustering to overcome the problem of limited search in tag spaces. The difference from our work, is that while we apply the traditional spectral algorithm [19], they combine the spectral bisection algorithm [17] and a modularity function $Q$, which measures the quality of a particular clustering of nodes in a graph. Technically, the spectral bisection algorithm is a extension of the spectral algorithm that bisects graphs into two graphs. Division into a larger number of graphs is usually achieved by repeated bisection. Another difference in comparison to our work is that we extend the weights for tag relatedness with similarity calculation while [3] only considers co-occurrence of tags. The final difference is that we have also performed an evaluation study based on compactness metrics.

In a medical domain, [8] propose a lightweight technique that uses multiple synchronized tag clouds to support iterative visual analysis and filtering of query results. The proposal was evaluated in a user study which presents typical search and comparison scenarios to users trying to understand heterogeneous clinical trials from a leading repository of scientific information. Unlike our work, they did not use any specific technique for analyzing the relatedness of tags. Therefore, our work provide a better solution for their problem as well. [1] introduce a new model for collaborative tagging in medical blogs, i.e. tagging blog entries with medical information. MTag includes two modules: the service module and the semantic module. The service module enables health professionals provide blog posts with auto-completed tags that represent actual medical terms and categorize their tags. Tags are mapped to URIs from online medical knowledge datasets to clarify their medical meaning. [4] describe a prototype which retrieves biomedical information from different sources, manages it to improve the results obtained and to reduce response time and, finally, integrates it so that it is useful for the clinician, providing all the information available about the patient at the POC. Moreover, it also uses tools which allow medical staff to communicate and share knowledge.

## 3    Tag Cloud Approach Based on Spectral Clustering

Figure 1 shows an excerpt of the MedWorm tag cloud (on the left side) and our generated tag cloud (on the right side). The first visible observation is that our tag cloud reduces the amount of tags in the cloud. Tags as "award, awards, Australia, ethics, advocacy" are not considered by our approach since they are not closely related to the other tags in the cloud. The second observation refers to the organization of the cloud itself. In the MedWorm cloud, many unrelated tags are located next to each other. Examples include "aids and alcohol", "awards and back pain" and "advocacy and affairs". In our tag cloud, we organize the "sub clouds" (clusters) per line and provide an allocation of tags based on their relatedness. Examples include "protein and aids" and "alcoholic and addiction". These sets are not found in the MedWorm tag cloud.

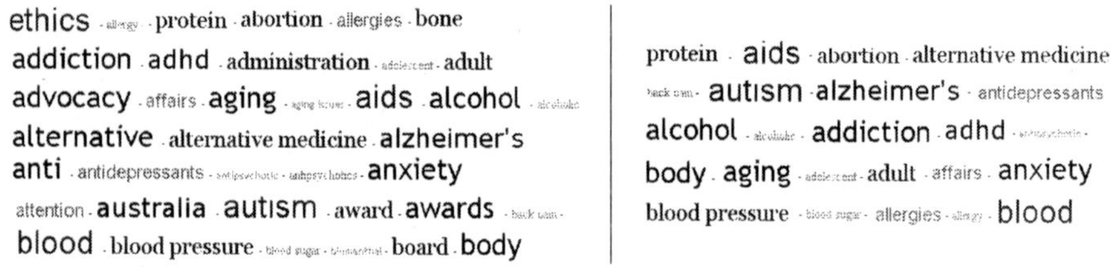

**Fig. 1.** An example of tag clouds from MedWorm dataset, on the left the original popularity based tag cloud and on the right generated by our approach

The tag cloud approach used in the Figure 1 is described bellow. It is based on two main steps: first, it calculates a similarity measure among tags, and, second, it runs a clustering technique on the tag cloud space to identify the sub clouds.

### 3.1    Calculating Tag Relatedness

We represent the tag space as a similarity matrix $W$ that captures the relatedness of all tags. Since our goal is to find strongly related tags, we use the frequency counts of all the co-occurred tag pairs (co-tags) and attempt to identify the significant co-tags. In order to do that, we determine the pairs of tags that co-occur more frequently, i.e., the pair of tags that are frequently assigned to the same article. In short, $W$ is calculated as:

$$W = \sum |tag_i \cap tag_j|, \tag{1}$$

where $tag_i \in T$ and $tag_j \in T$ and $T$ is the set of tags. The second step is to look for a cutoff point above which the co-tags are considered strongly related. The weakly related co-tags are discarded and not considered in further computations. The cutoff point is calculated based on the analysis of co-tags statistics and it is important to discard the noisy and weakly related co-tags which cause inaccurate clustering.

Once the strongly related co-tags are identified, we compute affinity among co-tags according to a similarity function. Different similarity measures can be exploited, but for this work, we opted for using cosine similarity because we obtained the best results in our preliminaries analysis [7]. The cosine similarity is calculated as follows:

$$Cosine(tag_i, tag_j) = \frac{2|I \cap J|}{\sqrt[2]{|I| \times |J|}} \qquad (2)$$

, where the amount of tag occurrences for $tag_i$ and $tag_j$ within all tag assignments is denoted by $|I|$ and $|J|$ respectively. The number of co-occurrences between $tag_i$ and $tag_j$ is given by $|I \cap J|$. This similarity measure is computed for every strongly related co-tag in the tag space, once we can transform the tag pair relations into a graph structure. It is an undirected weighted graph $G(V, E, W)$ consisting of:

- a set of nodes $V$, where a vertex $v_i$ of the graph corresponds to a tag $tag_i$.
- a set of edges $E$, where an edge $e_i$ connects vertices $v_i$ and $v_j$ if the tag $tag_i$ relates strongly to tag $tag_j$ or vice versa.
- weights are given by the affinity matrix $W$, where a weight $w_{i,j}$ corresponds to the similarity between $tag_i$ and $tag_j$.

As the graph $G$ is undirected, it holds that $w_{i,j} = w_{j,i}$ and the affinity matrix $W$ is symmetric. The next step is to group similar tags into clusters.

## 3.2   Clustering Tag Space

Once the graph $G$ is created, we then proceed to find (sub) clusters of tags that address the same topic. For instance, a cluster of tags addressing the topic "diet" could contain the tags "meal", "vitamin", "periodicity", while a cluster of tags addressing the topic "infectious diseases" could contain the tags "contamination", "virus", "oral contact". This requirement matches exactly the principle of spectral clustering algorithms, i.e. to cut a weighted graph into a number of disjoint pieces (clusters) such that the intra-cluster weights (similarities) are high and the inter-cluster weights are low [19]. To obtain clusters, we therefore rely on a spectral clustering algorithm which input is the undirected weighted graph $G$. The spectral clustering algorithm partitions the graph $G$ based on its spectral decomposition into subgraphs. The affinity matrix $W$ expresses the graph G, in such way that for each node the matrix $W$ contains a row with graph weights (similarities values) between a given node and all other nodes. The steps to run the spectral clustering are:

1. We build the Laplacian matrix $L = D^{-1/2}WD^{-1/2}$ derived from the affinity matrix $W$. The $D$ is $n \times n$ diagonal matrix whose $(i,i) - th$ element is the sum of $W$'s $i - th$ row, in other words it is degree of a given node $i$ - sum of all weights corresponding to the edges that are connected to a given node $i$. The Laplacian matrix $L$ is symmetric and has identical size as affinity matrix $W$.

2. We compute the $k$ largest eigenvectors of L, these obtained top $k$ eigenvectors are used as columns to create a new matrix $U \in \mathcal{R}^{n \times k}$. We consider each row of $U$ as a point in $\mathcal{R}^k$, hence we can apply standard K-means algorithm to cluster these points into $k$ clusters. In our experiment, we empirically tried different numbers of clusters to run our analysis and concluded that for our experiment and the dataset 10 clusters perform the best. This could however differ from a dataset to dataset and can even change with the evolution of the tag set. Thus, an approach that automatically defines the member of clusters is envisaged as part of our future works.

3. Finally, we map original node $i$ to the cluster $j$ if and only if row $i$ from matrix $U$ belongs to the same cluster $j$. We obtained disjoint groups of similar and related tags and we are able to build enriched tag cloud.

## 4    Evaluation

### 4.1    Dataset and Experimental Setup

**Methodology.** In order to evaluate the generated tag cloud, we analyzed the problem from a traditional information retrieval perspective. We used tags from each sub cloud as query terms and analyzed the search results issued by these tag queries. Indeed, we compared the set of tags assigned to returned results against the set of tags in the each sub cloud (or cluster). In this sense we could calculate three structural properties of the cloud: *coverage, overlap* and *relevance*. For issuing the queries, we utilized the *Apache Lucene* [2] as our search engine.

For the matter of comparison, we repeated the same procedure on the Med-Worm tag cloud. Since MedWorm's cloud relies on tag popularity and does not deal with explicit clusters, we decided to create "fake" clusters composed by tag neighbors located after and before a tag query $q$ present in our sub clouds. Thus, the clusters were made up around all tag queries common in both clouds. In this sense, we could build clusters of $T_{neighbors}$ for the MedWorm tag cloud and compare the results against our approach. The amount of clusters and size was the same as used in our approach. Regarding the amount of clusters for the cloud, we empirically set the number of cluster based on our observations of the cluster quality. After testing a tag cloud containing 5 to 20 clusters, we ran our experiments with 5, 10 and 15 clusters.

**Data and Queries.** We crawled medical articles from *MedWorm* repository and stemming out the entity attributes from the data. Thus, we obtained the

---

[2] http://lucene.apache.org/

tags, resources and its associations. The resulting dataset comprises 13,509 tags and 26,1501 documents. We also indexed the stemmed words from documents to build up the search space. Finally, the tag cloud was pre-processed according to the steps described in Section 3.

As noted before, all tags from the clusters of our generated tag cloud were utilized as individual queries as long as they were also found in the baseline tag cloud. In this sense, both approaches could be evaluated on the same search results. We justify the utilization of tags as queries to avoid using "arbitrary" terms (even medical related), that eventually could not retrieve results and thus not contributing the evaluation.

**Evaluation Metrics.** The quality of tag cloud has been studied in many studies [10,18]. In this work, we evaluate the quality of our cloud inspired by metrics established by [18]. In particular, we pay special attention to the *coverage, overlap* and *relevance* of the cloud. We understand that these metrics capture the structural properties of a cloud and indicate the its quality for representing the collection of tagged documents. In order to formally describe the metrics, let $T_c$ be the set of tags in a cluster $c$; and $C_q$ be the set of items retrieved when a query $q$ is issued.

- *Coverage of $T_c$:* Some items in $C_q$ may not be assigned with any tag from $T_c$. Then, these objects are not covered by $T_c$. Coverage gives us the fraction of $C_q$ covered by $T_c$. Thus, coverage $cov(T_c)$ is defined as:

$$cov(T_c) = \frac{|T_c|}{|C_q|}, \quad (3)$$

  This metric can take values between 0 and 1. If $cov(T_c)$ is close to 0, then $T_c$ is associated with a few items of $C_q$.
- *Overlap of $T_c$:* Different tags in $T_c$ may be assigned with the same item in $C_q$. The overlap metric captures the extent of such redundancy. Thus, given $t_i \in T_c$ and $t_j \in T_c$, we define the overlap $over(T_c)$ of $T_c$ as:

$$over(T_c) = avg_{t_i \neq t_j} \frac{|t_i \cap t_j|}{|C_q|}, \quad (4)$$

  This metric also lies in [0,1]. If $over(T_c)$ is close to 0, then the intersections of tags in the same cluster are small and redundancy is minor.
- *Relevance of $T_c$:* It says how relevant the tags in $T_c$ are to the original query $q$. To answer this, we treat each $t$ in $T_c - q$ as a query and we consider the set $C_t$ of items that this query returns. Since we decided to use one tag in $T_c$ as $q$, for obvious reasons, we set the constraint: $t \neq q$. The more $C_t$ and $C_q$ overlap, the more related $t$ is to $q$. If $C_t \subseteq C_q$, then $t$ is practically a sub-category of the original query $q$. Let us first define the relevance $rel(t,q)$ of a tag $t$ to the original query $q$ as the fraction of results in $C_t$ that also belong to $C_q$, i.e.:

$$rel(T_c) = avg_{t \in T_c} \frac{|C_t \cup C_q|}{|C_t|}, \quad (5)$$

The $rel(T_c)$ lies in [0,1]. The closer it is to 1, the more relevant is $T_c$ to the query $q$.

## 4.2   Evaluation Results

We generated our cloud based on the baseline MedWorm cloud containing 200 tags. This is the approximate amount of tags available on MedWorm web site. After generating our cloud, only 125 tags were considered. The 75 tags missing were discarded by the clustering algorithm. Only 70 tags from our tag cloud were also found in the baseline tag cloud. All those 70 tags were used as queries in the evaluation. Table 1 shows the comparative results of our analysis taking into account the three aforementioned metrics. The results on the left side of the table refer to MedWorm tag cloud while the results on the right side of the table are achieved from our approach. The results correspond to the mean values for the metrics assessed. As results show, our approach obtained significant advantage

**Table 1.** *Mean Values* for the Metrics Assessed

| # Cluster | MedWorm Tag Cloud | | | Our Tag Cloud | | |
|---|---|---|---|---|---|---|
| | Coverage | Relevance | Overlap | Coverage | Relevance | Overlap |
| 5 | 0.53 | 0.56 | 0.65 | 0.67 | 0.66 | 0.61 |
| 10 | 0.51 | 0.55 | 0.67 | 0.70 | 0.68 | 0.61 |
| 15 | 0.56 | 0.52 | 0.61 | 0.65 | 0.63 | 0.59 |

(on average) in terms of coverage and relevance at rates of 20.4% and 16.4% respectively. We also achieved better overlap rates than the MedWorm tag cloud at a satisfactory rate of 5.7%. As to the number of clusters, we observed best results with 10 clusters were considered.

Focusing exclusively on the coverage metric, we can argue that reorganization of the cloud in sub clusters of related terms made it more representative. This means that each tag covers a more expressive part of the whole indexed corpus. Although no significant improvements were observed for overlap, at least we could observe that tags assigned to the search results were more equally distributed thus reducing scarcity. The immediate benefit is that searchers if using the tags as queries might increase the chances for hits of desired documents. As to the relevance metric, we can argue that the clusters contribute to generate a more cohesive cloud that better cover and represent the information it links to. We outline two benefits of our approach: i)it demonstrates how closely related the tags are in the cloud and ii) how closely related the search results are to the sub clouds.

## 5   Conclusion and Future Works

In this paper we propose an approach to generate quality tag clouds by considering the relatedness of tags and separation of concerns. Our hypotheses was that the organization of the whole cloud considering the relatedness of tags could improve structural properties of the cloud and thereby enhance information retrieval capabilities.

According to our results, we reached higher levels of coverage, overlap and relevance compared to a baseline medical tag cloud. As a future work, we plan to investigate how different metrics may correlate to each other in order to determine which independent metrics make sense as optimizations objectives. In addition, it is possible that metrics may exhibit different correlation trends in different datasets. As previously said, we plan to utilize an clustering approach that automatically define the amount of clusters. Further, digital dictionaries as WordNet or even domain ontologies should be considered for calculation of tag relatedness. We also plan to compare the clustering algorithm using the bisection technique with the one used in this work. Finally, a task-based evaluation using a navigation tool is planned to better support the validity of the approach.

**Acknowledgment.** This work has been supported by FP7 ICT project M-Eco: Medical Ecosystem Personalized Event-Based Surveillance under grant number 247829 and FP7 ICT project KiWi: Knowledge in a Wiki under grant agreement No. 211932.

# References

1. Batch, Y., Yusof, M.M., Noah, S.A.M., Lee, T.P.: Mtag: A model to enable collaborative medical tagging in medical blogs. Procedia Computer Science 3, 785–790 (2011); World Conference on Information Technology
2. Bateman, S., Gutwin, C., Nacenta, M.: Seeing things in the clouds: the effect of visual features on tag cloud selections. In: Proceedings of the Nineteenth ACM Conference on Hypertext and Hypermedia, HT 2008, pp. 193–202. ACM, New York (2008)
3. Begelman, G., Keller, P., Smadja, F.: Automated tag clustering: Improving search and exploration in the tag space. In: Proceedings of the WWW Collaborative Web Tagging Workshop, Edinburgh, Scotland (2006)
4. Cabarcos, A., Sanchez, T., Seoane, J.A., Aguiar-Pulido, V., Freire, A., Dorado, J., Pazos, A.: Retrieval and management of medical information from heterogeneous sources, for its integration in a medical record visualisation tool. IJEH 5(4), 371–385 (2010)
5. Chakrabarti, K., Chaudhuri, S., Hwang, S.-W.: Automatic categorization of query results. In: Proceedings of the 2004 ACM SIGMOD International Conference on Management of Data, SIGMOD 2004, New York, NY, USA, pp. 755–766 (2004)
6. de Spindler, A., Leone, S., Geel, M., Norrie, M.C.: Using Tag Clouds to Promote Community Awareness in Research Environments. In: Luo, Y. (ed.) CDVE 2010. LNCS, vol. 6240, pp. 3–10. Springer, Heidelberg (2010)
7. Durao, F., Lage, R., Dolog, P., Coskun, N.: Exploring multi-factor tagging activity for personalized search. In: WEBIST 2011, Proceedings of the 7th International Conference on Web Information Systems and Technologies, The Netherlands, May 6-9 (2011)

8. Hernandez, M.-E., Falconer, S.M., Storey, M.-A., Carini, S., Sim, I.: Synchronized tag clouds for exploring semi-structured clinical trial data. In: Proceedings of the 2008 Conference of the Center for Advanced Studies on Collaborative Research: Meeting of Minds, CASCON 2008, pp. 4:42–4:56. ACM, New York (2008)

9. Koutrika, G., Zadeh, Z.M., Garcia-Molina, H.: Coursecloud: summarizing and refining keyword searches over structured data. In: Proceedings of the 12th International Conference on Extending Database Technology: Advances in Database Technology, EDBT 2009, pp. 1132–1135. ACM, New York (2009)

10. Kuo, B.Y.-L., Hentrich, T., Good, B.M., Wilkinson, M.D.: Tag clouds for summarizing web search results. In: Proceedings of the 16th International Conference on World Wide Web, WWW 2007, pp. 1203–1204. ACM, New York (2007)

11. Leone, S., Geel, M., Muller, C., Norrie, M.C.: Exploiting tag clouds for database browsing and querying. In: Aalst, W., Mylopoulos, J., Rosemann, M., Shaw, M.J., Szyperski, C., Soffer, P., Proper, E. (eds.) Information Systems Evolution. LNBIP, vol. 72, pp. 15–28. Springer, Heidelberg (2011)

12. Maslowska, I.: Phrase-Based Hierarchical Clustering of Web Search Results. In: Sebastiani, F. (ed.) ECIR 2003. LNCS, vol. 2633, pp. 555–562. Springer, Heidelberg (2003)

13. Nigam, K., McCallum, A.K., Thrun, S., Mitchell, T.: Text classification from labeled and unlabeled documents using em. Mach. Learn. 39, 103–134 (May 2000)

14. Rivadeneira, A.W., Gruen, D.M., Muller, M.J., Millen, D.R.: Getting our head in the clouds: toward evaluation studies of tagclouds. In: Proceedings of the SIGCHI Conference on Human Factors in Computing Systems, CHI 2007, pp. 995–998. ACM (2007)

15. Schrammel, J., Leitner, M., Tscheligi, M.: Semantically structured tag clouds: an empirical evaluation of clustered presentation approaches. In: Proceedings of the 27th International Conference on Human Factors in Computing Systems, CHI 2009, pp. 2037–2040. ACM (2009)

16. Sinclair, J., Cardew-Hall, M.: The folksonomy tag cloud: when is it useful? J. Inf. Sci. 34, 15–29 (2008)

17. Van Driessche, R., Roose, D.: An improved spectral bisection algorithm and its application to dynamic load balancing. Parallel Comput. 21, 29–48 (1995)

18. Venetis, P., Koutrika, G., Garcia-Molina, H.: On the selection of tags for tag clouds. In: Proceedings of the Fourth ACM International Conference on Web Search and Data Mining, WSDM 2011, pp. 835–844 (2011)

19. von Luxburg, U.: A tutorial on spectral clustering. Statistics and Computing 17, 395–416 (2007)

# Graph Access Pattern Diagrams (GAP-D): Towards a Unified Approach for Modeling Navigation over Hierarchical, Linear and Networked Structures

Matthias Keller and Martin Nussbaumer

Steinbuch Centre for Computing (SCC)
Karlsruhe Institute of Technology (KIT) D-76128 Karlsruhe, Germany
{Matthias.keller,martin.nussbaumer}@kit.edu

**Abstract.** In this paper we motivate the advantages of a unified, language-independent concept for describing and defining navigation systems based on underlying graph structures. We expect that such an approach will lower the effort for implementing navigation systems with application frameworks while increasing the configurability and reusability of navigation systems at the same time. It also allows adapting navigation components to new data sources easily. A visual notation called Graph Access Pattern Diagrams (GAP-Ds) is outlined and its expressivity is demonstrated by examples.

**Keywords:** Navigation Systems, Graphs, Content Organization.

## 1    Introduction

The non-scientific standard works on navigation design and Web information architecture (e.g. [1],[2] or [3]) distinguish between different basic types of content organization systems on the one hand and navigation systems build on top of it on the other hand. Organization systems define *relations* on content *items* on an abstract level. In contrast navigation systems provide *hyperlinks* between *pages* representing content items. The hyperlink structure differs from the content structure. In a hierarchical content structure e.g. the first level nodes and the third level nodes are not connected directly, but there will be a hyperlink from all third level pages to all first level pages in a global navigation system based on that hierarchy.

If the underlying organization system is modeled as graph, different navigation systems can be described by simple patterns (**Fig. 1**). For example a local navigation may render the hyperlinks to the page representing the parent item in the organization system and to all the children. The idea presented in this paper is to develop a formal notation for this kind of pattern. Our vision is a general, lightweight, application-independent concept for defining common navigation systems such as menus or navigation aids that are based on hierarchical, linear or networked content structures which can be modeled as graphs. According to [1] other forms of content organization are the database-model and social classification. The Web Engineering methods as WebML [4] or OOHDM [5] focus on the database-content-model and provide elaborated models for this purpose.

A. Harth and N. Koch (Eds.): ICWE 2011 Workshops, LNCS 7059, pp. 155–158, 2012.

We experienced that although the largest part of common navigation systems belong to one of a few types such as global, local, supplementary or courtesy navigation [2], there are a plethora of ways how navigation systems translate graphs into hyperlink structures. A navigation system implementing a hierarchy e.g. may always expand all levels or just the active level. Parent levels may be expanded or closed. Children may be visible permanently or only when the mouse pointer is moved over the parent element, etc.

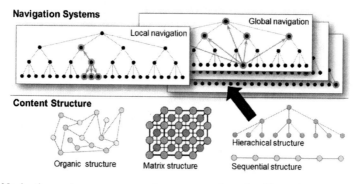

**Fig. 1.** Navigation systems as access patterns on top of graphs. Illustrations taken from [2].

We want to transform the intuitive concept of classifying navigation systems based on graphs into a small, simple and highly focused language. According to the idea of Domain-Specific Languages (DSLs) a Domain Interaction Model (DIM) as intuitive graphical notation is outlined in this paper [6].

Web application frameworks such as content management systems usually include components implementing the basic types of Web navigation on top of structures that can be modeled as graphs, e.g. folder-like structures (hierarchical graphs) or lists. A problem is that the navigation components provided, their behavior, the extent of configurability and the way they can be configured depends on the application.

## 2     Benefits

The proposed approach separates three common layers: The data layer, the navigation layer and the presentation layer. The data layer provides an abstraction for modeling the content organization as a graph with two types of relations. The *navigation layer* defines the hyperlink structure with GAP-Ds that is rendered by a processor e.g. in the form of nested lists. The presentation layer consists of presentation templates that guarantee a consistent visualization of all possible results.

We expect benefits for all three layers: On the data layer the graph model is an abstraction that allows adapting new data sources more easily. On the navigation layer GAP-Ds complement the concept of HCI interaction patterns [7] by a formal method for describing the behavior of navigation systems in detail. The current lack of such a method may be a reason for the low consensus on identified interaction patterns compared to software engineering design patterns that can be described by UML. GAP-Ds allow specifying navigation systems in corporate design style guides precisely and extending the configurability of navigation systems in application frameworks. GAP-Ds reduce the effort of implementing navigation systems. GAP-Ds can be reused and shared beyond the scope an application or framework. Considering GAP-Ds also makes presentation templates more universal and allows combining them with a broader range of navigation systems.

## 3    Outline of a Notation for GAP-Ds

In this section we outline the basic elements (**Fig. 2**) of a notation for GAP-Ds that we are discussing at the moment and demonstrate their expressivity by examples. Since in the proposed approach navigation systems are modeled with GAP-Ds on top of graphs, a notation for describing them is the foundation.

**Fig. 2.** GAP-D notation

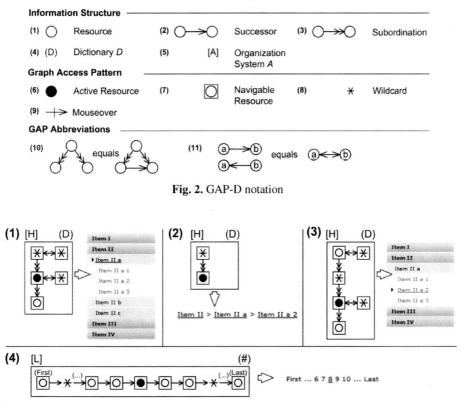

**Fig. 3.** GAP-D examples for a hierarchical organization system [H] and a linear organization system [L]: (1) All levels are expanded; (2) Active reference / breadcrumb; (3) First and current level and all ancestors and children are expanded (4) Paging

We propose to model organization systems as a graph with resources (1) as nodes and two types of edges, one representing succession (2) and the other representing subordination (3). When modeling hierarchies with the subordination relation, siblings are always considered as successors too (10). A graph representing an organization system can be named and referred by [*name*] (5). The model also contains dictionaries that associate names with resources (4). This allows using different labels for the same resource depending on the navigation system. GAP-Ds describe the navigation options depending on the active resource (6). The content relations are used to select neighbored resources. E.g. with the subordination symbol (3) all children of the active resource can be selected. A square indicates that that a hyperlink to a resource is displayed (7). A wildcard symbol models repetition (8). A line crossing a relation symbol (9) indicates a mouseover-effect. Finally an abbreviation for modeling bi-directional relations seems useful (11). The examples in **Fig. 3** illustrate the expressivity of these few elements.

# 4　　Discussion and Ongoing Work

Before developing tools, we want to include the feedback from the community in our considerations. We are also planning to analyze selected Web sites in order to evaluate which percentage of navigation systems can be described with GAP-Ds and how the notation can be extended while keeping the balance between simplicity and expressivity. It should be evaluated how quick developers can adopt and use the concept. Implementing a GAP-D editor and developing application-specific Solution Building Blocks [6] that are able to process GAP-Ds would be the next steps.

# References

1. Morville, P.: Information architecture for the World Wide Web. O'Reilly, Sebastopol (2007)
2. Garrett, J.: The elements of user experience: user-centered design for the web. American Institute of Graphic Arts, New Riders (2003)
3. Kalbach, J.: Designing Web navigation. O'Reilly, Beijing (2007)
4. Ceri, S., Fraternali, P., Bongio, A., Brambilla, M., Comai, S., Matera, M.: Designing Data-Intensive Web Applications. Morgan Kaufmann Publishers Inc. (2002)
5. Schwabe, D., Rossi, G., Barbosa, S.D.J.: Systematic hypermedia application design with OOHDM. In: Proceedings of the the Seventh ACM Conference on Hypertext, pp. 116–128. ACM, Bethesda (1996)
6. Nussbaumer, M., Freudenstein, P., Gaedke, M.: The Impact of Domain-Specific Languages for Assembling Web Applications. The Journal Engineering Letters 13, 387–396 (2006)
7. Kruschitz, C., Hitz, M.: Analyzing the HCI Design Pattern Variety. In: Proceedings of AsianPLoP 2010 (2010)

# Data-Driven and User-Driven Multidimensional Data Visualization[*]

Rober Morales-Chaparro, Juan C. Preciado, and Fernando Sánchez-Figueroa

Quercus Software Engineering Group, Universidad de Extremadura
{robermorales,jcpreciado,fernando}@unex.es

**Abstract.** Data Visualization on the Web is one of the main pillars for understanding the information coming from Business Intelligence based systems. However, the variety of data sources and devices together with the multidimensional nature of data and the continuous evolution of requirements is making this discipline more complicated as well as passionate. This paper outlines a process for obtaining a multidimensional data visualization driven by both, the data and the user, providing an automatic code generation. While the designer is automatically provided with a wide range of possible visualizations for a given data set, the user can change the visualization in several ways: the dominant dimension, the kind of visualization and the data set itself by adding, removing or grouping variables.

**Keywords:** Data Visualization, Web Engineering, Business Intelligence.

## 1 Introduction

Data Visualization is becoming more and more important in Web applications for Business Intelligence. Not only is important extracting the relevant information for the company but also showing it in the appropriate way. Company managers want to see their business' situation in a quick and easy way, in order to make decisions correctly, efficiently and on-time.

Different Data Visualization techniques are being widely used for this purpose [Bro08, TSD10]. Their interactive nature enables users to explore patterns, test hypotheses, discover exceptions, and explain what they find to others [Rob08].

These techniques have proven to be useful when the requirements do not change over time. However, for those applications with evolving requirements, this kind of systems generates a growing dissonance between what the users want to know, and what the application can show. Step by step, original requirements differ more and more from the actual necessities.

Under this situation, company managers have two options: managing more than one application and/or document to take decisions or contacting again the software company that developed the application to adapt it to the new requirements. The former has the problem of being an error-prone and tedious task, while the latter has the risk of not providing the information on-time for the company purposes.

---

[*] This work has been developed under the Spanish Contract MIGRARIA - TIN2011-27340 funded by Ministerio de Ciencia e Innovación.

A. Harth and N. Koch (Eds.): ICWE 2011 Workshops, LNCS 7059, pp. 159–166, 2012.

If the users know exactly how to see the information, why not letting them to drive and customize the presentation just to obtain the information in the most appropriate way? Several authors have identified this challenge as "interdisciplinary collaboration": there should be a communicative balance between visualization masters and application domain experts [KEM07]. So, it is time for user-driven visualization on the Web.

However, the variety of current data sources (query languages, APIs, etc.) together with the plethora of different devices for visualization and the ultimate practices coming from social applications for tagging information, are making data visualization on the Web even more challenging. The existence of semantic and/or contextual information around data is very useful for visualization purposes [Ber67]. This fact opens the opportunity to reason about data, bringing the possibility of automating Data Visualization. So, it is time for data-driven and user-driven visualization on the Web.

When combining several kinds of data, the visualization can be different depending on the dominant dimension (i.e. it is not the same showing the "hair color of some people", that showing "number of people with a certain hair color"). From a user-driven point of view, it would be interesting to play with different visualizations for the same set of data or even changing the dominant dimension just to find the information he is interested in. Under this multidimensional nature of data, we can say it is time for data-driven and user-driven multidimensional visualization on the Web.

Precisely, the main contribution of this paper is presenting a data-driven and user-driven process to visualize multidimensional data on the Web. The main benefits of the proposal are twofold. On the one hand, the possibility for the designer to reuse one visualization among different applications; on the other hand, the possibility for the user (and the designer) to have automatically more than one visualization for the same data set. Far from giving details, this paper outlines the whole process we are following in our research.

The rest of the paper is organized as follows. Section 2 introduces a motivating example while Section 3 presents the process. Finally, Section 4 outlines conclusions and related works.

## 2    Motivating Example

The restaurants manager of an international airport has a visualization software solution that shows up important data to her. The dashboard shown in Figure 1 summarizes data about time and target country of departures.

This solution fit well her needs in the past. However, now she wants to change the thematic of the airport restaurants, to be of cultures around the world: the menu at a given time will depend on the nationality of most of the passengers in the airport at that time. So it is needed to obtain which countries are the destinations/origins of most flights at different moments of the day. Desirably, she would be able to query the system, and the system able to answer.

From the system point of view: there are neither new data nor new casuistry among them or new actors. In addition, from the manager point of view: she knows better than everyone around the world how is the new visualization she needs. Despite this, her visualization software is not able to show her the data in the appropriate way. She needs a system that i) knows very well the nature of the data, ii) offers the possibility of choosing between different visualizations, playing with the number of items to be showed and the dominant dimension that drives the visualization.

Such a system is briefly introduced in next section. This system should be able to automatically show the dashboard of Figure 2.

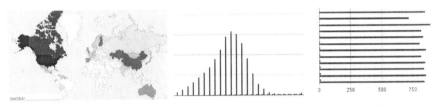

**Fig. 1.** Original dashboard. Left: average departures by target country. Center: average departures by hour. Right: average departures by month.

**Fig. 2.** Desired dashboard. At 9am and 3pm, frequency by target country.

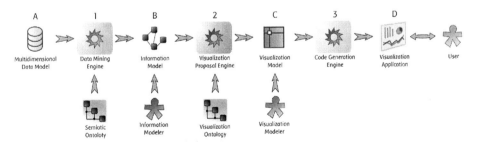

**Fig. 3.** Sequential steps of the process, from the data to the user

## 3    Proposal

The process is divided into three main sub-engines: data mining, visualization proposal and code generation (Figure 3). Next we briefly explain the whole process.

## 3.1   Data-Driven Concerns and the Multidimensional Challenge

Dimensions are the attributes of every object from the data set (i.e. name, age, gender,...), or the aggregations of attributes (i.e. average age, distinct name, count, etc.). Together with the name, their semantic annotations include (a) the type, (b) the range if applicable, (c) the relevance, (d) the relationship with other dimensions and (e) the organizational level (roughly: qualitative $\subset$ ordinal $\subset$ quantitative) [Ber67].

Each visualization has two parts. The first is constrained by the dominant dimension, which is usually mapped with the 2D position of the objects, i.e. used as the axis. The second is the selection of visual variables (mainly: color, intensity, size, orientation, grain and shape). Their accuracy for human perception is very well documented [CM84]. This part is usually summarized in a legend.

The "data mining engine" (Figure 3-1) is the entry point of the process. Its goal is to propose visualizations with the maximum utility and accuracy of perception. The utility is the capacity of showing the snapshot of the data that reveals potential non-obvious patterns. The accuracy of perception is about choosing the visual variables that best represents the selected attributes. To get these two goals, it automates every concern inferable from the multidimensional data. The input of the engine is a "data model" with semantic annotations (Figure 3-A). The output is an "information model", which stores all the decisions taken in the phase (Figure 3-B).

This phase is supported by a semiotic ontology, which contains the rating between the semantic markup of the dimensions and the visual variables, i.e., it stores that a quantitative dimension fits well with size but not with color.

The first task of the phase is building the most relevant perspectives: 1. Which is the dominant dimension of the data?   2. Which are the most relevant dimensions (which potentially will reveal patterns or trends)? and 3. Is it suitable to make groups, filters or annotations, to see the data better?

Then, it tentatively performs the matching of dimensions with visual variables: 1. Taking into account the dominant dimension: what is the best disposition of the object set? 2. For each output dimension: what visual properties do fit better? 3. Seeing the size of the dataset: is it needed managing filters, or perhaps the focus and the context?

In our motivating example, the input of the engine is the data model in Figure 4. Table 1 shows the first stage: the relevant perspectives that the system has found based on the data mining analysis of the data model. Table 2 represents the second task of the phase: the best visual variables for the dimensions of those perspectives. The decision takes into account, mainly, their organizational level as scored in the ontology (not shown). After that, the data-driven phase ends with an "information model": the composition of tables 1 and 2 (not shown).

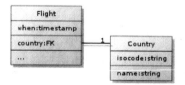

**Fig. 4.** Annotated data model

**Table 1.** Proposed perspectives

| Perspective | Dimensions | | |
| | dominant | outputs | group |
| --- | --- | --- | --- |
| Flights by hour | When | Count | Hour |
| Flights by month | When | Count | Month |
| Flights by country | Country | Count | Hour |

**Table 2.** Map between attributes and visual variables

| Dimensions | → | Organizatio nal level | → | Variables |
| --- | --- | --- | --- | --- |
| Count | | Qualitative | | Intensity, size |
| When | | Ordinal | | Hor. Axis |
| Country | | Qualitative | | map |

## 3.2    Model-Driven Flow

At this stage, the modeler has the option of improving the skeleton of the "information model". After this optional refinement, a "visualization proposal engine" selects the best patterns to display the perspectives (Figure 3-2).

Patterns are the formalization of a reusable graphical representation. The suitable patterns and their requirements are stored in the visualization ontology. For instance, one pattern is the "bar chart", which can be used for lots of different data sets, as long as the structure required for its usage is very common. While the input of the phase is the "information model", the output is a skeleton of a "visualization model" (Figure 3-C). Over that, the modeler can change the patterns and edit their preferences.

In our example, it is easy to see what the ontology will propose, seeing the output scoring at table 3: 1. Flights by hour → Bar chart; 2. Flights by month → Bar chart; 3. Flights by country → Intensity map.

Two facts must be observed: on the one hand, how the pattern "bar chart" can be used more than once. On the other hand, there is more than one pattern that could fit well for a given perspective; these are precisely two of the main benefits outlined in Section 1.

**Table 3.** Scoring of some patterns about displaying the indicated perspectives

| | bar chart | column chart | line chart | pie chart | heat map | time line | ⋮ |
| --- | --- | --- | --- | --- | --- | --- | --- |
| flights by hour | **0.8** | 0.7 | 0.5 | 0.4 | 0.0 | 0.3 | … |
| flights by month | **0.8** | 0.7 | 0.5 | 0.4 | 0.0 | 0.3 | … |
| flights by country | 0.5 | 0.4 | 0.0 | 0.3 | **0.9** | 0.0 | … |

The "code generation engine" (Figure 3-3) is intended to generate the runtime code for the system, using all the information previously collected. This is done by model transformations. It uses the "visualization model" as input, and outputs the final code of the application. Previous studies [JJK08] shows up the fact that web-native display technologies (HTML5, SVG, etc.) have the potential to expand the impact of visualization in some cases. So, we use them for the final code.

## 3.3    User Experience

Using the formal storage provided by ontologies, and, also, the formal representation of models, the proposed framework can now allow the user: a) maintaining the visualization patterns, editing their preferences (color, disposition, etc.) b) moving (maintaining the dominant dimension) from one visualization pattern to another, if the current one does not fit well with her interests. Afterwards, she optionally can perform a). c) changing the dominant dimension to get a new perspective, and then optionally b) and a). d) changing the dataset she wants (probably editing the filter), and then optionally c), b) and a).

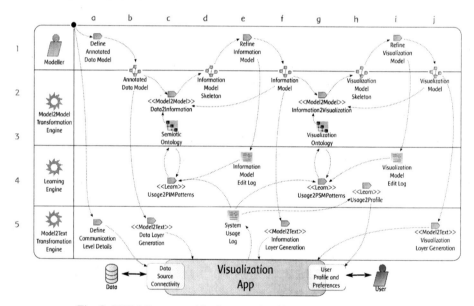

**Fig. 5.** SPEM diagram, with phases and artifacts of the methodology

Now, the example of the airport should be revisited from this perspective. Suppose that the user chooses the interaction referred as c). As expressed in the initial example: she wants to see "flights by hour and country". Then, the "data mining engine" finds new visual metaphors for the new dimensions and the "visualization proposal engine" searches for visualization patterns that best ranks the new combination. The user finally ends with the desired dashboard, like the one shown in Figure 2. A running demo of the motivation example can be seen at http://visualligence.com/airport_gv/. Although it has been manually developed, follows the process in order to show the viability and the possibility of automation.

### 3.4   SPEM Representation

The different parts of the proposal have been formalized in a SPEM representation (Figure 5). From row 1 to 3 it can be observed the correlation with the diagram in Figure 3. On row 5 there is the correspondence with the "code generation engine". The figure also reveals a learning process from selections performed by both, the designer and the user (row 4). The more frequent a pattern is selected, the more probably it will be automatically suggested for similar problems in the future. Also, it is useful storing those selections in the users' profile: so the system can adapt better to their preferences.

## 4     Conclusions and Related Work

This paper has presented a data-driven and user-driven approach for visualizing multidimensional data on the Web. Far from giving details, the paper has outlined the whole process with all its phases. This process is being integrated in RUX [LPSF07], a tool aimed to model advanced user interfaces. This integration is not over yet.

Table 4 shows some related works. Different features have been considered for them (user-driven, data-driven, model-driven, multidimensional, tool available and Web oriented). Although there are relevant works such as [BBC+11], to our knowledge there is not an existing approach considering all these issues.

**Table 4.** Summary of related proposals

|            | User | Data | MDE | High-dim | Tool | Web |
|------------|:----:|:----:|:---:|:--------:|:----:|:---:|
| [MLG+10]   | ✓    | ✓    |     |          | ✓    |     |
| [The03]    | ✓    |      |     | ✓        | ✓    |     |
| [BSL+01]   | ✓    |      |     | ✓        | ✓    |     |
| [SCB98]    | ✓    |      |     | ✓        | ✓    |     |
| [FPSSO96]  |      | ✓    |     | ✓        | ✓    |     |
| [Mac86]    |      | ✓    |     | ✓        | ✓    |     |
| [SH00]     | ✓    |      |     | ✓        | ✓    |     |
| [BBC+11]   |      | ✓    | ✓   | ✓        | ✓    | ✓   |
| Our proposal | ✓  | ✓    | ✓   | ✓        | ✓    | ✓   |

## References

[BBC+11]  Bozzon, A., Brambilla, M., Catarci, T., Ceri, S., Fraternali, P., Matera, M.: Visualization of Multi-domain Ranked Data. In: Search Computing, pp. 53–69 (2011)

[Ber67]   Bertin, J.: Semiologie Graphique: Les Diagrammes, Les Reseaux, Les Cartes (1967)

[Bro08]   Brooks, M.G.: The Business Case for Advanced Data Visualization (2008)

[BSL+01]  Buja, A., Swayne, D.F., Littman, M., Dean, N., Hofmann, H.: XGvis: Interactive data visualization with multidimensional scaling. Journal of Computational and Graphical Statistics, 1061–8600 (2001)

[CM84]  Cleveland, W.S., McGill, R.: Graphical perception: Theory, experimentation, and application to the development of graphical methods. Journal of the American Statistical Association 79(387), 531–554 (1984)

[FPSSO96]  Fayyad, U., Piatetsky-Shapiro, G., Smyth, P., et al.: Knowledge discovery and data mining: Towards a unifying framework. In: Proc. 2nd Int. Conf. on Knowledge Discovery and Data Mining, Portland, OR, pp. 82–88 (1996)

[JJK08]  Johnson, D.W., Jankun-Kelly, T.J.: A scalability study of web-native information visualization. In: Proceedings of Graphics Interface 2008, pp. 163–168. Canadian Information Processing Society (2008)

[KEM07]  Kerren, A., Ebert, A., Meyer, J.: Human-Centered Visualization Environments. Springer, Heidelberg (2007)

[LPSF07]  Linaje, M., Preciado, J.C., Sánchez-Figueroa, F.: Engineering Rich Internet Application User Interfaces over Legacy Web Models. IEEE Internet Computing 11(6), 53–59 (2007)

[Mac86]  Mackinlay, J.: Automating the design of graphical presentations of relational information. ACM Transactions on Graphics 5(2), 110–141 (1986)

[MLG+10]  Matković, K., Lež, A., Gračanin, D., Ammer, A., Purgathofer, W.: Event Line View: Interactive Visual Analysis of Irregular Time-Dependent Data. In: Taylor, R., Boulanger, P., Krüger, A., Olivier, P. (eds.) Smart Graphics. LNCS, vol. 6133, pp. 208–219. Springer, Heidelberg (2010)

[Rob08]  Roberts, J.C.: The Craft of Information Visualization (January 2008)

[SCB98]  Swayne, D.F., Cook, D., Buja, A.: XGobi: Interactive Dynamic Data Visualization in the X Window System. Journal of Computational and Graphical Statistics 7(1), 113 (1998)

[SH00]  Stolte, C., Hanrahan, P.: Polaris: a system for query, analysis and visualization of multi-dimensional relational databases. In: Proceedings of IEEE Symposium on Information Visualization 2000, INFOVIS 2000, pp. 5–14 (2000)

[The03]  Theus, M.: Interactive data visualization using mondrian. Journal of Statistical Software 7(11), 1–9 (2003)

[TSD10]  Turban, E., Sharda, R., Delen, D.: Decision support and business intelligence systems. Prentice Hall Press, Upper Saddle River (2010)

# Context-Aware and Adaptive Web Interfaces:
# A Crowdsourcing Approach

Michael Nebeling and Moira C. Norrie

Institute of Information Systems, ETH Zurich
CH-8092 Zurich, Switzerland
{nebeling,norrie}@inf.ethz.ch

**Abstract.** Web site providers currently have to deal with the growing range and increased diversity of devices used for web browsing. It is not only technically challenging to provide flexible interfaces able to adapt to the large variety of viewing situations, but also costly. We discuss the idea and challenges of adopting a crowdsourcing model in which end-users can participate in the adaptation process with the goal of enabling a much wider range of use contexts to which applications can adapt.

## 1 Introduction

Nowadays, web-based services are accessed from a wide range of devices with very different characteristics, not only in terms of screen size and resolution, but also supported input and output modalities. It is becoming increasingly difficult and also cost intensive for web site providers to cater for the large variety of client devices used today. We believe that the only feasible way to address this challenge is to adopt a crowdsourcing model in which end-users can become involved in the adaptation of web interfaces for different devices and preferences. To achieve this, we have started to address the technical challenges of designing a model, architecture, language and runtime system capable of supporting the dynamic definition and deployment of web site adaptations in a safe and efficient manner [1]. In this paper, we focus on the crowdsourcing principles underlying the approach and discuss how they relate to previous research on context-aware and adaptive interfaces and the many new forms of human computation [2].

We start by discussing different approaches to adaptation in Sect. 2. We then characterise our crowdsourcing approach in Sect. 3 and discuss how we aim to improve user participation, quality control and aggregation of contributions. Finally, Sect. 4 outlines remaining challenges and our ongoing research efforts.

## 2 Adaptation Approaches

In a recent study, we have shown that the majority of web sites today still use a fixed layout designed for a resolution of 1024x768 pixels despite the fact that average screen settings are much higher than that [3]. Rather than thinking of more flexible layout solutions, a number of web sites nowadays come in several

A. Harth and N. Koch (Eds.): ICWE 2011 Workshops, LNCS 7059, pp. 167–170, 2012.

special versions. However, the employed adaptations are typically designed for only a certain class of devices, e.g. for touchphones or tablets. The same is true for most of the advanced algorithms that promote automatic adaptation techniques, as these typically require substantial server-side processing [4], or only work for very specific scenarios, e.g. desktop-to-mobile adaptation [5]. The new approach for devices such as the iPhone or iPad is to provide special browser support, e.g. by enabling gestures for zooming and automatic scaling of the viewport, but this means that the problem is treated as a matter of input technique rather than an interface design issue and also requires user intervention.

Research in web engineering has focused on languages and model-driven approaches to support context-awareness and adaptivity in applications [6,7]. A second stream of research has looked at different abstraction levels of the user interface to be able to adapt to multiple user, platform and environment contexts [8]. The authoring of adaptive and multi-modal user interfaces has also been the subject of extensive research [9]. The suggested development processes typically start from some kind of domain or task model and logical descriptions of the interface. This is then followed by subsequent transformation steps to generate the final interface for a particular context of use. However, all these approaches rely on developers to specify the required forms of adaptation, which is almost impossible with the diverse and rapidly evolving range of settings.

Our new idea was to adopt a crowdsourcing model in which system developers provide an initial interface and adaptive features of the system can evolve at runtime with the help of users [1]. A number of interesting systems have been built to demonstrate the potential benefits of using crowdsourcing techniques. For example, Soylent [10] is an extension of Microsoft Word that allows users to create tasks related to the document, such as shortening of paragraphs or proof-reading, to be carried out by other users. Another useful system is HelpMeOut [11] which recommends potential solutions for compiler errors and runtime exceptions that other programmers have also encountered. While many crowdsourcing solutions tend to build on external services such as Amazon's Mechanical Turk[1], our goal was to *embed* crowdsourcing mechanisms into applications in order to provide end-users with the tools to collectively solve problems such as the lack of adaptivity. To achieve this, we first had to develop visual tools for end-users to be able to design new adaptations directly in the browser and then extend the common web application architecture with several components so that adaptations can also be shared between users and even across sites (Fig. 1). Popular examples of crowdsourcing platforms with somewhat similar goals are programmableweb.com and userscripts.org, where already large communities of active users maintain shared collections of web mashups and augmentations.

## 3   Crowdsourcing Approach

For a characterisation of our approach, we will use the taxonomy proposed by Quinn and Bederson [2].

---

[1] http://mturk.com

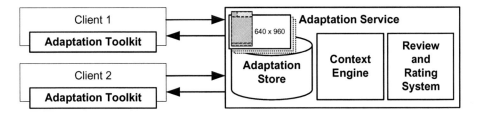

**Fig. 1.** Architecture showing two clients that contribute and consume web site adaptations for small-screen devices using the adaptation operations provided by the toolkit and server-side components for sharing and deployment of crowdsourced adaptations

*Motivation.* User motivation and participation can depend on many factors. Our intention was to provide end-users with simple, visual tools for customising directly the final interface according to the viewing situation without the need to understand the underlying languages or models. This makes it easy also for non-technical users. We expect a major effect on motivation by letting users see that the interface can improve through their actions and, similar to [12], by letting them know that other users can so benefit as well. Also, what to them may seem like a *personalisation* of the interface will in fact describe an *adaptation* for a particular use context when it is shared with the crowd. Even if only a few users share the adaptations created on their devices, then already many others using the same devices can directly benefit. Along the lines of Quinn and Bederson, this would mean that motivation in our approach is primarily guided by *implicit work* and a very light form of *altruism*.

*Quality.* In our crowdsourcing model where the viewing quality of a web site is primarily regulated by end-users, quality control may involve a number of schemes where we have given the highest priority to *defensive task design*. The main idea was to provide adaptation operations concerning only those aspects of the design that are directly related to the viewing context, such as size and position of web site elements, rather than content or functionality [1]. To increase the quality of adaptation scenarios, we capture precisely the context in which the adaptation process takes place by collecting all kinds of context information related to the device and the user. Finally, the recommender system used by our platform to determine the best-matching adaptations for a given context is complemented by a review and rating system. This enables *multilevel review* and a *reputation system* corresponding to [2], where system administrators, or promoted users, have a bigger say so that their approval or rejection have significant impact on the ranking and therefore the deployment of adaptations.

*Aggregation.* Also important for our crowdsourcing approach is the the idea of *iterative improvement*. Depending on the individual viewing situation and the current quality of adaptations, participating users may come up with whole new designs or only provide minor improvements over the original layout or other user-adapted versions. We support this by building on an adaptation technique that uses cascading stylesheet definitions and server-side components that are capable of managing different versions of adaptations for the same context [1].

# 4   Conclusion

Given the large variety of devices used for web browsing, we have started to explore a crowdsourcing approach to support web site providers in the design of flexible interfaces and to enable a much wider range of use contexts to which applications can adapt. As a first step, we developed a platform and visual toolkit for crowdsourced adaptations of web interfaces, which we discussed in this paper. We are currently carrying out extensive technical evaluations of this approach when it is applied to a number of existing web sites and used by a larger group of users. In particular, we are experimenting with different sharing and ranking modes for the controlled definition and deployment of new adaptations. This is important for cases when really a crowd of users contribute with web site adaptations and several different sets of adaptations have been defined for the same or similar contexts. The data we are collecting can provide interesting insight into adaptation requirements, help us improve both the underlying methods and the overall crowdsourcing approach and potentially lead to new web design patterns and guidelines for the wide variety of devices and platforms available today.

# References

1. Nebeling, M., Norrie, M.C.: Tools and Architectural Support for Crowdsourced Adaptation of Web Interfaces. In: Auer, S., Díaz, O., Papadopoulos, G.A. (eds.) ICWE 2011. LNCS, vol. 6757, pp. 243–257. Springer, Heidelberg (2011)
2. Quinn, A.J., Bederson, B.B.: Human Computation: A Survey and Taxonomy of a Growing Field. In: Proc. CHI (2011)
3. Nebeling, M., Matulic, F., Norrie, M.C.: Metrics for the Evaluation of News Site Content Layout in Large-Screen Contexts. In: Proc. CHI (2011)
4. Schrier, E., Dontcheva, M., Jacobs, C., Wade, G., Salesin, D.: Adaptive Layout for Dynamically Aggregated Documents. In: Proc. IUI (2008)
5. Hattori, G., Hoashi, K., Matsumoto, K., Sugaya, F.: Robust Web Page Segmentation for Mobile Terminal Using Content-Distances and Page Layout Information. In: Proc. WWW (2007)
6. Ceri, S., Daniel, F., Matera, M., Facca, F.M.: Model-driven Development of Context-Aware Web Applications. TOIT 7(1) (2007)
7. Frăsincar, F., Houben, G.J., Barna, P.: Hypermedia presentation generation in Hera. IS 35(1) (2010)
8. Calvary, G., Coutaz, J., Thevenin, D., Limbourg, Q., Bouillon, L., Vanderdonckt, J.: A Unifying Reference Framework for Multi- Target User Interfaces. IWC 15 (2003)
9. Paternò, F., Santoro, C., Mäntyjärvi, J., Mori, G., Sansone, S.: Authoring pervasive multimodal user interfaces. IJWET 4(2) (2008)
10. Bernstein, M.S., Little, G., Miller, R.C., Hartmann, B., Ackerman, M.S., Karger, D.R., Crowell, D., Panovich, K.: Soylent: A Word Processor with a Crowd Inside. In: Proc. UIST (2010)
11. Hartmann, B., MacDougall, D., Brandt, J., Klemmer, S.R.: What Would Other Programmers Do? Suggesting Solutions to Error Messages. In: Proc. CHI (2010)
12. Rashid, A.M., Ling, K.S., Tassone, R.D., Resnick, P., Kraut, R.E., Riedl, J.: Motivating Participation by Displaying the Value of Contribution. In: Proc. CHI (2006)

# Massive Multiplayer Human Computation for Fun, Money, and Survival

Lukas Biewald

CrowdFlower
3265 17th Street, Suite 302
San Francisco, CA 94110
lukas@crowdflower.com

**Abstract.** Crowdsourcing is an effective tool to solve hard tasks. By bringing 100,000s of people to work on simple tasks that only humans can do, we can go far beyond traditional models of data analysis and machine learning. As technologies and processes mature, crowdsourcing is becoming mainstream. It powers many leading Internet companies and a wide variety of novel projects: from content moderation and business listing verification to real-time SMS translation for disaster response. However, quality assurance can be a major challenge. In this paper CrowdFlower presents various crowdsourcing applications, from business to ethics, to money and survival, all of which showcase the power of labor-on-demand, otherwise known as the human cloud.

**Keywords:** Crowdsourcing, quality, democracy, data, labor, human.

## 1 Introduction

Before the Internet enabled human beings to connect as they do now, collecting large-scale datasets that require human computation was a time-consuming and expensive process. At CrowdFlower[2], we produce new datasets on-demand by routing tasks to large groups of distributed workers who work simultaneously. We see people collecting creative and innovative datasets for businesses, for fun, and even to improve the lives of others.

Topics of study in disciplines that focus on quantitative or technical data, like machine-learning research, have always been limited by the availability of datasets. For example, the Brown Corpus is a dataset compiled in the 1960s that has served as the basis for thousands of linguistics studies. It has been exhaustively parsed and tabbed. Graduate students would center entire research plans on the availability of previously collected data, and as a result, generations of papers on word disambiguation were tailored to the constraints of old data.

Crowdsourcing democratizes the data-collection process, cutting researchers' reliance on stagnant, over-used datasets. Now, anyone can gather data overnight rather than waiting years. However, some of the data collection may be sloppy. CrowdFlower addresses this issue by building robust quality-control mechanisms in order to standardize the results that come back from the crowd. The type of crowd, task design, and

A. Harth and N. Koch (Eds.): ICWE 2011 Workshops, LNCS 7059, pp. 171–176, 2012.

quality control tactics all affect the quality of the data. The important thing to remember is that crowdsourcing provides channels that allow researchers, businesses, or even armchair social scientists to gather data  having high quality data obviously affects the accuracy of the research.

The first time I used Amazon's Mechanical Turk[1] was at a search-engine startup, Powerset[6] (later acquired by Microsoft). I used Mechanical Turk to compare the quality of our search-relevancy algorithm against Yahoo! and Google. Initially, I thought it would be necessary to hire a team of people to compare the quality of results every day over the course of months. Instead, I set up an experimental task with no quality control, put in about $50, and let it run overnight. The data that came back was noisy, but I was able to find meaningful differences between the search engines.

The following examples showcase the role that crowdsourcing plays in data collection. Many of these are featured on our blog, and we often post new datasets and projects. We invite researchers to post new experiments on our site.

## 2   Crowdsourcing Applications

### 2.1   Ethics

Crowds can be used to source answers to philosophical questions. Stalin said, "A single death is a tragedy; a million deaths is a statistic." So what about 100 deaths? What about five? We tested this experimentally by asking people on Amazon Mechanical Turk to participate in the classic philosophical conundrum "The Trolley Problem,"[8] in which a person must decide whether to sacrifice one person in order to save several others.

The three sample scenarios are below. Here, the scenarios refer to saving five people, but we varied the number of people saved between 1 and 1,000 to see if it would affect the results.

Scenario A. A trolley is running out of control down a track. In its path are five people who have been tied to the track. Fortunately, you can flip a switch, which will lead the trolley down a different track to safety. Unfortunately, there is a single person tied to that track. Should you flip the switch?

Scenario B. As before, a trolley is hurtling down a track toward five people. You are on a bridge under which it will pass, and you can stop it if you drop something heavy in its way. As it happens, there is a very fat man next to youyour only way to stop the trolley is to push him over the bridge and onto the track, killing him to save five. Should you proceed?

Scenario C. A brilliant transplant surgeon has five patients, each in need of a different organ, each of whom will die without that organ. Unfortunately, there are no organs available to perform any of these five transplant operations. A healthy young traveler, just passing through the city the doctor works in, comes in for a routine checkup. In the course of doing the checkup, the doctor discovers that his organs are compatible with all five of his dying patients. Suppose further that if the young man were to disappear, no one would suspect the doctor. Should the doctor sacrifice the man to save his other patients?

How does our decision change based on the number of people who will die? The results were unexpected. For all three scenarios, subjects were increasingly willing to

**Decision Frequency**

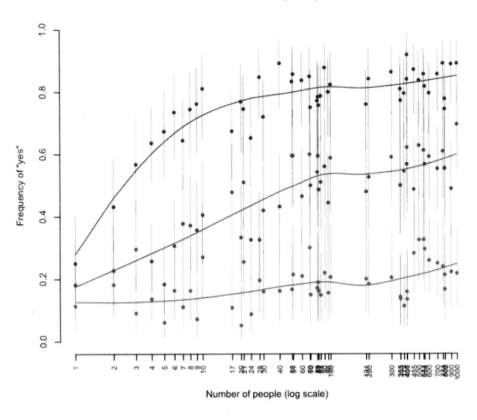

Number of people (log scale)

**Fig. 1.** Willingness to sacrifice a life

kill one person when it meant saving up to 100 people, but this willingness dipped when it meant saving between 100 and 200 people, and began to rise again when more than 200 people could be saved.

Each scenario also affected subjects' ethical calculus. Subjects were more willing to sacrifice a life when they controlled the trolley switch (Scenario A) than when someone else (i.e., the surgeon in Scenario C) acted as executioner (see Figure 1). By putting this experiment out to the crowd, we were able to gather responses from more than 100 subjects in a matter of hours[3].

## 2.2   Business

CrowdFlower provides a way for businesses to complete large tasks by giving them access to tens of thousands or hundreds of thousands of workers. By layering our technology across multiple labor channels, CrowdFlower enables access to a large sample of people. This means businesses can connect to a labor force in the cloud depending on their needs.

Just as cloud computing eliminated the need for businesses to predict how many servers they were going to need at any given time, crowdsourced labor eliminates the need for businesses to predict how many people they're going to need at any given minute. The quality-control algorithms we've developed ensure that workers are doing the tasks well, that they are trained when they make mistakes, and that they are removed if they are inefficient or spammy.

CrowdFlower has been able to assist clients in many ways, such as improving the accuracy of data for clients who publish business listings: e.g., business leader information (CEO and CFO names), contact information (phone, fax, and address), and company information (company name, description, and industry label).

In particular, our use of quality-controlled human intelligence excels at removing duplicate business listings that a computer program would gloss over. For example, a computer cannot say for certain whether the McDonald's restaurant in Manhattan and the McDonald's restaurant in New York City are the same place, but a person could do the additional research required to confirm whether the two restaurants are the same. In one instance, we improved the accuracy of a client's data by more than 20 percent.

## 2.3   The Greater Good

Crowdsourced data collection will continue to benefit businesses and revolutionize academic research. It can also benefit disenfranchised people by giving them access to dignified work.

For starters, the microtasks involved in crowdsourced labor mean that anyone anywhere can be productive, even if just for 10 minutes. They don't have to kill time playing solitaire at their computers or working on cross- words. Instead, they could be paid to do a job, earn virtual credits for an online game, or even give work to people in developing nations through a paired work program.

The developing world needs employment opportunities that crowdsourcing can provide by connecting women, youth, and refugees living in poverty to computer-based work. One of CrowdFlower's labor channels, Samasource[7], does just that.

CrowdFlower and Samasource created GiveWork[5], an iPhone app that allows users to support people in developing countries by completing short, on-screen tasks, which can either give a donation or an additional unit of work that is used for training purposes. People volunteer to tag a video or trace a road alongside someone who is learning computer skills. This is just the beginning for mobile-based crowdsourced labor.

Further, getting work to refugee populations is difficult whenever that work requires raw materials: e.g., building physical structures; but projects that require building information can move quickly and globally.

Crowdsourced labor has begun to level the playing field with respect to job access. This lends greater meritocracy to the job market: it is a natural extension of what the Internet has al- ready done, but rather than "who you know," the focus is on "what you know." Thus, a person in Berlin or Jakarta is not immediately ruled out of a job due geography.

## 2.4  Disaster Relief

Crowdsourcing also helps disaster relief efforts because disasters are, by definition, unpredictable, and relief requires a scalable workforce. The response to the Haitian earthquake in January 2010 demonstrated how a rapidly deployed workforce of far-flung volunteers can be critical to emergency relief efforts. After the quake, aid workers flooded Port-au-Prince, but they lacked information about who needed help, where the victims were, and what type of help they needed. FrontLineSMS[4] and the U.S. Department of State worked with Haitian telcom companies to set up an SMS short code, allowing Haitians to submit real-time reports using less bandwidth than the two-way audio that had caused system outages on the country's cell networks. The messages that came in were in Kryol and the aid agencies were unable to translate the messages fast enough.

CrowdFlower provided the infrastructure to route SMS texts to hundreds of thousands of Haitians (located by Samasource) who translated texts from Port-au-Prince in real time and categorized the victims' issues, allowing the agencies to direct specialists to the people who needed their services: e.g., getting potable water to thirsty people, routing doctors to injured people. Further, so that agencies could see hotspots, maps were created through Ushahidi[9], an open-source platform that allows people or organizations to collect and visualize information.

The rapid proliferation of broadband, wireless, and cell phone technology has revolutionized disaster relief efforts so that now, anyone with a computer or phone can provide assistance.

# 3  Conclusion

## 3.1  The Future of Democracy

What does the future look like for crowdsourcing, human computation, data exchange, and data transparency? When data is made widely available, it becomes widely analyzable, and through this process, crowdsourcing can empower us all.

# 4  Biography

Lukas Biewald is the CEO of CrowdFlower. Prior to co-founding CrowdFlower, he was a senior scientist and manager within the ranking and management team at Powerset, Inc., a natural language search technology company later acquired by Microsoft. Biewald has also led the search relevance team for Yahoo! Japan. He graduated from Stanford University with a BS in mathematics and an MS in computer science. He is an expert level Go player.

# References

1. Amazon Mechanical Turk, http://mturk.com
2. CrowdFlower, http://www.crowdflower.com

3. Crowdsourcing an Ethical Dilemma,
   http://blog.crowdflower.com/2009/01/crowdsourcing-ethics/
4. FrontLineSMS, http://www.frontlinesms.com
5. GiveWork,
   http://itunes.apple.com/us/app/give-work/id329928364?mt=8
6. Powerset, http://www.powerset.com
7. Samasource, http://www.samasource.org
8. The Trolley Problem,
   http://en.wikipedia.org/wiki/Trolley_problem
9. Ushahidi, http://www.ushahidi.com/

# Enterprise Crowdsourcing Solution for Software Development in an Outsourcing Organization

Ranganathan Jayakanthan and Deepak Sundararajan

TCS Innovation Labs – Web 2.0, Tata Consultancy Services, Chennai, India
jayakanthan@acm.org,deep.sun@tcs.com

**Abstract.** Enterprise Crowdsourcing has the potential to be a very powerful and disruptive paradigm for human resource deployment, project development and project management as we know them. This paper details ongoing work at TCS Innovation Labs – Web 2.0, Tata Consultancy Services, Chennai, India to develop an Enterprise Crowdsourcing Solution to tackle the various processes involved in the development of software by leveraging the untapped human resource in the organization. Large IT organizations have a lot of untapped manpower in the form of trainees, the bench strength and people involved in roles which do not fully employ their strengths in particular technologies they are experts in. This system aims to allow untapped talent to get access to challenging tasks part of other projects and work on them while providing a disruptive way to allocate resources in a conventional software development environment.

**Keywords:** Enterprise crowdsourcing, Crowdsourcing, Web 2.0, Collaborative work, Social networking.

## 1   Introduction

Jeff Howe's influential 2006 essay "The Rise of Crowdsourcing" starts off as, "Remember outsourcing? Sending jobs to India and China is so 2003. The new pool of cheap labor: everyday people using their spare cycles to create content, solve problems, even do corporate R & D." [1] This being 2011, outsourcing and crowdsourcing have both had tremendous growth in the meanwhile. This paper will look into an ongoing project to develop an enterprise crowdsourcing enabler for software development, inside a large outsourcing organization, attempting to fuse Howe's idea posited as an alternative to crowdsourcing, by subsuming it within the larger outsourcing paradigm. We have come full circle, in some sense!

### 1.1   Crowdsourcing

Howe presented developments in the 2006 essay [1] about how distributed, talented amateurs were disrupting the business models of established professionals through mechanisms which allowed them to reach out to potential employers and large business - buyers of their products and services, allowing them to provide previously inconceivable amounts of savings in terms of money as well as other resources. Since then, crowdsourcing has grown by leaps and bounds, transforming chimera like into various

A. Harth and N. Koch  (Eds.): ICWE 2011 Workshops, LNCS 7059, pp. 177–180, 2012.

avatars which result in radically different ways of looking at developing solutions to problems with enormous amounts of savings of resources with remarkable efficiencies achieved in attracting the right talent to work on the right problems.

## 1.2    Enterprise Crowdsourcing

Enterprise crowdsourcing posits the use of crowdsourcing in the enterprise to "access scalable workforce on-line." [2] Various organizations have succeeded at enterprise crowdsourcing by adopting various approaches. Organizations as diverse as GoldCorp and Proctor & Gamble have utilized crowdsourcing to attract the attention of external talent to tackle their hard problems. Enterprise crowdsourcing to attract talent from within the organization has mostly been restricted to uses such as knowledge sharing and idea generation.

In this paper we present an attempt inside a large outsourcing organization with 200,000 employees (and growing) to leverage untapped talent and target them towards software development subtasks. In our organization, as with many other such large outsourcing organizations, a significant percentage of the available human resources remain latent and untapped due to various reasons such as people being unallocated (on bench), in training and in projects in which all their relevant skills are not being utilized. Allocation of people into a project is a rigid, structured process, which involves multiple interviews and evaluation, processes that make it difficult to dynamically allocate resources to tackle smaller projects or problems. We detail a work-in-progress solution to apply enterprise crowdsourcing to outsourced software development.

## 2    Crowdsourcing Application

The TCS crowdsourcing application provides an integrated solution comprising of a marketplace for jobs (tasks), a workflow for creation of jobs, roles for users such as reviewer, requester and freelancer, a reputation mechanism, a virtual currency and a reviewing system. Let us look at some of the system.

### 2.1    Scope

The scope of the system is defined to address two types of requirements. The first is to cater to tasks that are generic and internal to the outsourcing company, TCS in this case. The second would be to crowdsource customer specific tasks. While the first is straightforward, the second would require an agreement with the customer and the tasks be made available only to the employees involved in the customer project.

### 2.2    Participants and User Roles

The participants of the system are the employees of TCS. They can be in internal projects, customer projects, undergoing training or in bench waiting for their next assignment.

The users in the system have roles such as requester (where they create jobs, invite participation, and manage jobs), freelancer (where they participate in a particular job) and reviewer (where they review work completed as part of a job.) Reviewers are nominated by the job requesters primarily on the basis of their reputation in the category the job was posted in. Users can have multiple roles.

## 2.3 Job Creation and Allocation

Tasks in the system are referred to as jobs. Task might involve a variety of subtasks which are part of the software development process in an outsourced IT firm. A wizard is provided for creating a job in the system. (Fig 1.) The job can be selected from among templates in the system with the ability to represent details dates, milestones and checklists, completion checklist, category and skillset, completion criteria along with the ability to nominate people to the job.

Once the job is created, it will be available in the Job Marketplace for the users to view and apply for the job.

The system will support three modes of job allocation according to the need of the requester. First, the requester will have the ability to nominate a freelancer or pick and choose a freelancer based on the applications received (applies for critical jobs). When there is need for more people to perform similar tasks – testing for instance, the requester can choose to allocate the job in a first come first served basis. Lastly, when the requester wants to get the best solution for a given problem, he can create a competition where any number of freelancers can take up the job and submit their solution.

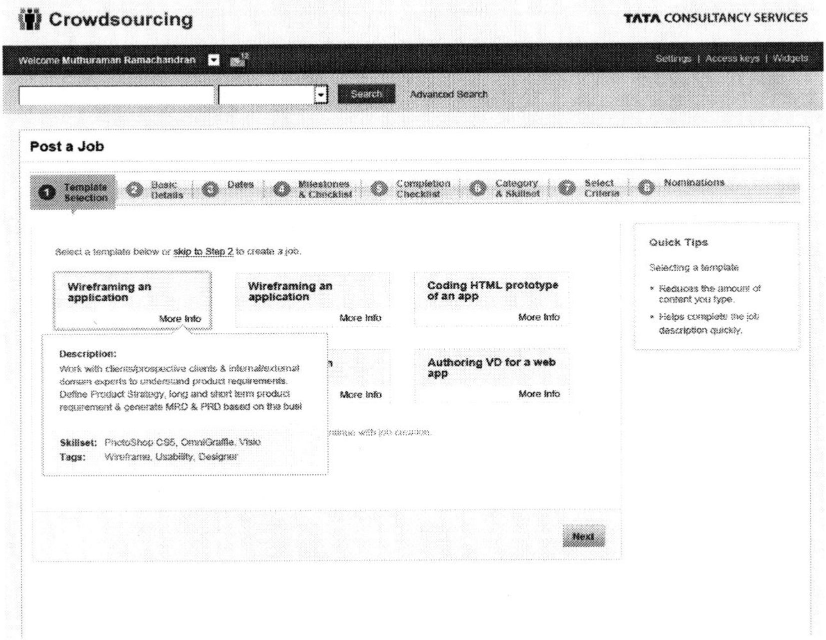

**Fig. 1.** Job creation wizard

# 3    Conclusion

The system provides a means to implement a crowdsourcing paradigm to traditional project management through a simplified job creation wizard, a marketplace and a reputation mechanism which apply salient social networking features to this problem. We look forward to deploying this application as a pilot with a selected number of projects in a month.

# References

1. Howe, J.: The Rise of Crowdsourcing. Wired 14(6) (2006)
2. Vukovic, M.: Crowdsourcing for Enterprises. In: 2009 Congress on Services I, pp. 686–692 (2009)

# A Model-Driven Framework for Developing Web Service Oriented Applications

Achilleas Achilleos, Georgia M. Kapitsaki, and George A. Papadopoulos

Department of Computer Science, University of Cyprus,
75 Kallipoleos Str., Nicosia, CYPRUS
{achilleas,gkapi,george}@cs.ucy.ac.cy
http://www.cs.ucy.ac.cy

**Abstract.** The advancements made in terms of the capabilities of mobile devices have shifted the interest of service engineering towards frameworks that are able to deliver applications rapidly and efficiently. The development of services that can be fully functional in mobile environments and operable on a variety of devices is an important and complex task for the research community. In this work, we propose a Model-Driven Web Service oriented framework that combines Model-Driven Engineering (MDE) with Web Services to automate the development of platform-specific web-based applications. The importance of this work is revealed through a case study that involves modelling and generation of a representative Web Service oriented mobile application.

**Keywords:** model-driven, web applications, code generation, mobile services, web services.

## 1 Introduction

Web Services (WSs) as the most representative implementation of the Service Oriented Architecture (SOA) are usually exploited in the field of Web-based applications for stationary devices. Lately, the advance of the field of mobile computing has introduced the need for developing Web Services that can be consumed through platform-specific clients in different environments, not only static ones, but also those dominating the mobile computing world [1]. End-users, constantly *on the move*, wish to be offered the same choices when working on their smartphones as on desktop devices [2]. In such environments, where users exploit a variety of devices in terms of complexity, size, computational capabilities etc., the need of developing services and applications that can target different mobile platforms arises.

At the same time the wide adoption of Model-Driven Engineering (MDE) from the research community has led to the advance of platforms and tools that facilitate the transformation of models between different abstraction levels resulting to functional code fragments at the final stage. Many of the approaches follow the paradigm of OMG's Model Driven Architecture (MDA) [3]. In MDA, a major separation mentioned includes the Platform Independent Model (PIM)

A. Harth and N. Koch (Eds.): ICWE 2011 Workshops, LNCS 7059, pp. 181–195, 2012.

and the Platform Specific Model (PSM). PIM is a rather abstract representation of a system and contains no information on implementation details. Conversely, PSM represents the system and takes into account platform specific properties. In the research community many attempts evolve around the issue of model transformation, where model transformation can be performed from PIM to PIM, PIM to PSM, PIM to code, etc. Although in MDE the *model* is the basic software component, models that do not result in functional applications have no practical use to the end-users and, consequently, nor to the service providers. For this reason, this paper focuses on the practicalities of the transformation conducted: the model to code step.

Taking the above challenges into account, in the framework of the current work, the issue of mobile application development for different platforms focusing on the Graphical User Interface (GUI) aspect is addressed. A number of code generators targeting different mobile platforms are defined (e.g., J2ME, C#) using as input the application model represented in the Presentation Modelling Language (PML). The PML, which was conceived and presented in previous work of the authors [18], provides means for designing GUI models that facilitate the generation of Web Service clients. The application modelling is complemented by the Web Services Description Language (WSDL) specification. The set of developed generators covers all major mobile and stationary device technologies. Using this approach, the development of functional Web Service Oriented applications for the following categories of devices is supported: (i) Resource-rich devices; e.g., desktops, laptops, (ii) Resource-competent devices; e.g., Netbooks, IPad, Kindle and (iii) Resource-constrained devices; e.g., mobile smartphones such as Google Nexus One, IPhone, HTC Desire, Nokia N8. This category set is based on the categorisation performed by Ortiz et al. [4], which was extended by adding the second category. The importance of the proposed framework lies in the high-degree of automation achieved, which improves the efficiency of the development process, since it allows developers to generate code for various platforms with limited effort.

The rest of the paper is structured as follows: Section 2 gives an overview of the related work in the field, whereas the description of the framework is provided in Section 3. This section is dedicated specifically to the details of the code generation process, which is the main and driving component of the proposed framework. The framework's applicability is exemplified in Section 4 through a mobile bookstore use case. Section 5 concludes the paper.

## 2   Related Work

In the literature various approaches exploiting the principles of MDE exist, either for the development of software applications in general or specifically for GUI development. Concerning modelling, it is important to keep the application's presentation independent from other layers (i.e., application's logic) so as to facilitate the integration with different technologies. Additionally, modelling GUIs in an abstract way facilitates mapping to different implementations.

Thus, we argue that a framework should provide components (e.g., architecture, code generators) to model and implement independently the GUIs and the WS implementation logic.

Initial work on GUI modelling focuses on the definition of the GUI structure using presentation diagrams and its behaviour using hierarchical statechart diagrams [5]. The definition of GUI structural and behaviour models is supported by the GuiBuilder tool, which allows the transformation from models to Java code. This work focuses simply on the development of Java-based GUIs, which can be used for implementing fully-functional multimedia desktop applications. Other examples of GUI modelling can be found in [6] and [7], although no details on the support for transformations to code are given.

Dunkel and Bruns [8] propose a simple and flexible approach for the development of mobile applications. They present a model-driven approach that allows defining the client's GUIs and the service workflow using graphical models, which are then transformed into XML-based descriptions (i.e., XForms code). The XForms W3C standard has been chosen because of its close correlation with the Mobile Information Device Profile (MIDP) of J2ME, which facilitates the mapping of XForm elements to MIDP elements. The approach is thus tailored towards J2ME and does not exploit the interoperability benefits of Web Services technology. Additional approaches [9], [10] overcome the issues faced by pure XML-based approaches, such as being data centric and the inability to expressively model behaviour, by developing graphical modelling environments that "speak" XML. This imposes though the overhead of developing and maintaining the modelling environments, which is a laborious and costly task. An extended discussion on various solutions for user interface design in application development is present in the survey of Perez-Media et al. [12].

Kapitsaki et al. [11] present an approach that automates the development of composite context-aware Web applications. The defined model-based approach proposes complete separation of the Web application functionality from the context adaptation. In particular, the methodology adopted utilises the Unified Modelling Language (UML) for the design and automatic generation of a functional context-aware Web application. The approach tackles and automates the development of context-aware Web applications, intended mainly for mobile users, which are formulated by third-party WSs. The use of UML should be replaced by standards that provide methods of accessing model stereotypes across different modelling tools.

The heterogeneity of mobile platforms in conjunction with the use of WSs is discussed also by Ortiz et al. [13]. The authors propose a service-side, aspect-oriented approach that allows developers to extend the implemented WS in order to enable the adaptation of the WS invocation result in accordance to the client device. The actual WS code is not directly affected, since additional aspect code is implemented, which intercepts the invocation of the service operation and adapts it according to the device type detected. This approach suffers from three main issues: the client-side implementation needs to include code that allows declaring from which device the WS is invoked, response time is slightly increased since the service-side aspect code requires to process and adapt the result, and implementation of different platform-specific service-clients is not considered.

In the area of Web development, not specific to Web Services, a number of tools have been proposed offering the means to model Web applications. Good examples can be found in UML-based Web Engineering (UWE[1]), where the application is modelled in UML notation containing a presentation model for the GUI properties, and Object-Oriented Hypermedia Design Method (OOHDM) [14], which targets hypermedia Web applications. Significant works, where Web Service-enabled applications are partially supported, can be found in the WebML CASE tool [15], a visual language used to represent the content structure of a Web application, and Hera [16], which focuses on Web Information Systems and hypermedia applications exploiting tools from the semantic Web, i.e., RDF (Resource Description Framework)) and RDFS. Although most of these works are quite mature, they differ from our approach in the motivation and in the target platforms supported, i.e., stationary devices in the above cases and mobile devices, which are the main focus in our case.

## 3   The proposed Framework

In this section the main steps of the development process are described; PML is briefly introduced, while particular emphasis is devoted to the transformation step. We emphasise on the specifics of the code generation phase in order to reveal the practicality and applicability of the transformation approach, which enables targeting different mobile but also stationary platforms. The description of the earlier steps is required and has been included in order to provide a comprehensive view of the proposed model-driven Web Service oriented framework.

### 3.1   Scope of Use and Overall Development Process

The proposed development process combines the characteristics of Web Services with the development directives given by Model-Driven Engineering. The presentation layer and the Web Service layer are kept distinct, in order to allow each one to be mapped to different implementations. This transformation logic is presented in Fig. 1, where each client is defined and developed in the form of GUIs and collection of Web Service communication classes. In the presentation particular focus is given on the GUI-related part depicted on the left side of the figure. Note that the Web Service implementation is conducted by the developer through a manual process. Nevertheless, the technology employed for implementing the WS main functionality does not restrict the client implementation to a specific platform. This is because Web Services allow the exchange of XML-based messages between entities regardless of the implementation details or the programming language used for the WS development.

---

[1] http://uwe.pst.ifi.lmu.de/

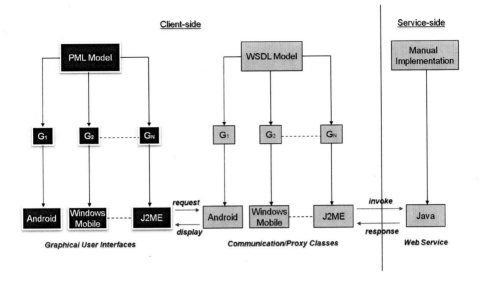

**Fig. 1.** Model-Driven, Web Service-oriented Architecture

The PML and WSDL models are designed at modeling time and act as input for the code generators that produce the respective code fragments. Regarding the WS part, existing WSDL code generation tools are used that enable the transformation of WSDL models to platform-specific proxy classes exploited for sending and receiving information via WS request and response messages.

In particular, the PML allows modelling GUIs in the form of screen layouts; as desired by the developer. The presentation models include the necessary abstract information on GUI elements (e.g., text box, label), properties (e.g., label's text) and relationships (e.g., panel contains button) of existing major mobile and stationary devices and platforms. A brief overview of PML is provided next. In accordance to the PML notation a number of platform specific code generators have been implemented for the technologies indicated in Fig. 1.

## 3.2   Brief Overview of PML

The Presentation Modelling Language is defined as an Eclipse Modeling Framework (EMF) based metamodel, using the Graphical Modelling Framework (GMF) Ecore diagram tool included in the environment presented in previous work [17]. The PML metamodel is presented in Fig. 2 and describes the graphical modelling elements, their associations and graphical properties, which enable the design of GUIs in the form of visual abstract models. The metamodel definition is based on an analysis and evaluation performed to identify elements, properties and associations that share similarities across different major platforms. Fig. 3 showcases that the metamodel definition is complemented by the Model-2-Code

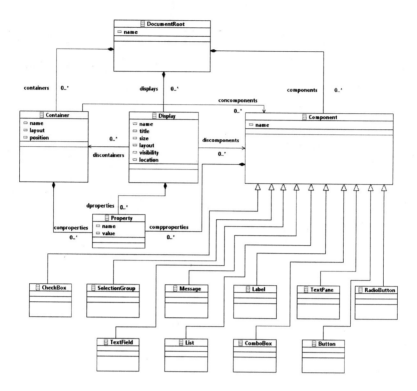

**Fig. 2.** Presentation Modelling Language metamodel

(M2C) transformation rules, which map abstract PML elements, properties and associations to platform specific implementation components, properties and associations (i.e., platform-specific code).

Most elements defined in the metamodel are self-explainable. *DocumentRoot* is the basic metaclass, where the rest of the model elements are aggregated, such as a number of displays corresponding to the screen of the mobile device (metaclass *Display*). The *discontainers* aggregation defines the containment relationship between the display and its container elements. The common graphical components are defined as children of the *Component* metaclass (e.g., *Message*, *Label*, *Button*). Similarly typical associations that exist between objects, such as the fact that container (e.g., panel) *includes* component (e.g., label), are also visible in the metamodel. The *Property* metaclass is an important element of the PML since it allows describing different graphical properties for the modelling elements. Each modelling element may contain various graphical properties, which are defined as instances of the *Property* metaclass. This provides the capability to extend easily and efficiently the PML by introducing new properties simply by adding parsing support within code generators.

The elements included in instances of the PML metamodel are analysed based on a number of transformation rules defined in the code generators. A deeper

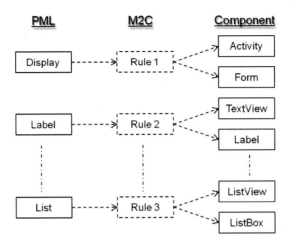

**Fig. 3.** Mapping PML to platform-specific implementations

analysis on the elements comprising PML is not included in the current paper. More information on the initial version of PML can be found in [18].

### 3.3 The Transformation Mechanism

The generation of the Web Service invocation part (from the client) is not addressed; instead, existing literature works on generating this part from WSDL descriptions are employed. WSDL, serving as the specification descriptor language for WSs, offers an abstract layer depicting the service functionality. Clients that wish to consume specific WSs rely on this WSDL specification, in order to discover the operations supported, the input arguments needed and the expected response details. WSDL code generators can be found in Java WS frameworks, such as the Novell exteNd Director development environment and the Axis2 Service Archive Generator Wizard offering the *wsdl2java* tool. .NET offers its own custom *wsdl* code generation tool. In the proposed framework the two latter tools have been employed along with the J2ME generator that forms part of the Sun Java Wireless Toolkit for CLDC. However, since no such tool is available for the Android platform, in the current stage of the presented work the WS communication classes were developed manually.

Further discussion on code generators for WSs has not been included, since the focus is given on the applicability of the presentation code generation tools on multi-platform environments. However, some works that exploit WS models and introduce tools for model transformation procedures in the framework of MDE exist. The reader can refer to relevant publications [19], [11].

In terms of the presentation layer, the code generation process allows transforming PML models to the appropriate platform-specific code. A set of generators targeting the following platforms of stationary and mobile devices have been implemented: Java, J2ME, Android, Windows Mobile and Windows Desktop. In this subsection two of the above generators have been chosen for demonstration purposes; specifically, the versions targeting Android and Windows Mobile are described in order to showcase also the main differences between the two technologies. In order to keep the paper comprehensive and due to space limitations, it is not possible to describe the whole generators set.

The Eclipse-based MDE environment, proposed in previous work [17], includes the openArchitectureWare (oAW) software tool that enables the development of code generators by defining model-to-text transformation rules. The tool comprises the *Xpand* template language, a text-editor, the workflow execution engine and two supplementary languages (i.e., *Check*, *Xtend*) with their individual text editors. Foremost, the *Xpand* language supports the definition of advanced code generators as templates, which capture the transformation rules and control the output document generation (e.g., XML, Java, C#, HTML). The transformation rules are defined using the *Xpand* text-editor and include references to extension functions specified using the *Xtend* language. In particular, extension functions are considered as utility functions (i.e., similar to Java utility functions), which support the definition of well-formulated generators and improve the structure of the generated code. Moreover, the Check language supports the definition of additional constraints using a proprietary language. Finally, the workflow execution engine drives the code generation on the basis of the defined templates and the input model.

The combination of the components supports the code generation process as depicted in Fig. 4. The transformation is executed via the workflow engine of oAW, on the basis of a workflow script that specifies information, such as the classes and components participating in the generation, output folders etc. The template definition, which drives code generation, constitutes the most important part of the transformation process. Appropriate templates have been defined for all participating platforms (i.e., C#, Java, J2ME, Android).

Listing 1 presents a sample part of the Android-specific template definition that allows demonstrating how code generation is achieved. Lines containing information such as generated files and package names have been omitted. The main part of the sample generator presented in this work is included in lines 31-74. This part is repeated for all display containers of the model enabling access to the graphical properties of the containers and the secondary components associated to them. For instance, line 34 illustrates how we can generate an Android *TableLayout* object and set accordingly its name in accordance to the name of

**Fig. 4.** The PML code generation process

the current container in the iteration, i.e., $<<discon.name>>$. The iteration through the collection of secondary components associated with each container is performed in the lines that follow (36-72). Depending on the type of element visited during the parsing of the PML model (indicated by the properties of *concomp*), the respective object creation with the appropriate name is generated. For example a new *TextView* object corresponds to each *Label* model element as indicated in lines 37-39, where the *keyword/property "text"* used at line 39 provides the capability to set the text on the label to the value parsed from the *Label* modelling element. The list of conditional statements allows to parse and generate other types of secondary components using the same reasoning.

*Listing 1. Sample for the Android-specific template*

```
1.   <<EXTENSION templates::AndroidPresentation>>
2.   <<DEFINE Root FOR presentation::DocumentRoot>>
     .....
30.  <<REM>>Starts iteration and creates a View for each container.<<ENDREM>>
31.  <<FOREACH this.discontainers AS discon->>
32.  public View <<discon.name+"View">>(){
33.     this.setTitle(<<discon.conproperties.select
                         (e|e.name.contains("title")).value.first()>>);
34.     <<discon.name>> = new TableLayout(this);
35.  <<REM>>Create the respective components contained in each View.<<ENDREM>>
36.  <<FOREACH discon.concomponents AS concomp->>
37.  <<IF concomp.metaType.name.matches("presentation::Label")->>
38.     <<concomp.name>> = new TextView(this);
39.     <<concomp.name>>.setText(<<concomp.compproperties.select
                         (e|e.name.contains("text")).value.first()>>);
40.  <<ELSEIF concomp.metaType.name.matches("presentation::TextField")->>
41.     <<concomp.name>> = new EditText(this);
     .....
71.  <<REM>>Ends the loop associated with the components collection.<<ENDREM>>
72.  <<ENDFOREACH>>
73.  <<REM>>Ends the loop associated with the containers collection.<<ENDREM>>
74.  <<ENDFOREACH>>
     .....
98.  <<ENDDEFINE>>
```

For the template definition targeting Windows Mobile a sample part is illustrated in Listing 2. The same approach has been employed for the remaining platform-specific code generators.

*Listing 2. Sample for the Windows mobile-specific template*

```
1.   <<EXTENSION templates::WindowsMobilePresentation>>
2.   <<DEFINE Root FOR presentation::DocumentRoot>>
     .....
23.  <<REM>>Create the constructor that creates Windows mobile main form.<<ENDREM>>
24.  public <<this.toFirstUpper()+"WindowsMobile">>(){
25.  <<FOREACH discontainers AS discon->>
26.  <<REM>>Set the name and title of the Windos mobile main form.<<ENDREM>>
27.       this.Name = <<discon.conproperties.select
                         (e|e.name.contains("title")).value.first()>>;
28.       this.Text = <<discon.conproperties.select
                         (e|e.name.contains("title")).value.first()>>;
29.  <<REM>>Create the components associated to each layout of the main Form.<<ENDREM>>
30.  <<FOREACH discon.concomponents AS concomp ITERATOR it->>
31.  <<IF concomp.metaType.name.matches("presentation::Label")->>
32.     <<concomp.name>> = new Label();
```

```
33.       <<concomp.name>>.Name = "<<concomp.name>>";
34.       <<concomp.name>>.Location = new System.Drawing.Point(0, 0);
35.       <<concomp.name>>.Size = new System.Drawing.Size(0, 0);
36.       <<concomp.name>>.TabIndex = <<it.counter0>> ;
37.       <<concomp.name>>.Text = <<concomp.compproperties.select
                       (e|e.name.contains("text")).value.first()>>;
39. <<ELSEIF concomp.metaType.name.matches("presentation::TextField")->>
40.       <<concomp.name>> = new TextBox();
41.       <<concomp.name>>.Name = "<<concomp.name>>";
42.       <<concomp.name>>.Location = new System.Drawing.Point(0, 0);
43.       <<concomp.name>>.Size = new System.Drawing.Size(0, 0);
44.       <<concomp.name>>.TabIndex = <<it.counter0>>;
45.       <<concomp.name>>.Text = "";
46. <<REM>> Ends the loop associated with the components collection. <<ENDREM>>
47. <<ENDFOREACH>>
48. <<REM>> Ends the loop associated with the containers collection. <<ENDREM>>
49. <<ENDFOREACH>>
    .....
70. <<ENDDEFINE>>
```

## 4   The Book Store Use Case

### 4.1   Overview

The chosen use case consists of a *BookStore* WS that provides means for searching and purchasing books. Specifically, the user exploiting the service can search for books, providing as input the book title. The WS returns all details of the book and gives the opportunity to the user to purchase the book. This latter operation is invoked by filling a number of necessary fields to complete the order and payment (including the customer information and the details of the payment method). Upon successful completion of the transaction a result page is shown.

Although not directly exploited in the context of the current work, the model of the *BookStore* WS is depicted in Fig. 5. The server side part of the *BookStore* prototype has been manually implemented in Java. The demonstration of this section concentrates on the generation of the presentation layer of the client side.

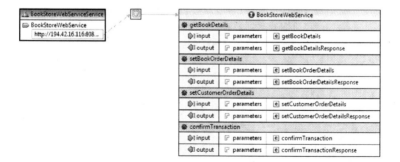

**Fig. 5.** The *BookStore* Web Service Description Language Model

## 4.2   Models Design and Code Generation

Due to the complexity of the WS and space limitations the PML model, which is degined manually by the application developer, is not provided in full; its basic parts demonstrating the use of the PML metamodel are given instead. The modeling part of the containers corresponding to distinct screens is shown in Fig. 6. At the top of the model an instance of the *Display* metaclass represents the main frame/display of the GUI. The display is associated with a number of container components that form instances of the *Container* metaclass. The first container, i.e., *searchForBooks*, corresponds to the first step of book searching, whereas the rest serve the book purchasing procedure.

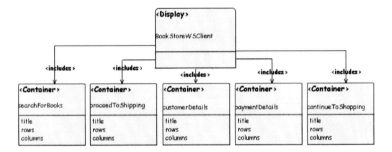

**Fig. 6.** Top level elements of the *BookStore* Presentation Model

Each container has its own properties and contains also secondary components, i.e., label, textfield, textpane and button elements, as shown for a specific container in Fig. 7. The secondary components are defined as instances of the respective metaclasses and include their own graphical properties. The *customerDetails* container corresponds to the phase, where the customer needs to provide as input her details with information, such as name and shipping address. These fields correspond to different GUI element types and are marked appropriately in the model.

*Listing 3. The GUI code generated for the Android target platform.*

```
1.  /** Called when the activity is first created. */
2.  public View searchForBooksView() {
3.        this.setTitle("BookStore - Multi-platform Web Service");
4.        searchForBooks = new TableLayout(this);
5.        bookTitle = new TextView(this);
6.        bookTitle.setText("Enter Book Title:");
7.        titleOfBook = new EditText(this);
8.        ... }
```

A segment of the generated code for the Android platform corresponding to lines 31-74 of Listing 1 is shown in Listing 3. These lines of code are the outcome of the transformation of the modelling elements corresponding to the *Display* and the individual graphical properties of two of the components of the searchForBooks *Container*. Although hidden in the models presented above, the name provided for the book store (i.e., *BookStoreWSClient*) forms part of the information that can be edited through the model properties editor view. In a similar fashion the generated code fragment corresponding to Windows Mobile is visible in Listing 4 following the specifics of the platform.

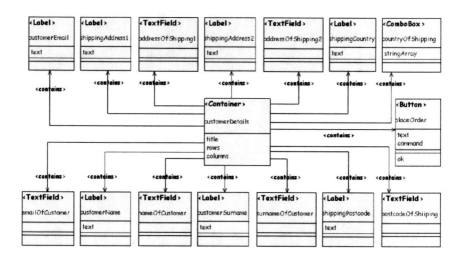

**Fig. 7.** Example container of the *BookStore* Presentation Model

Fig. 8 demonstrates some of the screenshots captured during the use of the *BookStore* WS on mobile clients deployed on the Android and the Windows Mobile platform. The screens for searching for a book, displaying the results and filling out the information for purchasing the book are shown. Alternated screenshots capture different steps in the functionality of the WS, while running on these platforms. Moreover, Table 1 presents a quantitative evaluation by comparing the generated code against the complete implementation (i.e., including manual code) for the examined platforms. Manual implementation for each platform is limited to: (i) calling the method that displays the next form, (ii) getting user input from form fields, (iii) calling the appropriate WS method (passing user input as arguments) via the proxy class and (iv) obtaining and displaying the WS response. The Lines of Code (LoC) belongs to the size metrics that can be used for analyzing the quality of model transformations in MDE. In future work, we aim to extend the evaluation by examining other software metrics, such as software cyclomatic complexity, and include a performance analysis evaluation that can provide more accurate results than the LoC metric.

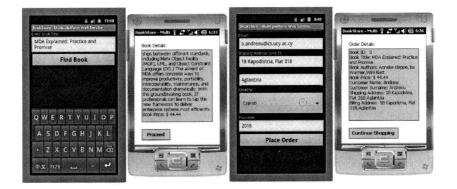

**Fig. 8.** The *BookStore* Web Service Deployed on Different Devices

**Table 1.** LoC percentage for the different platforms

| LoC Metric per Platform | Generated Code | Overall Code | Generated/ Overall (%) |
|---|---|---|---|
| *Java* | 189 | 334 | 56.59 |
| *J2ME* | 267 | 369 | 72.36 |
| *Android* | 244 | 361 | 67.59 |
| *Windows Mobile* | 360 | 481 | 74.84 |
| *Windows Desktop* | 360 | 475 | 70.30 |
| **All Platforms** | 1420 | 2020 | 70.30 |

*Listing 4. The GUI code generated for the Windows mobile target platform.*

```
1.   public BookStoreWSClientWindowsMobile(){
2.        this.Name = "BookStore - Multi-platform Web Service";
3.        this.Text = "BookStore - Multi-platform Web Service";
4.        bookTitle = new Label();
5.        bookTitle.Name = "bookTitle";
6.        bookTitle.Location = new System.Drawing.Point(20, 20);
7.        bookTitle.Size = new System.Drawing.Size(200, 20);
8.        bookTitle.TabIndex = 0;
9.        bookTitle.Text = "Enter Book Title:";
10.       titleOfBook = new TextBox();
11.       titleOfBook.Name = "titleOfBook";
12.       titleOfBook.Location = new System.Drawing.Point(20, 45);
13.       titleOfBook.Size = new System.Drawing.Size(200, 20);
14.       titleOfBook.TabIndex = 1;
15.       titleOfBook.Text = "";
16.       ...    }
```

The results show that each generator can be exploited in an efficient way, in order to automate a significant part of the implementation process (the average percentage is kept at 70.3%). Note that in the case of Java the percentage is lower, since it is not possible to generate the code that handles components placement for each screen. This is due to the layout choices offered by Java, which are missing in other technologies. For this reason the respective lines of code in Java need to be added manually.

## 5  Conclusions

In this work, a Model-Driven framework that automates the development of Web Service oriented applications has been presented. The process described allows modelling service-client GUI elements using the notation of the Presentation Modelling Language, whereas the key contribution refers to the transformation of PML models to functional code, targeting the different platforms encountered on mobile and stationary terminals (Java, Android, etc.). The code generators proposed have been implemented using a set of tools offered by the openArchitectureWare modelling component. Regarding the communication of the client with the Web Service, existing tools that support the transformation of WSDL models to corresponding proxy classes have been used.

The developed prototype and its applicability have been demonstrated through the book store WS, which was showcased running on mobile environments but deployed also on desktop devices (i.e., Java, Windows Desktop). The efficiency of the approach has been discussed on the basis of the use case and the results derived using the LoC metric. The proposed model-driven WS-oriented framework, consisting of the PML and WSDL along with the code generators set, has the capability to address heterogeneity when developing platform-specific applications. In particular, the approach allows users to automatically generate the required source code for Web Service client applications, which can consequently invoke Web Services from different devices and platforms. An interesting extension of this work is to consider the preferences of the user when adapting the Web Service, making this way the service user-aware. For instance, a user might want to receive the full book details even if she is using a resource-constrained device, while another user is satisfied with receiving the book's title and price.

## References

1. Bartolomeo, G., Blefari Melazzi, N., Cortese, G., Friday, A., Prezerakos, G., Walker, R., Salsano, S.: SMS: Simplifying Mobile Services - for Users and Service Providers. In: Advanced International Conference on Telecommunications and International Conference on Internet and Web Applications and Services, p. 209. IEEE Computer Society, Washington (2006)
2. Dern, D.: Cross-Platform Smartphone Apps Still Difficult. In: IEEE Spectrum. IEEE Press (2010)
3. Singh, Y., Sood, M.: Model Driven Architecture: A Perspective. In: IEEE International Advance Computing Conference, pp. 6–7. IEEE Computer Society (2009)
4. Ortiz, G., Garcia de Prado, A.: Adapting Web Services for Multiple Devices: A Model-Driven, Aspect-Oriented Approach. In: IEEE Congress on Services, pp. 754–761. IEEE Computer Society, Los Alamitos (2009)

5. Sauer, S., Duerksen, M., Gebel, A., Hannwacker, D.: GuiBuilder: A Tool for Model-Driven Development of Multimedia User Interfaces. In: Workshop on Model Driven Design of Advanced User Interfaces in MODELS 2006 (2006)
6. Link, S., Schuster, T., Hoyer, P., Abeck, S.: Focusing Graphical User Interfaces in Model-Driven Software Development. In: First International Conference on Advances in Computer-Human Interaction, pp. 3–8. IEEE Computer Society, Washington (2008)
7. da Cruz, A.M.R., Faria, J.P.: A Metamodel-Based Approach for Automatic User Interface Generation. In: Petriu, D.C., Rouquette, N., Haugen, Ø. (eds.) MODELS 2010. LNCS, vol. 6394, pp. 256–270. Springer, Heidelberg (2010)
8. Dunkel, J., Bruns, R.: Model-Driven Architecture for Mobile Applications. In: Abramowicz, W. (ed.) BIS 2007. LNCS, vol. 4439, pp. 464–477. Springer, Heidelberg (2007)
9. Paternó, F., Santoro, C., Spano, L.D.: User task-based development of multi-device service-oriented applications. In: International Conference on Advanced Visual Interfaces. LNCS, vol. 5726. ACM (2010)
10. Paternò, F., Santoro, C., Spano, L.D.: Model-Based Design of Multi-Device Interactive Applications Based on Web Services. In: Gross, T., Gulliksen, J., Kotzé, P., Oestreicher, L., Palanque, P., Prates, R.O., Winckler, M. (eds.) INTERACT 2009. LNCS, vol. 5726, pp. 892–905. Springer, Heidelberg (2009)
11. Kapitsaki, G.M., Kateros, D.A., Prezerakos, G.N., Venieris, I.S.: Model-driven development of composite context-aware web applications. Information and Software Technology 51(8), 1244–1260 (2009)
12. Pérez-Medina, J.-L., Dupuy-Chessa, S., Front, A.: A Survey of Model Driven Engineering Tools for User Interface Design. In: Winckler, M., Johnson, H. (eds.) TAMODIA 2007. LNCS, vol. 4849, pp. 84–97. Springer, Heidelberg (2007)
13. Ortiz, G., Garcia de Prado, A.: Mobile-Aware Web Services. In: International Conference on Mobile Ubiquitous Computing, Systems, Services and Technologies, pp. 65–70. IEEE Computer Society, Los Alamitos (2009)
14. Moura, S.S., Schwabe, D.: Interface Development for Hypermedia Applications in the Semantic Web. In: LA Web, pp. 106–113. IEEE CS Press (2004)
15. Brambilla, M., Ceri, S., Comai, S., Fraternali, P.: A CASE tool for modelling and automatically generating web service-enabled applications. International Journal of Web Engineering and Technology 2(4), 354–372 (2006)
16. van der Sluijs, K., Houben, G.J., Leonardi, E., Hidders, J.: Hera: Engineering Web Applications Using Semantic Web-based Models. In: de Virgilio, R., Giunchiglia, F., Tanca, L. (eds.) Semantic Web Information Management - A Model-Based Perspective, pp. 521–544. Springer, Heidelberg (2010)
17. Achilleos, A., Yang, K., Georgalas, N.: A Model Driven Approach to Generate Service Creation Environments. In: IEEE Global Telecommunications Conference, pp. 1–6. IEEE (2008)
18. Achilleos, A.: Model-driven Petri Net based Framework for Pervasive Service Creation. School of Computer Science and Electronic Engineering. University of Essex (2010)
19. Gronmo, R., Skogan, D., Solheim, I., Oldevik, J.: Model-driven Web services development. In: IEEE International Conference on e-Technology, e-Commerce and e-Service, p. 42045. IEEE Press (2004)
20. van Amstel, M.F., Lange, C.F.J., van den Brand, M.G.J.: Metrics for Analyzing the Quality of Model Transformations. In: 12th ECOOP Workshop on Quantitative Approaches on Object Oriented Software Engineering (2008)

# Developing Enterprise Web Applications Using the Story Driven Modeling Approach

Christoph Eickhoff, Nina Geiger, Marcel Hahn, and Albert Zündorf

University of Kassel, Software Engineering,
Department of Computer Science and Electrical Engineering,
Wilhelmshöher Allee 73,
34121 Kassel, Germany
{cei,nina.geiger,hahn,zuendorf}@cs.uni-kassel.de
http://se.eecs.uni-kassel.de

**Abstract.** Today's browsers, tools and Internet connections enable the growth of Enterprise Web Applications. These applications are no longer page-based and designed using HTML code. Enterprise Web Applications bring the capabilities and concepts of traditional desktop applications to the browser. We are used to the development of desktop applications for years and have defined our own process to enable the full model-driven development of applications without source code. Using this process and its tools, we are able to define not only data models for traditional applications and generate code out of it. Combined with the story-driven modeling approach, we are able to design the logic of applications using models and generate fully functional code. To use our knowledge and tools as well as our usual process for the development of Enterprise Web Applications, we investigated our process and adapted it to the new needs. As result we propose a new development process that combines the needs of complex software development with the implementation of web user interfaces and control flows between these user interfaces. The process is a guideline to use models and tools for the development of complex Enterprise Web Applications including data model, behaviour and user interface.

## 1   Introduction

We have developed traditional Java applications for years. Our main research area has been the model- and story-driven development of such applications. We have investigated ways to do the complete development of applications with our own development process and own tools: The Fujaba Process [2], [3] and Fujaba Toolsuite [9]. However, over the last years the type of applications changed. We more and more faced the challenge of developing so called Enterprise Web Applications. What we exactly mean by this term is further defined in section 2. Since we have gained expertise in the modeling of applications over years, the question we asked ourselves was: "Is it possible to develop web applications without the need to write any sourcecode, too?". We started by investigating our development of traditonal Java applications and apparently faced the differences

A. Harth and N. Koch (Eds.): ICWE 2011 Workshops, LNCS 7059, pp. 196–210, 2012.

between traditional software and web applications. First of all, web applications will mostly be divided into a client part and a server part. These two parts communicate using Remote Procedure Calls or other request technologies known in the web domain. These topics were not clearly addressed in the development process we used until now. Additionally, there is no full modeling and code generation support for these techniques inside the Fujaba Tool Suite, yet. Another point missing in the traditional Fujaba Process is the design of Graphical User Interfaces (GUIs) and the binding of application data to these interfaces (databinding). The last point had resided on our todo list even before web applications turned out to be the new research point. We thus decided to enhance our processes and tool integration to be able to do full development of Enterprise Web Applications, including distributed application parts and user interfaces. We therefore started to adopt and enrich the traditional Fujaba Process to be able to support all these new requirements. Also we tried to support the process with tool integration of the new requirements. We propose the use of the Google Web Toolkit (GWT)[1] as user interface and client side logic library. GWT automatically generates browser specific JavaScript code from Java Code. The Java code can easily be generated using the Fujaba Toolsuite code generation mechanisms. A first step towards modeling of databinding and support for server calls with GWT was already introduced with the Fujaba *Action Charts*, [5], in 2010. The design of user interfaces as well in source code as in story-driven modeling is a painstaking task. We therefore propose the use of the GWTDesigner[2] which is a visual GUI builder generating Java code. To enable the completely model driven development of web applications, we have to close the gap between Java code for the visual components and the diagrams modeling the rest of the application. We propose to use UML Lab [3] and its reverse engineering technologies to derive a structural representation of the GUI. This is sufficient to enable the modeling of client side behaviour, databinding, GUI listeners and server calls using story-diagrams and *Action Charts*. While the main points of the Web Fujaba Process have already been defined and will be presented in this paper, there are still some weak points. We currently do not explicitly state how the databinding will be incorporated into the process. Also, we have automatic test generation for the server parts, but not for the logical parts residing in the client and the user interface. These points will be handled in future revisions of the process. The remainder of this paper is structured as follows: Section 2 defines the class of targeted applications. After having defined the application class, we introduce the story-driven modeling approach, our adaptations needen for web applications, as well as a running example in section 3. As a result of our research, section 4 answers the question raised in the Introduction and defines the Web Fujaba Process and the associated toolchain. Section 5 shows similarities and differences to other modeling approaches. Section 6 finally concludes and gives information about work which still has to be carried out in the future.

---

[1] http://code.google.com/intl/de-DE/webtoolkit/
[2] http://code.google.com/intl/de-DE/webtoolkit/tools/gwtdesigner/
[3] http://www.uml-lab.com/

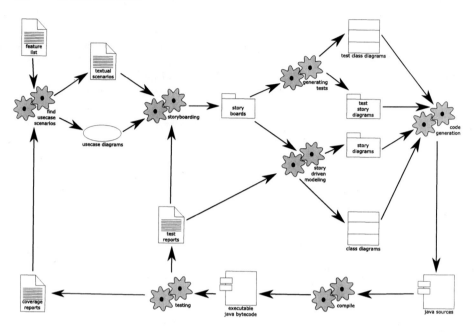

**Fig. 1.** The traditional Fujaba Process used for story-driven development of traditional applications

## 2    Targeted Applications - What We Call Enterprise Web Applications

As stated in section 1 our web application development process ist tailored to a special class of applications. We call these applications Enterprise Web Application and define them as follows:

- **Ajax based applications with excessive Document Object Model restructuring.** We explicitly do not target page based applications with traditional link infrastructure such as HTML links. Enterprse Web Applications will change the "page content" by resturucturing the Document Object Model of the web page. This way we do not have page reloads. This behaviour is also known from Rich Internet Applications.
- **Client side data model and logic.** We try to shift as much of the business logic of our applications to the client. The web browsers Ajax Engine takes care of computations and data model changes. This way, most of the application logic can be shifted to the client. The applications will only contact the server in special cases.
- **Desktop-like user interfaces.** Enterprise Web Applications have interfaces composed of so called widgets. We have controls similar to the ones known from desktop applications. Lists, buttons, dropdown-boxes and menus are used to provide access to the data model and logic.

- **Minimized server side code.** As stated above, we try to limit the server computations wherever possible. Only security critical issues are still computed by the server and persistent storage is carried out using the WebCoobra persistency and data replication framework.
- **Workflow driven.** This last item is no must. However, we state that most applications are developed to provide tool support for some kind of workflow. This is why we have introduced the workflow driven requirement into our application class as well as in our process. Workflow hereby does not mean to be forced to describe the work to be carried out using a Business Process Model. Nevertheless, recurring tasks may also form a workflow in some ways.

As example for what we call Enterprise Web Applications, the GoogleDocs[4] may be reviewed. While this application is also able to have multiple simultaneous users on one document, the technology used for this differs from our approach. However, the requirements to be of class Enterprise Web Application are fulfilled by GoogleDocs. Being similar in many cases, in contrast to traditional software the Enterprise Web Applications are accessible from everywhere in the world without the need to be installed. Being more flexible, this way, they still contain similar features than desktop software and are even more complex to develop due to the distributed nature. The story-driven development of this kind of applications is target to our research and development process.

## 3   Story-Driven Modeling of Enterprise Web Applications

The story-driven modeling approach is taught and researched by the Fujaba community for years now. There also exists a process, defining the steps needed to develop applications this way, the FUjaba Process (FUP). Figure 1 shows the complete process. The research of story-driven modeling of Enterprise Web Applications was based on this existing work, as described above. However, our targeted web applications still differ from the kinds of applications the FUP was targeted to. Nevertheless, FUP can still be used for the server parts and for parts of the data model of Enterprise Web Applications. A description of application development accourding to the FUP can be found in [3]. In the following, we will only give a short introduction on the main story-driven modeling features.

The development process starts by the definition of textual scenarios. One example scenario could be the following: *"Alice and Bob are playing Ludo. It is Alice's turn. She has rolled the dice which shows 2. Alice takes her red piece and moves it forward two fields."* The textual scenarios will then be translated to so called storyboards. Figure 2 shows the storyboard resulting from the example scenario shown above. These storyboards are used for automatic test generation. One Test is generated from every storyboard, testing the described scenario. Additionally, storyboards serve as starting point for the application development. As can be seen from Figure 2 the method `move(2)` is called on the `piece` object. This method can be implemented graphically using storydiagrams inside

---

[4] http://docs.google.com

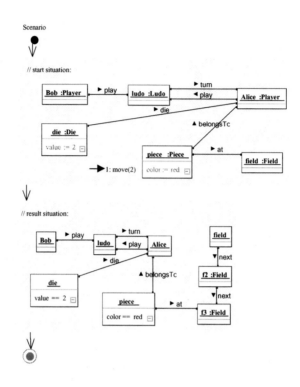

**Fig. 2.** Storyboard describing the example textual scenario of Alice and Bob playing ludo

the Fujaba Toolsuite. This way, the logic and data model changes are handled. The move() method will change the data model of the application by placing the piece object on a different Field. The diagram showing an example implementation of the move() method is shown in Figure 3. The Fujaba story-driven modeling techniques and capabilities are described in detail in [14]. Using the Fujaba Toolsuite and process, we are able to create classdiagrams for the data model as well as application logic using storydiagrams. All of these diagrams are used as input for the code generation process. This code generation results in Java source code implementing data model and application logic. The source code can be compiled using standard Java compilers and afterwards be executed within the Java Virtual Machine. The development of highly complex systems is possible this way. As an example: The code generation engine of Fujaba is bootstrapped and was developed using story-driven modeling approaches, itself.

The Fujaba development process described above in context of Enterprise Web Applications sufficient only for the server part and data model. There are some major issues missing in FUP concerning these kind of applications. The modeling of distributed systems is not clearly defined. These systems contain client and server part as well as communication between these parts. Additionally, the data model, which is created using the FUP techniques has to be bound to the client

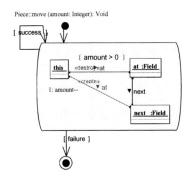

**Fig. 3.** Activity Diagram modeling the logic of the `move()` method

side user interface in some way. First steps towards the modeling of server calls and data bindings were introduced with the Fujaba *Action Charts* [5]. However, we have to provide modeling capabilities for the issues missing in this approach. The process for Enterprise Web Applications had to provide information on how to model server calls, do the databinding and create controller logic for the user interface. The implementation of graphical user interfaces is a painstaking task. This holds for hand coding as well as for modeling UIs with storydiagrams. However, we need support for visual user interface design in our process. Fortunately, the publication of Googles GWT-Designer[5] in 2010 opened a way for visual user interface definition. While the definition of UIs using the GWT-Designer makes life easier, the output of the graphical editor is Java source code. Since we intend to have a completely model-driven development process of Enterprise Web Applications we do not want to switch back to source code. We thus had to incorporate some kind of automatic mapping at this point. Following our process and using the associated toolchain we are able to generate source code, cross-compile it with the Google Web Toolkit and run a completely modeled web application. As a result of our research on the development of Enterprise Web Applications this paper presents our story-driven modeling approach defined in the Web Fujaba Process (WFUP).

### 3.1 Running Example

While the whole approach presented in this paper is still conceptual in some points, we needed an example application to test the whole process. This application had to be complex, support multiple users and have different user interfaces (views) for different kinds of tasks. Since Enterprise Web Applications will mostly be used to support some kind of workflow, as stated in 2 there also had to be a workflow with sufficient complexity to be solved by the example application. We choose a management workflow for the creation of animated computer films. The Enterprise Web Application modeled to support the whole

---

[5] http://code.google.com/intl/de-DE/webtoolkit/tools/gwtdesigner/index.html

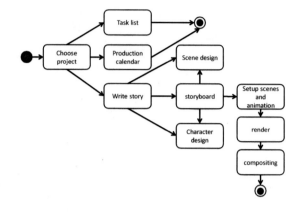

**Fig. 4.** Workflow of the example application to manage the creation of animated films

management of film productions like this will need to support the whole workflow shown in figure 4.

The application will need to manage different film projects from which the user can choose when starting the application. After this, information for the choosen project will be shown. Every step of the workflow shown will have its own user interface (view). The views will consist of similar items as user interfaces known from desktop applications, e.g. a calender with information about the project status, giving the project manager some kind of timely overview. Another view, the write story view (shown in Figure 5), will consist of a web editor, which will enable the user to define scenes, dialogues and the action taking place within the scene. This is done textually. Not every task of the workflow will be done within the webbrowser, 3D modeling, design and animation will as well be done with specified desktop applications as rendering and compositing processes. The web application will only show the current status of these action points. The example application serves as basis for the development of tool support for the proposed process. Therefore, we will develop the application according to this process. However, some parts of the application or process may be changed during development and further research. The process introduced in section 4 is the first version and will need further refinement. Even the workflow of the application might be changed, rearranged or further enriched. Maybe it might be necessary to define subworkflows for more complex action points.

## 4   The Web Fujaba Process (WFUP)

As a result to the question raised in section 1: "Is it possible to develop web applications without the need to write any sourcecode, too?" we propose the Web Fujaba Process. Combining the experience from traditional story-driven modeling and the research work introduced in section 3 we propose this process as guidance for the completely story-driven modeling of Enterprose Web Applications. The Web Fujaba Process hereby is based on the traditional Fujaba

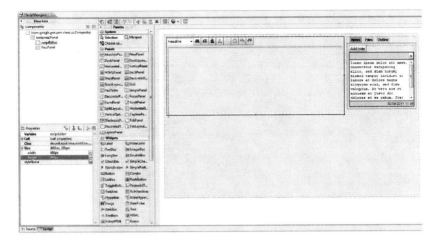

**Fig. 5.** Write story view from example application within GWT-Designer view in Eclipse

Process shown in figure 1. The Fujaba Process was further enriched with the description of user interface design and the possibilities to model UI controllers as well as server calls for distributed applications. However, the original process is still part of the development. The server parts of applications will be developed according to the original process. Figure 6 shows an overwiew of the Web Fujaba Process (WFUP).

The process starts by describing the intened application textually, as it was done in the old process. Taking the description as input, usecase scenarios are created and documented as well textually as in usecase diagrams. This step should be carried out together with the potential users or the customer. Since Enterprise Web Applications will be divided into a client- and a server part the process is divided at this point, too. The server part takes its textual and usecase scenarios and is further developed according to the FUP. This also is done for the application data model. This model can be designed the traditional way, resulting in class diagrams which can in turn be used inside the WFUP to do the data binding and controller parts. Since the applications we intend to create with the WFUP will deploy the data model both on server side and on client side, it is extremely necessary here, to integrate the model into both development steps. For the server part, the application data model can be used as in the development of traditional applications with the FUP. However, the controller structure will be able to do changes on the data model directly in the client, without the need to make server calls. This results in the need of having the class diagrams of the data model in the WFUP process, too. Having special annotations and interfaces in the application data model will enable the use of the WebCoobra Framework [1] for the data model. This gives us support for automatic replication of data between the server and multiple clients, enabling the system to keep consistency. These annotations and interfacing can easily be

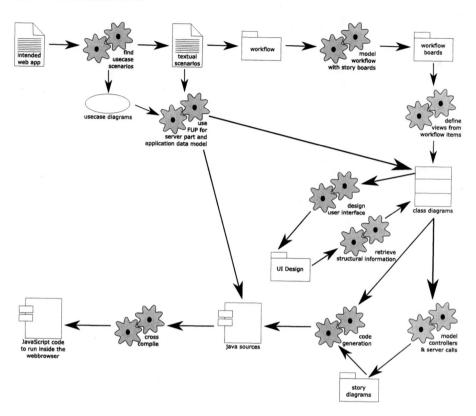

**Fig. 6.** The Web Fujaba Process, a proposal for story-driven development of Enterprse Web Applications with the Google Web Toolkit and Fujaba

done during the FUP for the server part and data model and do not have to be taken into account while developing the client side with the WFUP. The clients side code can handle every object of the data model directly, this way, which eases the modeling of controllers for the user interface. The client part of the application will be developed using the additional steps introduced in this paper. Enterprise Web Applications mostly will follow some kind of workflow. This is due to the case that applications will mostly be designed to carry out some kind of work. In our running example introduced in section 3.1 the application to be developed is designed to enable the management of animated film productions. Thus, there is a workflow driving the application - the steps to be carried out to manage an animated film production in our case. This is true to the major part of applications. Hence, we try to extract a workflow from the textual scenarios. This workflow is modeled using Fujaba and will result in so called workflow boards. For every workflow step there will be one graphical user interface instance - one view. The view for the workflow step should be designed to support the user in performing the task associated with the workflow step. To enable this, we define one view component for every workflow step. The view components are simply UI

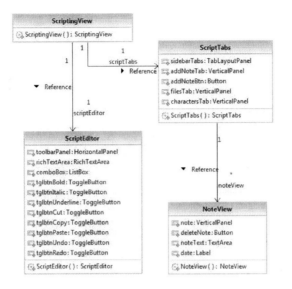

**Fig. 7.** Reverse engineered classdiagramm of script view user interface. This reverse engineering step is carried out by UML Lab, using the Java source code generated from the Google GWT-Designer.

classes inside a class diagramm. To link between the view class and the associated workflow step, we use a new kind of diagram, the UI board. The next step would be to further design the user interface. This will be done using the Google GWT-Designer. In a graphical way the user interface will be created and saved. As stated in 3 the GWT-Designer creates Java source code as output. We therefore retrieve back the structural information of the created classes to be able to use it within the remainder of the process. Figure 7 shows the classdiagram of the example view from Figure 5 after retrieving back the structural information from the GWT-Designer. The resulting class diagram has referenced classes to all the used user interface components as well as all the attributes set. Additionally, the structure of the view is represented by links between the different user interface classes in the diagram. After this step is finished, the structure of the view can be combined with the data model for the application, enabling the controller and application logic to perform model changes. The simplified version of the data model for the example application is shown in Figure 8. The logic of the controllers as well as the databinding can be modeled with Fujaba storydiagrams using the information of both of the classdiagrams shown above. The controllers in turn will result in a third classdiagram containing the controller structure. Every controller class will have methods which are automatically called by the associated user interface components when actions occur. The methods of these controller classes can be modeled with story driven techniques in Fujaba. After

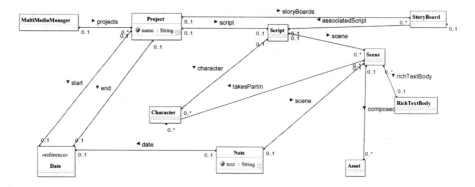

**Fig. 8.** Simplified data model for the example application in Fujaba notation

the modeling process is done, the runnable application will be created using code generation mechanisms.

The process described above enables the complete modeling of web applications including user interface components and client as well as server side logic. To support the user in carrying out this process, we started to implement tool support for this process. The suggested toolchain is further described in the following section.

### 4.1   WFUP Toolchain - Adding Tool Support to Our Process

The Fujaba Toolsuite already supports class and storydiagrams. However, the user interface designing process using Google GWT-Designer produces source code. We therefore need some kind of mapping from this source code to Fujaba's model here. We choose to retrieve back the structural informations of the designed user interfaces into Fujaba, here. This way, it would be possible to run further process steps with this structures. We found the tool support for this step in UMLLab. This tool is able to reverse engineer source code into structural model information and provide real-time synchronisation between model and code. The structural information gained from UML Labs reverse features enables us to close the gap between source code and model at this point. Still, the structural model gained through UML Lab does not help in the Fujaba development process because of incompatible meta models of both tools. Additionally, it is not possible to model the logical parts of web applications with story-driven modeling using UML Lab, yet. To overcome this problem, a real-time adapter between UML Lab and Fujaba has been created [6]. Using this adapter the structural information can be duplicated into Fujaba class diagrams and afterwards be used for the story-driven modeling of client side logic, controllers and databinding. The adapter also takes care of consistency between class diagrams residing within Fujaba and those within UMLLab. This means, we are able to apply changes to any of those diagrams later. To enable more comfortable access to the controllers, we have started to add right-click menus to the GWT-Designer. This way, we can add controllers to our user interface in a graphical way and only need to implement the logic of the controller afterwards. Having defined the whole application, the process takes the resulting diagrams; class diagrams of the view, story diagrams for the controllers and for server calls and generates code for all of these diagrams. Different code generation strategies will be used here, depending on the type and semantics of the diagram to be generated. This code generation step will result in Java source code that can be tested and debugged with the Google Plugins and which can be cross-compiled with the GWT cross compiler to gain the JavaScript code that is run inside the webbrowser and which can be deployed onto an application server. The tool support for the Web Fujaba Process is not yet completely implemented. However, the design of user interfaces, retrieval of structural information and design of user interface controllers and server calls can already be done using current versions of GWT-Designer, UML Lab and Fujaba.

## 5  Related Work

The approach and process proposed in this paper is not the only research work in the domain of model-driven development of web applications. However, we face on the development of a special class of applications: Enterprise Web Applications. Additionally, we want to be able to do this with the tool support we are used for the implementation of traditional applications. Thus, we try to broaden our modeling and graph transformation expertise to the domain of web application development. However, we will try to sum up some of the similarities and differences to other research work in this sector in the remainder of this section:

[7] shows the use of patterns for the development of Rich Internet Applications. The authors insist to use patterns on a higher abstraction layer, meaning in the modeling stage. The approach uses models of these patterns that are modeled once and then reused by model-to-model transformations or manually. Similar to our approach of Action charts [5] the authors introduce UML state diagrams for the modeling of user interface actions. The reuse of some patterns modeled to execute common user interface operations will be further invesitigated and might be included into our process in the future.

The Orchestration Model which is introduced in [10] in combination with the "Model-Driven Development Process for RIAs" follows similar steps than the process introduced here. However, there is a lot of model transformation between platform independent and platform specific models needed, following this approach. These meta layers often get confused as well from developers as customers. We have tried to hide these meta-information from the customer using our story-driven approaches in the past. Tests with students showed that application development following the story approach often is simpler for the customers and developers to understand and in additon there is always a document which can easily be understood by both. The simple notation of storyboards and usecase diagrams in some points enabled the customer to design parts of the development process on his own.

[12] contains activity diagrams for the generation of user interfaces as well as WYSIWYG user interface design. These diagrams are similar to our workflow

boards. However, we will use the information flow of workflow boards to generate the exchange of one view or parts of it by another. The user interface design will, like in [12] be carried out with graphical design. However, the approach introduced in [12] is designed for Enterprise Applications using Eclipse and SWT rather than web applications.

The UWE4JSF method [8] again uses similar approaches than the WFUP introduced above. However, it faces on JSF[6] applications rather than real Ajax applications. The navigation structure shown in this paper can be seen similar to our workflow boards, again. Nevertheless, transitions within our workflow boards will not trigger page changes. It will rather result in the Document Object Model Tree to be changed, meaning that part of the views or even complete views will be exchanged without the page to be reloaded.

[4] shows ways for multi-level testing of model driven web applications. This point will be start for future research of WFUP. While the traditional FUP enables testing and even automatic generation of test code, the WFUP currentls lacks this for the client side of applications. We will have to find ways to (semi)automatically incorporate tests into the WFUP in the future.

Another interesting idea is the model-driven way of importing user interface mockups into the real development process described in [11]. The implementation of this idea into our intended toolchain would really be nice to have. However, since the GWT-Designer is not yet open-source there is currently no plan to implement this into our process.

WebML is widely used in the domain of model driven web engineering. The approach and process presented on [13] are used to define applications which do not fit into our targeted application class as defined in section 2. While we target on Enterprise Web Applications without page reload and with client side application state, WebML is mainly targeted on traditional page based web applications. Thus, the process defined by WebML is not useful for the story-driven development of applications we want to create. We therefore defined our own process, which is exactly tailored to the needs of Enterprise Web Applications.

As far as we know, the completely story-driven modeling of web applications was not yet done in the community of web engineering. We tried to introduce the process we are used to and adopt it to the special needs of our targeted application class. Getting input from additional research in the are of web engineering will hopefully further enrich this process in the future and make it less experimental.

## 6   Conclusion and Future Work

This paper showed the research steps and methods carried out to design a completely story-driven approach for the development of Enterprise Web Applications. The Web Fujaba Process (WFUP) was introduced as our proposal for the development of these applications. The predecessor, the Fujaba Process, used for the development of traditional desktop applications was introduced. The changes

---

[6] Java Server Faces - http://java.sun.com/javaee/javaserverfaces

and enhancements made to extend this process for the development of Enterprise Web Applications including user interface design were shown. The work to be carried out to completely implement tool support and user friendly usage of the proposed tool chain is still going on. Since we intend to have a development process that resides completely within the model, without switching to source code writing, we still have some minor problems to face. At the moment there is still the need to combine different tools to develop applications. GWT-Designer for the user interface specification, UML Lab for the sturctural information retrieval, Fujaba for the main development of the rest of the application. While all of these applications can be combined at this point, there is still the need for better tool integration. The diagrams for databinding and controllers of user interfaces, as well as the ones for server calls will need some rework. Some new diagrams might be introduced for these purposes, in case we figure out that the traditional story diagrams will not suffice for our proposal. Additionally, there will have to be some wizards for the generation of complete web applications as well as for the creation of different kinds of diagrams. Having new diagrams will also mean to have to update code generation to fulfill the needs of web applications. There will be different semantics of storydiagrams, so we will have some kind of context-sensitive code generation here, depending on the purpose of the diagram. While there has to be done a lot of work with the distributed parts of the web application, the server parts can be designed and generated following the current standard FUP process. This means, there is automatic generation of test for the server part of the application. Hence, we will try to enable test generation for client parts as well. Since this is current research work, we do not yet know which ways of testing will be used within the web application process of Fujaba. There is still a lot of work to be carried out to enable complete story-driven development of web applications and have all the different tools and parts integrated well into each other. Nevertheless, we still want to stay with the model-centric and story-driven approach. This way, we hope to bring the common advantages of model-driven development to the web domain. The diagrams we propose to use might, in addition, often be better to read and understand by customers than this is the case with source code.

# References

1. Aschenbrenner, N., Dreyer, J., Hahn, M., Jubeh, R., Schneider, C., Zündorf, A.: Building Distributed Web Applications based on Model Versioning with CoObRA: an Experience Report. In: Proc. 2009 Intl. Workshop on Comparison and Versioning of Software Models, pp. 19–24. ACM (May 2009)
2. Diethelm, I., Geiger, L., Zündorf, A.: Systematic Story Driven Modeling. Technical Report (February 2004)
3. Diethelm, I., Geiger, L., Zündorf, A.: Systematic Story Driven Modeling, a case study. Edinburgh, Scottland (May 2004)
4. Fraternali, P., Tisi, M.: Multi-Level Tests for Model Driven Web Applications. In: Benatallah, B., Casati, F., Kappel, G., Rossi, G. (eds.) ICWE 2010. LNCS, vol. 6189, pp. 158–172. Springer, Heidelberg (2010)

5. Geiger, N., George, T., Hahn, M., Jubeh, R., Zündorf, A.: Using actions charts for reactive web application modelling (2010)
6. Koch, A.: Echtzeit synchronisierung von uml-modellen unterschiedlicher technischer basis am beispiel von uml lab und fujaba. Master's thesis, Kassel University, Fachbereich 16, Fachgebiet Software Engineering, Wilhelmshöher Allee 73, 34121 Kassel (September 2010)
7. Koch, N., Pigerl, M., Zhang, G., Morozova, T.: Patterns for the Model-Based Development of RIAs. In: Gaedke, M., Grossniklaus, M., Díaz, O. (eds.) ICWE 2009. LNCS, vol. 5648, pp. 283–291. Springer, Heidelberg (2009)
8. Kroiss, C., Koch, N., Knapp, A.: UWE4JSF: A Model-Driven Generation Approach for Web Applications. In: Gaedke, M., Grossniklaus, M., Díaz, O. (eds.) ICWE 2009. LNCS, vol. 5648, pp. 493–496. Springer, Heidelberg (2009)
9. Nickel, U., Niere, J., Zündorf, A.: The Fujaba Environment, Limmerick, Ireland, pp. 742–745. ACM press (June 2000)
10. Pérez, S., Díaz, O., Meliá, S., Gómez, J.: Facing interaction-rich rias: The orchestration model. In: Schwabe, D., Curbera, F., Dantzig, P. (eds.) ICWE, pp. 24–37. IEEE (2008)
11. Rivero, J.M., Rossi, G., Grigera, J., Burella, J., Luna, E.R., Gordillo, S.E.: From Mockups to User Interface Models: An Extensible Model Driven Approach. In: Daniel, F., Facca, F.M. (eds.) ICWE 2010. LNCS, vol. 6385, pp. 13–24. Springer, Heidelberg (2010)
12. Schramm, A., Preußner, A., Heinrich, M., Vogel, L.: Rapid UI Development for Enterprise Applications: Combining Manual and Model-Driven Techniques. In: Petriu, D.C., Rouquette, N., Haugen, Ø. (eds.) MODELS 2010, Part I. LNCS, vol. 6394, pp. 271–285. Springer, Heidelberg (2010)
13. The Web Modeling Language (2011), http://www.webml.org
14. Zündorf, A.: Rigorous object oriented software development. Habilitation Thesis, University of Paderborn (2001)

# Aspect-Oriented Modeling of Web Applications with HiLA

Gefei Zhang[1] and Matthias Hölzl[2,*]

[1] Arvato Systems Technologies GmbH
[2] Ludwig-Maximilians-Universität München
{gefei.zhang, matthias.hoelzl}@pst.ifi.lmu.de

**Abstract.** Modern web applications often contain features, such as landmarks, access control, or adaptation, that are difficult to model modularly with existing Model-Driven Web Engineering approaches. We show how HiLA, an aspect-oriented extensions for UML state machines, can represent these kinds of features as aspects. The resulting models achieve separation of concerns and satisfy the "Don't Repeat Yourself" (DRY) guideline. Furthermore, HiLA provides means to detect potential interferences between features and a declarative way to specify the behavior of such feature combinations.

## 1 Introduction

The history of Model-Driven Web Engineering (MDWE) is also a history of Separation of Concerns. Even in the early hours of MDWE, numerous modeling approaches, such as [3,8,10,18], which considered only the static web sites with primitive GUIs common at that time, were designed so that the domain model, the navigation model, and the presentation model, were separated from each other.[1] This way, the complexity of the models could be reduced, the legibility and maintainability improved.

While web applications evolved to modern, ubiquitous, adaptive applications implementing complex business processes presented by elaborate GUIs, new concerns also emerged and had to be taken into account. Unfortunately, models of these concerns are often tightly entangled with the rest of the application and therefore hard to separate. For instance, adapting the behavior of a web application to different navigation patterns of different users often means introducing changes throughout the model so that the adaptation mechanism is interwoven with the normal application behavior. This makes the effect of adaptation difficult to discern in the model and, even more importantly, makes it difficult to consistently modify the adaptive behavior. Similarly, access control in the context of web applications often requires checking the current user's rights throughout in the navigation structure.

The growing complexity of web applications also poses another challenge for the separation-of-concerns efforts of the MDWE research: the growing number of concerns

---

* This work has been partially sponsored by the EU project ASCENS, 257414.

[1] There were also approaches that did not care about separation of concerns, though. In these approaches the model just contained everything, i.e. navigation, presentation, etc. However, we think a clean separation of concerns is generally beneficial w.r.t. model readability. See also [11].

A. Harth and N. Koch (Eds.): ICWE 2011 Workshops, LNCS 7059, pp. 211–222, 2012.

in web applications increases the chance that some of them are interfering. Modeling the interaction of concerns, i.e. how concerns are combined with each other, is often quite unintuitive, changing the interaction logic an error-prone task.

It is therefore desirable to have a language which supports 1) the separate modeling of different concerns of web applications, and 2) a high-level, i.e. declarative definition of the combination of concerns. In this paper, we present the power of the language *High-Level Aspects* (HILA) in Model-Driven Web Engineering. HILA is an aspect-oriented extension of UML state machines [15] and can be used on top of state-machine-based MDWE approaches, such as [2,6,14,20]. In HILA, different concerns of a software system are modeled in *aspects*, separately from the base functionalities of the applications and from each other. Therefore, different behavioral concerns of a web application can be cleanly separated. Moreover, HILA is defined in such a way that potential interference between aspects can be detected mechanically, and that combination of aspects can be defined in a simple, declarative way. Hence, HILA can be very useful in model-driven engineering of modern web applications. HILA is integrated in the Hugo/RT UML model translator which supports formal software-engineering aproaches with model checking, theorem proving, and code generation for HILA models.

The remainder of this paper is organized as follows: in the following Sect. 2 we briefly overview the techniques of modeling web applications using UML state machines and point out some modularity problems. After a short introduction of the HILA language in Sect. 3 it is shown in Sect. 4 how HILA can help mitigate the problems. Combination of concerns is discussed in Sect. 5. Related work is discussed in Sect. 6 before we finally draw conclusions and sketch some future work in Sect. 7.

## 2   Modeling Web Applications with UML State Machines

The language of UML state machines is very popular for behavioral modeling. It is even considered "the most popular modeling language for reactive components" [7]. Therefore, it also provides a natural and widely-used way of modeling web applications, see e.g. [2,6,13,14,20]. Usually states model navigation nodes, transitions model links between the navigation nodes, and events model user input or system events.

For example, the state machine in Fig. 1 models a simple online book store. Very simply spoken, the user of this book store can browse over the books (state Browse), select a book (event book) and view either its summary (BookSummary) or detail information (BookDetail), and, after successfully logging in (Login), buy the book (Buy).

However, modularization in state machine models is generally difficult, see [23]. In particular, even this simple state machine containing only seven states shows some modularity deficiencies. This is also why Fig. 1 is not very easy to comprehend. In particular, the following features complicate the state machine and obscure (at least partially) the behavior of the web application:

1. In this application, the user can go back to the home of the application from every other site. This is modeled by a transition leaving every other state to Home. This is a violation of the *Don't Repeat Yourself* (DRY) principle.

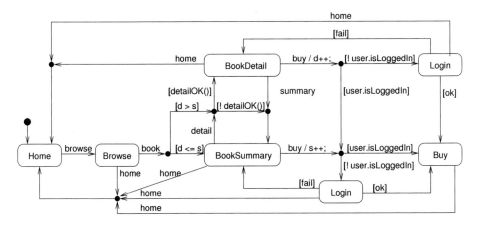

**Fig. 1.** Example: Modeling a book store with a UML state machine

2. In order for the user to buy a book, he is required to be logged in. Since there are two ways of entering Buy (from BookDetail and BookSummary), Login is also modeled twice. Again, the DRY principle is violated.
3. When the user finishes browsing and selects a book (event book), it is difficult to see which view, BookDetail or BookSummary is shown. In fact, two features are modeled in a tightly entangled way:
   (a) The system checks whether the summary or the detail view is more "commercially successful" and shows the user this view. That is, it stores in the two variables d and s (updated on the transitions leaving BookDetail and BookSummary) the frequencies of the user proceeding to buy the book from these views, and shows him the "right" view when the user has selected a book.
   (b) Meanwhile, the systems also checks if it is technically appropriate to show the detail view. Reasons for this view being inappropriate could be that the client device, due to factors like processing power, band width, or size of the display, does not support the display of the detail information. The detail of this check is modeled in a rather abstract function call detailsOK(). Only then this function returns true, the detail view is shown, otherwise the summary is shown instead.
4. The relation of the above two features is not easy to comprehend. Only after careful study of Fig. 1 is it clear that currently an AND relation is implemented, that is, both of the conditions must be satisfied for the book detail to be shown. Changing to OR or any other combination (e.g. the detail view should be shown as soon as it is more successful, no matter if the client is adequate or not) would be an error-prone task.

Such modularity problems of UML state machines can be addressed by HiLA. In the following, we first give a brief overview of HiLA and then show how it can be used in modeling web applications to improve the model modularity.

# 3   HILA in a Nutshell

High-Level Aspects (HILA) [23] is an aspect-oriented extension of UML state machines. It provides a new language construct to separately model parts of the system behavior, and thus enhances the modularity of the models.

This construct is called *aspect*. An aspect is applied to a UML state machine, which is called the *base machine*, and defines some additional or alternative behavior of the base machine at some points of time during the base machine's execution. The behavior is defined in the *advice* of the aspect; the points of time to execute the advice are defined in the *pointcut*. The advice also has the form of a state machine, except that the final states may carry a label, indicating which state should be activated when the advice is finished and the the execution of the base machine should be resumed. This state is referred to as the *resumption state*. The pointcut is a specification of the points of time when certain states of the base machine are just about to become active or have just been left, or the time spans during which certain states are active. Actually, the first two kinds of pointcuts can also be regarded as those points of time when some transition is fired: a state S is just about to become active whenever any transition leading to S is fired, and it has just been left whenever a transition leaving it is fired.[2]

Overall, an aspect is a graphical model element stating that at the points of time specified by the pointcut the behavior defined by the advice should be executed, and that thereafter the base machine should resume execution by activating the state given by the label of the advice's final state. Intuitively, it can also been understood as a statement that certain transitions should be "interrupted" (what we call *advised*) by the advice.

HILA also allows the definition of *history properties*. A history property contains a pattern, and yields the number of matches of this pattern in the execution history of the base machine. History properties can considerably reduce the complexity of the modeling of history-based features. Since HILA is an extension of the UML, UML templates as defined in [15] can be applied to reuse HILA aspects even more frequently.

Some examples of HILA aspects are given in Fig. 2. Aspect B in Fig. 2(a) states that whenever state S is just about to become active (≪before≫) (that is, the aspect advises every transition leading to S), an additional state X should be activated, and then, when the final state of the advice is activated, the base machine should resume execution at the source (label goto src) of the advised transition (which means that S will *en effet* never be active). Note this aspect is defined as a template. Instantiating S with different states will specify a multitude of points of time and advise a multitude of transitions. Aspect A in Fig. 2(b) advises every transition leaving A (≪after≫), activates state Y, and then returns to the original target (label goto tgt) of the advised transition. This aspect therefore defines an additional navigation node Y after the user has left T. Aspect W shown in Fig. 2(c) states that whenever the state U is active, and the current event is ev,

---

[2] Since UML state machines may actually contain concurrent regions, and there may be multiple active states at run time, pointcuts and labels actually are defined in terms of sets of states, see [23]. However, we currently do not have an example in which concurrent constructs of state machines are necessary for modeling web applications, and consider only the simple case of single-region state machines in this paper.

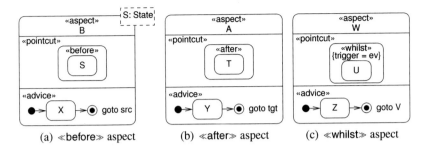

Fig. 2. HiLA Examples

the state Z should be activated, and, after that, the base machine should go to state V to resume execution.

The weaving algorithms of HiLA are described in [23]. The algorithms are prototypically implemented in HiLA/Hugo, an extension of the UML model translator and model checker Hugo/RT [12]. HiLA was applied to several case studies, including a larger-scale crisis management system, see [9].

## 4   Modeling Web Applications with HiLA

HiLA helps to achieve a better separation of concerns in modeling web applications as follows: first the modeler starts with a very simple state machine (which we call the *base machine*) to model the basic navigation structure. Typical hard-to-modularize features of web applications, such as *landmarks*, access control and adaption, are then modeled separately in aspects. This way, the basic navigation structure, as well as the other features, are kept simple and easy to read, hence the model is less error-prone. Potential interactions between the aspects are then resolved in a simple, declarative way.

### 4.1   Basic Navigation Structure

To keep the application model easy to understand and maintain, the base machine should be as simple as possible. Ideally, all information needed to determine the next transition to fire should be locally available in the source state, and there should be as little redundancy of model elements as possible. In the context of web applications this implies that the base machine should not model features like landmarks, access control, and adaptation rules. The basic navigation structure of our book store example is given in Fig. 3. The aforementioned out-sourcing of the more elaborate features makes it possible to start with a textbook state machine, i.e. one that is simple and intuitive.

### 4.2   Landmarks

"Landmarks" are navigation nodes that are supposed to be (directly) reachable from every other node. In order to avoid the violation of the DRY principle, some Web Engineering approaches, such as [8,16], define a keyword **landmark** to model landmarks.

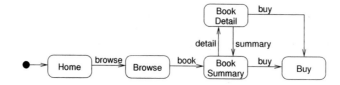

**Fig. 3.** Book store: basic navigation structure

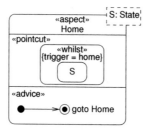

**Fig. 4.** Book store: aspect template defining a landmark

Unfortunately, this solution is not applicable to state-machine-based approaches, for it is not clear which event should fire the transition to the landmark. Moreover, this keyword can only be used to model landmarks that should be directly reachable from *every* other state and does not support modeling a navigation link for an arbitrary subset of the navigation nodes. In plain UML, composite states, which consist of one or more regions, are used to model common reaction of different states to the same event. Unfortunately, in the context of Web Engineering, composite states only provide partial help, but do not work if there exist landmarks which are supposed to be directly reachable from different sets of states upon different events, since a state can belong to only one region.

Using HILA, we only need a «whilst» aspect to overcome these problems, see Fig. 4: whenever state S is active (stereotype «whilst»), and the current event is home (tagged value trigger = home), the advice should be executed. Since the advice does not define any behavior (the transition leaving the initial vertex leads to the final state directly), but only tells the base machine to go to state Home (label goto Home), the aspect actually state that the state machine should go to Home from state S upon event home. This aspect is defined as a UML template, instantiating the formal parameter S with different states thus models a direct navigation link from each of the states to Home.

### 4.3 Access Control

Access control is also hard to modularize in web application since the same logic often has to be implemented on a multitude of navigation links and this often means violation of DRY, see also [25].

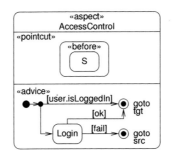

**Fig. 5.** Book store: aspect template for access control

Using HiLA, a simple «before» aspect often suffices to efficiently model access control, see Fig. 5: every time just before («before») state S gets active, it is checked (in the advice) if the user is currently logged in (user.isLoggedIn). If this is the case, the final state labeled goto tgt is activated, upon which the advice is finished, and the base machine resumes execution by going to the target of the advised transition. On the other branch, if the user is not logged in, a login site is shown (Login). Again, the base machine resumes at the target of the advised transition after a successful log in (ok), otherwise the user cannot goto the state, and is "pulled" back to the source of the advised transition (label goto src).

### 4.4 Adaptation

An adaptive web application is one that changes its behavior automatically to meet the preferences of the user. Adaptation is a cross-cutting concern that may easily be intertwining with other concerns of the application [1]. We show how HiLA can help to model adaptation of web applications in a highly modular fashion.

Checking whether showing details is appropriate on the client (rule 3b on page 213) before actually moving to BookDetail is pretty simple. Again, what we need is no more than a «before» aspect, see Fig. 6(a): whenever the state BookDetail is about to become active, function detailOK() is called. We do not specify this function in more detail in this paper, but simply assume that it returns true iff showing details of the current book on the client is appropriate w.r.t. the predefined conditions like network bandwidth and processing power, etc. If the function returns true, the final state labeled goto BookDetail is activated, and the base machine resumes execution at the state BookDetail, otherwise, an error message is shown (Error), and the base machine resumes execution at the state BookSummary (label goto BookSummary).

The other adaptation rule, showing the more successful view (rule 3a on page 213), defines a system behavior that is dependent on the navigation history of the user. We thus define two history properties, d and s in (the «history» compartment of) the aspect SuccessfulView (Fig. 6(b)): the pattern of d contains a transition from BookDetail to Buy. The value of d is the number of matches of this pattern in the execution history of the base machine, that is, the number of times of this transition was fired. Therefore, d is a counter of how often the user proceeded from the detail view (BookDetail) to buying the book. Similarly, the history property s counts how often the user proceeded from

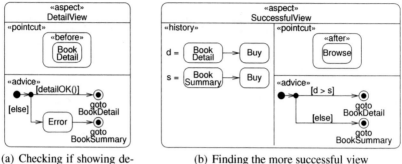

(a) Checking if showing details is fine with the client

(b) Finding the more successful view

**Fig. 6.** Book store: two aspects for two adaptation rules

the summary view (BookSummary) to buying the book. If $d > s$, i.e. it is more likely for the user to buy a book when he is viewing the details of the book, then the better view is the detail view; otherwise, if it is more likely for the user to buy a book when he is viewing the summary of the book, then the summary view should be shown after the user has selected a book from Browse.

## 5    Feature Combination

Modern web applications usually come with an array of different features. Although it is desirable to model these features in separation, more often than not they are supposed to work together, as a whole. For instance, the two adaptation rules in our simple book store are modeled separately, but since both of them restrict the navigation to the detail view of the book, their interference has to be carefully designed.

More concretely, each of the two rules defines a constraint that has to be satisfied for the system to show the detail view of the book, but what is the relation between these two constraints? Do they both have to be satisfied? Or only one of them? For (the designer of) a modeling language, the most important question to answer is probably how easy (or hard) it is to design such a relation or to switch to another.

The UML model Fig. 1 actually implements an AND of the two rules. Only when both of them are satisfied, the system will show the detail information of the book. Comprehension of this logic requires careful study of the guards of a whole array of transitions, switching to another combination requires careful modification of the guards.

In HILA, we therefore provides means both to detect pairs of aspects that can be interfering, and declarative ways to define their interaction.

### 5.1    Interference Detection

Checking whether any two aspects are possibly interfering requires checking if the labels of the final states, which finish the execution of the advices, are conflicting. Since in general an advice may contain more than one final states and not even the determination of the one that actually finishes the advice is decidable, we restrict ourselves to a conservative analysis, with the intention of finding all possible pairs of conflicting aspects, which are then subject to further investigations by more powerful instruments like model checking, or by human experts.

While the general analysis of HiLA aspects is pretty complex (see [23]), in our bookstore application, it suffices to apply a simple analysis rule: if the aspect of an aspect A1 contains a final state labeled goto G1, and another aspect A2 has a pointcut of the form «before» G1, then A1 and A2 may be interfering. Note that the two adaptation rules of the book store satisfy this condition: the advice in Fig. 6(b) contains a final state with the label goto BookDetail, while pointcut of the aspect in Fig. 6(a) has the form of «before» BookDetail. Therefore, these two aspects may be conflicting. Further investigations, for example by a human expert, show that the constraints of the conflicting labels, i.e. detailOK() in Fig. 6(a) and d > s in Fig. 6(b) can actually be simultaneously satisfied, and therefore the two aspects are actually conflicting.

## 5.2 Declarative Feature Combination

The definition of feature combination is declarative in HiLA. After finding all potentially interfering aspects, we simply define a resumption state for each combination of the aspects. Despite an exponential complexity in theory, this procedure is often sufficiently practicable, since the sets of interfering aspects are usually small enough.

**Table 1.** Book store: feature combination

| DateilView | SuccessfulView | Combined |
|---|---|---|
| goto BookDetail | goto BookDetail | goto BookDetail |
| goto BookDetail | goto BookSummary | goto BookSummary |
| goto BookSummary | goto BookDetail | goto BookSummary |
| goto BookSummary | goto BookSummary | goto BookSummary |

In our book store, the only interfering aspects are Fig. 6(a) and Fig. 6(b). Two different labels, hence two different resumption states are defined: BookDetail and BookSummary. Table 1 shows a possible combination of these two aspects, where the column Combined contains the value that should actually be used. It is easy to see that only when both of the aspects set BookDetail to be the resumption state, the detail view is shown. This is the same logic as the UML solution given in Fig. 1. In contrast to the UML state machine, switching to another combination is now a simple task.

## 6   Related Work

Aspect-orientation has been recognized by Web Engineering researchers as helpful for improving the modularity of software design models. In [1] aspect-oriented language constructs are defined for separate modeling of adaptation. Compared with this approach, which contains only four kinds of web-specific aspects, the general-purpose language of HiLA is much more expressive.

The approaches [4,17] also propose to use aspect-oriented techniques to model adaptation modularly. Compared to HILA, interference detection and declarative definition of aspect (feature) combination is not supported. In fact, even the more general topic, the interference between different parts of web design models, is surprisingly little investigated by the MDWE community, the only work that we are aware of being [21], which is not state-machine-based and not aspect-oriented, and our previous paper [22], which considered only navigation modeling, whereas the current paper also covers landmark and access control modeling.

Compared with other approaches of aspect-oriented state machines, the distinguishing feature of HILA is that it is high-level. That is, HILA aspects are defined *semantically*, based on the dynamic run time information of the base machine, whereas the other approaches, such as [5,19,26], are defined *syntactically*, based only on the static structure of the base machine. Due to this difference, HILA aspects are simpler and easier to comprehend, and detection of interference is also easier. For a more thorough discussion, see [23].

In the MDWE context, HILA may be applied on top of state-machine-based approaches like [2,6,14,20].

## 7    Conclusions and Future Work

We showed in this paper some modularity problems exhibited by UML state machines when they are used in the context of MDWE, and we showed how to use HILA to mitigate them. In particular, using HILA can considerably enhance the modularity and thus reduce the complexity of state machines when modeling web applications that involve landmarks, access control, and adaptation. One of the highlights of our approach is the automated detection of potential interference between the aspects, and the simple, declarative definition of feature combination.

Future work includes code generation out of HILA aspects, and extending HILA to model other concerns of web applications. In particular, the aspect-oriented approach of modeling rich user interface defined in [24] should be integrated in HILA.

## References

1. Baumeister, H., Knapp, A., Koch, N., Zhang, G.: Modelling Adaptivity with Aspects. In: Lowe, D., Gaedke, M. (eds.) ICWE 2005. LNCS, vol. 3579, pp. 406–416. Springer, Heidelberg (2005)
2. Busch, M.: Integration of Security Aspects in Web Engineering. Diplomarbeit, Ludwig-Maximilians-Universität München (2011)
3. Cachero, C., Gómez, J., Pastor, Ó.: Object-Oriented Conceptual Modeling of Web Application Interfaces: the OO-$\mathcal{H}$ Method Abstract Presentation Model. In: Bauknecht, K., Madria, S.K., Pernul, G. (eds.) EC-Web 2000. LNCS, vol. 1875, pp. 206–215. Springer, Heidelberg (2000)
4. Casteleyn, S., Van Woensel, W., van der Sluijs, K., Houben, G.-J.: Aspect-Oriented Adaptation Specification in Web Information Systems: A Semantics-Based Approach. The New Review of Hypermedia and Multimedia (NRHM) 15(1), 39–71 (2009)

5. Clarke, S., Baniassad, E.: Aspect-Oriented Analysis and Design. Addison-Wesley (2005)
6. Dolog, P.: Engineering Adaptive Web Applications. PhD thesis, Universität Hannover (2006)
7. Drusinsky, D.: Modeling and Verification Using UML Statecharts. Elsevier (2006)
8. Hennicker, R., Koch, N.: A UML-Based Methodology for Hypermedia Design. In: Evans, A., Kent, S., Selic, B. (eds.) UML 2000. LNCS, vol. 1939, pp. 410–424. Springer, Heidelberg (2000)
9. Hölzl, M., Knapp, A., Zhang, G.: Modeling the Car Crash Crisis Management System with HiLA. Trans. Aspect-Oriented Software Development (TAOSD) 7, 234–271 (2010)
10. Houben, G.-J., Frasincar, F., Barna, P., Vdovjak, R.: Modeling User Input and Hypermedia Dynamics in Hera. In: Koch, N., Fraternali, P., Wirsing, M. (eds.) ICWE 2004. LNCS, vol. 3140, pp. 60–73. Springer, Heidelberg (2004)
11. Int. Wsh. Aspect-Oriented Modeling (April 17, 2011), http://dawis2.icb.uni-due.de/aom/home
12. Knapp, A., Merz, S., Rauh, C.: Model Checking - Timed UML State Machines and Collaborations. In: Damm, W., Olderog, E.-R. (eds.) FTRTFT 2002. LNCS, vol. 2469, pp. 395–414. Springer, Heidelberg (2002)
13. Knapp, A., Zhang, G.: Model Transformations for Integrating and Validating Web Application Models. In: Mayr, H.C., Breu, R. (eds.) Proc. Modellierung (MOD 2006). Lect. Notes Informatics, vol. P-82, pp. 115–128. Gesellschaft für Informatik (2006)
14. Meliá, S., Gómez, J., Pérez, S., Díaz, O.: A Model-Driven Development for GWT-Based Rich Internet Applications with OOH4RIA. In: Schwabe, D., Curbera, F., Dantzig, P. (eds.) Proc. 8th Int. Conf. Web Engineering (ICWE 2008), pp. 13–23. IEEE (2008)
15. Object Management Group. OMG Unified Modeling Language (OMG UML), Superstructure, Version 2.4. Specification, OMG (2010), http://www.omg.org/spec/UML/2.4/Superstructure
16. Rossi, G., Schwabe, D., Lyardet, F.: Web Application Models Are More Than Conceptual Models. In: Kouloumdjian, J., Roddick, J., Chen, P.P., Embley, D.W., Liddle, S.W. (eds.) ER Workshops 1999. LNCS, vol. 1727, pp. 239–253. Springer, Heidelberg (1999)
17. Schauerhuber, A.: AspectUWA: Applying Aspect-Orientation to the Model-Driven Development of Ubiquitous Web Applications. PhD thesis, Technische Universität Wien (2007)
18. De Troyer, O., Leune, C.J.: WSDM: A User Centered Design Method for Web Sites. Computer Networks 30(1-7), 85–94 (1998)
19. Whittle, J., Moreira, A., Araújo, J., Jayaraman, P. K., Elkhodary, A.M., Rabbi, R.: An Expressive Aspect Composition Language for UML State Diagrams. In: Engels, G., Opdyke, B., Schmidt, D.C., Weil, F. (eds.) MODELS 2007. LNCS, vol. 4735, pp. 514–528. Springer, Heidelberg (2007)
20. Winckler, M., Palanque, P.A.: StateWebCharts: A Formal Description Technique Dedicated to Navigation Modelling of Web Applications. In: Jorge, J.A., Jardim Nunes, N., Falcão e Cunha, J. (eds.) DSV-IS 2003. LNCS, vol. 2844, pp. 61–76. Springer, Heidelberg (2003)
21. Wu, H.: A Reference Architecture for Adaptive Hypermedia Applications. PhD thesis, Technische Universiteit Eindhoven (2002)
22. Zhang, G.: Aspect-Oriented Modeling of Adaptive Web Applications with HiLA. In: Kotsis, G., Taniar, D., Pardede, E., Khalil, I. (eds.) Proc. 7th Int. Conf. Advances in Mobile Computing & Multimedia (MoMM 2009), pp. 331–335. ACM (2009)
23. Zhang, G.: Aspect-Oriented State Machines. PhD thesis, Ludwig-Maximilians-Universität München (2010)

24. Zhang, G.: Aspect-Oriented UI Modeling with State Machines. In: Van den Bergh, J., Sauer, S., Breiner, K., Hußmann, H., Meixner, G., Pleuss, A. (eds.) Proc. 5th Int. Wsh. Model-Driven Development of Advanced User Interfaces (MDDAUI 2010), pp. 45–48 (2010)
25. Zhang, G., Baumeister, H., Koch, N., Knapp, A.: Aspect-Oriented Modeling of Access Control in Web Applications. In: 6th Int. Wsh. Aspect Oriented Modeling (AOM 2005), Chicago (2005)
26. Zhang, J., Cottenier, T., van den Berg, A., Gray, J.: Aspect Composition in the Motorola Aspect-Oriented Modeling Weaver. Journal of Object Technology 6(7), 89–108 (2007)

# Model-Driven Web Form Validation
# with UML and OCL

Eban Escott[1], Paul Strooper[1], Paul King[2], and Ian J. Hayes[1]

[1] The University of Queensland, School of Information Technology
and Electrical Engineering, Brisbane, QLD, 4072, Australia
[2] ASERT, Level 23, 127 Creek St, Brisbane, QLD, 4001, Australia
{eescott,pstroop,ianh}@itee.uq.edu.au,
paulk@asert.com

**Abstract.** Form validation is an integral part of a web application. Web developers must ensure that data input by the user is validated for correctness. Given the importance of form validation it must be considered as part of a model-driven solution to web development. Existing model-driven approaches typically have not addressed form validation as part of the model. In this paper, we present an approach that allows validation constraints to be captured within a model using UML and OCL. Our approach covers three common types of validation: single element, multiple element, and entity association. We provide an example to illustrate an architecture-centric approach.

**Keywords:** Model-driven, web engineering, web form validation.

## 1 Introduction

The user experience of any web application is crucial to its success. This experience is influenced by many factors, including form validation. Users will fill out forms that are submitted to the server and these forms must be validated to ensure that the data entered is acceptable. Subsequently, this data could be used for some immediate operations, such as email or to invoke a web service. It could also be stored in a database for later use. No matter the intended use of the data, it is imperative that it is validated for correctness.

Form validation can be achieved on either the client-side or server-side of the application. Client-side validation offers a richer user experience by using technologies such as JavaScript and AJAX. Solely relying on client-side validation is a risk as a user may disable JavaScript via a browser setting. Therefore, server-side validation is a necessity that should not be avoided. For this reason, and to reduce scope, we focus only on server-side validation, although our approach could be applied to client-side validation as well.

Given the importance of form validation it must be considered as part of a model-driven solution to web development. There are many proposed web-modelling languages, but most do not address form validation. In this paper, we categorise form

A. Harth and N. Koch (Eds.): ICWE 2011 Workshops, LNCS 7059, pp. 223–235, 2012.
© Springer-Verlag Berlin Heidelberg 2012

validation and propose a model-driven solution that uses UML [1] and OCL [2]. UML is a general purpose modelling language and OCL augments UML to make more precise models. We analysed four different web application frameworks to ensure our approach can be used for a number of target platforms and show an example of generating form validation for one framework.

Section 2 discusses the related work and how other web modelling languages have included form validation. Section 3 shows how form validation is coded in a web application framework. This demonstrates the code that we must generate as part of our solution and in Section 4 we give an example of how to achieve this using UML and OCL. Section 5 discusses the results of using the approach on the example and relates the approach to generating form validation code for other web application frameworks. We conclude in Section 6 and summarise our future work.

## 2    Related Work

There are many different ways of applying model-driven development and each has its goals and priorities. We subscribe to Architecture-Centric Model-Driven Software Development (AC-MDSD) [3] in which the goals are development efficiency, software quality, and reusability. This is in contrast with other well-known approaches, such as the Model Driven Architecture (MDA) [4], where the goals are interoperability and software portability.

Stahl and Völter [3] describe AC-MDSD alongside an iterative two-track development process in which there is an implementation track, which is the target application, and a modelling and transformation track[1]. The implementation track is responsible for building the *reference implementation* that is used to derive the models and transformations. Stahl and Völter recommend that the implementation track should be one development iteration in front of the modelling and transformation track. The implementation track emphasises the importance of web application frameworks, which we discuss in Section 3. It may seem counter-intuitive to build a *reference implementation* as this creates an extra cost, but when considering that the outcome of AC-MDSD is to build many applications of the same software family, this cost is offset by later gains. This is not too dissimilar to a software product line where an initial investment must be made [5].

Existing web modelling languages have rarely discussed the issue of form validation. During our literature review of OOWS [6], OOHDM [7], UWE [8], IDM [9], WebML [10], Hera [11], and WSDM [12], we did not find references addressing form validation. Additionally, the code generators UWE4JSF [13] for UWE, OOHDMDA [14] for OOHDM, and HPG [15] for Hera, do not have form validation included. WebRatio [16] for WebML includes form validation by adding validation rules to entry units that are part of its domain-specific language (DSL). The tool

---

[1] Stahl and Völter refer to the two-track development process as having a *domain architecture* track and an *application* track. We refer to these as the *implementation* track and the *models and transformations* track respectively. We believe these terms are more intuitive in the context of this paper.

generates code for the Struts [17] web application framework but the details are not published as the tool is proprietary.

The only web modelling language openly addressing form validation is WebDSL [18]. WebDSL maintains separation of concerns while integrating its sublanguages, enabling consistency checking and reusing common language concepts. Groenewegen and Visser [19] have designed a WebDSL sublanguage for form validation and categorised form validation into *value well-formedness*, *data invariants*, *input assertions*, and *action assertions*. *Value well-formedness* checks that the input conforms to its expected type, *data invariants* are constraints in the domain model, *input assertions* are for form elements which are not directly connected to the domain model, and *action assertions* are validation checks during the execution of actions.

The WebDSL approach contrasts with our work as we apply a reusable UML-compliant solution, not a textual DSL specific to WebDSL. The WebDSL validation categories of *value well-formedness* and *action assertions* are not considered relevant in our context. For us, *value well-formedness* is handled by the web application framework and *action assertions* are not applicable to standard web form validation, which is the scope of our research. WebDSLs *input assertions* do not warrant a new category in our research as our UML profile can be applied to multiple models as discussed in Section 4.4. The last WebDSL category of *data invariants* is comparable to our validation categories. We use a finer-grained approach that is suited for specific web application frameworks.

We believe that the target web application framework is important. WebDSL attempts to create an implementation-neutral language that can be applied to multiple code generators. This approach has merit but risks missing opportunities to utilise features that exist in one web application framework and not in another. This point relates to the goals and priorities given the model-driven philosophy discussed at the beginning of this section and elaborated further in Section 5.

## 3    Web Application Frameworks

In our approach, the target architecture is closely aligned with a chosen web application framework. We examined four such frameworks and what the generated code might look like. This is part of an AC-MDSD approach whereby a developer should start by building the *reference implementation* first. Subsequently, this is used to abstract to the models and drive the transformations.

Web application frameworks form the backbone of modern web development. The features available for each framework vary but they all have some built-in mechanism to support form validation. For our research, we analysed four frameworks all with different programming languages. The frameworks are Spring MVC [20], Ruby on Rails [21], Grails [22], and ASP.NET MVC [23] using programming languages Java, Ruby, Groovy, and C# respectively. Spring MVC is used for our example in Section 4 based on its popularity in the market place, but we believe any of the four frameworks could be used as discussed in Section 5.

The Spring MVC web framework validation is based on JSR:303 Bean Validation [24] by the Java Community Process. JSR:303 allows developers to define declarative validation constraints based on annotations. For example, in the following program code on lines 6 and 7, a persons age has a minimum of 0 and a maximum of 110.

```
1  public class PersonForm {
2
3     @NotNull
4     private String name;
5
6     @Min(0)
7     @Max(110)
8     private int age;
9     ...
10 }
```

The annotations are applicable to single HTML elements only. If the developer needs to validate multiple elements or ensure entity associations are correct then they must use a custom validator. The following program code is a custom validator for Spring. The method *validate* on line 7 is invoked and provides an opportunity for developers to add in custom validation beyond what is available via JSR:303 annotations, or implement validation without annotations as shown in the following program code.

```
1  public class PersonValidator implements Validator {
2
3     public boolean supports(Class clazz) {
4        return Person.class.equals(clazz);
5     }
6
7     public void validate(Object obj, Errors e) {
8        ValidationUtils.rejectIfEmpty(e, "name", "empty");
9        Person p = (Person) obj;
10       if(p.getAge() < 0) {
11          e.rejectValue("age", "negativevalue");
12       } else if(p.getAge() > 110) {
13          e.rejectValue("age", "too.old");
14       }
15    }
16 }
```

All of the four web application frameworks we analysed have some mechanism for standard validation and custom validation. It is important to recognise the target code generation as this will become the *reference implementation* in the iterative two-track development process described in Section 2. In AC-MDSD, it is the implementation track that drives the modelling and transformation track.

# 4    Example

Our example shows how we use UML and OCL for form validation. The example involves generating a web application and manually testing the form validation. The generated web application provides create, read, update, and delete (CRUD) functionality for applicable parts of the domain. Fig. 1 is the domain model for our example and it is part of a typical e-commerce web application. A product belongs to a brand, can be categorised, and purchased via a shopping cart.

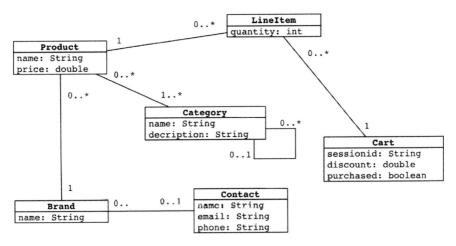

**Fig. 1.** Domain Model

In Section 4.1 we discuss the scope of the HTML elements we will consider for validation. In Section 4.2 we categorise the different types of validation and in Section 4.3 we describe our model-driven solution. The UML Profile is presented in the Section 4.4.

## 4.1    Target Elements

The W3C develops standards to ensure the long-term growth of the Web. At the time of writing this paper, the current version of HTML is 4.0.1[2]. We will be focusing our validation on these HTML elements. Section 17 of the HTML 4.01 specification [25] lists all possible form elements. Fig. 2 shows example HTML with a typical rendering below. A developer can place an element on a form to allow a user to input some data.

There are technologies available that allow for more complex elements by combining these elements together in a meaningful way. For example, a developer can use JSF [26] to create custom controls, or mixing HTML with JavaScript different input types are possible. At this stage, we have considered HTML 4.01 elements only though the approach is extensible and part of our future work.

---

[2] HTML 5.0 is not finalised but our approach could include new elements from the specification.

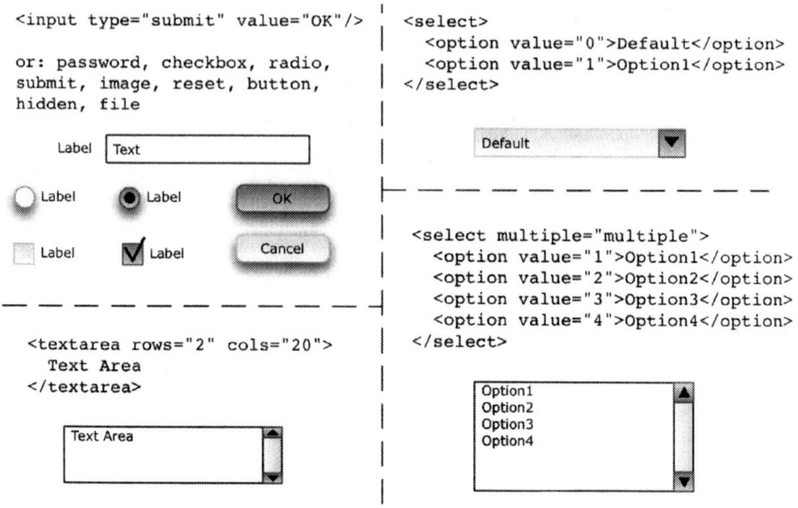

**Fig. 2.** HTML 4.01 form elements

## 4.2    Validation Categories

We conducted an analysis of several web sites to categorise different types of validation. These categories are used to determine how the validation will be included in the meta-models and eventually transformed into generated code for the target web application framework. The three categories we found are: *single element, multiple element,* and *entity association.*

*Single element* refers to validation that occurs on one HTML element only. For example, a text field must not be empty, or the integer entered must be less than ten. Depending on the type of HTML element, different web application frameworks provide built-in validation. All frameworks allow setting minima and maxima for numerical types and string lengths. They also all have some way to use regular expressions for validation; for example, email addresses, credit cards, dates, etc.

*Multiple element* validation occurs when the value entered by a user on one element has an effect on what is expected in another element. For example, if a checkbox is ticked then a text field must not be empty, or a date entered in an element must be before another date in a different element.

*Entity association* refers to the class relationships that exist in the domain. The domain is included in the majority of web modelling languages, e.g. in UWE it is known as a content model. UML class diagrams and the associations between the classes have a multiplicity, e.g. a one-to-many relationship. In this case, unlike a zero-to-many, it may be required that the one multiplicity is required.

All of the three validation categories are included in our example. Fig. 3 is a screen capture of the validation that occurs when a user attempts to save a new product without filling in any of the form. The error messages are displayed to the right of the element. The form has been generated and is part of a web application.

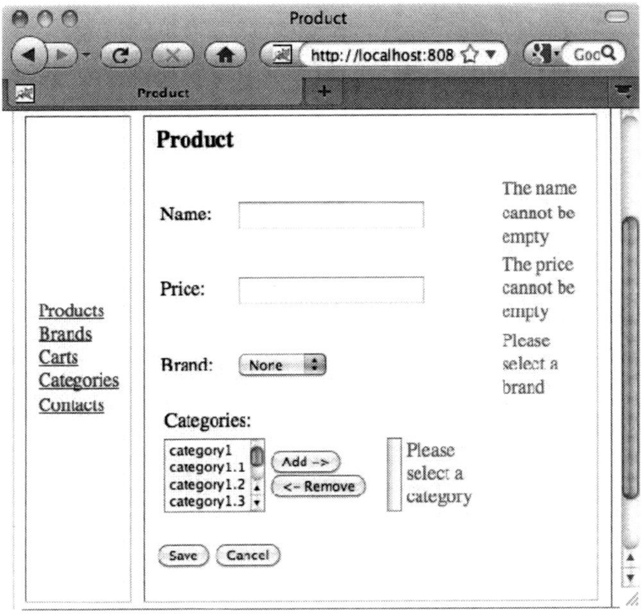

**Fig. 3.** Example of Product form validation

### 4.3    Modelling and Transformations

Our model-driven solution to web form validation is part of a solution that generates web applications using Spring MVC and Hibernate [27]. For the context of this section we will give a brief summary of our models and transformations. Since the majority of web application frameworks are based on MVC we create three models, one model for each of the MVC-triad. We name our models the same: *Model, View*, and *Controller*. These models form the basis of our graphical DSL for web applications.

We build our target application and then, through a process of abstraction, map the application to the models. Stahl and Völter [3] describe AC-MDSD alongside a two-track iterative development process and we have had success in generating web applications with this approach. A full description of our models and transformations is beyond the scope of this paper, although recognition of the included models is needed to understand this section.

**Single Element.** UML stereotypes are used to model single element validation. By analysing the target web application framework, in this case Spring using JSR:303, we identify that the annotations can be generated using UML stereotypes. For example, as shown in Fig. 4, the *Product's* name is stereotyped <<NotEmpty>> and the price is stereotyped <<Min>>. The <<Min>> stereotype has a property that is used in the transformation and, in this case, the developer has set the value to zero.

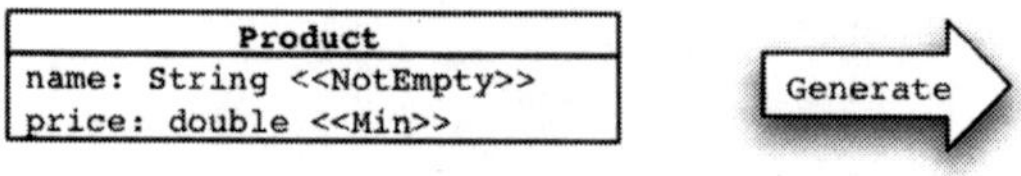

```
1  public class ProductForm {
2
3     @NotEmpty
4     private String name;
5
6     @Min(0)
7     private Double price;
8
9     ...
10 }
```

Product
name: String <<NotEmpty>>
price: double <<Min>>

Generate

**Fig. 4.** Product with stereotypes

We use the Eclipse Modelling Project [28] and subprojects for our modelling and transformation track. The models are UML2 [29] with Profiles using JET [30] for the model-to-code transformations. JET uses templates and we implement a multi-stage generator that uses intermediate XML beans.

**Multiple element.** We use OCL constraints (invariants) to represent multiple element validation, as UML stereotypes do not provide sufficient flexibility. For example, a *Contact* must input an email address, a phone number, or both. The OCL invariant is:

```
email.size() > 0 or phone.size() > 0
```

We place these invariants on the UML class in the domain model. If an invariant is found during the transformations, we use the Eclipse subproject OCL [31] to assist generate the form validation code. OCL has an abstract syntax tree and we have implemented a *visitor* (pattern) that produces Java expressions. The following program code shows how the OCL constraint is created on line 1; and on line 3 the expression is visited by our OCL to Spring Visitor which outputs the required Java code.

```
1 OCLExpression query = helper.createQuery(expression);
2 OCL2SpringVisitor visitor = new OCL2SpringVisitor();
3 String code = query.accept(visitor);
```

The Java code is stored as a string and further along the transformation process it is passed to a JET template that is responsible for producing the Spring validator class shown below. The boolean expression for the if statement on lines 7 and 8 is the code produced by our visitor. It is the negation of the OCL constraint, which is the condition that should reject the value.

```
1  public class ContactValidator implements Validator {
2     public boolean supports(Class clazz) {
3        return ContactForm.class.equals(clazz);
4     }
5     public void validate(Object obj, Errors e) {
6        ContactForm form = (ContactForm) obj;
7        if((form.getEmail().length() <= 0) &&
8           (form.getPhone().length() <= 0)) {
9           e.rejectValue("contact.multiple");
10       }
11    }
12 }
```

The result of an OCL expression is true or false, making it well suited for form validation. By visiting an OCL expression we are able to create the equivalent Java expression needed to be placed in the web application custom validator. Eclipse OCL does model checking prior to our transformations ensuring that the OCL is syntactically correct and references valid attributes in a UML class diagram.

**Entity Association.** Enforcing multiplicities on class associations is dependent on the requirements of the web application. Some projects do not require this to be validated while others do. For our example, when an entity is either created or updated the association multiplicities are enforced. This entails checking the associations and if an association had a value of '1', we then add in validation. In Fig. 3, this can be seen as a *Product* has a *..1 association to a *Brand*. So, the user must select a brand before saving.

No additional UML stereotypes or OCL needs to be included. The UML class associations can have multiplicities and during the transformation we check for these. When one is found we add validation to the appropriate validator as shown in the following code. Line 7 checks that the user has selected a *Brand* other than the default value of '0'. Fig. 3 shows the validation working in a browser.

```
1   public class ProductValidator implements Validator {
2     public boolean supports(Class clazz) {
3       return ProductForm.class.equals(clazz);
4     }
5     public void validate(Object obj, Errors e) {
6       ProductForm form = (ProductForm) obj;
7       if(form.getSelectedBrand()[0].equals("0")) {
9         e.rejectValue("brand.atLeastOne");
10      }
11    }
12 }
```

### 4.4   UML Profile

Fig. 5 shows part of the UML Profile used for *single* and *multiple element* validation. All stereotypes inherit from *Bundle*, which has two properties: errorMessage and errorCode. In our generated web application, these are transformed into a resource bundle that is used by Spring MVC to display error messages to the user.

The *Single* stereotype is abstract and subclassed for each annotation of JSR:303. For brevity, Fig. 5 only shows some of the JSR:303 annotations. A *Single* stereotype can be applied to a Property, which is called an extension and is depicted by an arrow with the head filled in [1, p.659]. Similarly, the Multiple stereotype can be a applied to a Class. The extension restricts the UML elements that the stereotype can be applied to.

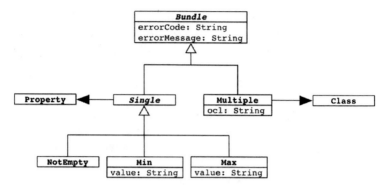

**Fig. 5.** Validation Profile

We have illustrated by example in this section how to apply our UML profile to a domain model. It is possible to have form elements that are not directly related to an entity from the domain model. These form elements may need to be validated. In WebDSL, this category of validation is called *input assertions*. We do not have a separate category, as we are able to apply the UML profile to our *View* model and reuse all of the same validation. It is beyond the scope of this paper to explain our *View* model in depth, but the UML profile enables us to apply validation to other models than the domain.

## 5     Discussion

Stahl and Völter [3] recommend that target artefacts are hand-written at least once in AC-MDSD. So, we build a *reference implementation* and then infer our model and transformations. If we wanted to include client-side validation we would start with making changes to the *reference implementation*. Once we were satisfied with the client-side validation we would then update our transformations and include any extra information necessary in the model. Similarly, for new HTML 5 elements we would include them following this same process.

So, if we were to follow the process again, but for a different web application framework, would we be able to reuse this approach with UML and OCL? Each of the four frameworks we analysed has some standard validators as shown in Table 1. Additionally, each framework provides custom validation whereby the developer can validate any of the form input. Therefore, it would be possible to use our approach again as *single element* validation can use UML stereotypes with a simple one-to-one mapping with the standard validators in Table 1. *Multiple element* validation and *entity association* would again need to be implemented via a custom validator.

The AC-MDSD goals of development efficiency, software quality, and reusability differ from the MDA goals of interoperability and software portability. MDA aims to achieve these goals via transformations from the platform independent model (PIM) to the platform specific model (PSM) and subsequently to the code. In our example, by mapping the web application framework standard validators to UML stereotypes we are making our models specific to that web application framework, effectively creating PSMs. If we were interested in creating a PIM we would need a suitable approach that would cover the standard validators as seen in Table 1. Using OCL for *single element* validation could be a viable solution and this is part of our future work.

**Table 1.** Standard validators for web application frameworks. In addition, each framework has the ability to provide custom validation.

| Framework | Validation |
|-----------|------------|
| Spring | AssertFalse, AssertTrue, DecimalMax, DecimalMin, Digits, Email, Future, Length, Max, Min, NotNull, NotEmpty, Null, Past, Pattern, Range, Size, Valid |
| ASP.NET MVC | Range, RegularExpression, Required, StringLength |
| Ruby on Rails | validates_acceptance_of, validates_associated, validates_confirmation_of, validates_each, validates_exclusion_of, validates_format_of, validates_inclusion_of, validates_length_of, validates_numericality_of, validates_presense_of, validates_size_of, validates_uniqueness_of |
| Grails | blank, creditCard, email, inList, matches, max, maxSize, min, minSize, notEqual, nullable, range, scale, size, unique, url |

## 6    Conclusion

Form validation is an important part of a web application and must be considered in model-driven web development. In this paper, we present an example of applying AC-MDSD using a two-track development methodology. Our models are UML and OCL compliant and the scope of our example is HTML 4.01 form elements with server-side validation. Client-side validation and complex form elements are future work.

We categorised validation into *single element, multiple element*, and *entity association*. We used UML stereotypes for single element and OCL for multiple element validation. Entity association is expressed as part of the domain model, which is a UML class diagram. In our transformations we checked the multiplicity of the associations and applied validation accordingly. We were able to successfully generate a Spring web application from our models and display them in a browser for manual testing.

Our analysis of web application frameworks included four frameworks with different programming languages. We observed some similarities between the different frameworks and this could be exploited to create a validation meta-model to be applied to more than one implementation. This approach does have an inherent risk that attempting to apply a general model for all implementations may miss some features of a framework. This issue will be addressed as part of our future work.

**Acknowledgements.** We would like to thank the Australian Postgraduate Award, The University of Queensland.

# References

1. Unified Modeling Language (April 10, 2011),
   `http://www.omg.org/spec/UML/2.2`
2. Object Constraint Language (April 10, 2011),
   `http://www.omg.org/spec/OCL/2.2`
3. Stahl, T., Völter, M.: Model-Driven Software Development: Technology, Engineering, Management. John Wiley, Chichester (2006)
4. Model Driven Architecture, `http://www.omg.org/mda`
5. Bockle, G., Clements, P., McGregor, J.D., Muthig, D., Schmid, K.: Calculating ROI for Software Product Lines. IEEE Software 21(3), 23–31 (2004)
6. Valderas, P., Fons, J., Pelechano, V.: Transforming Web Requirements into Navigational Models: AN MDA Based Approach. In: Delcambre, L., Kop, C., Mayr, H.C., Mylopoulos, J., Pastor, Ó. (eds.) ER 2005. LNCS, vol. 3716, pp. 320–336. Springer, Heidelberg (2005)
7. Rossi, G., Schwabe, D.: Modeling and Implementing Web Application with OOHDM. In: Rossi, G., Pastor, O., Schwabe, D., Olsina, L. (eds.) Web Engineering: Modelling and Implementing Web Applications, pp. 109–155. Springer, Heidelberg (2008)
8. Hennicker, R., Koch, N.: A UML-Based Methodology for Hypermedia Design. In: Evans, A., Kent, S., Selic, B. (eds.) UML 2000. LNCS, vol. 1939, pp. 410–424. Springer, Heidelberg (2000)
9. Bolchini, D., Garzotto, F.: Designing Multichannel Web Applications as "Dialogue Systems": the IDM Model. In: Rossi, G., Pastor, O., Schwabe, D., Olsina, L. (eds.) Web Engineering: Modelling and Implementing Web Applications, pp. 193–219. Springer, Heidelberg (2008)
10. Ceri, S., Fraternali, P., Bongio, A.: Web Modeling Language (WebML): a modeling language for designing Web sites. Computer Networks 33(1-6), 137–157 (2000)
11. Houben, G.J., Sluijs, K., Barna, P., Broekstra, J., Casteleyn, S., Fiala, Z., Frasincar, F.: HERA. In: Rossi, G., Pastor, O., Schwabe, D., Olsina, L. (eds.) Web Engineering: Modelling and Implementing Web Applications, pp. 263–301. Springer, Heidelberg (2008)
12. Troyer, O.D., Casteleyn, S., Plessers, P.: WSDM: Web Semantics Design Method. In: Rossi, G., Pastor, O., Schwabe, D., Olsina, L. (eds.) Web Engineering: Modelling and Implementing Web Applications, pp. 303–351. Springer, Heidelberg (2008)
13. Kroiss, C., Koch, N., Knapp, A.: UWE4JSF: A Model-Driven Generation Approach for Web Applications. In: Gaedke, M., Grossniklaus, M., Díaz, O. (eds.) ICWE 2009. LNCS, vol. 5648, pp. 493–496. Springer, Heidelberg (2009)
14. Schmid, H., Donnerhak, O.: OOHDMDA – An MDA Approach for OOHDM. In: Lowe, D., Gaedke, M. (eds.) ICWE 2005. LNCS, vol. 3579, pp. 569–574. Springer, Heidelberg (2005)
15. Rutten, B., Barna, P., Frasincar, F., Houben, G.J., Vdovjak, R.: HPG: a tool for presentation generation in WIS. In: Proceedings of the 13th International World Wide Web Conference on Alternate Track Papers & Posters, pp. 242–243. ACM (2004)
16. Acerbis, R., Bongio, A., Brambilla, M., Butti, S.: WebRatio 5: An Eclipse-Based CASE Tool for Engineering Web Applications. In: Baresi, L., Fraternali, P., Houben, G.-J. (eds.) ICWE 2007. LNCS, vol. 4607, pp. 501–505. Springer, Heidelberg (2007)

17. Apache Struts, `http://www.struts.apache.org`
18. Visser, E.: WebDSL: A Case Study in Domain-Specific Language Engineering. In: Lämmel, R., Visser, J., Saraiva, J. (eds.) Generative and Transformational Techniques in Software Engineering II. LNCS, vol. 5235, pp. 291–373. Springer, Heidelberg (2008)
19. Groenewegen, D.M., Visser, E.: Integration of Data Validation and User Interface Concerns in a DSL for Web Applications. In: van den Brand, M., Gašević, D., Gray, J. (eds.) SLE 2009. LNCS, vol. 5969, pp. 164–173. Springer, Heidelberg (2010)
20. Spring Framework (March 1, 2011), `http://www.springsource.org`
21. Ruby on Rails (March 1, 2011), `http://www.rubyonrails.org`
22. Grails (March 1, 2011), `http://www.grails.org`
23. ASP.NET MVC (March 1, 2011), `http://www.asp.net.mvc`
24. JSR: 303 (March 1, 2011), `http://jcp.org/en/jsr/detail?id=303`
25. HTML 4.0.1 Specification, `http://www.w3.org/TR/html401/`
26. Java Server Faces (March 1, 2011),
    `http://java.sun.com/javaee/javaserverfaces/`
27. Hibernate (March 1, 2011), `http://www.hibernate.org`
28. Eclipse Modeling Project (March 15, 2011),
    `http://www.eclipse.org/modeling/`
29. UML2 (March 15, 2011),
    `http://www.eclipse.org/modeling/mdt/?project=uml2`
30. JET (March 15, 2011),
    `http://www.eclipse.org/modeling/mdt/?project=jet`
31. OCL (March 15, 2011),
    `http://www.eclipse.org/modeling/mdt/?project=ocl`

# Modernization of Legacy Web Applications into Rich Internet Applications*

Roberto Rodríguez-Echeverría, José María Conejero, Pedro J. Clemente,
Juan C. Preciado, and Fernando Sánchez-Figueroa

University of Extremadura Spain,
Quercus Software Engineering Group
{rre,chemacm,pjclemente,jcpreciado,fernando}@unex.es
http://quercusseg.unex.es

**Abstract.** In the last years one of the main concerns of the software industry has been to reengineer their legacy Web Applications (WAs) to take advantage of the benefits introduced by Rich Internet Applications (RIAs), such as enhanced user interaction and network bandwith optimization. However, those reengineering processes have been traditionally performed in an ad-hoc manner, resulting in very expensive and error-prone projects. This situation is partly motivated by the fact that most of the legacy WAs were developed before Model-Driven Development (MDD) approaches became mainstream. Then maintenance activities of those legacy WAs have not been yet incorporated to a MDA development lifecycle. OMG Architecture Driven Modernization (ADM) advocates for applying MDD principles to formalize and standardize those reengineering processes with modernization purposes. In this paper we outline an ADM-based WA-to-RIA modernization process, highlighting the special characteristics of this modernization scenario.

**Keywords:** Web Models Transformations, Software Modernization, Software Reengineering, Rich Internet Applications.

## 1 Introduction

Rich Internet Applications (RIAs) have emerged as the most promising platform for Web 2.0 development by the combination of the lightweight distribution architecture of the Web with the interface interactivity and computation power of desktop applications, with benefits on all the elements of a WA (data, business logic, communication, and presentation). Among others, RIAs offer online and offline capabilities, sophisticated user interfaces, the possibility to store and process data directly on the client side; they offer high levels of user interaction, usability and personalization. RIAs also minimize bandwidth usage, and separate presentation and content at the client side [16].

---

* This work has been developed under the Spanish Contract MIGRARIA - TIN2011-27340 funded by Ministerio de Ciencia e Innovación, FEDER and Junta de Extremadura.

A. Harth and N. Koch (Eds.): ICWE 2011 Workshops, LNCS 7059, pp. 236–250, 2012.

To take advantage of these new capabilities, the industry is performing a reengineering of their legacy WAs to produce RIA clients. Unfortunately, a huge number of those legacy WAs were developed before most promising Model-Driven Web Engineering (MDWE) [18] methodologies were mature enough for mainstream. Then the industry posses a wide catalogue of complex WAs that were developed without following any MDD principle or technique. And the maintenance activities of those legacy WAs cannot be incorporated to the MDA development lifecycle of a company. Among other negative consequences, a lot of those legacy applications may lack a comprehensive up-to-date documentation and they may have been poorly maintained integrating new technologies without a defined strategy. In this complex scenario, the industry demands formalization and standardization of reengineering processes to reduce the expensive costs and high risks introduced by ad-hoc reengineering processes. In this setting, OMG Architecture-Driven Modernization (ADM) advocates for the application of Model-Driven Development (MDD) techniques and tools to formalize and standardize software reengineering processes.

Precisely, the major objective of the work presented in this paper is to define a flexible framework for the systematic and semi-automatic modernization of legacy non-model-based data-driven WAs into RIAs following OMG ADM principles. This paper shows then part of our work performed inside a complete modernization project we are currently developing in partnership with a national software company. In concrete, in this paper we only present a brief outline of our process, focusing specially on the RIA pattern identification activity. We conceived WA-to-RIA modernization as the process of building a RIA client from the legacy WA presentation and navigation layers and the required service-oriented connection layer with the underlying business logic at server side. Besides, we consider a RIA client is characterized for satisfying a set (or subset) of RIA features (presented in Section 2).

According to the OMG Architecture-Driven Modernization (ADM), the main objectives of our work may be summarized as follows:

- Legacy WA knowledge discovery. Our framework tries to define which information from the legacy system should be of interest for the modernization. And it tries to refine the knowledge extracted to alleviate the modernization costs. The acquired knowledge could be very heterogeneous covering aspects from technical (e.g. components, flow controls, etc.) to business domains (e.g. tasks, business rules, etc.).
- Target architecture definition. Recently, many approaches have appeared [6][14][22] in the Web Engineering community for the definition of RIA architectures. We try to apply the results of those proposals in our intent to derive a conceptual description of RIAs, which was independent of any particular technological platform and was useful on modernization processes.
- Transformation steps from the original system to the target one. Our framework tries to define the necessary sequence of steps to transform a legacy WA into a RIA, keeping the required flexibility to cope with different modernization scenarios.

The rest of the paper is structured as follows. Section 2 presents the collection of RIA features we consider to define the RIA client concept. Section 3 defines the system we use to illustrate our approach. Section 4 introduces our approach. The related work is commented in Section 5. Finally, main conclusions and future work are presented in Section 6.

## 2    Main Features of RIAs

In order to give a definition to the RIA client concept and to identify the relevant information to extract from the legacy WA for modernization, we have performed a deep analysis of the RIA-extended MDWE approaches and collected all the RIA features covered by them from a conceptual point of view. We have performed the collection and annotation of RIA features in a high level of abstraction, trying to avoid low level or technological concerns, and trying to provide a unified vision of them.

We consider the work in [16] as the starting point in the evolution and extension of a set of MDWE approaches in order to fulfill the new expressivity requirements introduced by the RIA development. According to that decision, we have only considered works published since 2005. Among the different proposals available in literature, we have studied both the most mature ones and also the recent proposals under development that may have some impact in the next future: WebML4RIA [6], OOHDM-RIA [19], OOH4RIA [11], UWE for RIA [7], RUX-Method [9], UWE-R [10], OOWS 2.0 [22], ADRIA [5] and IAML [24].

Following we present the collecion of RIA features we have:

- RF01. Data storage on client side. This feature refers to the capability of the client side to store data in a volatile or persistent way. The persistent data storage on client side is becoming a clear trend for current RIAs (key feature of HTML 5 standard).
- RF02. Multiple data sources or types. Actual RIAs can connect to different data providers (databases, Web services, Web APIs, etc.) and use different data formats (raw datasets, XML, JSON, etc.).
- RF03. Multimedia and Animation Support. Temporal Behavior. This feature refers to the capability of the client side to manage complex animations and multimedia content properly in order to enhance the user interaction.
- RF04. Logic execution on client side. It refers to the capability of the client side to execute part of the business logic inside its own runtime. Together with RF01 may reduce considerably server roundtrips and enhance user experience and productivity.
- RF05. Multithreading or concurrency. This feature refers to the capability of the client side to launch simultaneously different functionality threads. Its most widespread use is the ability of the client side of keeping a responsive interface while requesting data from the server side.
- RF06. Multidevice User Interface. This feature refers to the capability of a RIA to be accessed from a wide range of heterogeneous client terminals (user agents or devices). In the last years, RIAs have spreaded to the mobile

market and they have become one of the most preferred approaches to deploy applications because of their independence of technology.

- RF07. Single-Page Paradigm or Partial Page Refresh. This feature refers to the capability of a RIA client to present a desktop-like user interface avoiding the Click-Wait-and-Refresh-Cycle, characteristic of Web clients. This feature could be seen as a consequence of RF04 and RF12, at least.

- RF08. Rich UI Components (widgets). This feature refers to the capability of a RIA client to use a whole constellation of interactive and complex controls and components for UI composition. It supposes logic execution on client side.

- RF09. Rich User Interaction. This feature refers to the capability of a RIA client to define enhanced interactions and complex UI behaviours by expliciting orchestrations among widgets and server-side logic.

- RF10. Client runtime control. This feature refers to the capability of a RIA client to use and control partially the functionality of its runtime and to change its default behaviour, e.g. the back button of a Web browser.

- RF11. Communication started on server side (push model). This feature refers to the capability of a RIA to overcome the request-response communication model of Web applications. In a RIA both tiers (client and server) can innitiate a communication process with the other one.

- RF12. Asynchronous communication. This feature refers to the capability of a RIA client to send a request to the server without blocking until a response is sent back. A RIA can keep working normally and handle the response when necessary.

- RF13. Bulk data client-to-server transfers. It refers to the capability of a RIA client to send a collection of data to the server at once to reduce the server roundtrips. A RIA client stores collections of related data produced by the normal execution process and, at a given time, it sends the whole set of data to the server at once.

- RF14. Synchronization between client and server tiers. This feature refers to the capability of a RIA to keep data consistency among the different tiers of the application. This is a high level feature and then it can be decomposed in communication sequences between tiers. This feature could be seen as a combination of RF01, RF04, RF13, and a concrete synchronization policy.

- RF15. Offline mode. This feature refers to the capability of a RIA client to change seamlessly its operation mode between standalone, without live connection to the server, and online modes, with connection to the server. This is also a high level feature (referred as an architectural feature in some works) and then it can be seen as a consequence of the application of RF01, RF04, RF07 and RF14, at least.

## 3   Illustrative Example

In order to illustrate the main steps of our approach, let us consider JAVA Pet Store[1] Demo (Petstore) as our legacy WA. Petstore 1.3.2 was built on 2003 by JAVA BluePrints team to exemplify the development of a WA by means of the J2EE SDK technologies. Following we present the main reasons to select this sample legacy WA.

- The source code is publicly available. And it is a medium-size system.
- There exists a comprehensive documentation because it is conceived as a training project.
- It could be considered a well-known sample application and the baseline code of many WAs developed during those years.
- Its development is based on the BluePrints Web Application Framework (WAF), which inspired next JAVA Web application frameworks. So it presents the main elements of current MVC-based Web Application Frameworks.
- We think it is representative enough to illustrate the main points of the proposed approach.
- Additionally, Petstore has been evolving along with the JEE SDK to illustrate the features of the new versions. So, with the release of JEE 5 SDK, Petstore was reengineered to illustrate how the Java EE 5 platform can be used to develop an AJAX-enabled Web 2.0 application.

In this setting, Petstore WA is perfectly suitable to be used as our case study since the original application is used as the input for our approach whilst the new Petstore 2.0 WA represents the desired output of the approach.

Basically, Petstore WA provides customers with online shopping. Through a Web browser, a customer can browse the catalog, place items to purchase into a virtual shopping cart, create and sign in to a user account, and purchase the shopping cart contents by placing an order with a credit card.

As one of our main goals consists on modernizing the presentation tier, we have focused on the catalog functionality of the Storefront component. In concrete, we are interested in product and item page shown in figure 1. These two web pages are dinamycally generated from application data. The former displays a product listing (all items of Chihuahua product in figure). The latter shows the details of a concrete item (Adult Male Chihuahua in figure). Every product item of the product page links with its corresponding item page. Clearly a Master/Detail relationship is set between the main data displayed by both pages.

From a RIA viewpoint, contrary to the multipage solution presented by Petstore 1.3.2, this scenario of data relationship is realized in a single page by applying the Master/Detail screen pattern [20]. This is an ideal pattern for creating an efficient user experience by allowing the user to stay in the same screen while navigating between items. Moreover, as figure 2 illustrates, Master/Detail screen pattern is the solution adopted by the Petstore 2.0[2] implementation for

---

[1] Version 1.3.2: [Aug 04, 2003]
   http://java.sun.com/blueprints/code/jps132/docs/index.html
[2] http://java.sun.com/developer/technicalArticles/J2EE/petstore/

**Fig. 1.** Master/Detail relationship between product and item pages

**Fig. 2.** Master/Detail Screen pattern merging legacy product and item pages

the scenario depicted above. This modernization scenario is precisely the case study we have selected to illustrate our approach.

## 4   The Approach

As aforementioned, the approach presented in this work briefly introduces and outlines our modernization process of a legacy WA. As figure 3 shows, the main objective of our process is to generate a RIA client of the legacy WA and the necessary service-oriented connection layer with the underlying business logic. The RIA client could be composed of a rich UI (highly interactive), the data stored at client side, the logic processed at client side, and the infrastructure logic for server communication and synchronization. Most of the server-side code would remain unmodified so the system could keep working as a WA. With that purpose, a connection layer would be built between the new RIA client and the original business logic. This layer aims to cope with the derived data and logic distribution concerns and seamlessly integrate an asynchronous communication model between client and server.

As depicted in figure 4, our modernization process consists on 5 main phases: (1) static and dynamic information extraction from the source (data, logic and presentation) and the configuration files of the original WA; (2) knowledge representation and refinement on a technology independent language (we use KDM),

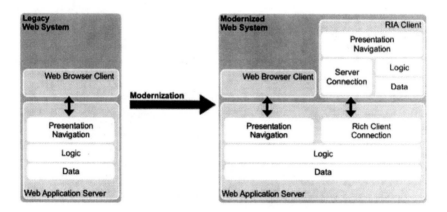

**Fig. 3.** Target system architecture

the extracted information is incorporated in a model with a higher level of abstraction; (3) optional projection of the conceptual system to a specific RIA-extended MDWE approach; (4) optional Web models refinement by applying RIA patterns at more concrete level; and (5) final code generation.

According the ADM horseshoe model proposed by OMG [21], which defines 3 modernization domain levels (technology, application & data, and business), we argue our approach would be located at the second domain level (application and data architecture) because we think it involves major changes (beyond technical domain) that clearly affect the application architecture. Fundamentally, these changes are related to:

- The UI structure and organization (RF06-RF08). The multipage structure of the legacy WA presentation layer should be frequently modified according to the single-page paradigm (RF07) characteristic of RIA clients. A componentization process should be performed to map plain HTML display elements and controls into RIA widgets. And all the main elements of the legacy UI layout should be rearranged according to the new paradigm.
- The UI control flow (RF05, RF09-RF10). The hyperlink-based interaction model should be transformed to an event-based interaction model. In a RIA client navigation is not conceived as a sequence of hyperlinked page. Navigation is realized as a sequence of UI state transitions driven by events. Some of those transitions could not imply a request to the server. An UI state transition could be basically defined as an update (screen update) of the current UI components or as a new components load (new screen load).
- The client to server communication (RF11-RF14). RIA clients frequently interact with server logic following a service-oriented model, which may imply major changes on server side logic interface. Additionally, single-page RIA clients require an asynchronous communication model to maintain a responsive UI.

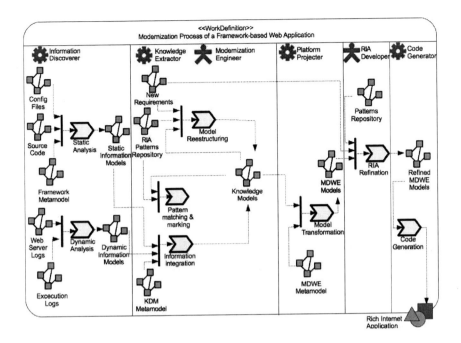

**Fig. 4.** Modernization process overview

- The offline work mode (RF15). Many RIA clients provide their users with the capability of switching between online and offline modes. Obviously, this is a highly device-dependant feature, because at client side: data should be stored (RF01); and business logic should be executed (RF04).

Following, we try to provide a more detailed vision of the main stages of our modernization process, using the Petstore sample WA to illustrate them. We will take special attention to the RIA pattern recognition step in phase 2.

## 4.1  Information Extraction and Representation

As shown in figure 4, the first phase of our process tries to reduce the complexity of the modernization process by switching from the heterogeneous world of implementation technologies to the homogeneous world of models. For this purpose, following ADM recommendations, we have used available solutions for code to model transformation (static analysis), such as MoDisCo discoverers and metamodels for Java, JSP and XML (Specific Abstract Syntax Tree Metamodels, SASTM[3]). Language-dependent models representing the whole legacy WA are then obtained as final products of this phase. Then, the process provides us, thus, with the ability of working directly with models since this moment. Further we have considered the convenience of specifying additional metamodels to

---

[3] http://www.omg.org/spec/ASTM/

capture supplemental information from the legacy WA, e.g. WAF information. But we decided to postpone that goal to the next iteration of our approach.

According to our goal of generating a RIA client, the most relevant information to extract accurately is the one involved in the following concerns:

- UI Layout. Commonly, legacy WAs have been built to keep a uniform UI structure and organization to increase usability and to present a recognizable look&feel. To capture that UI Layout is then a preponderant requirement of our modernization process. So the legacy WA look&feel could be regenerated in the RIA client. That is a difficult task. Our approach consists on extracting that kind of information from the template system used by the Web application framework. In the concrete case of our example, we get some basic UI Layout information from the configuration file of the template system. Figure 5 (left side) shows the UI Layout of the item page.

- Web page and data relationships. Dynamic Web pages are generated on the fly to display different values of the application data. So every dynamic Web page defines a concrete view of application data. The correct specification of those views and the related data entities are key to infer the proper componentization of the legacy WA UI. Figure 5 (right side) shows the JSP code excerpt that relates the item page to the item data.

- Navigational map. In order to generate a RIA client according to the single page paradigm (RF07) is necessary to extract and process the whole navigational map of the legacy WA. So grouping and clustering activities could be performed to assist on the componentization process. In our example, the navigation information could be extracted from different sources: JSP pages, template system configuration file, request mapping file (concrete responses to client request may be specified) and Java code, indeed. For this work, we are only considering the navigational map extracted from the JSP pages.

- Operational map. This map is a subset of the navigational map concerning only the requests dispatched by the controller component of the legacy WA as action calls to the business layer. The operational map is useful to discover the request flows between client and server tiers (communication model) and to identify the operations performed over the data. In our example, the operational map could be extracted from JSP pages and the request mapping file.

```
<screen name="item">
  <parameter key="title" value="Item" direct="true"/>   <c:set value="${catalog.item}" var="item" />
  <parameter key="banner" value="/banner.jsp" />
  <parameter key="sidebar" value="/sidebar.jsp" />      <p class="petstore_title">
  <parameter key="body" value="/item.jsp" />              <c:out value="${item.attribute}"/>
  <parameter key="mylist" value="/mylist.jsp" />          <c:out value="${item.productName}"/>
  <parameter key="footer" value="/footer.jsp" />        </p>
</screen>
```

**Fig. 5.** Legacy code

Finally, we introduce an activity to analyze dynamically the legacy WA. We argue that the analysis of the runtime traces could provide us with valuable information about user interaction. That interactivity information could drive modernization decisions to take in following phases of the process.

### 4.2   Knowledge Inference and Representation

This is the main phase of the modernization process. The goal of this phase would be to derive an enriched conceptual specification of the legacy system in a technology-independent model (knowledge model) from the information stored inside the static and dynamic models generated on the previous phase. Moreover, the knowledge model will be continuously refined according to the modernization goals. From an overall viewpoint, this phase is composed of three fundamental steps:

1. Transformation of the intermediate static models (SASTM) onto the technology-independent knowledge model (KDM[4]), integrating all the extracted information. ADM suggests to use a M2M transformation to perform this step, as [15][4][3] exemplified.
2. Enrichment of the KDM models from the dynamic information obtained.
3. Intermediate model refinement by finding expressions of characteristic RIA patterns.

On one hand, figure 6 shows an excerpt of the KDM representation (simplified) of the Petstore sample WA, as an example of the output of the first step of this phase. As shown, we are only considering UI and Code KDM Packages. In the UI Packages JSP pages are modeled as instances of the *Screen* metaclass, product and item *Screen* instances in the figure. Both *Screen* instances are related by a *UIFlow* instance that represents a navigation flow from the product *Screen* instance to the item *Screen* instance. We are considering only the main area of the JSP pages. So both *Screen* instances are only composed of *UIField* instances representing the data to be displayed. Every *UIField* is related with a *Member Unit* instance by a *Display* relationship. In this case, the *Member Unit* instances represent members of the item instance of *Class Unit*. That way both screens specify a different view of the item *Class Unit*. Additionally (not shown in the figure), the product *Screen* instance actually displays a collection of instances of item *Class Unit*.

On the other hand, the model refinement step is performed in two sequential activities: (1) identification of pattern expressions in the knowledge model; and (2) restructuring of the knowledge model according to the patterns identified.

First of all, we try to refine the model by locating automatically RIA pattern expressions in the knowledge model. This activity is performed by a pattern matching process. Selected RIA patterns stored in the repository are processed sequentially. Marks are introduced in the model knowledge to signal pattern

---

[4] http://www.omg.org/spec/KDM/1.1/

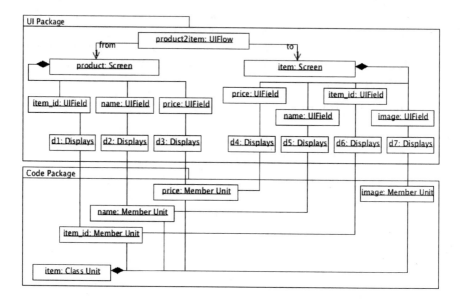

**Fig. 6.** Mater/Detail Screen Pattern in KDM (simplification)

identifications. As mentioned in section 3, the illustrative scenario we are considering is the detection of the Master/Detail screen pattern. In this case, basically, we try to locate two instances of the *kdm::ui::Screen* metaclass related in a sequential flow and displaying the same data entity but at different level of detail. In concrete, the master page will display less data than the detail page. This scenario is precisely the situation depicted in figure 6. To automatize this activity we are trying to use the QVT[5] language. Current results are promising, but the precision of the pattern matching process is still low. One reason of this low precision could be related with the high level of abstraction of the KDM UI Package which may lack necessary elements to represent Web user interfaces as [2] suggests. Probably we should also review the way we are using KDM. Another reason could be the lack of contextual information that could lead to detect false positives. To alleviate that situation we think it would be necessary to get additional information to semantically define both Web pages (and the data displayed) and their relationship within the whole system.

After pattern recognition and signalling, the knowledge model is ready to be restructured according to the patterns identified. We considered this activity requires human intervention. The modernization engineer should review all the marks introduced in the knowledge model and select one of the available restructurings for each one, keeping a valid model. Returning to our example, the engineer could select between 2 restructuring choices: (1) applying the Master/Detail Screen pattern as mentioned in section 3; or (2) applying the Quicklook pattern

---

[5] http://www.omg.org/spec/QVT/

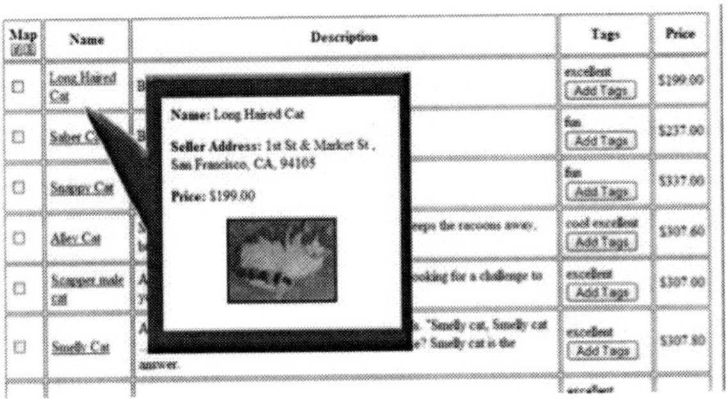

**Fig. 7.** Quicklook pattern in the search results page

(hover text) as the search page of Petstore 2.0 does to present details of the search results (figure 7).

### 4.3  Platform Projection

We have decided to introduce an optional step previous to the generation of the final code of the RIA client. This step consists on projecting the refined knowledge models of the legacy WA into RIA-extended MDWE models. Current techniques and tools of M2M transformation could assist on this projection. We consider this optional step could provide the engineer with the following advantages:

- The target system would be specified in a language nearer to Web and RIA domains. So it could be processed at a fine-grained level.
- Some tool or tool chain to support the development of the system, e.g. WebRatio for WebML [1], would assist the engineer in the modernization process or future maintenance activities.
- A repository of patterns could be used to leverage the stored know-how on system refinement [17], and to detect potential problems generated during the modernization process.
- A code generation engine that appears as a fundamental requirement for the forward engineering stage of the modernization process.

### 4.4  Code Generation

Following our idea of reusing MDD techniques and tools, final code generation could be performed by means of available code generation engines. On one hand, for instance, to generate the client side we could use the generation engines of the toolkits of main MDWE-RIA approaches, such as WebRatio and RUX-Tool [8]. On another hand, for server side connection layer generation we should evaluate the application of different model to code transformation tools, such as OMG MOF Model to Text, JET, Xpand, etc.

## 5  Related Work

Due to the wide scope and complexity of the process presented here, there is a high number of related approaches and they are really heterogeneous. This section points out some of these works as example of this heterogeneity.

During the last decade, as stated in [13], important works in the reverse engineering domain have been developed. VAQUISTA [23] proposes the utilization of different reverse engineering techniques to make the migration of the user interface of a WA to different platforms easer. Similarly, the work in [12] applies reverse engineering techniques to migrate a multipage interface of a WA to a single page interface (Web 2.0). All these approaches are closely related to the reverse engineering phase of the modernization process presented here.

[19]and [17] propose approaches to systematically incorporate RIA features into legacy WAs. However, contrary to the work presented here, these approaches are applied to legacy WAs that were developed by using MDD techniques and methodologies.

On the other hand, in the last years there have appeared some approaches to the application of MDD principles and techniques for the maintainability of software systems, e.g. in activities of software migration or modernization. In that sense, MoDisco [3] is a generic, extensible and open source approach for software modernization that makes an intensive use of MDD principles and techniques. Our work presents a specialization of the framework defined by MoDisco to be applied in concrete modernization scenarios from legacy WAs into RIAs.

## 6  Conclusions and Future Work

This work present an outline of our approach for the definition of a systematic process for WA-to-RIA modernization, by applying MDE principles, techniques and tools. One main requirement of this process is to make an extensive use of ADM related specifications. In concrete, the main goal of the modernization process presented consists on generating a RIA client from the legacy WA presentation and navigation layers and its corresponding service-oriented connection layer with the underlying business logic at server side. We have specially focused on the RIA pattern identification activity. Master/Detail Screen pattern and Quicklook pattern has been proposed as possible solutions for multipage master/detail relationships on the legacy WA.

Moreover, this work also depicts a collection of essential RIA features we have collected to understand the concept of RIA client. On one hand, these features provided us with the necessary information to define a conceptual modernization architecture in KDM. On another hand, they helped us on the specification of the kind of information we should extract from the legay WA in order to perform its RIA modernization.

Regarding the tool support, we are currently involved in the definition of our tool chain to systematize the modernization process by assisting the engineer team in the many and complex tasks to accomplish. For the reverse engineering phase, we are evaluating the possibility of adopting MoDisco as tool framework. Meanwhile, for the forward engineering phase, we may use mainstream MDWE methods and tools, e.g. WebRatio and RUX-Tool.

Given the extension and complexity of every modernization process and the initial stage of our approach, we have a great amount of related researching lines to follow. Among them, we are principally interested in 3: (1) extracting more accurate dynamic information (interaction models) from the legacy WA in order to infere the necessary knowledge to drive the data and logic distribution between client and server sides; (2) extending the application of ADM specifications to the whole process and considering business domain modernization; and (3) integrating properly the modernization tool chain to reduce costs and to leverage modernization knowledge reuse. Additionally, to confirm our RIA features relevance we will try to validate them with practitioners.

# References

1. Acerbis, R., Bongio, A., Brambilla, M., Butti, S., Ceri, S., Fraternali, P.: Web Applications Design and Development with WebML and WebRatio 5.0. In: Bertrand Aalst, W., Mylopoulos, J., Sadeh, N.M., Shaw, M.J., Szyperski, C., Paige, R.F., Meyer (eds.) TOOLS EUROPE 2008. LNBIP, vol. 11, pp. 392–411. Springer, Heidelberg (2008)

2. Barbier, F., Deltombe, G., Parisy, O., Youbi, K.: Model Driven Reverse Engineering: Increasing Legacy Technology Independence. In: Second India Workshop on Reverse Engineering, Thiruvananantpuram (2011)

3. Bruneliere, H., Cabot, J., Jouault, F.: MoDisco: A Generic And Extensible Framework For Model Driven Reverse Engineering. In: IEEE/ACM International Conference on Automated Software Engineering, pp. 1–2 (2010)

4. Izquierdo, J.L.C., Molina, J.G.: An Architecture-Driven Modernization Tool for Calculating Metrics. IEEE Software 27(4), 37–43 (2010)

5. Dolog, P., Stage, J.: Designing Interaction Spaces for Rich Internet Applications with UML. In: Baresi, L., Fraternali, P., Houben, G.-J. (eds.) ICWE 2007. LNCS, vol. 4607, pp. 358–363. Springer, Heidelberg (2007)

6. Fraternali, P., Comai, S., Bozzon, A., Carughi, G.T.: Engineering rich internet applications with a model-driven approach. ACM Transactions on the Web 4(2), 1–47 (2010)

7. Koch, N., Pigerl, M., Zhang, G., Morozova, T.: Patterns for the Model-Based Development of RIAs. In: Gaedke, M., Grossniklaus, M., Díaz, O. (eds.) ICWE 2009. LNCS, vol. 5648, pp. 283–291. Springer, Heidelberg (2009)

8. Linaje, M., Preciado, J.C., Morales-Chaparro, R., Rodríguez-Echeverría, R., Sánchez-Figueroa, F.: Automatic Generation of RIAs Using RUX-Tool and Webratio. In: Gaedke, M., Grossniklaus, M., Díaz, O. (eds.) ICWE 2009. LNCS, vol. 5648, pp. 501–504. Springer, Heidelberg (2009)

9. Linaje, M., Preciado, J.C., Sanchez-Figueroa, F.: Engineering Rich Internet Application User Interfaces over Legacy Web Models. IEEE Internet Computing 11(6), 53–59 (2007)

10. Machado, L., Filho, O., Ribeiro, J.: UWE-R: an extension to a web engineering methodology for rich internet applications. WSEAS Transactions on Information Science and Applications 6(4), 9 (2009)

11. Meliá, S., Gómez, J., Pérez, S., Díaz, O.: A Model-Driven Development for GWT-Based Rich Internet Applications with OOH4RIA. In: 2008 Eighth International Conference on Web Engineering, pp. 13–23 (July 2008)
12. Mesbah, A., van Deursen, A.: Migrating Multi-page Web Applications to Single-page AJAX Interfaces. In: 11th European Conference on Software Maintenance and Reengineering (CSMR 2007), pp. 181–190 (March 2007)
13. Patel, R., Coenen, F., Martin, R., Archer, L.: Reverse Engineering of Web Applications: A Technical Review. Technical Report July 2007, University of Liverpool Department of Computer Science, Liverpool (2007)
14. Pérez, S., Díaz, O., Meliá, S., Gómez, J.: Facing Interaction-Rich RIAs: The Orchestration Model. In: 2008 Eighth International Conference on Web Engineering, pp. 24–37 (July 2008)
15. Pérez-Castillo, R., De Guzmán, I.G.-R., Piattini, M.: Business Process Archeology using MARBLE. In: Information and Software Technology (2011)
16. Preciado, J.C., Linaje, M., Sanchez, F., Comai, S.: Necessity of methodologies to model Rich Internet Applications. In: Seventh IEEE International Symposium on Web Site Evolution (2005)
17. Rodríguez-Echeverría, R., Conejero, J.M., Linaje, M., Preciado, J.C., Sánchez-Figueroa, F.: Re-engineering legacy Web applications into Rich Internet Applications. In: 10th International Conference on Web Engineering (2010)
18. Rossi, G., Pastor, O., Schwabe, D., Olsina, L.: Web Engineering: Modelling and Implementing Web Applications. Human-Computer Interaction Series (October 2007)
19. Rossi, G., Urbieta, M., Ginzburg, J., Distante, D., Garrido, A.: Refactoring to Rich Internet Applications. A Model-Driven Approach. In: 2008 Eighth International Conference on Web Engineering, pp. 1–12 (July 2008)
20. Scott, B., Neil, T.: Designing Web Interfaces: Principles and Patterns for Rich Interactions. O'Reilly Media (2009)
21. Ulrich, W.: Modernization Standards Roadmap, pp. 46–64 (2010)
22. Valverde, F., Pastor, O.: Facing the Technological Challenges of Web 2.0: A RIA Model-Driven Engineering Approach. In: Vossen, G., Long, D.D.E., Yu, J.X. (eds.) WISE 2009. LNCS, vol. 5802, pp. 131–144. Springer, Heidelberg (2009)
23. Vanderdonckt, J., Bouillon, L., Souchon, N.: Flexible reverse engineering of web pages with VAQUISTA. In: Proceedings Eighth Working Conference on Reverse Engineering, pp. 241–248 (2001)
24. Wright, J.M.: A Modelling Language for Interactive Web Applications. In: 2009 IEEE/ACM International Conference on Automated Software Engineering, pp. 689–692 (November 2009)

# Quality Models for Web [2.0] Sites:
# A Methodological Approach and a Proposal

Roberto Polillo

University of Milano Bicocca, Dept. of Informatics, Systems and Communication,
Building U14, Viale Sarca 336, 20126 Milano Italy
roberto.polillo@unimib.it

**Abstract.** This paper discusses a methodological approach to define quality models (QM) for Web sites of any kind, including Web 2.0 sites. The approach stresses the practical use of a QM, in requirement definition and quality assessment, during design & development processes or during site operation. An important requirement for such QMs is *organization mapping*, which allows who is in charge of quality management to easily identify the actors in the organization responsible for implementing or improving each specific quality characteristic. A family of QMs is proposed and compared with ISO/IEC 25010 QMs for software products and software-intensive computer systems.

**Keywords:** quality, quality model, web, web engineering, web 2.0, ISO/IEC 25010.

## 1 Introduction

According to ISO/IEC 25000:2005 [1], a *quality model* (QM) is a "defined set of characteristics, and of relationships between them, which provides a framework for specifying quality requirements and evaluating quality."

QMs are very important in Web engineering. Having a good QM at hand can be extremely useful in all phases of a Web site life cycle. In the requirement specification phase, a QM helps in eliciting and orderly describing all important facets of the site to be designed. Indeed, the table of contents of a good requirement specification document could strictly mirror the QM, by assigning to each model characteristic a specific section of the document [2]. During the development process, a QM helps the project team in keeping their eyes on all desired quality attributes of the system to be implemented. In assessing the quality of an existing site, or different sites for comparison or benchmarking, a QM provides a structured approach to the evaluators, helping them to stay focused on the important issues. In the operation phase, a QM provides the site management with a "compass" to keep its evolution on the right track. Indeed, all Web sites are very dynamic; their evolution is constant and substantial: it is therefore essential to continuously monitor their quality, to avoid that the frequent changes disrupt piecemeal an initially sound project. This is particularly important for Web 2.0 sites, whose evolution is determined not only by the site management, but also by the (possibly large and uncontrollable) user community. A "suitable" QM is the necessary supporting tool for these monitoring actions.

A. Harth and N. Koch (Eds.): ICWE 2011 Workshops, LNCS 7059, pp. 251–265, 2012.
© Springer-Verlag Berlin Heidelberg 2012

But *how* do we choose it? The selection of a QM is a delicate task, because it may have a large impact on the site's success, and is not trivial at all, for two main difficulties: *orthogonality* and *measurability* of characteristics.   Orthogonality is difficult to achieve because the quality attributes of a Web site interact in complex ways; measurability, because many of them are subjective.

The literature on Web quality is very large, and a number of QMs for Web sites have been proposed over the years, approaching the problem from different perspectives. QM characteristics may be chosen on the basis of their semantic orthogonality, their measurability, the feasibility of their automatic evaluation, their relationship with the Web site development process, or with the use of statistic or probabilistic models (among others: [3],[4],[5],[6],[7]). Some QMs address specific types of Web sites, such as e-commerce or information portals; others analyze specific attributes, like data quality or quality in use (e.g. [8], [9], [10], [11]). Most of them are in some way related with the ISO quality standards. However, there seems to be no general consensus on their definition and characteristics.

This paper will contribute to this debate, by proposing an approach specifically oriented to the needs of the people responsible for the *management* of a Web site, and by sketching a QM family which can be proficiently used by project managers and Web properties managers both in the development and operation phase. This is a revision and extension of a simple QM for Web 1.0 sites previously defined by the author [4], following its experimentation in the Web site development road-map described by the author in [2] and the Web evolution of recent years.

In Section 2 the ISO approach to QMs for software and computer systems is summarized. Section 3 will discuss the main peculiarities of Web sites with respect to traditional software systems, and lay down a few basic requirements for Web sites QMs, also considering the evolution of the role of users in Web 2.0 sites. Section 4 will describe the proposed QM family, and Section 5 will briefly compare it with the ISO standard. Finally, Section 6 will contain some conclusions.

## 2    The ISO System and Software Quality Models

In the software engineering literature, software QMs have been discussed for many years. The ISO/IEC 9126, issued as an International Standard (IS) in 1991 [12] and revised in 2001 [13], is the best known reference in this area. Part 1 of this multi-part document provides a very general QM for software products external and internal quality, based on a set of 6 *quality characteristics* (*Functionality, Reliability, Usability, Efficiency, Maintainability, Portability*) and 27 *sub-characteristics*. A second QM defines 4 characteristics for *Quality in use, i.e.* "the user view of the product". This IS has been recently canceled, and replaced by ISO/IEC 25010 [14], which updates the previous QMs in various ways. It addresses "software products and software-intensive computer systems" of any kind, and defines two QMs. The *Product quality model* encompasses internal and external qualities of the system, and is composed of 8 characteristics and 31 sub-characteristics (Fig.1).

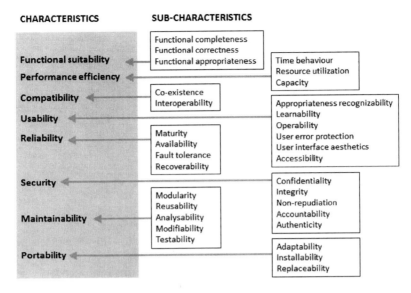

**Fig. 1.** Product quality model according to ISO/IEC 25010

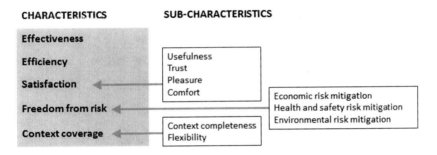

**Fig. 2.** Quality in use model according to ISO/IEC 25010

The *Quality in use model* is now composed of 5 characteristics and 9 sub-characteristics (Fig.2). Note that quality in use is a superset of usability, classically defined in [15] as "the degree to which a product or system can be used by specified users to achieve specified goals with effectiveness, efficiency and satisfaction in a specified context of use."

Each QM sub-characteristic may be further hierarchically decomposed. Quality characteristics and sub-characteristics at any level should be *measurable*, either directly or indirectly, through a set of associated *measurable properties*.

Fundamental in the ISO approach is the distinction between the *internal properties* of a product (which contribute to the *internal quality*), its *external properties* (which contribute to the *external quality*), and its *quality in use properties*, i.e. properties which

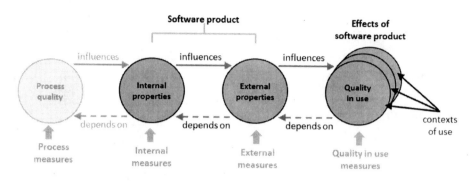

**Fig. 3.** Conceptual approach to quality, according to ISO/IEC 25010

can be measured when the product is actually in use in specific contexts. All these properties influence each other and the resulting quality in a complex way, as schematized in Fig.3.

ISO/IEC 25010 belongs to the SQuaRE series of International Standards (see [1]). In SQuaRE, ISO/IEC 25012 [16] defines a third QM, for data retained in a structured format within a computer system, composed of 15 characteristics: *Accuracy, Completeness, Consistency, Credibility, Currentness, Accessibility, Compliance, Confidentiality, Efficiency, Precision, Traceability, Understandability, Availability, Portability* and *Recoverability.*

# 3    Quality Models for Web Sites: Why They Should Be Different

## 3.1    Web Sites Peculiarities

The ISO standards provide a very general conceptual framework for defining QMs for complex systems with a substantial software component. The basic approach of defining a hierarchy of quality *characteristics*, and *measurable properties* which can be aggregated to obtain quantitative measures of characteristics provides a sound foundation for defining *any* QM, in *any* domain. Moreover, the ISO model is the result of three decades of discussions about the basic quality dimensions of software-based systems. Its categorization and terminology can be discussed and - in a few cases - may also be considered somehow obscure, but certainly cannot be ignored in any approach to quality in software engineering.

On the other hand, it should be clearly understood that the ISO documents only provide a *conceptual framework*, and not a ready-to-use QM. To be of practical use, this framework must be tailored to the specific [class of] system[s] under consideration. This may not be a simple task, especially when these systems do not fit well with the systems considered in classical software engineering, such as ERP, command & control, embedded systems. This is the case of Web sites, which possess a number of peculiarities that greatly differentiate them from the above systems:

*Information content.* In the large majority of cases, unstructured information content prevails on structured data. Emphasis is on user navigation, not on data management and computation. Therefore, a fundamental dimension of quality relates to *information architecture* [17]. Information architects are more and more involved in large Web sites, together with *content editors*, who create and manage its information content. Information-rich sites may employ large editing staffs, with an organization in some ways similar to that of traditional magazines.

*Communication.* In most cases, Web sites can be considered machines whose main purpose is communication, rather than computing and data management. This is also true for e-commerce or other sites offering online services. Web sites address a global audience, in a strongly competitive, "open" environment. There is no user lock-in: competition is only a few clicks away, so visitors' loyalty must be won on a day-by-day basis. User attention span can be extremely short, so his/her interest must be captured in brief time-intervals. So big efforts are required on communication and branding, and professionals typically not seen in traditional software projects are necessary (visual designers, art directors, communication and marketing people).

*Continuous evolution.* Web sites are living organisms. Their contents are constantly updated, and even their information architecture changes frequently. This is true for *any* site, not only for information portals. Visitors of a site often expect the content to be updated practically in real time. Site managers must strive hard to comply with these expectations, just to keep their site reputation. Interactive services and the user interface are frequently modified and improved. According to the *perpetual-β* concept, the software behind these services is continuously modified to better serve user needs. These – in turn – change as new possibilities are discovered, in a constant *co-evolution* of usage patterns and system functions. In a word, managing the evolution of a Web site sets pressing requirements to site administrators, and this should be taken into account seriously in any QM designed for these systems.

## 3.2     Web Site Quality Actors

By [*quality*] *actor* we mean any system stakeholder with an active role in creating/maintaining some quality attribute, such as Web designers, visual designers, content editors, software developers. Actors of a Web site are more numerous and more varied than in traditional software systems. Indeed, the development of any site is really a multi-disciplinary project, involving many different roles (Fig.4).[1]

In a typical Web 1.0 site, end users have a passive role, so they are not considered actors because they do not contribute to its quality: they only navigate the site and possibly interact with it in predefined transactions (as in e-commerce). In Web 2.0 sites the situation is completely different. The users can typically create and upload content, embed content from other sites, tag, comment or rate content created by other users and share it with their "friends", and interact with them in public. This is not only true for large social networks such as Facebook, Twitter, YouTube and Flickr, but also for an increasingly large number of small sites, due to the many available tools which allow to easily implement these functions, such as share buttons, plugins, html snippets. Therefore, in Web 2.0 sites, *the users themselves must be considered quality actors* and critical ones indeed, since they can have a big impact on the global functioning of the site. Even a perfectly designed and implemented site can fail as a

---

[1] Different roles may not necessarily be played by different people. For very small sites, all of the above roles may also be impersonated by the same person.

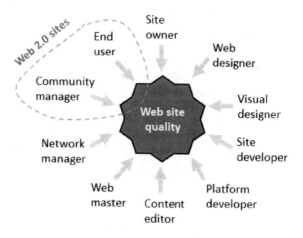

**Fig. 4.** The main quality actors of a Web site

consequence of "bad" (or unexpected) user behavior. So users must be continuously monitored and in some way controlled or stimulated, requiring the presence of new roles (denoted as *community management* in Fig.4), and in some cases the evolutionary modification of specific site functions, intended – so to speak – to improve the user-generated quality. A typical example is the evolution of the community content moderation mechanisms in Yahoo!Answer, where they had to oppose the unexpected volume of user spam and troll activity, that seriously risked crashing the site [18].

### 3.3   Organization Mapping

The ISO definition of a QM, quoted in Section 1, emphasizes the practical purposes of any QM, which is not viewed as a mere categorization of the quality attributes of a system, but rather as a *practical tool*, to steer design ("specifying requirements") and evaluation ("evaluating quality") processes. In our view, this should be constantly kept in mind when defining any QM. To this end, we require that there be as simple as possible relation between quality [sub-]characteristics and the roles (actors) responsible for implementing and improving them. In this way, responsibility for different quality characteristics can be easily allocated and tracked, being always clear who is responsible for what. We call this attribute of a QM *organization mapping*. In Fig. 5, mapping on the left can be considered better than the mapping on the right, because responsibilities are better isolated and quality characteristics improvements are easier to manage.

A good mapping is a crucial requirement of a Web site QM because, as shown in Fig.4, the actors involved in Web projects are many, and the involved skills are extremely varied. In a multi-disciplinary team, different cultures, practices and value systems may sometimes create interaction difficulties, as anybody involved in medium to large Web site development or operations may have experienced. To avoid these problems, it is necessary that the teams be correctly organized, with a clear allocation of responsibilities on the different system components and associated quality characteristics.

Of course, the goodness of the mapping does not depend only on the QM, but also on the actual organization which develops and manages the site. A chaotic organization will nullify the practical utility of even the best QM. Nevertheless, after fifteen years of Web engineering experiences, the roles and functions of the different quality actors in e Web project are today sufficiently well understood. This allows to define good QMs which are reasonably applicable to most Web organizations.

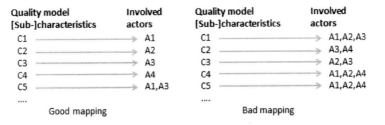

**Fig. 5.** Organization mapping of quality models

### 3.4    Requirements for Web Sites Quality Models

With the above premises, we can now lay down the main requirements for our QM.

*Requirement 1. QM should have an organization mapping as simple as possible*, as discussed in 3.3. We do not require that it be related to a *specific* project organization schema, but simply that the quality [sub-]characteristics be associated in a simple way to the quality actors of Fig.4. It is rather evident that the ISO QM of Fig.1 does not satisfy at all this requirement.

*Requirement 2. QM should be tailorable to the class of sites under consideration.* Web sites are enormously diversified. They may differ in size, in technology, in purpose, in complexity, in relationship with the front users (from purely informative to interactive to social), in impact on their activities (from critical to non-critical). So there will be no universal QM. Tailoring the QM would mean adding or dropping some sub-characteristics or specializing some of them with further levels of detail. Sometimes we would also assign *different weights* to the [sub-]characteristics, to express their importance in the particular context.

*Requirement 3. QM should be subsettable according to its specific purpose.* Some [sub-]characteristics should be droppable from the QM, when they are not needed in its actual context of use. E.g., when using a QM to compare a site with its competition, we usually do not have access to information on their internal structure. Thus, we would drop all [sub-]characteristics associated to internal properties from the QM.

*Requirement 4. QM should be scalable according to site complexity.* Any site (even the simplest) is really a very complicated system, as briefly discussed in 3.1. But it is totally unrealistic to pretend that small organizations (which own the large majority of sites) may (or want to) deal with all the subtleties of a conceptually sound and complete QM. Simple users need simple tools. Therefore, a scalable QM would be available in simplified versions to be used in simple contexts.

*Requirement 5. QM should be universally usable and accessible.* Last but not least, if we want to have a real impact on the quality of the present day Web, we should design QMs that, as much as possible, are *universally usable and accessible.* This would entail the use of broadly understood concepts described in a simple language, with easy and free accessibility. [2]

The stated requirements imply that we need a *family of closely related QMs,* and not a single QM, if possible with a common set of top-level characteristics. These are the "foundations" of the QM, and therefore should be easily recognizable by anybody as the basic dimensions of the quality of *any* Web site. They would constitute the main sections of the requirement specifications of *any* Web development project, and the main aspects to be considered in *any* assessment or evaluation. QM personalization should then be localized in the lower levels of the hierarchy of characteristics, to cope with specific Web applications (Req.2), purpose (Req.3), site complexity (Req.4) and to the complexity of the organization (Req.5). This will be mostly done by adding/dropping sub-characteristics or defining lower levels in the characteristics tree.

# 4     A Quality Model Family for Web Sites

## 4.1     Defining the Top-Level Characteristics

Rather than start from the ISO model and modify it piecemeal to comply with the stated requirements, it seems more reasonable to start anew, and see where this approach leads. Requirement 1 suggests to start by defining a general model of a Web site, showing its main logical components (the quality of which we wish to take under control), its main quality actors and the relationship between actors and components. This can be done a)- considering the Web site design & development process, or b)-considering the Web site in operation. The second approach seems more comprehensive because of the constantly evolving nature of Web sites (which are not "frozen" when they are published online after development) and because it allows to consider the role of end users as quality actors, which is fundamental in a Web 2.0 context. Thus this paper will use approach b).[3]

---

[2] Lack of usability and accessibility are, in our opinion, the main problems with the ISO QMs, which hinder their large scale adoption by the general community of Web practitioners. ISO documents are difficult to read and organized in a complex structure, which is continuously evolving. To understand the status of the ISO document system and to identify the documents relevant to a particular activity, it is not easy and very costly, since documents are not freely available, but cost a lot of money. Regrettably, this is also true for quality related standards, which should be, in our opinion, as openly available as possible.

[3] Approach a) has been used in the previous version of this QM, dealing only with Web 1.0 sites [4], using the design & development model described in [2], in which the quality of a Web site is formed incrementally, through an ordered iterative process. Not unexpectedly, the results are the same, since the same actors and components are present in both approaches. Lack of space does not allow to further comment on this issue here.

Therefore, a Web site in operation will be modeled as a set of nested logical components, as shown in Fig.6. The *Site* component is nested in a *Site platform*, typically representing the used Content Management System (CMS) and related software components (e.g., DBMS). In turn, the *Site platform* is nested in the *Server & Network Platforms* component, representing the server(s) hosting the site and the network infrastructure. The *Site* component is in turn decomposed in five components: *Information architecture & navigation*, *Graphics & branding*, *Software functions* and *Content* components, which are self-explaining.

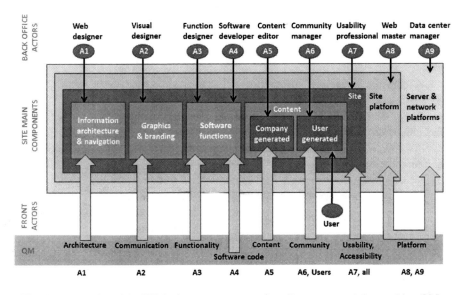

**Fig. 6.** A general model of Web site components and quality actors, and the resulting QM

Each logical component is associated to its (prevailing) quality actor. For example, the *Company generated content* component is under the responsibility of *Content editor(s)*. Actors are all members of the back-office organization, except in Web 2.0 sites, where the users are also considered actors. The bottom line in Fig.6 shows the 9 top-level characteristics of the proposed QM: *Architecture, Communication, Functionality, Software code, Content, Community, Usability, Accessibility, Platform*.

Here, the term *Architecture* refers exclusively to information architecture [17], including site navigation facilities, and not to internal software architecture. Its associated actor is therefore the Web designer (or information architect).

*Communication* refers to all aspects of site communication, typically embodied in the site Style Guide, defining graphics, typography, multimedia usage and user experience issues. The associated actors are the visual designers because in small/medium sites this responsibility is usually assigned to them. Note, however, that larger sites may have a more complex organization, involving art directors, communication departments, and the like.

Like the ISO *Functional suitability* [14], *Functionality* means "the degree to which the site provides functions that meet stated and implied needs when used under specified conditions". Note that this does not include navigation functions (menus, breadcrumbs, and so on), which are part of the site *Architecture*.

*Content* collects all the quality characteristics related to the company-generated information/data content of the site, under the responsibility of the content editors.

*Community* is mostly used only for Web 2.0 sites, and considers user-generated content: associated actors are site users and site community managers.

*Platform* considers the site platform (CMS, DBMS, and similar components, under responsibility of the Web master), the hardware and software of the hosting servers, and the network infrastructure. Its quality characteristics are both static (i.e.: are they suitable for the context?) and dynamic (i.e.: are their operations well managed? Are their performances adequate?). Here the quality actors may differ depending on the specific organization: in Fig.6 we consider the case when server and network management are outsourced to an external organization, and there is a data center manager interfacing the service.

*Usability* and *Accessibility* have the usual meaning of the ISO documents. Since these characteristics are the result of the cooperation of all involved actors, in Fig.6 we have indicated a usability professional, as the actor with the responsibility of managing the usability and accessibility issues of the site.

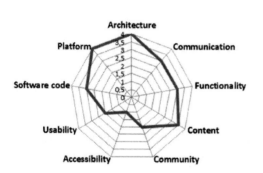

Fig. 7. The quality profile of a Web site

Finally, *Software code* refers to the quality of the software specifically developed for the site (therefore excluding platform components acquired on the market), under responsibility of the software developers.

Note that in most cases there is a one-to-one relationship between characteristics and actors, as shown in the bottom line of the schema, thus the QM has a good *organization mapping*, as required.

Because the names chosen for the top-level characteristics are very mundane, the site quality profile can be easily communicated to *all* site stakeholders, e.g. with a simple radar diagram, as in Fig.7.

## 4.2    Defining the Sub-characteristics

The definition of sub-characteristics is less critical. Once the top-level framework is stable and well understood, the lower levels can be tailored to specific contexts and improved over time, as experience in their use increases and Web applications evolve.[4] Our proposal is based on 33 sub-characteristics (Fig.8), including internal quality (*Standards conformance, Code* and *Platform Maintainability*) and Web 2.0 sites (*Community Management*).[5] These should be dropped when assessing only external quality and quality in use of Web 1.0 sites, as in [4].

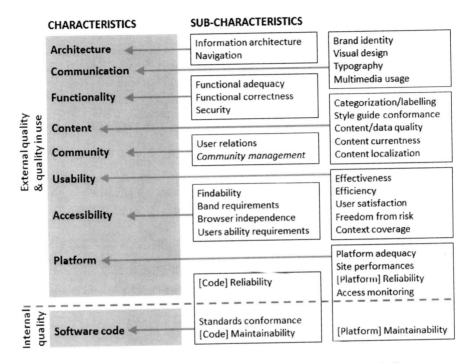

**Fig. 8.** The proposed QM. Sub-characteristics for Web 2.0 are in italics

In most cases, the meaning of sub-characteristics is self-evident.

For *Content*, we evaluate separately the content categorization (*Categorization/labelling*),[6] the conformance to organization-defined style guides – possibly including external standards (*Style guide conformance*), the timeliness of content updating (*Content currentness*), and the quality of internationalization and localization of the site (*Content localization*). Finally, *Content/data* quality would consider such attributes as accuracy, completeness, and so on of the content elements (including structured data stored in data bases), such.

---

[4] The ISO standard itself explains that "the set of sub-characteristics associated with a characteristic have been selected to be representative of typical concerns without necessarily being exhaustive" (see [14], pag.2).

[5] *User relations* concern the management of user requests, and applies also to Web 1.0 sites.

[6] Note that, while the *Architecture* characteristic deals with the overall information architecture and navigation of the site, the *Categorization/labelling* sub-characteristic deals with the organization of the site contents. They are considered separately, because one is defined by the Web designer, the other by the content editors.

Note that here *Accessibility* is intended in its wider meaning, as the characteristic that can limit the digital divide. Therefore, its sub-characteristics are: *Findability, Band requirements, Browser independence* and *User ability requirements*, i.e. accessibility for people with disabilities.

For *Usability*, we used, for simplicity, the characteristics of the ISO/IEC 95010 model for *Quality in use*.[7]

Under *Platform, Platform adequacy* collects all issues referring to the static properties of CMS, DBMS, server and network infrastructures (hardware and software), while *Site performances* deals with their dynamic properties (time behavior, resource utilization, and so on). *Access monitoring* evaluates SEO and Web analytics activities.

We considered *Reliability* and *Maintainability* separately for the site-specific *Software code*, and for the (often standard) *Platform*, since the involved quality actors are usually different.

A number of third-level characteristics should be further defined, tailored to specific classes of sites. This is typically the case of *Functional adequacy*, to deal with specific classes of functionalities, such as *Shopping functions adequacy* for e-commerce, *Uploading functions adequacy* for file sharing sites, *Identity profiling functions adequacy* for social networks, and so on.

As we shall see in the following sections, a number of ISO/IEC 25010 sub-characteristics can be used at the third or fourth level of our QM. For *Content/data quality*, sub-characteristics of the ISO/IEC 25012 data quality model may be used, such as *Accuracy, Completeness, Consistency, Credibility, Precision, Traceability*, and so on.

## 5    Comparison with the ISO Standard

A comparison between ISO 25010 and the proposed QM shows the following main differences and analogies:

1.  Top-level characteristics *Architecture, Communication, Content* and *Community* and their sub-characteristics, which differentiate Web sites from traditional software systems, are not considered in ISO/IEC 25010 models. (Structured data - but not textual and multimedia information - are considered in ISO/IEC 25012).
2.  *Functionality* is included in both models (though with slightly different names). In our model, *Security* is a sub-characteristic of *Functionality* (as it was in ISO/IEC 9126:2001), but it might be considered a top-level characteristic as well if desired (this would be advisable, e.g. in Web banking applications).
3.  *Usability* is included in both models. As sub-characteristics, we considered the characteristics of *Quality in use* (Fig.2).

---

[7] Indeed, the ISO/IEC 25010 itself specifies that "Usability can either be specified or measured as a product quality characteristic in terms of its sub-characteristics, or specified or measured directly by measures that are a subset of quality in use." (§4.2.4) We prefer the second option, closer to the "classical" definition of usability [15].

**Table 1.** Comparison of ISO/IEC 25010 vs the proposed QM

| ISO/IEC 25010 Product QM | Corresponding level in the proposed QM |
|---|---|
| **Functional suitability** | 1   (name changed to Functionality) |
| Functional appropriateness | 3   (under Functional adequacy) |
| Functional completeness | 3   (under Functional adequacy) |
| Functional correctness | 2   (under Functionality) |
| **Performance efficiency** | Not used |
| Time behaviour | 3   (under Site performance) |
| Resource utilization | 3   (under Site performance) |
| Capacity | 3   (under Platform adequacy) |
| **Compatibility** | 3   (under Platform adequacy) |
| Co-existence | 4   (under Compatibility) |
| Interoperability | 4   (under Compatibility) |
| **Usability** | 1   (uses sub-attributes of ISO Quality in use QM) |
| Appropriateness recognizability | Not used |
| Learnability | Not used |
| Operability | Not used |
| User error protection | Not used |
| User interface aesthetics | Not used |
| Accessibility | 1   (top-level characteristic) |
| **Reliability** | 2   (under Software code and Platform) |
| Maturity | 3   (under Reliability) |
| Availability | 3   (under Reliability) |
| Fault tolerance | 3   (under Reliability) |
| Recoverability | 3   (under Reliability) |
| **Security** | 2   (under Functionality) |
| Confidentiality | 3   (under Security) |
| Integrity | 3   (under Security) |
| Non-repudiation | 3   (under Security) |
| Accountability | 3   (under Security) |
| Authenticity | 3   (under Security) |
| **Maintainability** | 2/3  (under Software code and Platform adequacy) |
| Modularity | 3/4  (under Maintainability) |
| Reusability | 3/4  (under Maintainability) |
| Analysability | 3/4  (under Maintainability) |
| Modifiability | 3/4  (under Maintainability) |
| Testability | 3/4  (under Maintainability) |
| **Portability** | 3   (under Platform adequacy) |
| Adaptability | 4   (under Portability) |
| Installability | 4   (under Portability) |
| Replaceability | 4   (under Portability) |

4.  We put *Accessibility* at the top-level, given its importance in many Web sites (in ISO it is a sub-characteristic of *Usability*).
5.  While *Maintainability*, *Portability* and *Compatibility* are given much emphasis in ISO/IEC 25010, they do not need a front-line position in present day Web sites, more and more built on-top of widely used and compatible platforms, in some cases maintained by large communities of developers. We considered *Maintainability* separately for the site-specific *Software code*, and for the (often standard) *Platform,* as a second level characteristic. *Compatibility* and *Portability* do not appear in Fig.8, as they may be considered third level characteristics under *Platform adequacy,* for the evaluation of the selected platform, and a component of *Browser independence*, under *Accessibility.*

In summary, with respect to ISO/IEC 25010, the proposed QM considers some new characteristics related to the Web sites specificities, has an higher level of abstraction and allocates common sub-characteristics in a different way, according to their level of importance in Web sites and to the organization mapping requirement.

A detailed mapping between ISO/IEC 25010 and the proposed QM is shown in Table 1. Here, the shaded [sub-]characteristics are not used in our QM, but might be added at third or fourth level in the hierarchy, where indicated in the table. If this is done, our QM can be said to conform to the ISO standard, being a superset of it.[8]

## 6   Conclusion

This paper has proposed a methodological approach to define QMs for Web sites of any kind, including Web 2.0 sites and applications. The approach stresses the practical use of a QM, in requirement definition and quality assessment, during design & development processes or during site operations. Therefore, the main driver for QM definition has been what we called *organization mapping*, as opposed to the conceptualization of abstract quality characteristics. Organization mapping allows who is in charge of quality management to easily identify the actors in the organization responsible for implementing or improving each specific quality characteristics. This is much more important for Web sites than in traditional software systems, given the high number and diversity of the actors involved, and the possibility of conflicts arising from their diverse approaches.

Accordingly, a simple QM family has been proposed, starting from a very general model of Web site, mapping its main logical components to the actors responsible for their quality. This QM defines the characteristics down to the second level: it is general enough to be applicable to a very large class of sites and to be used as a viable table of contents for requirement definition documents. It should be specialized and tailored for specific classes of Web sites and applications, intended purposes and organizations, typically by dropping the sub-characteristics which are not relevant to the particular context, and defining lower levels of the hierarchy.

---

[8] According to ISO/IEC 25010, "any quality requirement, quality specification, or evaluation of quality that conforms to this International Standard shall either; a)- use the quality models defined in it or b)- tailor the quality model giving the rationale for any changes and provide a mapping between the tailored model and the standard model".

A comparison with the ISO QMs for software and software intensive systems has shown differences and similarities, originating from the particular nature of Web sites and applications, and the approach adopted in the QM construction. The proposed QM is essentially a superset and an abstraction of the ISO/IEC 25010 Product QM, where the common parts are allocated differently in the hierarchy of characteristics, mainly to comply to the organization mapping requirement.

# References

1. ISO/IEC 25000:2005: Software Engineering – Software Product Quality Requirements and Evaluation (SQuaRE) – Guide to SQuaRE (2005)
2. Polillo, R.: Plasmare il Web – Road map per siti di qualità. Apogeo, Milano (2006)
3. Mich, L., Franch, M., Gaio, L.: Evaluating and Designing the Quality of Web Sites. Journal IEEE Multimedia 10(1), 34–43 (2003)
4. Polillo, R.: Il Check-up dei Siti Web. Apogeo, Milano (2004)
5. Signore, O.: A Comprehensive Model for Web Sites Quality. In: Proc. of WSE 2005 – 7th IEEE Int. Symposium on Web Site Evolution – Budapest, pp. 30–36 (2005)
6. Moraga, A., Calero, C., Piattini, M.: Comparing Different Quality Models for Portals. Online Information Review 30(5), 555–468 (2006)
7. Malak, G., Sahraoui, H., Badri, L., Badri, M.: Modeling Web Quality Using a Probabilistic Approach: An Empirical Evaluation. ACM Transactions on the Web 4(3) (2010)
8. Stefani, A., Xenos, M.: E-Commerce System Quality Assessment Using a Model Based on ISO 9126 and Belief Networks. Software Quality Control 16(1), 107–129 (2008)
9. Herrera, M., Moraga, M.Á., Caballero, I., Calero, C.: Quality in Use Model for Web Portals (QiUWeP). In: Daniel, F., Facca, F.M. (eds.) ICWE 2010. LNCS, vol. 6385, pp. 91–101. Springer, Heidelberg (2010)
10. Lew, P., Olsina, L., Zhang, L.: Quality, Quality in Use, Actual Usability and User Experience as Key Drivers for Web Application Evaluation. In: Benatallah, B., Casati, F., Kappel, G., Rossi, G. (eds.) ICWE 2010. LNCS, vol. 6189, pp. 218–232. Springer, Heidelberg (2010)
11. Moraga, C., Moraga, M.A., Calero, C., Caro, A.: SQuaRE-Aligned Data Quality Model for Web Portals. In: QSIC 2009 Proc. of the 2009 9th Int. Conf. on Quality Software, pp. 117–122. IEEE Press, Los Alamitos (2009)
12. ISO/IEC 9126:1991: Information Technology – Software Product Evaluation – Quality Characteristics and Guidelines for their Use (1991)
13. ISO/IEC 9126-1:2001: Software Engineering – Product Quality – Part 1: Quality Model (2001)
14. ISO/IEC 25010:2011: System and Software Engineering – Systems and Software Quality Requirements and Evaluation (SQuaRE) – System and Software Quality Models (2011)
15. ISO/IEC 9241-11:1998: Ergonomic Requirements for Office Work with Visual Display Terminals – Part 11: Guidance on Usability (1998)
16. ISO/IEC 25012:2008: Software Engineering – Software Product Quality Requirements and Evaluation (SQuaRE) – Data Quality Model (2008)
17. Morville, P., Rosenfeld, L.: Information Architecture for the World Wide Web. 3rd edn. O'Reilly Media (2007)
18. Farmer, F.R., Glass, B.: Building Web Reputation Systems. O'Reilly Media (2010)

# Exploring the Quality in Use of Web 2.0 Applications: The Case of Mind Mapping Services

Tihomir Orehovački[1], Andrina Granić[2], and Dragutin Kermek[1]

[1] University of Zagreb, Faculty of Organization and Informatics
Pavlinska 2, 42000 Varaždin, Croatia
{tihomir.orehovacki,dragutin.kermek}@foi.hr
[2] University of Split, Faculty of Science
Nikole Tesle 12, 21000 Split, Croatia
andrina.granic@pmfst.hr

**Abstract.** Research in Web quality has addressed quality in use as the most important factor affecting a wide acceptance of software applications. It can be conceived as comprising two complementary concepts, that is, usability and user experience, which accounts for the employment of more user-centred evaluations. Nevertheless, in the context of Web 2.0 applications, this topic has still not attracted sufficient attention from the HCI community. This paper addresses the quality in use of Web 2.0 applications on the case of mind mapping services. The evaluation methodology brings together three complementary methods. The estimated quality in use is measured by means of the logging actual use method, while the perceived quality in use is evaluated by means of the retrospective thinking aloud (RTA) method and a questionnaire. The contribution of our work is twofold. Firstly, we provide empirical evidence that the proposed methodology in conjunction with the model, set of attributes, and measuring instruments is appropriate for evaluating quality in use of Web 2.0 applications. Secondly, the analysis of qualitative data reveals that performance and effort based attributes considerably contribute to mind mapping services success.

**Keywords:** Web 2.0, Quality in Use, Evaluation Methodology, Study Results.

## 1 Introduction

Usability evaluation plays an essential role in the human-centred design process of interactive software applications. *Usability*, as a quality of use in context [4], is related to ease-of-use and ease-of-learning. More recently, a concept of *user experience* (UX) [9] has been gaining popularity, leading to a switch in the research focus from product-centred evaluation to more user-oriented one. Furthermore, due to the emergence of Web 2.0 applications, the role of user experience in the assessment process has become even more important. As a result of these developments, latest research in Web quality has been addressing *quality in use* that is considered to be one of the most important factors affecting a wide acceptance of software applications in general.

A. Harth and N. Koch (Eds.): ICWE 2011 Workshops, LNCS 7059, pp. 266–277, 2012.
© Springer-Verlag Berlin Heidelberg 2012

## 1.1    Research Background

In recent research in the field of usability, user experience and quality in use, e.g. [3], [6], [11], [13] along with the latest quality standard [10], no agreement has so far been reached on attributes which reflect the 'real quality' of a software application. Moreover, it is not clear how the concept of quality in use should be defined in the context of Web 2.0 applications. According to the ISO standard on quality models [10], usability (along with flexibility and safety) is a characteristic of quality in use, with effectiveness, efficiency and satisfaction as its sub-characteristics. In accordance with ISO 25010, Bevan perceived usability as performance in use and satisfaction in terms of its relation with user experience [3]. To encompass the overall user experience, satisfaction needs to be concerned with both pragmatic and hedonic user goals. Lew *et al.* [11] proposed extending the ISO 25010 standard to incorporate new characteristics, in particular information quality and learnability. They also argued for including usability and user experience concepts into the modelling framework. Taking the above into consideration, quality in use could be seen as comprising two complementary concepts: (i) usability, which refers to the product-centred evaluation of pragmatic attributes through the use of both subjective and objective measuring instruments as well as (ii) user experience (UX), which concerns the use of subjective measuring instruments for the assessment of hedonic attributes.

HCI literature offers a lot of different models, methods and standards aimed at evaluating the quality and usability of software applications. However, research related to the evaluation of Web 2.0 applications in general has been deficient. Recent studies suggested that the reason for that might be the inappropriateness of current approaches for evaluation of those applications. A research into usability assessment carried out by Hart *et al.* [8] revealed that the popular social networking site Facebook complies with only two of ten heuristics originally proposed by Nielsen [12]. They also reported that the attributes such as ease of use, usefulness and playfulness have a major impact on users' loyal behaviour. When subjected to conventional usability evaluation, YouTube appears to score badly as well, meeting only two traditional heuristics [17]. Thompson and Kemp [18] argued that one of the main reasons why Web 2.0 applications such as Flickr, Wikipedia and YouTube have a large number of active users is their focus on user experience. Moreover, they extended and modified a set of Nielsen's traditional heuristics with an objective to evaluate the usability of Web 2.0 applications. However, the validity of the proposed set of heuristics has so far not been empirically confirmed. In addition, current research is usually focused on the development of methods and models aimed for the evaluation of particular quality aspects (e.g. information quality [1]) or types of Web 2.0 applications (e.g. mashups [5]). All the afore-mentioned findings motivated us to initiate our research into the design of a methodology that would enable the evaluation of the quality in use of Web 2.0 applications, regardless of their type and the context in which they are used [14].

## 1.2    Proposed Classification of Quality in Use Attributes

Our analysis of relevant recent research in the field of Web quality and usability assessment resulted in a set of attributes that may have a significant role in the evaluation of the quality in use of Web 2.0 applications [16]. The developed conceptual model shown in Figure 1 classifies quality in use attributes into six basic categories: system quality (SYQ), service quality (SEQ), information quality (INQ), performance (PFM), effort (EFO), and acceptability (ACP).

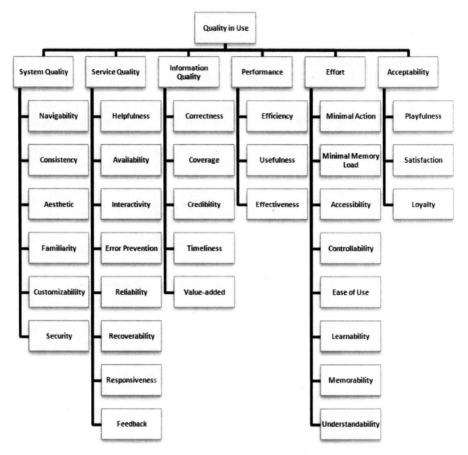

**Fig. 1.** Proposed model for evaluating Quality in Use of Web 2.0 applications [16]

*System Quality* (SYQ) measures quality in use of Web 2.0 application at the level of its interface features. It is comprised of six attributes: *navigability* (NVG, degree to which interface elements are well organized and alternative navigation mechanisms are provided), *consistency* (CNS, degree to which the same structure, design, terminology and components are used throughout a Web 2.0 application), *aesthetic* (AES, degree of visual attractiveness of a Web interface), *familiarity* (FML, degree to which a Web interface is similar to previously used applications), *customizability* (CUS, degree to which interface elements can be adapted to the characteristics of the task or user), and *security* (SCR, extent to which personal data and files are protected from unauthorized access). *Service quality* (SEQ) is the extent of quality of interaction between the user and a Web 2.0 application. This category is further decomposed into eight attributes: *helpfulness* (HLP, degree to which a Web application contains modules for user's assistance), *availability* (AVL, degree to which interface elements are continuously available), *interactivity* (ITR, degree to which a Web 2.0 application creates the feeling of use of a desktop application), *error prevention* (ERP, degree to which a Web application prevents the occurrence of errors), *reliability* (RLB, degree to which a Web 2.0 application works without errors or interruptions), *recoverability* (RCV, the extent to which a Web 2.0 application can recover from errors and interruptions in its running), *responsiveness* (RSP, extent of the speed of a Web 2.0 application's response to users' requests and actions), and *feedback* (FDB, extent to which a Web 2.0 application displays its status or progress at any time). *Information Quality* (INQ) captures the quality of the content which proceeds out of using a Web 2.0 application. This category contains five different attributes: *correctness* (CRC, degree to which information content is free of errors), *coverage* (CRG, degree to which information content is appropriate, complete and compactly represented), *credibility* (CDB, degree to which information content is unbiased, trustworthy, and verifiable), *timeliness* (TLS, degree to which information content is up to date), and *value-added* (VAD, degree to which information content is advantageous). *Performance* (PFM) refers to the quality of performing assignments by means of a Web 2.0 application interface functionalities. This category includes three attributes: *effectiveness* (EFE, degree to which an assignment can be achieved with accuracy, and completeness), *usefulness* (UFL, degree to which the user perceives a Web 2.0 application as the most appropriate solution for performing the assignment), and *efficiency* (EFI, degree to which a goal can be achieved with minimal consumption of resources). *Effort* (EFO) is the extent of perceived and estimated mental and physical energy when executing a task with Web 2.0 applications. This category is subdivided into eight attributes: *minimal action* (MAC, degree to which an assignment solution can be achieved in a minimum number of steps), *minimal memory load* (MEL, amount of information the user needs to remember when carrying out tasks), *accessibility* (ACS, extent to which a Web 2.0 application can be used by people with a widest range of disabilities), *controllability* (CTR, level of user's freedom while completing the task), *ease of use* (EOU, degree to which a Web 2.0 application can be used without help), *learnability* (LRN, which measures how easily the user can learn to use a Web interface functionalities), *memorability* (MRB, which measures how easy it is to memorize and remember how to use a Web 2.0 application), and *understandability* (UND, extent to which interface elements are clear and unambiguous to the user). To facilitate data collection in this study, two theoretically separated attributes, that is, minimal action and minimal memory load, are logically combined into a single attribute that is named physical and mental effort (PME). *Acceptability* (ACP) consists of attributes that directly contribute to the success of a Web 2.0 application, including *playfulness* (PLY, extent to which using a Web 2.0 application is fun and stimulating), *satisfaction* (STF, extent to which a Web 2.0 application can meet user's expectations) and *loyalty* (LOY, the users' intention to continue to use a Web application or to recommend it to their colleagues). The main aim of this paper is to investigate to what extent the proposed model and associated measuring instruments are appropriate for evaluating the quality in use of Web 2.0 applications, particularly mind mapping services.

## 2    Methodology

**Participants.** A total of 86 respondents (70.9% male, 29.1% female), aged 20.31 years (SD = 1.868) on average, participated in the survey. Participants were students of Information Science from the University of Zagreb. All of them had been using popular Web 2.0 applications (Facebook and YouTube) on a regular basis (71% and 77.9%, respectively, did that twice a day or more often). The study was conducted within the Data Structures course. It should be noted that students had not participated in similar studies before.

**Procedure and apparatus.** The study adopted a within-subjects design contrasting four different Web 2.0 applications for mind mapping. During one semester, students had to solve four different programming tasks. In addition to writing the programming code, an integral part of each task was to graphically display an algorithm by means of a mind map. All the tasks were of equal complexity. Before the experiment started, we had defined which Web 2.0 application must be used when performing a particular task. Web 2.0 applications that were involved in the study are presented in Figure 2.

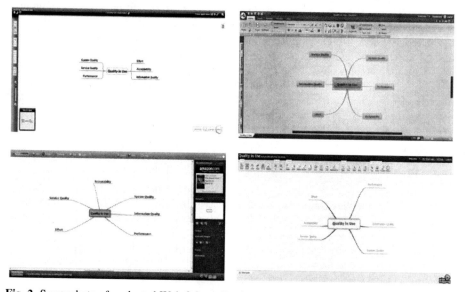

**Fig. 2.** Screenshots of evaluated Web 2.0 applications (clockwise, starting from top left: Mind 42, Mindomo, Wise Mapping, and Mindmeister)

Data were gathered by both objective and subjective means. Objective quality in use attributes (efficiency and effort) were measured using a Mousotron [2], which kept track of timing, mouse movements, mouse clicks, and keystrokes. To ensure maximum data accuracy, students were given detailed written and oral instructions at the beginning of each assignment. In the first step, students had to create an account and log in. Once the working environment had been loaded, it was necessary to run Mousotron and start task execution. Immediately after the task was completed, students needed to stop the data collecting process. The results gathered by means of Mousotron and the solutions for the assignment were supposed to be uploaded to the e-learning system. In order to obtain as much data about the advantages and disadvantages of the used mind mapping Web 2.0 applications as possible, the retrospective thinking aloud (RTA) method was employed. RTA allowed students to complete the assignment first, and then describe their experiences of working with a

Web 2.0 application. Immediately after they had completed the educational activity, students had to provide a critical review of the mind mapping application and deliver it in the form of a written report. One of the authors conducted a two-phase analysis of the data collected with the RTA method. Firstly, positive and negative comments related to the particular Web 2.0 applications were extracted from reports. Subsequently, each comment was attached to quality in use attributes whose definition they fit most closely. At the end of the semester, the perceived quality in use was evaluated by means of a post-use questionnaire.

**Measures.** Effort was measured by means of three metrics: distance traversed, mouse clicks, and keystrokes. *Distance* refers to the number of millimeters traversed by the user while moving the mouse between two points. *Mouse clicks* are the sum of all the mouse clicks (left, right, middle) that were made while reaching the task solution. Double clicks were not specifically analyzed, but were recorded as left clicks. *Keystrokes* denote the total number of keys on the keyboard that the user clicked while reaching the task solution. Other parameters that potentially affect the amount of physical effort, such as the number of the mouse wheel scrolls, are beyond the scope of this study. The sum of previous three metrics is referred to as *estimated effort*. Apart from physical effort, efficiency in use was also measured. *Time* is the amount of time expressed in seconds required to complete the task. *Mouse moving speed (MMS)* is the ratio of distance and time expressed in millimetres per minute (mm/min). *Keyboard typing speed (KTS)* is the ratio of keystrokes and time expressed in the number of keystrokes per minute (ks/min). *Mouse clicking speed (MCS)* is the ratio of mouse clicks and time expressed in the number of mouse clicks per minute (mc/min). The sum of keyboard typing speed, mouse moving speed and mouse clicking speed is referred to as *estimated efficiency*. Given that the execution of assignments was not time limited, objective assessment of the effectiveness was beyond the scope of this study. The post-use questionnaire was used for gathering data about perceived quality in use of the evaluated Web 2.0 applications. Each quality in use attribute was measured with between three and eight items. Responses were modulated on a five point Likert scale (1-strongly agree, 5-strongly disagree). In addition, overall preferences were assessed directly by a 4-point semantic differential item (1-best, 4-worst) in which users were asked to rank the quality in use of mind mapping Web 2.0 applications. The Cronbach's alpha values (presented in Table 1) ranged from .701 to .896, thus indicating a high reliability of the scale. Combining three different methods (logging actual use, questionnaire and RTA), complementary data of the estimated and perceived quality in use of the mind mapping applications was gathered. In this way, the process of detection of problems in Web 2.0 applications usage was accelerated, while the identification of key quality in use attributes was facilitated. The research results are presented in more detail in the following section.

**Table 1.** Internal reliability of scale

|  | **Mind 42** | **Mindmeister** | **Mindomo** | **Wise Mapping** |
|---|---|---|---|---|
| System Quality | .779 | .767 | .798 | .794 |
| Service Quality | .720 | .701 | .732 | .741 |
| Information Quality | .811 | .789 | .769 | .788 |
| Performance | .816 | .741 | .774 | .796 |
| Effort | .896 | .868 | .884 | .885 |
| Acceptability | .855 | .850 | .863 | .831 |

# 3    Results

Given that data were not normally distributed (K-S 1,2,3,4 > 0.05), the analysis was conducted by means of non-parametric tests. All the reported results are expressed as the median value.

## 3.1    Estimated Quality in Use

**Effort.** The analysis of the data revealed statistically significant differences among the four Web 2.0 interfaces in terms of mouse movements during task execution ($\chi2(3) = 23.255$, p < .001). The Wilcoxon Signed-Rank Tests with Bonferroni pairwise comparisons revealed that participants needed to make significantly fewer mouse movements to solve the task using the Mind 42 than either Mindmeister (Z = -3.585, p = .000, r = - .27) or Mindomo (Z = -4.433, p = .000, r = - .34). Both effects were medium in size with the significance level set at p < .008. No significant differences were observed in other pairwise comparisons.

The type of the Web 2.0 application used significantly affected the amount of mouse clicks made by users during the mind map design ($\chi2(3) = 11.102$, p < .05). A comparison of the number of mouse clicks among all four Web 2.0 applications revealed that users made much fewer mouse clicks using Mind 42 or Mindmeister than using Mindomo or Wise Mapping. Therefore, the number of required comparisons in the post-hoc analysis was reduced and the significance level set at p < .0125. A significant difference in the number of mouse clicks was found between Mindmeister and Wise Mapping (Z = -2.995, p = .003, r = - .23), Mind 42 and Wise Mapping (Z = -2.824, p = .005, r = - .22), and Mindmeister and Mindomo (Z = -2.556, p = .011, r = - .19), respectively, while the difference between Mindmeister and Mindomo was not significant (Z = -1.955, p = .051). All the effects were small in size. No significant difference was found among all four Web 2.0 applications in terms of the amount of keystrokes made when reaching the task solution ($\chi2(3) = 1.806$, p = .614).

**Table 2.** Results of objective measure effort for four selected mind mapping Web 2.0 applications (note that a lower score means a better result)

|               | Mind 42 | Mindmeister | Mindomo | Wise Mapping |
|---------------|---------|-------------|---------|--------------|
| Distance (mm) | 30759   | 38049       | 41313   | 39411        |
| Keystrokes    | 554     | 536         | 612     | 561          |
| Mouse clicks  | 292     | 286         | 353     | 361          |
| **Effort**    | **31610** | **38993** | **42693** | **40248**  |

There was a significant difference in the amount of estimated effort among all four Web 2.0 applications ($\chi2(3) = 22.858$, p < .001). Pairwise comparison revealed a significant difference between Mind 42 and Mindomo (Z = -4.407, p = .000, r = - .37), and between Mind 42 and Mindmeister (Z = -3.563, p = .000, r = - .27). The difference between Mind 42 and Wise Mapping was on the verge of the significance level (p < .0125). According to the summary of the results presented in Table 2, students experienced less effort using Mind 42 than any of the three remaining Web 2.0 applications.

**Efficiency.** Friedman's ANOVA revealed a significant difference among four different Web 2.0 applications in the speed of moving the mouse during task solving ($\chi2(3) = 40.083$, p < .001). As a follow up for this finding, a post-hoc analysis with the significance level set at p < 0.125 was applied. A significant difference in the speed of mouse movements was found between Mind 42 and Mindmeister (Z = - 4.567, p = .000, r = - .35), Mind 42 and Mindomo (Z = -4.825, p = .000, r = - .37), Wise Mapping and Mindmeister (Z = -4.192, p = .000, r = - .32), and between Wise Mapping and Mindomo (Z = -3.718, p = .000, r = - .28), respectively. Neither the keyboard typing ($\chi2(3) = 1.806$, p = .614) nor mouse clicking ($\chi2(3) = 6.402$, p = .094) speeds were significantly different among all four evaluated Web 2.0 applications. A significant difference in the estimated efficiency of evaluated Web 2.0 applications was discovered ($\chi2(3) = 41.829$, p < .001). A post hoc analysis showed a significant difference in the overall efficiency between Mindomo and Mind 42 (Z = - 4.851, p = .000, r = - .37), Mindmeister and Mind 42 (Z = -4.549, p = .000, r = - .35), Wise Mapping and Mindmeister (Z = -4.231, p = .000, r = - .35), and Wise Mapping and Mindomo (Z = -3.757, p = .000, r = - .29). According to the results presented in Table 3, of all four evaluated Web 2.0 applications, Mindmeister was the most efficient in accomplishing the assignments.

**Table 3.** Results of objective measure efficiency for four selected mind mapping Web 2.0 applications (note that a higher score means a better result)

|  | Mind 42 | Mindmeister | Mindomo | Wise Mapping |
|---|---|---|---|---|
| MMS (mm/min) | 1952 | 2573 | 2550 | 2074 |
| KTS (ks/min) | 35 | 34 | 35 | 33 |
| MCS (mc/min) | 18 | 19 | 19 | 20 |
| Efficiency | 2013 | 2635 | 2604 | 2122 |

## 3.2    Perceived Quality in Use

**Rank.** A significant value of chi square ($\chi2(3) = 37.381$, p < .001) indicates the existence of differences in the subjective ranking measure among the evaluated Web 2.0 applications. A post-hoc procedure with the significance level set at p < .0167 revealed differences between Wise Mapping and Mindmeister (Z = -4.800, p = .000, r = - .37), Wise Mapping and Mindomo (Z = -4.668, p = .000, r = - .36), Mindomo and Mind 42 (Z = -2.864, p = .004, r = - .22), Mindmeister and Mind 42 (Z = -2.671, p = .008, r = - .20), and Wise Mapping and Mind 42 (Z = -2.605, p = .009, r = - .20). The results of overall subjective preferences presented in Table 4 indicate that Mindomo has the highest rank of perceived quality in use.

**Table 4.** Results of subjective measure rank for four selected mind mapping Web 2.0 applications (note that a lower score means a better result)

|              | M Rank | $\chi^2$ | df | p      |
|--------------|--------|----------|----|--------|
| Mind 42      | 2.65   | 37.381   | 3  | < .001 |
| Mindmeister  | 2.19   |          |    |        |
| Mindomo      | 2.04   |          |    |        |
| Wise Mapping | 3.12   |          |    |        |

**Questionnaire.** The results show that the scores of the four applications differ significantly ($\chi^2(3) = 27.599$, p < .001). Wilcoxon Signed-Rank Tests with a Bonferroni correction were used to follow up on this finding. Significant differences were found between Wise Mapping and Mindomo (Z = -4.394, p = .000, r = - .34), Mindomo and Mind 42 (Z = -4.073, p = .000, r = - .31), Wise Mapping and Mindmeister (Z = -3.926, p = .000, r = - .30), and between Mindmeister and Mind 42 (Z = -2.915, p = .004, r = - .22). All the effects were medium in size. The summary of the results obtained from the post-use questionnaire is presented in Table 5.

**Table 5.** Results of overall perceived quality in use of four selected mind mapping Web 2.0 applications (note that a lower score means a better result)

|              | Median | SD     | $\chi^2$ | p      |
|--------------|--------|--------|----------|--------|
| Mind 42      | 334.00 | 50.471 | 27.599   | < .001 |
| Mindmeister  | 328.00 | 46.658 |          |        |
| Mindomo      | 321.50 | 47.000 |          |        |
| Wise Mapping | 338.50 | 46.962 |          |        |

**Retrospective Thinking Aloud.** Data analysis revealed that students had generated a total of 1711 comments related to the advantages (63.18%) and disadvantages (36.82%) of the used Web 2.0 applications. In general, effort and performance based attributes were reported in most cases during RTA sessions, while the attributes related to the information quality were mentioned rather rarely. In particular, the most important quality in use attributes reported by students are ease of use, effectiveness, controllability and interactivity, while in the context of Web 2.0 applications used for mind mapping the attributes such as consistency, feedback, accessibility and memorability are of little importance. Based on overall results presented in Table 6, the best ratio of reported advantages and disadvantages in use belongs to Mindomo, followed by Mindmeister, Mind 42, and Wise Mapping.

**Table 6.** Results of Retrospective Thinking Aloud (RTA) method

| | Mind 42 | | Mindmeister | | Mindomo | | Wise Mapping | |
|---|---|---|---|---|---|---|---|---|
| | Pros | Cons | Pros | Cons | Pros | Cons | Pros | Cons |
| NVG | 27 | 5 | 16 | 7 | 17 | 5 | 9 | 14 |
| CNS | | | | | | | | |
| AES | 12 | 3 | 14 | 6 | 12 | | 5 | 7 |
| FML | 5 | 1 | 5 | | 22 | 1 | 4 | 5 |
| CUS | 1 | 13 | 15 | 15 | 21 | 5 | 5 | 17 |
| SCR | | | | | | | | 1 |
| HLP | 1 | | 3 | 3 | 7 | | 7 | 1 |
| AVL | 1 | 1 | 6 | 8 | 12 | 5 | 5 | 1 |
| ITR | 24 | 1 | 24 | | 27 | 5 | 15 | 18 |
| ERP | 10 | 3 | 8 | 4 | 5 | 5 | 2 | 9 |
| RLB | 7 | 1 | 10 | 6 | 14 | 2 | 7 | 13 |
| RCV | | | | | 1 | | 1 | 1 |
| RSP | | | 1 | | 3 | 5 | 1 | 4 |
| FDB | | | | | | | | |
| CRG | 4 | 7 | 3 | 12 | 13 | 3 | 4 | 20 |
| EFE | 24 | 37 | 28 | 24 | 52 | 8 | 16 | 38 |
| UFL | 14 | 2 | 17 | 1 | 11 | 2 | 3 | 10 |
| EFI | 15 | 1 | 11 | 3 | 14 | 5 | 8 | 16 |
| PME | | | | | 2 | | | 1 |
| ACS | | | | | | | | |
| CTR | | 40 | 7 | 20 | 17 | 10 | 4 | 26 |
| EOU | 64 | 2 | 53 | 5 | 71 | 3 | 42 | 14 |
| LRN | 3 | 3 | 7 | 4 | 12 | 1 | 5 | 5 |
| MRB | | | | | | | | |
| UND | 16 | 1 | 6 | 5 | 15 | 4 | 6 | 13 |
| PLY | 1 | | 1 | | 1 | | | |
| STF | 34 | 14 | 26 | 9 | 39 | 7 | 15 | 20 |
| LOY | 1 | 4 | | 1 | 1 | | | 1 |
| CMP* | | | 3 | 1 | 3 | | | 23 |

\* Attribute was not included in model proposed in [16]

## 4    Discussion and Concluding Remarks

The objective of the research described in this paper was the design of a methodology for evaluating quality in use of Web 2.0 applications [14]. In order to accomplish the research goal, the quality in use of mind mapping applications was evaluated with three different methods: logging actual use, questionnaire, and retrospective thinking aloud.

The purpose of the experiment presented in this paper was twofold. Firstly, we aimed to determine to what extent the conceptual model and the corresponding measuring instrument we developed would be suitable for the evaluation of Web 2.0 applications. The analysis of the data gathered by means of the logging actual use method revealed that in the analysis and comparison of Web 2.0 applications the following can be used: distance traversed, number of mouse clicks and mouse moving speed. Namely, through the use of these objective metrics a statistically significant difference between the evaluated Web 2.0 applications can be determined. However, the measures of numbers of keystrokes, keyboard typing and mouse clicking speeds did not show discriminant validity. We believe that this occurred because the experiment was not time-limited. Another possible reason may be a narrow specialization of evaluated applications. Accordingly, the results obtained from the post-use questionnaire showed statistically significant differences among all four evaluated Web 2.0 applications. This suggests that Web 2.0 applications can be ranked by mean values.

Secondly, we aimed to identify the importance that users attach to certain attributes of quality in use and to detect whether the set of the most important attributes depends on the type of Web 2.0 application. The results gathered by means of the retrospective thinking aloud (RTA) method revealed the importance of effort (28.99%) and performance (21.43%) based attributes of quality in use. In particular, participants felt highly satisfied and comfortable working with Web 2.0 applications meeting the following quality in use attributes: ease of use, effectiveness, controllability, interactivity, navigability, customizability, efficiency, information content coverage, understandability, and reliability. In addition, data analysis showed that some attributes (consistency, feedback, accessibility, and memorability) were not mentioned at all during the RTA session. Possible reasons may be: majority of users not having any kind of disability; the ability to evaluate memorability when the application is re-used with a time lag, etc. On the other hand, compatibility, i.e. the degree to which a Web 2.0 application works equally well within different browsers, operating systems, or devices, which was not included in the proposed model, has proven to be an important indicator of problems in use of Web 2.0 applications. The results were similar to the findings presented in [15] which suggest that: (i) there is a general set of attributes that needs to be measured independently of the type of Web 2.0 applications; (ii) the weight of an attribute depends on the type of the evaluated Web 2.0 application; and (iii) there is a set of attributes aimed for measuring the quality in use of specific types of Web 2.0 applications. In our research, the results of the estimated and perceived quality in use do not match. Such findings are in accordance with those presented in e.g. [7]), indicating that quality in use should be measured with both subjective and objective instruments since they are aimed for evaluating different aspects of Web 2.0 applications. In addition, we must emphasize that a homogeneous set of four evaluated applications is a fairly modest sample on the basis of which generalizable sound conclusions on the importance of each category on the quality in use of Web 2.0 applications can not be drawn. Therefore, our future work will be focused on: (i) applying the proposed model to evaluate the quality in use of various Web 2.0 applications in a different context of use; (ii) revision of attributes, model and measuring instruments; (iii) improvement of a proposed methodology with an aim to facilitate analysis and comparison of the evaluated Web 2.0 applications.

# References

1. Almeida, J.M., Gonçalves, M.A., Figueiredo, F., Pinto, H., Belém, F.: On the Quality of Information for Web 2.0 Services. IEEE Internet Computing 14(6), 47–55 (2010)
2. Blacksun Software (2011),
   http://www.blacksunsoftware.com/mousotron.html

3. Bevan, N.: Extending Quality in Use to Provide a Framework for Usability Measurement. In: Kurosu, M. (ed.) HCD 2009. LNCS, vol. 5619, pp. 13–22. Springer, Heidelberg (2009)
4. Bevan, N., Macleod, M.: Usability measurement in context. Behaviour & Information Technology 13, 132–145 (1994)
5. Cappiello, C., Daniel, F., Matera, M.: A Quality Model for Mashup Components. In: Gaedke, M., Grossniklaus, M., Díaz, O. (eds.) ICWE 2009. LNCS, vol. 5648, pp. 236–250. Springer, Heidelberg (2009)
6. Chiou, W.-C., Lin, C.-C., Perng, C.: A strategic framework for website evaluation based on a review of the literature from 1995-2006. Information & Management 47, 282–290 (2010)
7. Frøkjær, E., Hertzum, M., Hornbæk, K.: Measuring usability: Are effectiveness, efficiency, and satisfaction really correlated? In: Proceedings of the ACM CHI Conference on Human Factors in Computing Systems, pp. 345–352. ACM, New York (2000)
8. Hart, J., Ridley, C., Taher, F., Sas, C., Dix, A.: Exploring the Facebook Experience: A New Approach to Usability. In: 5th Nordic Conference on Human-Computer Interaction: Building Bridges, pp. 471–474. ACM, Lund (2008)
9. Hassenzahl, M., Tractinsky, N.: User experience - a research agenda. Behaviour & Information Technology 25(2), 91–97 (2006)
10. ISO/IEC 25010:2011. Systems and software engineering - Systems and software Quality Requirements and Evaluation (SQuaRE) - System and software quality models (2011)
11. Lew, P., Olsina, L., Zhang, L.: Quality, Quality in Use, Actual Usability and User Experience as Key Drivers for Web Application Evaluation. In: Benatallah, B., Casati, F., Kappel, G., Rossi, G. (eds.) ICWE 2010. LNCS, vol. 6189, pp. 218–232. Springer, Heidelberg (2010)
12. Nielsen, J.: Heuristic evaluation. In: Nielsen, J., Mack, R.L. (eds.) Usability Inspection Methods, John Wiley & Sons, New York (1994)
13. Olsina, L., Sassano, R., Mich, L.: Specifying Quality Requirements for the Web 2.0 Applications. In: Proceedings of 7th International Workshop on Web-oriented Software Technology (IWWOST 2008), pp. 56–62. CEUR, Bratislava (2008)
14. Orehovački, T.: Development of a Methodology for Evaluating the Quality in Use of Web 2.0 Applications. In: Campos, P., Graham, N., Jorge, J., Nunes, N., Palanque, P., Winckler, M. (eds.) INTERACT 2011, Part IV. LNCS, vol. 6949, pp. 382–385. Springer, Heidelberg (2011)
15. Orehovački, T.: Perceived Quality of Cloud Based Applications for Collaborative Writing. In: Pokorny, J., et al. (eds.) Information Systems Development – Business Systems and Services: Modeling and Development, pp. 575–586. Springer, Heidelberg (2011)
16. Orehovački, T.: Proposal for a Set of Quality Attributes Relevant for Web 2.0 Application Success. In: 32nd International Conference on Information Technology Interfaces, pp. 319–326. IEEE Press, Cavtat (2010)
17. Silva, P.A., Dix, A.: Usability – Not as we know it! In: 21st British HCI Group Annual Conference on HCI 2007: People and Computers XXI: HCI...But not as We Know It, vol. 2, pp. 103–106. ACM, University of Lancaster (2007)
18. Thompson, A.-J., Kemp, E.A.: Web 2.0: extending the framework for heuristic evaluation. In: 10th International Conference NZ Chapter of the ACM's Special Interest Group on Human-Computer Interaction, pp. 29–36. ACM, New Zealand (2009)

# Detecting Conflicts and Inconsistencies in Web Application Requirements

Matias Urbieta[1,3], Maria Jose Escalona[2], Esteban Robles Luna[1], and Gustavo Rossi[1,3]

[1] LIFIA, Facultad de Informática, UNLP, La Plata, Argentina
{murbieta,esteban.robles,gustavo}@lifia.info.unlp.edu.ar
[2] IWT2 Group. University of Seville, Spain
mjescalona@us.es
[3] Conicet

**Abstract.** Web applications evolve fast. One of the main reasons for this evolution is that new requirements emerge and change constantly. These new requirements are posed either by customers or they are the consequence of users' feedback about the application. One of the main problems when dealing with new requirements is their consistency in relationship with the current version of the application. In this paper we present an effective approach for detecting and solving inconsistencies and conflicts in web software requirements. We first characterize the kind of inconsistencies arising in web applications requirements and then show how to isolate them using a model-driven approach. With a set of examples we illustrate our approach.

## 1 Introduction

Eliciting web application requirements implies understanding the needs of different stakeholders, those that are related with the same underlying enterprise business. Most of the times, requirements are agreed by stakeholders in such a way that the semantics and meanings of each used term is well understood; however when different points of view [11] of the same business concept exist, ambiguities and/or inconsistencies may arise, being them detrimental to the Software Requirement Specification (SRS). Traditionally, conciliation tasks are performed using meeting-based tools, in order to eliminate requirements ambiguity and inconsistence. When requirement inconsistencies are not detected on time -being this one of the most severe reason of project cost overrun [12][17]-, they may become defects in the web software. In this context, the effort to correct the faults is several orders of magnitude higher than correcting requirements at the early stages [12].

Inconsistencies may also arise from new requirements, which introduce new functionality or enhancements to the application or, even, for existing requirements that change during the development process. For example, an online e-commerce site may plan a promotion for Christmas, where some products have free shipping for a period of time; meanwhile other products keep the usual shipping cost. This new

A. Harth and N. Koch (Eds.): ICWE 2011 Workshops, LNCS 7059, pp. 278–288, 2012.

requirement introduces changes that are perceived by the user because he can see promotional banners in different pages. It is noteworthy that the existing "shipping" requirement is overridden (and contradicted) with the shipping cost exception, introducing ambiguities: what products have the free shipping promotion? In which way users are notified? How long will the promotion be available?

In this paper we present a model-based validation and inconsistency detection technique for web application requirements, particularly for those that reflect themselves during navigation and interaction, two aspects are the key features of web applications. Though we exemplify our technique with WebSpec[15], the same ideas can be easily applied to other similar approaches such as WebRE[8] or Molic[6]. By using this technique we reduce the risk of errors and costs caused by inconsistencies detected in the final stages of software development.

The main contributions of this paper are threefold: a characterization of web application requirement inconsistencies depending on a taxonomy for conflicts; a modular approach for detecting inconsistencies that can easily complement any web application engineering process no matter its style: agile or unified; and a set of running examples to illustrate our approach.

The rest of this paper is structured as follows. Section 2 presents some related work in requirements validation. Section 3 introduces the background for the paper. Section 4 presents our characterization of web requirement conflicts. Section 5 describes our approach to detect and deal with inconsistencies. Section 6 presents a tool which provides support for conflict detection analysis. Finally Section 7 concludes this work discussing the lessons learned, our main conclusions and some further work on this subject.

## 2    Related Works

The analysis and detection of conflicts in the requirements phase are one of the most critical tasks in requirements engineering [15]. A global view presented in [7] divides this phase in three main tasks: requirements capture, requirements definition and requirements validation. The detection of conflicts is normally executed in the last one. In [7] the authors surveyed the way in which web engineering approaches dealt with these three phases and conclude that requirements validation is one of the less treated. Besides, none of these techniques offers a systematic detection of conflicts in requirements. Approaches studied in this survey support four main techniques for requirements validation: reviews, audits, traceability matrix and prototypes. In [16] this set is enriched adding requirements test. It consists in the generation of early test cases derived from requirements, which enables the early validation with users.

Recently, some web design approaches, such as WebML[5], support this idea using the model-driven paradigm. However, even offering systematic (or even automatic) support for early testing, the detection of inconsistencies in the requirements specification continues being "too artisanal" and depends on the analyst's experience and his/her capability for supporting the review with customers and users.

Focusing only on the detection of conflicts, in [3], an approach to detect conflict in concerns is presented. In this approach, the authors propose the use of a Multiple Criteria Decision Making method to support aspectual conflict management in aspect oriented requirements. The main limitation of this approach it that it is oriented to aspect-oriented requirements treatment and it only deals with concern conflicts.

In other phases of the life cycle, the conflict detection process has been researched intensively by the model-driven community mainly focused to UML model conflicts. In [1] the author proposes detecting conflict in a twofold process: analyzing syntactic differences raising candidate conflicts and understanding these differences from a semantic view.

# 3     Background

In this work we focus on detecting conflicts in web applications requirements which are modeled using WebSpec, a web requirement meta-model describing interactions, navigations and interface aspects.

WebSpec[15] is a visual language; its main artifact for specifying requirements is the WebSpec diagram which can contain *interactions*, *navigations* and *rich behaviors*.

A WebSpec diagram defines a set of scenarios that the web application must satisfy. An *interaction* (denoted with a rounded rectangle) represents a point where the user can interact with the application by using its interface objects (widgets). *Interactions* have a name (unique per diagram) and may have widgets such as labels, list boxes, etc. In WebSpec, a *transition* (either *navigation* or *rich behavior*) is graphically represented with arrows between *interactions* while its name, precondition and triggering actions are displayed as labels over them. In particular, its name appears with a prefix of the character '#', the precondition between { } and the actions in the following lines.

The scenarios specified by a WebSpec diagram are obtained by traversing the diagram using the depth-first search algorithm. The algorithm starts from a set of special nodes called "starting" nodes (*interactions* bordered with dashed lines) and following the edges (*transitions*) of the graph (diagram).

As an example of WebSpec's concepts we present in Fig. 1 the specification for the user story: "As a customer, I would like to search products by name and see their details" in an e-commerce application. *Home* represents the starting point of the specification and it contains 2 widgets: *searchField* text field and *search* button (see [15] for further details).

# 4     Characterizing Requirements Conflicts in Web Applications

During requirement specification, there may be cases where two or more scenarios that reflect the same business logic differ subtly from each other producing an inconsistency. When these inconsistencies are based on contradictory behaviors, we are facing a conflict of requirements [10]. Conflicts are characterized by differences of objects' features, logical (what is expected) or temporal (when is expected) conflicts between actions, or even difference of terminology that creates ambiguity.

In this analysis, we will emphasize on web application navigation, as well as user interaction peculiarities that are not covered in the traditional characterization of requirement conflicts [10]. Consequently, we provide an interpretation of each conflict type in the web application realm, using simple but illustrative examples. We use WebSpec terminology to specify the requirements.

**Fig. 1.** WebSpec diagram of the *Search by name* scenario

Structural conflicts stand for a difference in the data expected to be presented in one web page by different stakeholders. A stakeholder may demand a data to be shown in a web page that contradicts other stakeholder requirement. For example, a stakeholder expects a product content description just as a read-only label, while another one may expect the content as a list of packaged items with an overall description contradicting the first requirement.

Two web application requirements may contradict the way in which links are traversed producing navigational conflicts, e.g. having a single source node but two targets. The target nodes are different, but the event that triggers the navigation and the condition guards are the same, producing an ambiguity of such requirement. In WebSpec terms, for a given navigation sequence (or path) composed with *interactions* and *navigations*, there are two navigation alternatives triggered by the same event. For instance, a WebSpec *navigation* can define that after clicking the "Buy" button at the Product *interaction*, a shopping cart is presented. On the other hand, the same *navigation* has as target the PaymentMethod *interaction*, which allows selecting a payment method instead of presenting the Shopping cart.

A semantic conflict occurs when the same real world object is described with different terms. This situation may generate a false negative in the conflict detection process, since a conflict may not be detected and new terms are introduced into the system space thus increasing its complexity. As a consequence the same domain object is modeled in two entities having different terminology. For instance, an e-commerce site can wrongly define two entities that stand for the same concept: Good and Product.

## 5    Detecting and Correcting Conflicts

Next we present our approach that helps detecting conflicts checking the existences of false positives and false negatives conflicts. The approach comprises the following steps, depicted in Fig. 2 (notice that steps 1 and 2 are already part of any development process; therefore the novel contribution begins in step 3):

1. Requirement gathering: Using well-known requirement elicitation techniques such as meetings, surveys, Joint Application Development (JAD), etc. a Software Requirement Specification (usually in natural language) is produced. In the case of an agile underlying development process, a briefer description is usually produced with user stories [4]; use cases are often used in a unified process style.

2. Requirement modeling: Web application requirements are formalized using a requirement domain specific language (DSL) (e.g. WebSpec, WebRE or Molic). This formalization is essential during the validation process with stakeholders. By means of using a requirement DSL, the validation process can automated.

3. Structural analysis of the web requirements model: by means of an algebraic comparison of models, candidate structural and navigational conflicts are detected. Additionally, navigation paths are evaluated for checking their consistency.

4. Semantic analysis: candidate conflicts are analyzed and semantic equivalences are detected. For each candidate conflict, both the new requirement and the compromised requirement are translated from a high abstraction level (the requirements DSL) to a minimal form, using an atomic constructor in order to detect semantic differences.

5. Conciliation process: once the existence of a conflict is confirmed, we must start conciliating requirements. This process demands the establishment of a communication channel among those stakeholders concerned to the conflict.

6. Refinement: When a conflict is confirmed some adjustment and tuning must be done in order to remove the detected conflict and reach a consistent state.

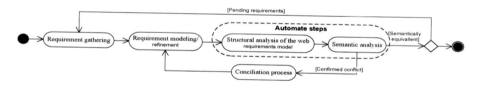

**Fig. 2.** The overall process for detecting requirement conflicts

The process is applied iteratively each time a new set of requirement rises. The new incoming set of requirements is checked with each one of the already consolidated requirements of the system space. In Fig. 2, those steps that can be implemented to be automated are grouped with a dashed box and those steps outside the dashed box are manually elaborated.

| Show product information | Show product summary |
|---|---|
| **As a customer**<br>**I want** to be able to see quickly product's information from a list of products<br>**So that** i can see a detailed view of product features | **As a customer**<br>**I want** to be able to see quickly product's summary when listed<br>**So that** i can see product's features |

**Fig. 3.** User stories for gathered requirements

## 5.1    Requirement Gathering and Requirement Modeling (Steps 1 and 2)

In order to describe clearly and accurately the aforementioned process, we use as a running example the development and extension of an e-commerce site. In Fig. 3, user stories [4] derived from gathered requirements are shown. Instead of including in this section the corresponding WebSpec diagrams, we show them in each of the subsequent steps.

## 5.2    Detecting Syntactic Differences (Step 3)

A candidate conflict arises when the set of syntactic differences between requirement models is not empty. These differences may be a consequence of the absence of an element in one model but present in the other, the usage of two different widgets for describing the same information, and finally a configuration difference in an element such as the properties values of a widget. This situation may arise when two different stakeholders have different views of a single functionality, or when an evolution requirement contradicts an original one. As the result of having a formal tool for describing requirements, the detection task can be implemented by reasoning over the specification. In this case using the WebSpec support tool [15], this task can be performed using OCL [14] sentences or RDF [9] queries.

Structural conflicts detection can be implemented by a comparison operation between interactions, in order to detect the absence of elements or elements constructions differences. Since WebSpec *interactions* are containers of widgets, we can apply set's difference operations in order to detect inconsistencies. For example, a Product interaction version called Product[1] have *Name*, *Valorization* and *Content* Labels, and an *addToShopping* Button and, on the other hand, a different version called Product[2] comprises a *Name*, and *Description* Label, and a list of *PackageItem* Labels. After applying the symmtric difference, following widgets differs: *Valorization*, *Content*, *addToShoppingCart*, *Description*, and a list of *PackageItem*.

Notice that for the comparison operation, two elements are equal if and only if they have the same identifier and have the same widget type and compatible configuration.

To detect navigational conflicts, outgoing navigations from a given node with identical triggering events but different targets must be detected. The task is pretty straightforward; since *navigations* are described by a guard and a set of actions that trigger them, the *navigations* for a given *interaction* must be compared to each other taking into account their guards and set of actions. The main challenge of this procedure is to check whether or not the sets of actions that correspond to navigations are semantically equivalent considering that the actions can be syntactically different.

Next we introduce an analysis process that helps avoiding false positives.

## 5.3    Semantic Analysis (Step 4)

As the result of the structural analysis of models, a list of candidate conflicts is reported; this list must be verified in order to detect false positives, i.e. conflicts that actually are not conflicts since the compromised specifications describe the same requirement. This issue has been already studied in [1][13] where models are analyzed in order to expose their underlying goals. When the underlying goals are different, we are facing a confirmed conflict.

We use an approach proposed in [1] and based on having an additional semantic view of requirements that complements the existing syntactic view. For achieving this, requirements models are downgraded in terms of abstraction, obtaining a refined model formed only with semantically simple elements. The resultant model is larger than the source diagram but has the same semantics.

This approach is twofold: a meta-model called semantic view, defined as a reduced subset of the web application requirement DSL is specified, and a transformation is specified that takes elements from the source model to the "semantic view".

The compromised models (the new and the stable one) are transformed into a semantic view where the derived models are finally compared syntactically. For each conflict detected in step 3, this approach helps detecting false positives because the semantically equivalent constructions imply that different models specify the same requirement. In the other hand, models are compared when no conflict is detected to expose false negative cases.

We will use as semantic view a simplified WebSpec meta-model where the Transition's hierarchy and Container widgets are removed. The transition hierarchy is formed by two specializations - Navigation and RichBehavior - that are removed in order to focus on determining what is the intent of the *interaction*, independently of the used interaction pattern: traditional navigation or RIA interaction. When containers do not have a name, they are removed in order to reduce composition complexity and avoid unnecessary object aggregations.

Finally a model transformation must turn a WebSpec model into a semantic one in order to provide a simpler understanding.

In the transformation, a set of rules closely related to the Web requirement meta-model used are applied over the input model obtaining the semantic view. These rules are based on heuristics defined by the requirement engineer and the available set of rules must be improved iteratively by means of lessons learned of its application.

If other Web requirement meta-model is used such as WebRE, a different set of rules must be defined where each one must increase the abstraction level in such a way the intent of the model is emphasized.

Some of the rules for WebSpec meta-model comprised by the transformation are:

- Disabled TextFields are translated to Labels. As disabled TextFields do not allows user inputs these are replaced by simple Labels.
- Links are translated to buttons. Links and Buttons are usually used for describing an action triggering. Therefore, links are normalized to buttons.
- Navigations and RichBehavior are simplified into a single transition abstraction. This rule makes the diagram focus more on the data itself instead of the way in which it is accessed. Finally, Navigation´s and RichBehavior ´s actions are removed.

In order to detect if the syntactic conflict is in fact a conflict, the semantic transformation is applied over both requirement specifications. Both transformations produce the same model that is formed by Labels and a Button. Thus, as both semantic views are equal, there is not conflict at all.

The following example aims at illustrating how semantic conflicts are detected; in particular a false negative case. In Fig. 4 two requirements, namely "show product information" and "show product summary" represent the same interaction idea but use two different interaction patterns: traditional web navigation and RIA´s mouse hover pattern.

The left-hand image specifies that after clicking the name of a product, the link is traversed and a product detail is shown. On the other hand, in the picture at the right, when the mouse´s pointer is place over the product´s name, a product detail is popped-up. It is remarkable that both requirements´ models have the same intent but are described with distinct WebSpec constructors.

The resultant of applying the transformation to both conflicted WebSpec is a pair of normalized diagrams that must be syntactically compared in order to detect differences. Fig. 5.a and Figure 5.b show the result of applying the transformation to the examples presented in Fig. 4.a and 4.b respectively where Navigations and RichBehavior were normalized into the more abstract Transitions, and the Home link was removed because it is not referenced anymore.

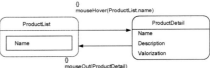

**Fig.  4a.** Specification  of  conventional navigation requirement.

**Fig. 4b.** Interaction based on a RIA feature.

**Fig. 5a.** Normalized conventional navigation model into Semantic view.

**Fig. 5b.** Normalized RRIA feature model into Semantic view.

Then a semantic conflict is detected because both models are not syntactically equal in the semantic view because Price and Description Labels are not present in both ProductDetail interactions (Fig. 5.a and Fig. 5.b).

There are cases were both traditional navigation and RIA features are required, in this case the raised warning for a false negative conflict must be omitted.

## 5.4    Conciliation Process (Step 5)

So far, we have shown how to detect conflicts that must be resolved in order to keep the SRS sound and complete. Next we will introduce a set of heuristics that helps resolving structural and navigation conflicts and that have been implemented as suggested refactorings in our tool support.

In the case of structural conflicts, the absence of a given widget in a model but present in the other, we can take an optimistic position understanding that the best solution is to include the construction as an improvement when it is not present. This idea comes from the fact that new requirements may improve others requirement´s functionality; therefore the new requirement widget may enrich an existing interaction.On the other hand, the widget type incompatibility demands a deeper analysis understanding the context of the difference.

Navigational conflicts express ambiguity in the way in which the web application is browsed, having two targets (WebSpec *interactions*) in a *navigation* triggered by the same event. This situation is naturally resolved enriching the scenario in such a way that the conflict is dissolved because the scenario detail is increased. Since we are using WebSpec as a requirement modeling tool, there are two strategies available for disambiguating: adding precondition clauses or extending the scenario path; both increase scenario detail.

As we have previously introduced, different stakeholders may provide slightly different specification for the same application goal. Nonetheless, there are scenarios where it is more prone to face inconsistencies such as the presence of business objects' hierarchies. At the requirement elicitation stage, hierarchies of business objects may not be clearly detected and defined, and as a consequence several business objects structurally different are referenced with the same name.

## 6     Tool Support

We have extended the WebSpec tool [15] with a reasoning support that helps detecting inconsistencies in the requirement modeling process. The tool provides a consistency checker engine based on the Eclipse EMF OCL[14] query system. By means of executing OCL queries over diagrams both structural and navigational inconsistencies are detected. The tool automates the structural analysis of web requirement models, transformation of requirements into semantic view and the syntactic analysis discussed in Section 5. Its main intent of use is during the requirement gathering and requirement modeling steps of the process, as it aids analysts in the requirement modeling, requirement management, and consistency checking activities. The tool provides a consistency report is generated showing detected conflicts and compromised widgets. Finally, when inconsistencies are detected, candidates list of automatic and semiautomatic (those that require an input parameter) refactorings that correct inconsistencies are presented. Since conflicts can not be trivially resolved, the tool provides a list of refactorings that could be applied to resolve the problem. The analyst should decide which option is the best to be applied, and afterwards the tool will perform automatically the refactoring over the WebSpec diagrams.

## 7     Concluding Remarks and Further Work

We have presented a novel approach for detecting conflict and inconsistencies in web application requirements in the early stages of software development. The presented approach leans on a web requirement meta-model used for specifying, in a formal way, the application requirements. Any new requirement is checked against the consolidated requirement set in order to detect conflicts. By means of syntactic and semantic analysis inconsistencies are detected. The approach is modular so it can be plugged in any software engineering approach to ensure application consistency, validate requirements, and save time and effort to detect and solve error in latest software development steps. Our support tool helps to automate the analysis and correction of these inconsistencies.

We have presented some simple examples that illustrate the approach feasibility but it still requires further work. We are currently working on the following issues: complete the approach with a set of ontology matching algorithms in order to improve semantic conflicts detection; extend the available heuristics for resolve detected conflicts in order to provide automated conflict detection and solving solution; and carry out an experiment instantiating the approach in order to provide evidence and to measure the time and effort effectively saved.

# References

[1] Altmanninger, K.: Models in Conflict - Towards a Semantically Enhanced Version Control System for Models. In: MoDELS Workshops 2007, pp. 293–304 (2007)

[2] Boehm, B.W., Grünbacher, P., Briggs, R.O.: Developing Groupware for Requirements Negotiation: Lessons Learned. IEEE Software 18(3) (2001)

[3] Brito, I.S., Vieira, F., Moreira, A., Ribeiro, R.A.: Handling Conflicts in Aspectual Requirements Compositions. In: Rashid, A., Aksit, M. (eds.) Transactions on AOSD III. LNCS, vol. 4620, pp. 144–166. Springer, Heidelberg (2007)

[4] Cohn, M.: Succeeding with Agile: Software Development Using Scrum, 1st edn. Addison-Wesley Professional (2009)

[5] Ceri, S., Fraternali, P., Bongio, A., Brambilla, M., Comai, S., Matera, M.: Designing Data-Intensive Web Applications. Morgan Kaufmann Publishers Inc., San Francisco (2002)

[6] de Paula, M.G., da Silva, B.S., Barbosa, S.D.: Using an interaction model as a resource for communication in design. In: CHI 2005 Extended Abstracts on Human Factors in Computing Systems, Portland, USA, April 02-07, pp. 1713–1716 (2005)

[7] Escalona, M.J., Koch, N.: Requirements Engineering for Web Applications: A Survey. Journal of Web Engineering II(2), 193–212 (2004)

[8] Escalona, M.J., Koch, N.: Metamodeling Requirements of Web Systems. In: Proc. International Conference on Web Information System and Technologies (WEBIST 2006), INSTICC, Setúbal, Portugal, pp. 310–317 (2006)

[9] Euzenat, J., Shvaiko, P.: Ontology Matching, 1st edn. Springer, Heidelberg (2007) ISBN: 978-3540496113

[10] IEEE Recommended Practice for Software Requirements Specifications. IEEE Std 830-1998 (1998)

[11] Kotonya, G., Sommerville, I.: Requirements engineering with viewpoints. Software Engineering Journal 11(1), 5–18 (1996)

[12] Leffingwell, D.: Calculating the Return on Investment From More Effective Requirements Managament. American Programmer 10(4), 13–16 (1997)

[13] Li, C., Ling, T.W.: OWL-Based Semantic Conflicts Detection and Resolution for Data Interoperability. In: ER (Workshops) 2004, pp. 266–277 (2004)

[14] Object Management Group, Object Constraint Language, Version 2.2,
`http://www.omg.org/spec/OCL/2.2/`

[15] Luna, E.R., Garrigós, I., Grigera, J., Winckler, M.: Capture and Evolution of Web Requirements Using WebSpec. In: Benatallah, B., Casati, F., Kappel, G., Rossi, G. (eds.) ICWE 2010. LNCS, vol. 6189, pp. 173–188. Springer, Heidelberg (2010)

[16] Sommerville, I.: Software Engineering. Addisson Wesley (2002); Van Der Straeten, R., Mens, T., Simmonds, J., Jonckers, V.: Using Description Logic to Maintain Consistency Between UML Models. In: Stevens, P., Whittle, J., Booch, G. (eds.) UML 2003. LNCS, vol. 2863, pp. 326–340. Springer, Heidelberg (2003)

[17] Yang, D., Wang, Q., Li, M., Yang, Y., Ye, K., Du, J.: A survey on software cost estimation in the chinese software industry. In: ESEM 2008, pp. 253–262 (2008)

# Streamlining Complexity: Conceptual Page Re-modeling for Rich Internet Applications

Andrea Pandurino[1], Davide Bolchini[2], Luca Mainetti[1], and Roberto Paiano[1]

[1] University of Salento, Department of Innovation Engineering
Graphics and Software Architectures Lab
Via Monteroni - 73100 Lecce (LE), Italy
{andrea.pandurino,luca.mainetti,roberto.paiano}@unisalento.it
[2] Indiana University, School of Informatics at IUPUI
User Simulation and Experience Research Lab
535 W. Michigan St., 46202 Indianapolis, IN, U.S.A.
dbolchin@iupui.edu

**Abstract.** The growth of Rich Internet Applications (RIAs) calls for new conceptual tools that enable web engineers to model the design complexity unleashed by innovative interaction (with increasing communication potential) and to carefully consider the impact of the design decisions on the optimal flow of the User Experience (UX). In this paper we illustrate how is particularly relevant for RIA engineering not only to capture existing RIA technologies with suitable design artifacts but also to model an effective dialogue between users and RIA interfaces. Through a case study, we propose a set of conceptual design primitives (Rich-IDM) to enable web engineers to characterize the fluid, smooth and organic nature of the user interaction, and to take design decisions which meet both usability and communication requirements.

**Keywords:** User Experience, Rich Internet Application, Dialogue Modeling, Information Architecture, UX Requirements.

## 1 Introduction

The technologies enabled by RIA offer designers the opportunity to experiment with a novel interaction grammar that is radically changing the *dialogue rules* between the application and the user. The metaphor of the dialogue seems appropriate to represent the new communication aspects enabled by RIA technologies; in fact, for long time, Human-Computer Interaction (HCI) researchers assume that a sort of dialogue is established between the user and the interactive application during its use [2]. On this basis, every element of the application interface can be considered as a dialogue fragment that can be built using several "dialogue types and techniques" (such as form filling, menu selection, icons, direct manipulation, etc.) [8]. It is our opinion that RIAs are completely changing the core vocabulary of the dialogue for two reasons:

A. Harth and N. Koch (Eds.): ICWE 2011 Workshops, LNCS 7059, pp. 289–301, 2012.

(i) the set of interface primitives is raised through the introduction of new widgets; (ii) the interface primitives respond to more interaction events (such as mouse-over, drag-and-drop) than the corresponding primitives in a standard Web Application (WA). These new events allow users to enrich the dialogue with the application.

Two principal flaws could affect the design of RIAs if they are modeled using standard WA methods: (i) *underutilization* of the features of the RIA interface because the used methodology does not consider expressly the new primitives. Thus, the application interface has the same behavior of a standard WA and simply the system is re-written using a new technology; (ii) *weak use* of the RIA interface primitives: the designer models the new features of RIAs considering only the technological aspects, without evaluating the impact on the UX. This can cause serious problems to the interaction quality of the entire web application. To better understand this important aspect, in section 2 we report some examples of this defect using a commercial web site. Here we propose a design approach that can mitigate these flaws. Our approach, called Rich-IDM, can help designers to consider properly the RIA interface features, taking under control the communication aspects of the application. Rich-IDM can improve the dialogue between users and application, and, thus, the design of the UX because its primitives are characterized by a strong semantics (based on the metaphor of web-as-dialogue) derived by the information model. The dialogue is the bridging metaphor between the need to plan a product (design) and its UX, as defined in [11] "a representation of designers' hypotheses on experiences of the user needs or wants to have with the product in the future" or in [12] "a dynamic, context-dependent and subjective concept, which stems from a broad range of potential benefits users may derive from a product", which is in line with the UX definition proposed by ISO (2008) [10]: "A person's perceptions and responses that result from the use or anticipated use of a product, system or service."

The paper is organized as follows: section 2 provides the reader with a brief introduction to the poor RIA design problem caused by the introduction in RIA features considering only as technological improvements; section 3 gives a brief presentation of our methodological approach in order to address these issues; section 4 reports on key related work in the area of RIA engineering approaches and User eXperience (UX) requirements design; finally, in section 5 the conclusions summarize our key messages and sketch future research directions.

## 2    Potential and Weaknesses of RIA Design

The features of RIAs tend to exhibit potential flaws that can negatively affect the usability of the interaction. In detail: (i) at the micro-interaction level, the aesthetic impact of the presentation layer can obscure the real intent of the page at any given moment of the interaction, diverting the user's attention; (ii) recurring attention tunneling can easily bring users to misplace the saliency of the overall message of the page content. This problem can be summarized by implicit questions of the user: What is the designer showing me now? What is the main intent of this page? What is the message of this page?; (iii) users may have difficulty in capturing the underlying conceptual model of the designers, which should ideally match the user's mental model, thus starting an errant mental model; and (iv) the massive use of animations (such as sliding windows), that trigger continuous changes of the interface, greatly stresses user working memory by forcing users to recall their specific position in the local and global information architecture, the affordance of specific controls, and their location. In a previous work [16], we presented a set of case studies providing examples of flaws derived by the analysis of real web sites. For lack of space, here we limit our analysis to only one example.

**Case study.** A clear example of user working memory stressing can be found in the homepage of the Verizon corporate (Fig. 1), a communication carrier of the North America. The intent of the page is to show the features of the offered services. The page content is not so dense, but the page is long and requires the use of the mouse scroll to be completely viewed.  The page presents various mechanisms that allow users to change (hide/unhide) completely the provided information without a page reload: (i) the menus in the highlighted area 1 (see Fig. 1) are composed of several items that inside have multiple columns with buttons and advanced options; (ii) the images of the area 3 allow to change completely the content showed in the area 2; (iii) the area 4 contains a set of messages "what's HOT" automatically updated or by user choice through the specific button in the same section; (iv) the area 6 controls the vertical banners, which are sliding elements with contents.

**Fig. 1.** www.verizon.com, homepage (April 2010)

Summarizing, there are 6 areas and 17 contents that can contain other dynamically showed elements.

The information presented *one-shot* to the user is few if compared to the global quantity of information of the page but, to have a complete schema of the page content, the user should access all the hided elements, which are mutually exclusive. Then, to reach specific product, the user must remember its position and the corresponding path; moreover, in order to compare two products (not displayed at the same time), the user must remember the features of the first while he/she is reading the other one. This situation is a clear example of poor user experience caused by a weak application of the RIA features.

In order to prevent the flaws described in the case study and the UX defects analyzed (but not reported) in this paper, in the following paragraph we present our conceptual approach called Rich-IDM.

## 3    Disciplined RIA Modeling for Improved UX Requirements

The new features of the RIA have changed radically the UX and put new questions that must be carefully evaluated during the design time. From this point of view, as described in the related work section, the existing approaches reach the goal to formalize the technological aspects of RIAs but they do not consider how to evaluate the changes in the UX and how it evolves. Thus, it is clear that it is necessary to define a methodological layer in which the single primitive has a well-defined communication semantics able to model the interaction and navigation paradigms of RIAs.

On the basis of these needs, in the following we present a conceptual approach (Rich-IDM) based on the Interactive Dialogue Model (IDM) [3]. First, we give a brief introduction to IDM (see Table 1), then we present all the primitives of Rich-IDM considering their notation and semantics (see Table 2). To give an example of the effectiveness of the Rich-IDM primitives to prevent and to correct UX poor usability situations, we report an artifact of the reengineering activity we did on the homepage of www.verizon.com, already used to describe the interface flaw.

### 3.1    A Brief Introduction to IDM

The idea to use the concepts of the dialogue as basis to describe the human-computer communication is not new. For long time, the research in the field of the Human–Computer Interaction (HCI) assumes that between the user and the interactive application a sort of dialogue is established during its use [1]. Often, in HCI literature, "dialogue" is used as synonymous "interaction". On this basis, every element of the application interface such as the information retrieved from a database, the pop-up windows, the buttons, and other widgets, can be considered as dialogue fragments that can be built using several "dialogue types and techniques" (such as such form filling, menu selection, icons, direct manipulation, etc. [7]). Hence, the design of the interaction is often called "dialogue design" and, therefore, it is defined as the activity of modeling the structure of the conversation between the user and the system.

A complete model of a dialogue must describe all its aspects: the information and its structure, the relationships among information pieces and how this information must be showed and delivered to the user. Starting from this perspective and considering that often the new features of RIAs affect the quality of the dialogue, raveling the user interface and forcing the user to understand the interaction paradigms, we choose to extend IDM that is a dialogue-based design technique for shaping the communicative structure of information-intensive interactive applications.

IDM is based on proven hypermedia/web design concepts and dialogue theories. It can be used to describe the essential interactive and navigation features of information-intensive applications at the proper conceptual level, by focusing on the dynamics of the dialogue. The main advantages of IDM may be summarized as follows: a) easiness of use and understandability of the design primitives employed with respect to their expressive power; b) primitives semantics based on dialogue concepts, thus more accessible by novice designers without a technical background; c) separation between channel-independent (or technology-independent) design (determining the expected deep structure and dynamics of the dialogue) and channel-dependent design (conceptual specification for the applications available on different devices). IDM primitives are organized in two main design layers: Conceptual IDM (C-IDM) and Logical IDM (L-IDM).

C-IDM is used to describe the "conceptual schema" of the application. It is simple to grasp and effective enough in representing the most relevant features of the application, defining the topics of the dialogue and relations between its elements; in other word, it is used to shape the deep dialogic structure of the interaction. Starting from the C-IDM design, the logical design models the decisions that are typically dependent on a specific fruition channel through which the application may be conveyed. The conceptual schema is unique in the application because defines the overall interaction strategy; while, the designers can develop one or more logical schemas, one for each specific channel they want to design the application for.

The L-IDM is used to shape the application dialogic features specific of a given channel or technologies of fruition such as standard web browsers, mobile devices, screen readers, etc. IDM breaks down the application information (according to its semantics) defining the topics (core content entities) and dialogue acts (interaction units) in a L-IDM schema. Considering the goal of this paper, the main L-IDM primitives (used in the case studies) are described in the Table 1.

Readers interested in a complete introduction to IDM can refer to [3]. Currently, IDM is being used in several research and industrial projects allowing capturing the dialogue features of the applications, and providing a valid design to project the non-technical aspects.

## 3.2   The Rich Extension of IDM

In the rest of this section we provide readers with a brief introduction to Rich-IDM, which is our extension of IDM to cover RIAs. Table 2 shows all Rich-IDM design primitives at a glance; after, for each primitive, we describe its semantics and its specific features.

**Table 1.** The IDM design primitives.

| Name | Notation | Design Semantics |
|------|----------|------------------|
| Topic / <br><br>Multiple Topic | Topic <br><br> Multiple Topic | It is the dialogue subject: the argument of a dialogue between user and application. A topic should contain information with a precise sense for the final user independently from the application and from the arguments presented inside. <br><br> If the topic has more instances, it is a multiple topic. |
| Content Dialogue Act | ● | A piece of dialogue that represents contents for users. The information of a topic can be structured using the content dialogue acts. |
| Transition Dialogue Act | ◉ | A piece of dialogue that allow users to navigate from a topic to an other one. Its goal is to enable users to change dialogue arguments, following semantic relationships. |
| Introductory Dialogue Act / <br><br>Parametric Dialogue Act | Introductory <br><br> Parametric | A piece of dialogue that allows starting a dialogue from a specific topic. The main message of an introductory act is a list of instances of the same topic. <br><br> It may be multiple. |
| Relevant Relation | - - ▶ | A relevant semantic relation represents the possibility to move the attention from a topic to other one that is semantically related to the same argument. |

**RIA-Page Element.** In Rich-IDM, the minimum piece of information is called RIA-Page Element and it is managed as a unique block. In detail, the RIA-Page Element is defined as a coherent atomic fragment of RIA page, which displays a specific content with its proper meaning for the users. It could be specialized in: (i) Introductory RIA-page Element which main goal is to introduce the specific content and, often, is related to an introductory dialogue act; (ii) Content RIA-page Element that, mapping one or more content dialogue acts, displays to the user the payload of the dialogue; and (iii) Transition RIA-page Element that shows the semantic information (taken from transition dialogue act) that links two topics. The specific semantics of this set of primitives allows establishing a direct link with the functions of the contents inside. Thus, it is possible to evaluate in the early phase of the design the balance between the different types of delivered contents. The UX model is improved because the designer has the tools to assess into the page the correct quantity of information, avoiding pages without contents and stuffed with links represented by graphical elements that are more usual in RIAs.

**Table 2.** The Rich-IDM design primitives

| Name | Notation | Design Semantics |
|------|----------|------------------|
| Content RIA-Page Element | | A coherent, atomic fragment of RIA page, which displays a *content* unit, as directly mapped from IDM content dialogue acts. |
| Introductory RIA-Page Element | | A fragment of a RIA page which displays mechanisms to enable *access* to multiple instances of a dialogue topic, as directly mapped to an introductory dialogue act of the IDM logical design. |
| Transition RIA-Page Element | | The reification of an IDM transition dialogue act on the RIA page. It allows users to follow the semantic relation of two dialogue topics. |
| RIA-Handle | | An interaction affordance, which enables users moving within two or more page elements of the same User Experience Core. |
| User Experience Core | | A connected composition of page elements, which communicates the semantic nucleus of what is offered to the user at a given moment. |
| Context View | | A set of User Experience Cores, which maintains navigational context, orientation, organic, and fluid transition between the cores. |
| Default Element | | Indicate the default RIA-Page Element showed to the user. |

**RIA-Handle.** After the definition of the RIA-Page Elements, that are the interaction objects, it is necessary to define a new primitive able to model the mutual relation between the elements of the page. This new concept is the RIA-Handle, which main goal is to model all the dynamic aspects of the UX. The RIA-Handle is a directional relationship between the RIA-Page Elements involved in a user action. The RIA-Handle captures the syntactic of RIA interaction, on top of the semantics modeled by the other elements. From the methodological point of view, the RIA-Handle allows designers to represent all the relations contained in the information architecture.

**User Experience Core.** In RIAs, many information elements (that could not be semantically directly connected) can be collapsed in the same page. Thus, the core of the dialogue is not directly related with the displayed elements. To satisfy this need, the User Experience Core is defined. Its main goal is to model clearly the elements of the Rich-IDM design that must be the heart of the dialogue with the users. The

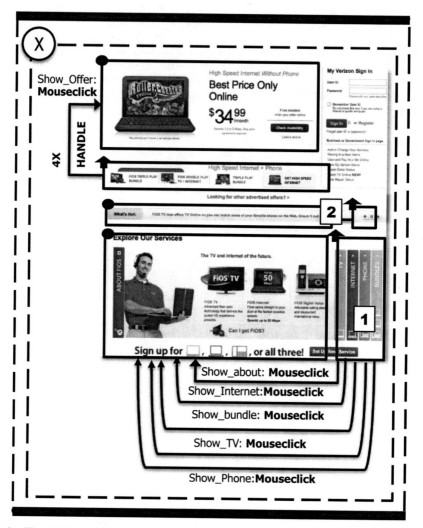

**Fig. 2a.** The AS-IS model of the www.verizon.com homepage (April 2010) described using the Rich-IDM notation

designer must carefully manage the elements contained in the User Experience Core because their perception affects strongly the sense and the quality of the message delivered to the user. On this basis, the semantics of the User Experience Core is to define the unit of perception of the dialogue. Formally, the User Experience Core is a container of the RIA-page Elements. At the start of the navigation, the default RIA-page Elements showed to the user is marked with the Default Element described in Table 2. The RIA-Handle mechanism is used to model the navigation between the User Experience Cores independently if they are (or not) part of the same Context View.

**Context View.** The look&feel of the RIA is relevant and often the visualization aspects are used to define specific areas of the application and delimitate related arguments. To capture these characteristics crucial for the quality of the dialogue flow, designers need to define the User Experience Cores that must be shown in the same way to the user. The Context View enables designers to define a specific navigational context allowing harmoniously connecting related User Experience Cores.

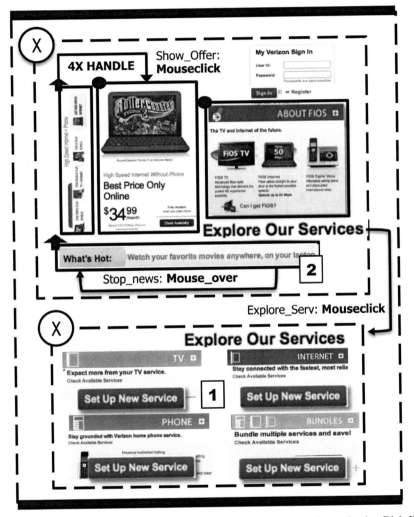

**Fig. 2b.** The TO-BE model of the www.verizon.com homepage reengineered using Rich-IDM. The UX has been transformed reducing the stress of the user working memory to compare options. This model avoids the sliding elements (lower UX Core) of the AS-IS page (Fig. 2a) and allows the user to compare the services in a one-shot view (upper UX Core). Both UX Cores are contained in a unique Context View that guarantees a uniform navigational context.

Formally, the Context View is a container of User Experience Cores. Its name is due to the idea that the User Experience Cores of the same view are shown to the user in uniform manner, thus providing a common (and stable) visualization environment to the user. In order to better explain the usefulness of Rich-IDM to improve the UX, we report in Fig. 2b the Rich-IDM reengineering of a homepage fragment of the Verizon web site; then we compare the TO-BE model with the AS-IS model showed in Fig. 2a.

At the beginning of the reengineering phase, in the TO-BE model we created two User Experience Cores: the first one groups the information about the company and the news; the second one (in the bottom of Fig. 2b) shows the information contained in the sliding elements of the Fig. 2a (marked with box "1"). Then, we focused on the middle of the homepage where there is the "What's up" news (marked with box "2") with a button to stop them. In Fig. 2b, we have removed the control button and we have implemented a "mouse over" event that the user can use to block the news.

At the end of the reengineering activity, we have removed six navigation links and one button, and we have introduced a new User Experience Core that allows users to compare all the carrier's products.

## 4      Related Work

Researchers approach the RIA design mainly modeling: (i) the information of the application, the core objects and their behavior; (ii) the navigation through the information nodes; (iii) the interface as "what the user perceives"; and (iv) the interaction between the user and the application, specifying the available events on the interface.

The Object Oriented Hypermedia Design Method [19] (OOHDM) proposes a model process structured according five steps: requirements modeling, conceptual modeling, navigation design, interface design, and implementation. The interface design is defined using the Abstract Data View (ADV) [5] that enables specifying the status and the behavior of each interface objects using state charts.

WebML for RIAs [4] extends the WebML method considering two aspects: (i) a well-defined separation between the client side and the server side; (ii) a better definition of the application interface. The data design is based on the Entity-Relationship (E-R) model that is extended considering the levels of persistence. The business logic model provides the specification of operations at the client side and server. WebML adopts the Rich Internet Application User eXperience (RUX) model [13] to design the interface aspects.

The RUX method defines the interface of an application through four levels: concepts and tasks, abstract interface, concrete interface, and final interface. The concepts and tasks level describes the data and business logic, and can be modeled using a web design methodology such as WebML. The abstract interface level describes the aspects of the interface common to all RIA technologies. The concrete interface level is the implementation of the abstract interface and it defines three presentation sublevels: spatial presentation, temporal presentation, and interaction presentation. The final interface level translates the designed model into the specific RIA concrete technology.

UML-based Web Engineering [17] (UWE) is a method for systematic and model-driven development of web applications. It exploits an UML profile to provide a specification of the domain-relevant information of a web system. To design RIAs, UWE integrates the RUX method. UWE propose to apply patterns [18] at a high abstraction level to minimize the design efforts and to maximize the expressiveness of model artifacts, describing the behavior of the RIA features. UWE-R [14] is a light-weighted extension of UWE for RIAs, covering navigation, process and presentation aspects.

OOH4RIA [15] has the main goal to cover the entire development lifecycle of RIAs. It is based on model-driven approach that specifies the artifacts to model a complete RIA for the GWT framework [9]. The starting point of the OOH4RIA design is the definition of the OOH domain model to represent the domain entities and the navigational connections. Also, OOH4RIA enable transforming the navigation model into the presentation model.

OOWS [20] is a methodological approach to develop web applications in an OO modeling oriented software development environment. It integrates appropriate models to capture the structure, behavior, navigation and presentation requirements of a web application. Also, it proposes an extension to support Web 2.0 application development.

ADRIA [6] is method for designing RIAs departing from the results of an object-oriented analysis; it employs interaction spaces as the basic abstraction mechanism coherently throughout all the design activities; its notation is based on UML.

Internet Application Modeling Language (IAML) [21] aims to provide modeling support for all of the fundamental concepts of RIAs. Along with operations and domain objects, it models events and conditions as first-class citizens, also promoting users and security as first-class. It uses concepts from existing languages where appropriate, such as ECA rules, ER diagrams, and UML Activity and Class diagrams.

Whereas these approaches provide support for abstracting existing RIA technologies and to design (and generate) the development artifacts, they lack in bridging the fluid, smooth and organic nature of the user interaction and navigation in RIAs to the design.

To meet this challenge, we propose to extend this perspective to examine the connection between RIA interface modeling and the requirements for the user experience. This perspective is only partially covered by existing works (RUX and ADV, in particular).

# 5    Conclusions

Due to the superior user interaction unleashed, RIAs require web engineers to balance the potential sophistication of the user interface and the need to ensure proper usability, cognitive workload, and efficiency. To meet this challenge, we have proposed a set of high-level modeling constructs, which bridges UX requirements and RIA design. Through a case study and extending the IDM method, we have shown some relevant features of our approach: expressiveness to capture interaction grammars and semi-formality to facilitate the establishment of a common ground between UX designers and web engineers. In detail, we proposed new primitives with a strong semantics: the User Experience Core, the Content / Introduction / Transition RIA-Page Element, the RIA-Handle, and the Context View.

Future research will concern the execution of measurements exploiting model metrics we are working on, in order to provide quantitative feedbacks on the level of transformative improvements the Rich-IDM can introduce in UX design of RIAs.

# References

1. Andersen, P.B.: A Theory of Computer Semiotics. Cambridge Univ. Press, Cambridge (1997)
2. Andersen, P.B.: A Theory of Computer Semiotics. Cambridge University Press (1997) [2]
3. Bolchini, D., Paolini, P.: Interactive Dialogue Model: A Design Technique for Multi-Channel Applications. IEEE Trans. on Multimedia 8(3), 529–541 (2006)
4. Ceri, S., Fraternali, P., Bongio, A.: Web Modeling Language (WebML): a modeling language for designing Web sites. Computer Networks: The International Journal of Computer and Telecommunications Networking 33(1-6), 137–157 (2000)
5. Cowan, D., Pereira de Lucena, C.: Abstract Data Views: An Interface Specification Concept to Enhance Design for Reuse. IEEE Trans. on Software Eng. 21(3), 229–243 (2005)
6. Dolog, P., Stage, J.: Designing Interaction Spaces for Rich Internet Applications with UML. In: Baresi, L., Fraternali, P., Houben, G.-J. (eds.) ICWE 2007. LNCS, vol. 4607, pp. 358–363. Springer, Heidelberg (2007)
7. Hewett, T., Baecker, R.M., et al.: Dialogue Techniques. In: ACM SIGCHI Curricula for Human-Computer Interaction ACM Special Interest Group on Computer-Human Interaction Curriculum Development Group, http://sigchi.org/cdg/cdg2.html
8. Hewett, T., Baecker, R.M., et al.: Dialogue Techniques. ACM SIGCHI Curriculum Development Group, http://www.sigchi.org
9. Houben, G.J., Van der Sluijs, K., Barna, P., Broekstra, J., Casteleyn, S., Fiala, Z., Frasincar, F.: Hera: Chapter 10. In: Web Engineering: Modelling and Implementing Web Applications. HCI Series, pp. 263–301. Springer, Heidelberg (2008)
10. ISO DIS 9241-210:2008. Ergonomics of human system interaction - Part 210: Human-centred design for interactive systems (formerly known as 13407). International Organization for Standardization (ISO), Switzerland (2008)
11. Kankainen, A.: Thinking model and tools for understanding user experience related to information appliance product concept. In: Dissertation of Degree of Doctor of Philosophy, pp. 1–59. Helsinki University of Technology, Espoo (2002)
12. Lai-Chong Law, E., Roto, V., Hassenzahl, M., Vermeeren, A., Kort, J.: Understanding, scoping and defining user experience: a survey approach. In: Proc. of the 27th International Conference on Human Factors in Computing Systems (CHI 2009), pp. 719–728. ACM, New York (2009)
13. Linaje, M., Preciado, J.C., Sánchez-Figueroa, F.: A Method for Model Based Design of Rich Internet Application Interactive User Interfaces. In: Baresi, L., Fraternali, P., Houben, G.-J. (eds.) ICWE 2007. LNCS, vol. 4607, pp. 226–241. Springer, Heidelberg (2007)
14. Machado, L., Filho, O., Ribeiro, J.: UWE-R: An Extension to a Web Engineering Methodology for Rich Internet Applications. WSEAS Trans. Info. Sci. and App. 6(4), 601–610 (2009)

15. Meliá, S., Gómez, J., Pérez, S., Diaz, O.: A Model-Driven Development for GWT-Based Rich Internet Applications with OOH4RIA. In: Proc. of ICWE 2008, pp. 13–23. IEEE, New York (2008)
16. Pandurino, A., Bolchini, D., Mainetti, L., Paiano, R.: Rich-IDM: Extending IDM to Model Rich Internet Applications. In: Proc. of 12th ACM iiWAS Int. Conf., pp. 145–152 (2010)
17. Preciado, J.C., Linaje, M., Morales-Chaparro, R., Sanchez-Figueroa, F.: Designing Rich Internet Applications Combining UWE and RUX-Method. In: Proc. of ICWE 2008, pp. 148–154. IEEE, New York (2008)
18. Preciado, J.C., Linaje, M., Morales, R., Sánchez-Figueroa, F., Zhang, G., Kroiß, C., Koch, N.: Designing Rich Internet Applications Combining UWE and RUX-Method. In: Proc. of 8th Int. Conf. on Web Engineering (ICWE 2008), pp. 148–154. IEEE, New York (2008)
19. Schwabe, D., De Almeida Pontes, R., Moura, I.: OOHDM-Web: an environment for implementation of hypermedia applications in the WWW. ACM SIGWEB Newsl. 8(2), 18–34 (1999)
20. Valverde, F., Pastor, O.: Facing the Technological Challenges of Web 2.0: A RIA Model-Driven Engineering Approach. In: Vossen, G., Long, D.D.E., Yu, J.X. (eds.) WISE 2009. LNCS, vol. 5802, pp. 131–144. Springer, Heidelberg (2009)
21. Wright, J.M., Dietrich, J.B.: Requirements for Rich Internet Application Design Methodologies. In: Bailey, J., Maier, D., Schewe, K.-D., Thalheim, B., Wang, X.S. (eds.) WISE 2008. LNCS, vol. 5175, pp. 106–119. Springer, Heidelberg (2008)

# A Flexible Graph-Based Data Model Supporting Incremental Schema Design and Evolution

Katrin Braunschweig, Maik Thiele, and Wolfgang Lehner

Database Technology Group, Faculty of Computer Science,
Technische Universität Dresden,
01062 Dresden, Germany
{katrin.braunschweig,maik.thiele,wolfgang.lehner}@tu-dresden.de

**Abstract.** Web data is characterized by a great structural diversity as well as frequent changes, which poses a great challenge for web applications based on that data. We want to address this problem by developing a schema-optional and flexible data model that supports the integration of heterogenous and volatile web data. Therefore, we want to rely on graph-based models that allow to incrementally extend the schema by various information and constraints. Inspired by the on-going web 2.0 trend, we want users to participate in the design and management of the schema. By incrementally adding structural information, users can enhance the schema to meet their very specific requirements.

**Keywords:** data integration, schema flexibility, schema evolution, web data, graph theory.

## 1 Introduction

Recent years have seen a rise in data-driven technologies and applications on the web. Data on a wide range of topics is made publicly available following the trend towards open data. This data is inherently heterogenous in its structure and subject to frequent change. Due to these characteristics, it is a very complex task for application developers to handle web data efficiently. This is particularly true for so-called situational analytics and mashups which are developed by users with very different skill levels. To leverage the heterogenous resources on the web and to provide a uniform interface for applications, it is necessary for the data to be integrated into a queryable and consistent, but also flexible data model.

This challenge of integrating data from a number of diverse sources bears resemblance to ETL (extract, transform and load) processes common in data warehouse scenarios. Data from different sources, conforming to different schemas, is integrated using a mediated schema. This schema remains unchanged for long periods of processing and is only rebuild when it is required due to significant changes in the original schemas. In the context of the web, we need to integrate not only data with structural diversity, but also data that is schema-free. The main challenge, however, is the volatility of the resources. In contrast to

A. Harth and N. Koch (Eds.): ICWE 2011 Workshops, LNCS 7059, pp. 302–306, 2012.

the resources of a data warehouse, resources on the web change frequently and erratically. Traditional data models, such as the relational data model, do not provide the flexibility required to efficiently deal with these characteristics. Instead, we take a graph-based approach towards a flexible data model supporting the integration as well as the continuous evolution of web data. The model is meant to form the basis of a data repository for web applications. Inspired by the Web 2.0 trend of user participation, we plan to provide users with tools to collaboratively and incrementally enhance the integration of the data.

## 2    Research Problems and Objectives

The main problem we want to address in our research is the heterogeneity of web data and the resulting issues for applications regarding the integration and management of the data. In this scenario we have identified the following challenges, which we will address in our research. First of all, schema management should be flexible enough to handle both, structured and unstructured data. To achieve this, schema information should be optional so that different levels of structure can appear simultaneously in the system. This will, for example, enable unstructured data to be imported without extensive transformations. Inconsistencies in the schemas of different sources of structured data need to be addressed through mapping techniques. Furthermore, the query functionality should be determined by the amount and quality of metadata available. Due to the volatility of resources on the web, we need to take the evolution of the schema into consideration as well. However, extending and changing schema information should be non-destructive, which means it should not require the re-building of application processes. This requires a balance between flexibility and consistency regarding the schema. Additionally, we need to incorporate schema versioning, to ensure that schema changes do not invalidate previously existing applications. Apart from these features, which are closely related to the data integration and schema design challenge, there are further related topics that need to be studied in this context, but which are not the primary focus of our research. They include amongst others transaction support, permission and privacy issues, efficient data storage and distribution.

## 3    Research Methodology and Approach

To achieve the outlined objectives we will build on existing data models and query languages. Instead of enforcing a static mediated schema during the data load process, we plan to enable incremental extraction and enhancement of schema information. Leveraging the current web trend, we want to encourage users to participate in the management and integration of their data by collaboratively building schemas as they are required for querying. Automated extraction and integration techniques will be incorporated to support users through, for example, recommendations. An overview of our approach is depicted in Figure 1.

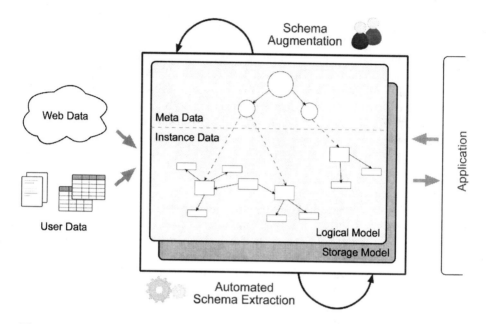

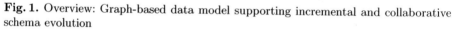

**Fig. 1.** Overview: Graph-based data model supporting incremental and collaborative schema evolution

## 3.1  Graph-Based Data Model

The traditional relational data model is a well established choice for structured data. However, it is not considering the heterogeneity and volatility of web resources. Instead, we use a directed, labeled multi-relational graph, a common model in graph databases, as a basis for our approach. Vertices and edges in the graph represent entities and relationships respectively. Both, vertices and edged, can be labeled with name/value pairs which represent properties. Schema information can be stored in a schema graph that defines entity types, primitive types and relationship types. Instance data is stored in an instance graph which contains concrete entities, primitive values as well as concrete relationships. We take a graph based approach due to a number of characteristic features that support our proposition. First of all, the graph structure supports different levels of complexity within the same graph. Not all instances are required to have the same amount and type of properties and relationships. Additionally, a tight coupling of data and meta data is achieved by representing both as graphs that are connected. This leads to a natural integration of metadata into the system and facilitates meta data querying. Finally, graph structures are easy to interpret, which is beneficial for our plan to enable strong user participation.

## 3.2  Tentative Research Plan

The tentative plan for our research consists of the following steps:

1. First, we have to define a uniform data model that enables efficient integration of structurally diverse data and flexible evolution of the schema. So far, we have selected the graph model described above as a suitable basis for our data model.
2. Our next task is the development and incorporation of basic operators for the definition, manipulation and querying of both, data and metadata. Our goal is to exploit the natural features of the graph structure for the operators as much as possible. For example, we can utilize graph traversal techniques for the propagation of schema modifications. These operators include operators that enable users to incrementally enhance the schema.
3. Additionally, we will consider suitable techniques to ensure stability for applications despite schema changes. Therefore, schema inconsistencies with regard to the applications must be compensated to a certain degree in order to delay expensive reorganizations.
4. In connection with schema evolution we will study options for supporting schema versioning in our data model.
5. In addition to studying the flexible schema design and evolution on a theoretical level, we will implement our approach in a prototype to validate our assumptions. In order to evaluate the flexibility, scalability and efficiency of our approach, we will look for a suitable benchmark [4].

## 4   Related Work

In addition to the relational data model, which is often the standard when dealing with structured data, a number of alternative data models have emerged in the context of the web. Often associated with the term "NoSQL databases", these alternatives include basic key/value stores, column-oriented stores, document stores and graph databases. The main concerns of these systems are on the one hand scalability that meets the requirements of big web applications and on the other hand, relaxation of the tight schema requirements of relational systems towards a schema-free solution. In our research we focus on graph databases which offer the highest flexibility. Angeles et al. [1] provide an extensive survey of existing graph database models including various graph query languages. In [6], a hypergraph model is introduced. Based on this model, storage, querying as well as indexing techniques are described. A well established open source graph database is Neo4j[1]. In [2], Bollacker et al. present Freebase, a graph database for storing human knowledge in a structured manner. Freebase provides tools for users to collaboratively augment the data and schema. In contrast to our approach, data in Freebase has to conform to predefined types, which can be extended by the user, but do not provide the flexibility we aim to achieve.

The incremental extraction of metadata from unstructured data has been addressed in [3]. Chu et al. propose a relational approach based on the interpreted storage format using three basic operators (extract, integrate and cluster) to incrementally discover and extract structure. It maintains the flexibility of schemaless models, since keyword search can be applied at any time, but also enables

---

[1] http://neo4j.org/

the user to run complex queries as soon as more schema information has been extracted. A similar concept for structured data can be found in research regarding dataspace systems [5]. Data sources, that have not been integrated fully, can be queried through keyword search, for example. If more complex operations like data mining are requested, the data sources can be integrated incrementally. This approach is often referred to as "pay as you go", which also inspired the web-scale data integration architecture PayGo by Madhavan et al. [7]. PayGo aims at incrementally integrating structured data found on the Web by applying techniques for automated schema mapping and schema clustering as well as techniques for discovering additional relationships between data.

## 5  Conclusion

The heterogeneity of data resources on the web present a difficult challenge for web application developers. Many existing data integration solutions are not flexible enough to handle both structured and unstructured data and are not designed to address the volatility of data sources on the web. We have presented our concept for a graph-based solution, which utilizes a combination of automated techniques and user participation to achieve flexible data integration and evolution.

## References

1. Angles, R., Gutierrez, C.: Survey of graph database models. ACM Comput. Surv. 40 (2008)
2. Bollacker, K., Evans, C., Paritosh, P., Sturge, T., Taylor, J.: Freebase: a collaboratively created graph database for structuring human knowledge. In: SIGMOD 2008 (2008)
3. Chu, E., Baid, A., Chen, T., Doan, A., Naughton, J.: A relational approach to incrementally extracting and querying structure in unstructured data. In: VLDB 2007, pp. 1045–1056 (2007)
4. Curino, C.A., Tanca, L., Moon, H.J., Zaniolo, C.: Schema evolution in wikipedia: toward a web information system benchmark. In: Enterprise Information Systems (2009)
5. Franklin, M., Halevy, A., Maier, D.: From databases to dataspaces: a new abstraction for information management. SIGMOD Rec. 34 (2005)
6. Iordanov, B.: HyperGraphDB: A Generalized Graph Database. In: Shen, H.T., Pei, J., Özsu, M.T., Zou, L., Lu, J., Ling, T.-W., Yu, G., Zhuang, Y., Shao, J. (eds.) WAIM 2010. LNCS, vol. 6185, pp. 25–36. Springer, Heidelberg (2010)
7. Madhavan, J., Jeffery, S.R., Cohen, S., Dong, X.L., Ko, D., Yu, C., Halevy, A., Inc, G.: Web-scale data integration: You can only afford to pay as you go. In: CIDR 2007 (2007)

# ProLD: Propagate Linked Data

Peter Kalchgruber

University of Vienna, Faculty of Computer Science, Liebiggasse 4/3-4, A-1010 Vienna
peter.kalchgruber@univie.ac.at

**Abstract.** Since the Web of Data consists of different data sources maintained by different authorities the up-to-dateness of the resources varies a lot. However a number of applications are built upon that. To tackle the problem of out-dated resources, we propose to develop a framework that utilizes the linkage between Linked Data nodes to propagate updates in the cloud. For that purpose we have observed propagation strategies developed in the database domain and have created a list of currently unsolved problems which emphasize the difference between the propagation in the Web of Data and state of the art approaches. Apart from the improvement of the up-to-dateness of data, by following the approach of propagation the network improves and inconsistencies will be reduced.

## 1 Introduction

The Web of Data is growing continuously[1]. As of today, a large amount of applications[2] already utilize data from the Linked Open Data (LOD) cloud; however, the experience of such applications closely correlates with the data quality of the underlying data. Bizer [1] illustrates that the timeliness beside others (accuracy, completeness) is one of the most popular dimension of information quality.

The Web of Data reflects knowledge about things of the real world. Changes in the real world, in terms of updates, will be executed in the Web, by the maintaining data node owner or local community. The problem is, that currently it takes a long time, until all concerned resources in the cloud become updated and a consistent status is achieved. For example, taken the actual political changes in the country Egypt, it is expected, that the Parliament website, will update the change of government directly. Only after the time $\Delta t$, news sites, encyclopedias and other data nodes will update their Web resources. $\Delta t$ varies depending on the maintaining data node owner or community and the underlying technology. For example, due to the required manual effort, data of the most linked

---

[1] In May 2009 the Linked Data cloud of 4.7 billion triples [2]. By February 2011 it had grown to 27 billion triples.
http://www4.wiwiss.fu-berlin.de/lodcloud/state/#structure

[2] http://www.w3.org/wiki/SweoIG/TaskForces/CommunityProjects/
/LinkingOpenData/Applications

A. Harth and N. Koch (Eds.): ICWE 2011 Workshops, LNCS 7059, pp. 307–311, 2012.

data node DBpedia is currently only updated about semiannually. The example[3] demonstrates that, real world updates are visible in the Web of Data, but they are not propagated to data sets they are interlinked with.

Our objective is to propagate updates of resources to all linked resources with the same identity in the cloud. Although it is obvious to use database propagation approaches to tackle the problem, we discovered several problems on using them in Section 2. As a possible solution we present our prototypical framework in Section 3.

## 2    Background and Related Work

Globally, the Web of Data contains huge sets of redundant partially linked data. Thus it bears some similarities with databases, also in context of propagation of updates. But we found a list of differences and open problems displaying the non-triviality of propagation in the Web of Data. Based on the following list, we discuss the approaches in related work and define our field of research:

- Schema mapping (neither unique IDs, nor unique vocabulary)
- Availability of data nodes (online/offline)
- Properties stating equality between resources not always reliable
- Synchronization with relational databases (Wikipedia ↔ DBpedia)
- Trust / Authority (every triple must be read as claim from the corresponding data node not as a fact [8])
- Propagation of triples which do not exist at all nodes
- Behavior if data nodes drop their data and do a general dump import (as DBpedia is built on a regularly basis)

As known from related domains (e.g. Distributed Database Management Systems) updating distributed data sources is a critical issue. The approach of propagation in the Web of Data expose similar characteristics as data propagation [10] and data replication [6]. However the linkage between data nodes is neither symmetric nor complete and due to the AAA principle[4] (data can be incomplete or inconsistent) the use of this traditional approaches are not applicable in the Web of Data.

Data nodes use a mix of commonly used vocabularies for describing their data. This mix is often not sufficient, and therefore expanded with proprietary terms [3]. This results in heterogeneity and problems with the interoperability of metadata. It is still difficult to map metadata with the same semantic meaning together although there are already different approaches to map metadata [9,3] or match ontologies [5]. However our tests have shown that they are not implemented broadly.

---

[3] Change of government in Egypt: Only the data node Freebase has updated its data about the recent change of the regime. However DBpedia, DBpedia Live, New York Times still hold data of the previous state, although they are linked as identical.

[4] Anyone can say Anything, Anywhere

Another problem is the *non-assured availability* of data sets. Anytime a server can be temporarily unavailable, or stop its service. If a data node is offline for a while, it needs to receive the missed updates, after it has recovered. It cannot know which server has propagated updates in the meanwhile. Since there is no master server, as in traditional distributed databases, this information must be saved in the cloud.

*sparqlPuSH* [11] allows clients to get informed about data updates in RDF stores via *PubSubHubbub*[5], a simple open server-to-server publish/subscribe protocol. *sparqlPuSH* uses the *PubSubHubbub* infrastructure to notify clients over hubs via a push based approach. *sparqlPuSH* can only be used for the notification use case and could be used in the framework to notify remote datasets about updates.

The property `owl:sameAs` of the Web Ontology Language (OWL)[6] per definition [4] is interconnecting equivalent resources between two data sets. It indicates that two resources exhibiting different URIs actually refer to the same resource - they share the same "identity". But sometimes, historical resources (e.g. the resource *East Berlin*) are set equivalent with new ones [7], or no distinction is made between the context of resources (e.g. Republic of Ireland vs. Island Ireland). Strategies for the aggregation of equivalent resources are proposed in [4]. A more detailed ontology of `owl:sameAs` has been proposed by Halpin [7]. However, the currently inappropriate usage of `owl:sameAs` makes it difficult to build a framework on it.

## 3   Approach

Our overall objective is to develop an efficient update strategy for Linked Data. Once a resource at a single node become updated, by means of propagation all resources with the same identity in the cloud, should receive this update, too. Our framework called *ProLD* is based on RDF properties that define the equality between linked resources (e.g. `owl:sameAs`). ProLD follows links between same identities on distributed data nodes to propagate the updates in the cloud.

It can be used as an add-on to existing services, to help data node owners to propagate updates made on datasets that are under their control and to receive updates from other datasets, which propagate their updates. The ProLD Framework consists of three elements:

- The *Observer* is responsible to detect local changes at a dataset. It searches for equivalent resources (e.g. marked with `owl:sameAs`), compose a propagation package and handle it to the *Propagator*. The Observer has an interface to commonly used RDF storages such as Virtuoso, Jena, or 4store.
- The *Receiver* receives updates sent from the *Propagator* of other data nodes, does integrity checks and triggers the changes at the local dataset.
- The *Propagator* receives a list from the Observer containing update packages for remote resources. It propagates the updates to the cloud.

---

[5] http://code.google.com/p/pubsubhubbub/
[6] http://www.w3.org/TR/owl-ref/

The Observer can be informed about changes at the local triple store by change logs created by triple stores, or by adding triggers to the database. Once it becomes informed about a change at a local data set, it scans the local resource for equivalent resources in the cloud. An object with the collected information will be sent to the Propagator. The Propagator creates a unique hash value of the package and saves it with a time stamp in a local buffer. Thereafter, it sends a package to all servers listed in the `owl:sameAs` field of the local resource. The Receiver at the remote data set is listening to receive packages. After the integrity check, it asks the Propagator, whether the package was already processed by comparing hash-values with a buffer list. If the information about the updated resource is new, there are different ways to proceed: Either the tool is configured in automatic mode, it will do the changes at the local resource, scan for `owl:sameAs` values and hand the package (as described above) to the Propagator. Alternatively, in semi-automatic mode the update could be reviewed by local quality review programs, a community or the data node owners.

In case of an update, the modification package will always include the old and the new triples. This enables the Receiver to decide carefully based on rules whether a.) the subject resource of the package is equal to the local resource and b.) both triples refer to the same property. Thereby it use schema concepts such as sub-property or super-property to take a decision. It is also being considered to add more surrounding triples to the modification package, to help to distinguish between similar resources by the identification of the resources by fingerprints.

### 3.1 Scenario Open Government Data

Governments increasingly use the cloud to expose their data. The owners of *data.gov.eg*, DBpedia and Freebase have installed ProLD on their data nodes. The government of Egypt will update the form of government at the local resource **eg:Government** to "Military junta". The Observer detects the change and sends the required update information to the Propagator. Data nodes with identical resources (e.g. DBpedia or Freebase) listed as `owl:sameAs` at `eg:Government` will receive this propagation package. Before they process the content, each Receiver proofs if the package was not processed earlier by comparing the hash-value and timestamp with the list of already processed packages. If so, it drops the package. Otherwise the Receiver updates the local resource, looks for local `owl:sameAs` resources and forwards the package to their data nodes.

## 4    Research Methodology

Currently, there is no solution to handle update propagation in the Web of Data. The previous section indicates that there are several solutions for partial problems but also many open problems. But research about a general view of the problem has not been done so far.

In particular we are concerned with the following research questions:

- Which protocols and techniques are available and which are required to allow propagation in the Web of Data?
- How can propagation of updates be performed considering its scalability?

Our methodology to solve the research questions consists of three phases: First additional research in the state of the art and technology evaluation needs to be done. Based on the results a prototype will be developed. It will be improved and extended incrementally through testing in real life scenarios. Finally, the third phase contains the evaluation of the framework. There the time until updates appear in data nodes using ProLD is compared with data nodes not using the framework. Furthermore the rate of successful updates should be compared with error cases.

## 5    Conclusion

In this paper we have discussed several problems concerning the propagation of updates in the Web of Data. Although the Web of Data can be seen as a big distributed database, research in the field of propagation of updates in the cloud has shown that there are so far several unsolved problems. The combination of existing approaches reveals that propagation is reasonable and possible. A sketched rough concept of our framework gives an overview, how propagation could be done in the cloud. Thus, the time until updates in the cloud are performed can be reduced to a minimum.

## References

1. Bizer, C.: Quality-Driven Information Filtering- In the Context of Web-Based Information Systems. VDM Verlag, Saarbrücken (2007)
2. Bizer, C., Heath, T., Berners-Lee, T.: Linked data – the story so far. Int. J. Semantic Web Inf. Syst. 5(3), 1–22 (2009)
3. Bizer, C., Schultz, A.: The R2R Framework: Publishing and Discovering Mappings on the Web. In: COLD 2010, Shanghai (2010)
4. Ding, L., Shinavier, J., Finin, T., McGuinness, D.L.: owl:sameAs and Linked Data: An Empirical Study . In: Proc. of the 2nd Web Science Conference, Raleigh NC, USA (April 2010)
5. Euzenat, J., Shvaiko, P.: Ontology Matching. Springer, Berlin (2007)
6. Gifford, D.K.: Weighted voting for replicated data. In: Proc. of the 7th ACM SOSP, SOSP 1979, pp. 150–162. ACM, NY (1979)
7. Halpin, H., Hayes, P.J.: When owl:sameAs isn't the Same: An Analysis of Identity Links on the Semantic Web. In: CEUR Workshop Proceedings (2010)
8. Hartig, O., Langegger, A.: A database perspective on consuming linked data on the web. Datenbank-Spektrum 10, 57–66 (2010)
9. Haslhofer, B.: A Web-based Mapping Technique for Establishing Metadata Interoperability. PhD thesis (November 2008)
10. IBM. IMS DataPropagator Implementation Guide. IBM, 650 Harry Road San Jose, 3 edn. (2002)
11. Passant, A., Mendes, P.N.: sparqlpush: Proactive notification of data updates in rdf stores using pubsubhubbub. In: 6th Workshop on Scripting and Development for the Semantic Web (May 2010)

# Causal Relation Detection for Activities from Heterogeneous Sources

Philipp Katz and Alexander Schill

Technische Universität Dresden, Germany
Department of Computer Science, Chair of Computer Networks
philipp.katz@tu-dresden.de

**Abstract.** On the web, information representing specific activities is often scattered over different systems. Although, causal relations exist between these activities, these are usually not obviously visible to the user, unless explicitly given. This paper outlines the difficulties which are caused by missing relations. The core contribution of this work will be a system which is capable of identifying cause-effect relations between single activities. The system will use these relations to form coarse-grained groups consisting of sequences with single activities. The intended goal is to employ the detected relations to reduce information overload while increasing accountability, clarity, and traceability for its users. The research is conceived under the assumption of handling heterogeneous sources of information. A further objective is to create a highly generic and flexible system which can be adapted to different use cases. The system will be evaluated with concrete case studies, one of them analyzing relations on software development sites such as SourceForge.

**Keywords:** Internet Information Extraction, Information Aggregation, Information Integration, Relation Extraction, Data Linking.

## 1 Introduction

Over the last years, the WWW has evolved into a highly dynamic and interactive medium. In conjunction with the buzzword "Web 2.0", so called user-generated content, published on different platforms such as blogs, wikis, social networks, or media portals, is gaining influence. As well as the number of different sources, the amount and frequency of generated information is increasing continuously. Besides the general and often discussed phenomenon of "information overload", which has already been characterized in various different sources [1], a further problem can be observed: "information scattering", where information concerning one specific topic is usually published across various different sources. In [2], information scattering is described as a situation, where few sources exist, "that contain many items of relevant information, while most sources have only a few". Although, their analysis is influenced by a standpoint of library science, their general notion can be transferred to the heterogeneity and diversity of the WWW, including user-generated content.

A. Harth and N. Koch (Eds.): ICWE 2011 Workshops, LNCS 7059, pp. 312–316, 2012.
© Springer-Verlag Berlin Heidelberg 2012

## 2   Terminology and Scenario

In this work, the term "activity" is defined as an atomic event occurring at a certain time. A source propagating activities is called "activity generator". Obviously, activities exist which are triggered by other activities, leading to causal relations between pairs of activities, which can be considered as "cause-effect relations".

To substantiate the idea behind this work, consider the following concrete usage example: The workflow of a typical open source software project is organized using various tools such as an issue tracker, a version control system, discussion forums, and mailing lists as depicted in Fig. 1. End users experiencing issues with the software, use the forums or mailing lists to start a discussion. Different users and developers are involved in this discussion, and finally a bug report is posted to the tracker. After a period of time, a developer reads about the problem, commits a bug fix to the version control system, and closes the ticket. The described scenario consists of various activities; the bug report is triggered by the forum discussion, the committed fix is triggered by the bug report.

The scenario outlines the difficulty to get the current situation of the project. While there obviously exists a latent sequence of activities triggered by the initial discussion, it is later difficult to reconstruct such a process, as events are scattered over different heterogeneous sources. Decisions which had an impact on activities are hard to trace from a retrospective point of view. Support is complex, as users need to search for information concerning a specific problem on different sources, manually synthesizing a causal chain representing a decision process.

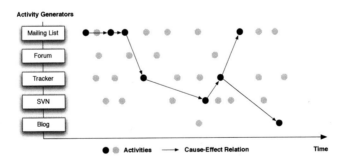

**Fig. 1.** Example for an activity flow in an open source software project

## 3   Research Questions

Based upon the outlined scenario in the preceding section, the following three research questions form the main contributions of this work:

**How can a system to reduce information overflow and scattering be designed?** The goal of this work is to address the problem of information overflow by establishing relations between single pieces of information, forming semantically related groups. Such a group can be characterized as an abstraction of single, fine-grained pieces of information, which are connected by cause-effect relations. Such representations help users to gain a view on "the global picture", making it possible to understand compound, scattered activities formed of single events. The notion of activities will be employed to reduce the information overflow, allowing the user to filter out irrelevant information, only getting into detail where applicable. To establish these relations in a precise way, suitable algorithms need to be employed and necessary components of the system need to be identified.

**How can the system cope with highly heterogeneous types of data?** The sources considered by the system can be characterized as highly heterogeneous. Where, from a low-level and technical standpoint, the term "heterogeneous" can be used to describe varying formats and standards, on a more abstract level, a great spectrum of quality in respect to the actual data has to be considered. Different sources usually provide diverse amounts and types of metadata. Besides explicit features which can be extracted directly from their sources, also implicit information will be taken into account, which needs to be induced by the system automatically. This might include correlations between different authors, temporal aspects, or characteristics concerning different sources. Those features will be employed to create a generic model for the data, which forms the foundation for the applied algorithms. Due to the heterogeneous nature of the considered data, the potential sparsities and unequal distributions concerning the presence of those features need to be taken into account.

**Which methodologies can be applied to ensure the adaptiveness of the system to various usage scenarios and domains?** The general aim of this work is a highly generic and flexible system, which is capable of covering a wide range of potential use cases. Therefore, a parametrizable and configurable framework which can furthermore be integrated into various existing workflows needs to be provided.

## 4    Related Work

In the domain of network monitoring and management, event correlation and filtering systems (ECS) are employed to diagnose network failures. Various proposals for approaches and practical implementations exist [3,4,5], sharing the general goal to identify "root causes" for specific problems and to filter the massive amount of single events by correlating and aggregating them to more abstract, "conceptual" events [6]. Obviously, these approaches focus on technical events generated by machines such as servers or routers. To the author's knowledge, there have been no efforts on mapping the concepts from ECS to honor the specific properties of event streams with content generated by and for human users.

Research in the area of Topic Detection and Tracking (TDT), which was initiated under a DARPA program, is analyzing textual and audio-visual data from news broadcast sources in order to perform a topic based characterization and to detect links between pieces of information [7]. More recently, efforts have been conducted to identify events in data from community and social media sources such as Flickr, Youtube, or Facebook [8,9,10] employing document clustering techniques to identify groups of information associated to a specific event. As a general constraint, each instantiation of the mentioned approaches allows to consider only one specific source, disregarding the possibility to establish relations between different types of heterogeneous data spread over various sources.

Work on Process Mining deals with extracting process models from event log data [11]. However, this data is generated by technical systems and therefore conforms to a very strict, well-defined and homogeneous structure which is in general not reflected by user-generated content on which this work puts its focus.

## 5   Current Progress

For an initial analysis, a crawler for SourceForge[1] was developed. The crawler was used with the phpMyAdmin project, aggregating activity feeds, tracker data, messages from mailing lists, forum posts and commit messages from their source code repositories. The resulting dataset consists of over 180,000 individual items spanning a time interval of approximately ten years. After a first naïve experiment using text clustering techniques based on a plain term model to identify causal relations, it can be concluded, that more elaborate approaches need to be employed in order to achieve reasonable results.

The outlined dataset contains a set of explicit features which can be taken into consideration for creating connections between pairs of items. These features include hyperlinks between items or indicators such as revision or tracker IDs given in the text, which can be extracted using patterns. They will be employed for building a preliminary baseline and for evaluating the initial results. Further iterations will be measured with regard to this baseline.

With PRISMA[2], a system architecture for handling the information overload in an enterprise context has been described [12]. The implementation of this system will provide the framework for evaluating the algorithms from this work.

## 6   Future Work Plan

In the short term, the future work will focus on extracting further features from the given dataset. Therefore, an extensive feature engineering will be performed, evaluating implicit features which can be extracted from the data. In general, these might include structural, temporal, statistical, linguistical or semantic features, regarding individual properties.

---

[1] http://sourceforge.net/
[2] PeRsonalization of Information StreaM Aggregates.

In the medium term, following a bottom-up approach, an abstraction from the knowledge gained from practical experiments concerning the data from Source-Forge will be performed. Regarding further use cases, an evaluation is neccessary, on how the model needs to be generalized and extended, in order to allow for the aimed adaptiveness. Therefore, a further concrete scenario which considers the domain of Wikipedia content will be described. The objective is to research the impact of pieces of news published by different sources on Wikipedia articles. Evidently, a great amount of edits performed in the Wikipedia is triggered by current events of the day. In the long term, an instantiation of the system will be used as a component within PRISMA.

**Acknowledgments.** The PRISMA project is funded by the Free State of Saxony and the EU (European Social Fund).

# References

1. Richtel, M.: Lost in E-Mail, Tech Firms Face Self-Made Beast, http://www.nytimes.com/2008/06/14/technology/14email.html (retrieved March 7, 2011)
2. Bhavnani, S.K., Wilson, C.S.: Information Scattering. In: Encyclopedia of Library and Information Sciences, 3rd edn., pp. 2564–2569 (2010)
3. Vaarandi, R.: Platform Independent Event Correlation Tool for Network Management. In: Proc. of the 2002 IEEE/IFIP Network Operations and Management Symposium (2002)
4. Liu, G., Mok, A.K., Yang, E.J.: Composite Events for Network Event Correlation. In: Proc. of the Sixth IFIP/IEEE International Symposium on Integrated Network Management, pp. 247–260 (1999)
5. Jiang, G., Cybenko, G.: Temporal and Spatial Distributed Event Correlation for Network Security. In: Proc. of the 2004 American Control Conference, vol. 2, pp. 996–1001 (2004)
6. Hasan, M., Sugla, B., Viswanathan, R.: A Conceptual Framework for Network Management Event Correlation and Filtering Systems. In: Proc. of the Sixth IFIP/IEEE International Symposium on Integrated Network Management, pp. 233–246 (1999)
7. Allan, J.: Introduction to Topic Detection and Tracking. In: Topic Detection and Tracking: Event-Based Information Organization, Springer, pp. 1–16. Springer, Heidelberg (2002)
8. Becker, H., Naaman, M., Gravano, L.: Learning Similarity Metrics for Event Identification in Social Media. In: Proc. of the Third ACM International Conference on Web Search and Data Mining, pp. 291–300 (2010)
9. Sayyadi, H., Hurst, M., Maykov, A.: Event Detection and Tracking in Social Streams. In: Proc. of International Conference on Weblogs and Social Media, ICWSM (2009)
10. Zhao, Q., Mitra, P., Chen, B.: Temporal and Information Flow Based Event Detection From Social Text Streams. In: Proc. of the 22nd National Conference on Artificial Intelligence, vol. 2, pp. 1501–1506 (2007)
11. van der Aalst, W.M.P., Schonenberg, M.H., Song, M.: Time prediction based on process mining. Information Systems 36(2), 450–475 (2011)
12. Katz, P., Lunze, T., Feldmann, M., Röhrborn, D., Schill, A.: System Architecture for handling the Information Overload in Enterprise Information Aggregation Systems. In: Proc. of the 14th International Conference on Business Information Systems (2011)

# XML Document Versioning, Revalidation and Constraints*

Jakub Malý and Martin Nečaský

Faculty of Mathematics and Physics
Charles University in Prague, Czech Republic
maly@ksi.mff.cuni.cz

**Abstract.** One of the prominent characteristics of XML applications is their dynamic nature. When a system grows and evolves, old user requirements change and/or new requirements accumulate. Apart from changes in the interfaces used/provided by the system or its components, it is also necessary to modify the existing documents with each new version, so they are valid against the new specification. In this doctoral work we will extend an existing conceptual modeling approach with the support for multiple versions of the model. Thanks to this extension, it will be possible to detect changes between two versions of a schema and generate revalidation script for the existing data. By adding integrity constraints to the model, it will be able to revalidate changes in semantics besides changes in structure.

**Keywords:** XML schema, schema evolution, conceptual modeling, constraints.

## 1 Introduction and Motivation

Recently, XML has become a corner stone of many information systems. It is a de facto standard for data exchange and it is also a popular data model in databases [1]. XML applications are very dynamic in their nature. Requirements change during the life cycle of the system and so do the XML schemas. Without any tools to help, the old and new schema need to be examined by a domain expert. Each change must be identified, analyzed and all the relevant components of the system modified accordingly. Moreover, all the existing documents must be updated. This can be a time-consuming and error-prone process, but, in fact, a significant portion of the operations could be performed automatically.

Applications usually utilize XML in two scenarios: either 1) XML documents are used for data exchange in intra/inter-system communication and XML schemas define interfaces of the individual components and systems themselves, while the data itself are stored in another (usually relational) data storage or 2) XML documents are also used to store the physical data and XML schemas are used to describe the structure and check the validity of these documents.

* This work was supported in part by the Czech Science Foundation (GAČR), grant number P202/10/0573, and by the grant SVV-2011-263312.

A. Harth and N. Koch (Eds.): ICWE 2011 Workshops, LNCS 7059, pp. 317–321, 2012.

As schemas change with a new version of the system, the system needs to be updated, but it is also usually required to accept data valid against the old version, at least for some transitional period of time. In the first scenario, the affected component can be equipped with some *adapter* component that modifies the structure of the document. In the second scenario, the existing documents stored in the system need to be augmented to conform to the new version of the schemas (this process is usually called *revalidation*). In both cases, the problem can be solved by accompanying the new version of the schema with some kind of "revalidation script" every time schemas change and using this script to either preprocess incoming data or update the existing internal documents. The revalidation script can be either a script in an implementation language (XSLT, XQuery Update Facility), or a sequence of formalized update operations.

## 2    Current Approaches

For the goal of determining whether documents are no longer valid against the new version, the system must recognize and analyze the differences between the old version $(\mathcal{S}')$ and the new version $(\widetilde{\mathcal{S}'})$ of the schema. There are two possible ways to recognize changes:

a) Recording the changes as they are conducted during the design process (and propagate each change immediately to the documents [2,3] or propagate all changes in one batch [4])
b) Comparing the two versions of the diagram [5,6]

All the existing evolution frameworks work only in the scope of one schema. However, in a complex system, the specification can be comprised of hundreds of schemas with interrelated changes. When new data needs to be added to the existing documents (e.g. when new mandatory element is added to the schema) the existing frameworks offer only trivial solutions (creating only the empty structure, the content must be filled by the user). But in a sound and consistent model, the content can be added automatically, as we will outline later. In some schema evolution scenarios, elements, attributes or whole subtrees are moved from one location in the document to another. These so-called *migratory* operations are not supported in many frameworks or the support is insufficient. None of the existing frameworks deal with the semantics of the changes (e.g. when `time-spent` attribute is moved from `Task` element to `Project` element, its value should be equal to the sum of all the values in `Task` elements in the old version) or integrity constraints.

## 3    Conceptual Modeling with Versioning and Revalidation

This doctoral work will follow the work on conceptual modeling of XML data. In [7], a two-layered model *XSEM* was introduced, with platform-independent

(PIM) and platform-specific (PSM) layers. A PIM schema (UML class diagram) models a problem domain at the conceptual level. A PSM schema is an extended (necessary for modeling hierarchical XML data) UML class diagram that models one XML schema. It is proven that a PSM schema is equivalent to regular tree grammars (RTG). Components of the PSM schemas in the system are linked to concepts in the PIM and thus correctness and coherence can be maintained during initial design and further evolution phase (e.g. change in a concept `Purchase` in the PIM schema can be easily propagated to all the PSM schemas where `Purchase` is referenced) – the two-layered design is made to measure to the scenarios, where there are multiple XML schemas (modeled by PSM schemas) sharing a common problem domain (modeled by PIM schema), each XML schema representing a different view on some part of the domain (e.g a PIM concept `Purchase` is referenced in a `purchase-request` and `yearly-report` schema, both using different attributes and associations of `Purchase`).

Also, having separate PIM and PSM makes possible to add additional models (e.g. model of a relational database) and linked them to PIM too. This way it is possible to depict the relation between XML schema constructs and RDB tables and columns via the links to common PIM.

To date, XSEM was enhanced with support for multiple versions in order to support schema evolution (*XSEM-Evo* [8]). XSEM-Evo uses combination of the methods mentioned in Section 2. The core of the algorithm uses schema comparison, but besides the two versions of the schema, it requires the set of *version links*, which connect the same concept in different versions (e.g. the old version and the new version of the concept `Purchase` will be linked). These version links can be maintained automatically as user edits the schema (this idea comes from the change recording approach), entered manually or by heuristics matching the similar concepts. Combined approach of schema comparison with version links sufficiently handles the addition, removal and also migratory changes in schemas, additional annotations enable it to handle non-trivial migratory operations mentioned in the previous section. The experimental implementation was incorporated into *XCase* editor [9]).

## 4    Research Objectives and Methodology

The aim of this doctoral work is to further enhance capabilities of XSEM-Evo in two main perspectives: 1) increase the power of XSEM model via introducing constraints at both PIM and PSM layers and 2) fully utilize the links to PIM layer during document revalidation, especially for adding missing content to the revalidated documents.

*Constraints in XML*    UML allows the designer to specify constraints and invariants in the model via *Object Constraint Language* (OCL) in those situations, where classes and associations do not describe the model precisely enough. At the level of XML schemas, constraints are required too. And some types of constraints are impossible to define via languages based on RTGs, such as DTD and classic XML Schema. Examples of such constraints are choices between groups of attributes or so called co-occurrence constraints (e.g. element $E_1$ must occur only if the value of element $E_2$ is $v_2$ – classic XML Schema cannot do better than to declare $E_1$ as optional). To allow such constraints, XML Schema was extended with the possibility to declare non-RTG based constructs *assert* and *test* and even a separate schema validation language *Schematron* was designed for this purpose.

As we modified UML to serve us in XML modeling, we plan to modify OCL to serve us to define constraints in XML schemas. Our PSM schemas can be translated to XSDs and it will be possible to translate the PSM level constraints to Schematron schemas analogously.

From the evolution point of view, with OCL constraints, it will be possible to track changes in semantics. For example, the request for customer history returned the list of all purchases in the old version, but in the new version, the list will contain only realized purchases. The structure of the schema will remain unchanged, but in the new version, a new constraint will be added. The evolution algorithm will be able to revalidate the document accordingly via deleting all the unrealized purchases. Since all the existing evolution frameworks only deal with structure and do not recognize semantics, none of them is even capable to detect such change, let alone revalidate it.

*Adding content.* To date, XSEM-Evo is able to deal with changes that modify the structure and data present in the document. However, sometimes, new data need to be added to the document (e.g. when new mandatory attribute is added to some document). The existing approaches also offer only insufficient solutions. They either only a) create the minimal empty structure (elements and attributes without values) or b) use default values (same in all instances) or c) require the new content to be provided by the user.

Possible link to other models, in particular relational database model (RDM), besides PSM was suggested in Section 3. With RDM linked to PIM, one possible solution (for the first scenario from Section 1) for adding content suggest itself – the required values for the content can be retrieved via a query from the database. E.g. when new attribute `date-of-birth` is added to element `student`, the system can trace the attribute being linked to PIM attribute `date-of-birth` of class `Person` and this can be traced to be stored in a column `PERSON_BIRTHDATE` of table `T_PERSON`. From this table, the value can be retrieved via a query during revalidation.

Another solution for the same problem would be to provide the algorithm with an additional input data document $D_i$ (for the previous example that would be the list of birth dates of the people in the system) and generate the revalidation script so that it will query the document $D_i$ when assigning values for `date-of-birth` attributes. The improvement brought by either of the two solutions is that the revalidation script will again be able to process all the existing documents automatically without requiring user's input.

Both extensions described above will be based on a strictly formal model.

Another possibility of adding data not already present in any form in the system, is by retrieving it from the external sources, e.g. from the Web.

# 5  Conclusion

Our approach to XML schema evolution and data revalidation can considerably simplify the process of transition to the new version. With the proposed enhancements, XSEM-Evo framework will be able to detect changes in the revalidation schema, decide, whether the detected changes may invalidate existing documents and in that case it generate a revalidation script.

Thanks to the two-layer architecture of XSEM, it is possible to define conceptual changes in one place on the PIM level and let the system to consistently propagate them to all the PSM schemas, where they may have impact. Constraints at both the PIM and PSM levels will complete the structural consistency with proper semantics and consistency of content/values.

The two-layer architecture also enables us to link XML schemas to other components of the system (e.g. relational database). With the introduction of constraints, the ability to detect changes in semantics and provide proper revalidations will be further improved. Together, XSEM framework will facilitate both initial design and further evolution with (special emphasis on consistency and coherence) of the systems, applications and specifications, especially in the area of web engineering, where XML, XML schemas and related technologies are utilized to a large degree.

# References

1. Bourret, R.: XML and Databases (September 2005),
   http://www.rpbourret.com/xml/XMLAndDatabases.htm
2. Guerrini, G., Mesiti, M., Sorrenti, M.A.: XML Schema Evolution: Incremental Validation and Efficient Document Adaptation. In: Barbosa, D., Bonifati, A., Bellahsène, Z., Hunt, E., Unland, R. (eds.) XSym 2007. LNCS, vol. 4704, pp. 92–106. Springer, Heidelberg (2007)
3. Su, H., Kramer, D.K., Rundensteiner, E.A.: XEM: XML Evolution Management, Technical Report WPI-CS-TR-02-09 (2002)
4. Klettke, M.: Conceptual xml schema evolution — the codex approach for design and redesign. In: Workshop Proceedings Datenbanksysteme in Business, Technologie und Web (BTW 2007), Aachen, Germany, pp. 53–63 (March 2007)
5. Domínguez, E., Lloret, J., Rubio, Á.L., Zapata, M.A.: Evolving XML Schemas and Documents Using UML Class Diagrams. In: Andersen, K.V., Debenham, J., Wagner, R. (eds.) DEXA 2005. LNCS, vol. 3588, pp. 343–352. Springer, Heidelberg (2005)
6. Kwietniewski, M., Gryz, J., Hazlewood, S., Van Run, P.: Transforming xml documents as schemas evolve. Proc. VLDB Endow. 3, 1577–1580 (2010)
7. Nečaský, M., Mlýnková, I.: When Conceptual Model Meets Grammar: A Formal Approach to Semi-Structured Data Modeling. In: Chen, L., Triantafillou, P., Suel, T. (eds.) WISE 2010. LNCS, vol. 6488, pp. 279–293. Springer, Heidelberg (2010)
8. Malý, J.: XML Schema Evolution Master Thesis (2010),
   http://www.jakubmaly.cz/master-thesis.pdf
9. XCase – tool for XML data modeling, http://www.ksi.mff.cuni.cz/xcase/

# A Reuse-Oriented Product-Line Method for Enterprise Web Applications

Neil Mather and Samia Oussena

School of Computing and Technology
University of West London, London, UK, W5 5RF

**Abstract.** Software product line engineering (SPLE) is a methodology for achieving systematic asset reuse in a family of software. The author of this proposal is producing a range of enterprise web portal products for Higher Education Institutions. The commonalities and variabilities of this product family suggest a SPLE approach would be beneficial. However, research indicates that full-blown, proactive SPLE is not always suited to small businesses. Efforts exist to reduce the overheads of SPLE. In this vein, this research proposes to develop a method for applying software product line engineering to enterprise web application development that makes efficient use of existing frameworks. This research falls into the domain of model-driven processes and methods for web engineering.

## 1 Introduction and Motivation

This research involves the creation of a software product line for enterprise web portals. The portals from this product line are to be deployed to Higher Education Institutes (HEIs) in various domains, such as nursing, social care, occupational therapy and teaching, for the administration of practice-based learning.[1]

While there are many similarities between practice-based learning in each of these domains, there are also many subtle (and not-so-subtle) differences. These differences are not just between domains, but also between HEIs. The variabilities can be in many places. There can be differences in the concepts and business processes in the domain. For example, while a nursing student may have a "mentor", in social work this may be their "practice educator" – a similar yet different concept. Similarly, the process of sending a student on placement varies from HEI to HEI. There can also be differences in the basic functionality of a portal for each HEI – each has its own set of requirements for basic functionality and customisations such as branding and available features. In developing software systems for practice-based learning across domains and HEIs, techniques are required to account for these commonalities and variabilities. Traditional approaches to software reuse are not suited to this purpose. This research seeks to utilise SPLE to enable efficient reuse in the creation of these enterprise portals, and to investigate the use of SPLE in web applications at large.

---

[1] Practice-based learning is a form of higher education wherein a significant portion of a student's education is spent training in real-world environments.

A. Harth and N. Koch (Eds.): ICWE 2011 Workshops, LNCS 7059, pp. 322–326, 2012.
© Springer-Verlag Berlin Heidelberg 2012

## 2    Background

SPLE is a systematic approach to achieving software reuse. It aims to minimise the overheads incurred when building a family of software products that have significant shared features, yet various differences. SPLE and its reuse-oriented methodology has many purported advantages, both financial and technical, and a number of industrial case studies document the successes it can bring [9,14]. Yet due to its relative newness and its perceived overheads it is not yet in widespread use in small- to medium-sized enterprises [8, p. 205]. Efforts exist to bring the benefits of SPLE to companies less able to absorb its large up-front analysis times [7,5,11].

SPLE is commonly split into two main processes: domain engineering and application engineering [13, p. 20]. In *domain engineering* the scope of the domain of the product family is defined, and common and variable parts across products are identified. *Variability management*, a key component of SPLE, is used to manage these commonalities and variabilities. *Feature modelling* is the most common method for variability management [3]. In *application engineering* concrete products are produced from the assets and models that have been produced in the domain engineering process. This requires the production of a *configuration specification* of the variability model, which defines the features to be included (and excluded) from the product in question. A transformation process must then take place, mapping the assets and the configuration specification into a concrete product. While frequently the goal is for this mapping to be automated, human intervention in the process is often required.

Enterprise portals are web-based systems that provide the means for researching, collaborating and manipulating data within the enterprise. They provide functionality such as targeted information provision, easy content management, inter-personnel communication and collaboration, business intelligence reporting and quick access to line-of-business data [4]. The utility of enterprise portals has infiltrated the corporate consciousness enough for several pre-fabricated, commercial portal frameworks to exist, which can be used by companies to 'roll their own' portal without having to start entirely from scratch. These portal frameworks are predominantly component-based architectures.

Web systems are seen as an area where the rapid response times of SPLE for new products can be beneficial. However, the high upfront costs can be off-putting to small- to medium-sized enterprises. The extractive and reactive approaches are ways around these costs [7], and similarly the use of pre-existing tools can be another time-saving measure [8]. Despite this, much prior work in integrating the SPLE paradigm with web applications and portals has involved the construction of a new, custom-built portal framework each time [12,8,2,1]. This is a missed opportunity for software reuse. This research will suggest that a process for variability management and application engineering using an *existing* portal framework will further increase the productivity gains of SPLE in the sphere of the web.

## 3   Aims and Objectives

The specific aims of this research are:

- To demonstrate that the software reuse savings of SPLE can be further increased by making use of existing portal and web frameworks.
- To build upon prior work and develop the concepts around SPLE and web systems, and to define new concepts where required.
- To develop a methodology that describes how to take an 'off-the-shelf' portal/web framework and apply variability management and SPLE techniques to produce applications in a product line.

## 4   Research Methodology

This research will begin with a design science creational phase, followed by an empirical evaluative stage [10]. The first stage will create the software artifacts and methodologies, and the second stage will empirically investigate the utility of these artifacts in a real-world context.

The first stage will utilise the *Formulative-Process* research approach, and the research method will be *Concept Implementation*. These are the most predominant approaches in software engineering research [6]. These methodologies will be used to create the research artifacts of this research – newly defined concepts for the use of SPLE with web systems; a general methodology for reusing frameworks for web systems; and an instantiation of this methodology in one technology.

The product-line will be defined in a reactive fashion based on demand, as opposed to the heavy up-front analysis of the proactive approach [7]. The core and variable assets and models will evolve as new portals are created for new customers. Initial portals will go through the software product life-cycle of requirements engineering, analysis, design, implementation and testing. As the portal product-line is produced, the toolkit for portal generation will be developed. This artifact will take the form of a generator that, given a configuration specification (derived from a variability model such as a feature model), will produce a generator script. This script will compile and install the required assets in the portal framework to produce an individual product. This toolkit will be used to inform the definition of the generalised methodology for reusing portal frameworks in an SPLE approach.

The initial evaluation of the method will be based on the *proof by implementation* research method. The construction of a fully-operational product line from which applications can be produced and sold will be taken as partial validation of the method. It is important, however, to more rigorously validate the method in comparison to alternative methods. This can be performed quantitatively by analysing the reduction in developer-written lines of code by the method. Further software reuse metrics can also be employed. In addition to this, empirical evaluation via case study will be performed in the second stage of the research.

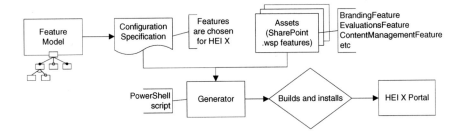

**Fig. 1.** Process for generating a portal from a configuration specification and pre-built assets. Selected assets are installed by the Generator. Future iterations will allow for variability within individual assets, for example through compilation-time bindings in source code, or run-time parameterisation.

## 5   Research Plan

Work to date has involved the production of conceptual models, business process models, and domain glossaries of the social work and nursing domains of practice-based learning. Research into portal frameworks has been performed, as has research into product line and variability management techniques. Initial requirements engineering has been performed with one HEI in the social work domain. Use cases have been created and a prototype portal has been developed using C#, ASP.NET, and Microsoft SharePoint. This portal is currently being tested by the HEI. A prototype version of the toolkit for portal generation has been produced, as shown in Figure 1.

Going forward into the 2nd year, the reactive SPLE approach will be used as portals are produced for other HEIs. This will define the practice-based learning portal product-line as variability is incorporated into the existing models and assets. As this process occurs, concepts for web systems product-lines will be defined, with a focus on reuse of the portal framework infrastructure and components. The toolset with which to automate the generation of new web applications from product-family assets will be enhanced. The concepts of this toolset will be generalised to describe a methodology applicable to portal frameworks and web systems in general. In the 3rd year of research, empirical, evaluative analysis of the utility of the methodology and its instantiation will be made via case study. This will be achieved at the company as more portals are rolled out to customers.

## 6   Contributions to Web Engineering

The main contributions of this research will be:

- Definition of concepts related to SPLE and enterprise web systems. This will include variability management techniques for enterprise ontologies and business processes, and investigations into aspect-oriented programming for web-related software product lines.

– A general methodology with which existing portal/web frameworks can be used in the software product line engineering paradigm.
– An instantiation of the methodology – i.e. a toolkit that can be used to generate enterprise web applications incorporating the reuse of one existing framework technology.
– An empirical, industrial case study of the methodology in practice.

# References

1. Balzerani, L., Di Ruscio, D., Pierantonio, A., De Angelis, G.: A product line architecture for web applications. In: Proceedings of the 2005 ACM Symposium on Applied Computing, pp. 1689–1693. ACM (2005)
2. Capilla, R., Dueñas, J.C.: Light-weight product-lines for evolution and maintenance of Web sites. In: Proceedings of the Seventh European Conference on Software Maintenance and Reengineering, pp. 53–62. IEEE Computer Society (2003)
3. Chen, L., Babar, M.A.: A Status Report on the Evaluation of Variability Management Approaches. In: 13th International Conference on Evaluation and Assessment in Software Engineering (EASE). BCS (2009)
4. Dias, C.: Corporate portals: a literature review of a new concept in Information Management. International Journal of Information Management 21(4), 269–287 (2001)
5. Ghanam, Y., Maurer, F.: Extreme Product Line Engineering: Managing Variability and Traceability via Executable Specifications. In: Proceedings of the 2009 Agile Conference, pp. 41–48. IEEE Computer Society (August 2009)
6. Glass, R.: Research in software engineering: an analysis of the literature. Information and Software Technology 44(8), 491–506 (2002)
7. Krueger, C.W.: Easing the transition to software mass customization. In: Software Product-Family Engineering, pp. 178–184 (2002)
8. Laguna, M., González-Baixauli, B., Hernández, C.: Product Line Development of Web Systems with Conventional Tools. In: Proceedings of the 9th International Conference on Web Engineering, pp. 205–212. Springer, Heidelberg (2009)
9. Van Der Linden, F., Schmid, K., Rommes, E.: Software product lines in action: the best industrial practice in product line engineering. Springer, Heidelberg (2007)
10. March, S.T., Smith, G.F.: Design and natural science research on information technology. Decision Support Systems 15(4), 251–266 (1995)
11. McGregor, J.D.: Agile Software Product Lines - A Working Session. In: Proceedings of the 2008 12th International Software Product Line Conference, vol. 7. IEEE Computer Society (September 2008)
12. Pettersson, U., Jarzabek, S.: Industrial experience with building a web portal product line using a lightweight, reactive approach. In: Proceedings of the 10th European Software Engineering Conference, vol. 30, pp. 326–335. ACM (September 2005)
13. Pohl, K., Böckle, G., Van Der Linden, F.: Software Product Line Engineering: Foundations, Principles and Techniques. Springer, Heidelberg (2005)
14. Software Engineering Institute. Catalog of Software Product Lines (2010)

# A Flexible Architecture for Client-Side Adaptation

Sergio Firmenich[1,2], Gustavo Rossi[1,2] , Silvia Gordillo[1,3], and Marco Winckler[4]

[1] LIFIA, Facultad de Informática,
[2] Universidad Nacional de La Plata and Conicet Argentina
[3] CiCPBA
{sergio.firmenich,gordillo,gustavo}@lifia.info.unlp.edu.ar
[4] IRIT, Université Paul Sabatier, France
winckler@irit.fr

**Abstract.** Currently the Web allows users to perform complex tasks which involve different Web applications. Anyway they still have to face these tasks in a handcrafted way. Although it is possible to build service-based software, such as mashups, to combine data and information from different providers, many times this approach has limitations. In this paper we present an approach for Client-Side Adaptation aimed to support complex concern-sensitive and task-based adaptations with user-collected data. Our approach improves user experience by supporting user tasks among several Web applications.

## 1    Research Context

The evolution of the web has given more and more capabilities to users. From only allowing them browsing contents, at present users not only modify and add new ones but that they choose the way in which the content is presented. Nowadays, users perform several tasks on the Web in general using more than one application. As a consequence they have to perform some extra work when they change the Web application in use and want to continue their task in it. With each switch the work context is generally lost. It means that both what the user was doing and the relevant information which was used is lost when he navigates. As part of a solution to this problem, users can combine contents and services from different resources in order to generate new applications like mash-ups. Another current trend is to adapt Web sites on the client-side, which implies modifying the original contents of Web applications by adding, removing or modifying elements into the Web sites DOMs. This phenomenon of Client-Side Adaptation (CSA) has given new capabilities to users, who now can adapt Web sites correspondingly with their preferences or requirements even those which are not contemplated by Web applications developers.

CSA is a promising trend since at the Client-Side all information about the user activity is available even outside the boundaries of a single Web application. However, while CSA provides a new opportunity to integrate information from several Web sites this power does not seem to be fully exploited. Our first step was to apply concern-sensitive navigation (CSN) at the Client-Side [2]. CSN is a conceptual tool to improve the user experience by taking into account his concern while he navigates the Web. Suppose the user is navigating from A to B; then when he arrives to application B, the application is adapted with information or functionalities

A. Harth and N. Koch (Eds.): ICWE 2011 Workshops, LNCS 7059, pp. 327–331, 2012.

according with the user concern in A, but if the user would be navigated from C the adaptation would be different. The main idea of CSN is to adapt the current node considering the contents of previous ones in the navigation. CSN can occur in two ways. When both pages A and B belong to the same Web application we say that it is *intra-application* CSN. On other hand, CSN is *inter-application* when target and source nodes belong to different applications.

In this work we show a flexible architecture to support CSN and other kinds of adaptations. We have developed a set of tools for supporting users in developing adaptations, which can be shared such as in a crowdsourced development structure.

This paper is organized as follows: in section 2 we introduce the objectives of our research; in section 3 we present a software structure to support all our approach. Finally, section 4 presents conclusions and further works.

## 2    Research Objectives

The research proposal of this position paper tries to answer the following research question: *How can adaptation of existing Web applications be directed in order to improve the user's experience by empowering him with mechanism to fulfil volatile adaptation requirements while he navigates different Web applications to accomplish his tasks?*

Different objectives were identified in order to success deal with the main research question. The first one is to clearly *identify which information is available at the Client-Side*. In comparison with typical approaches for adaptation, CSA gives us new possibilities. For our approach two kinds of information are mainly relevant:

- Navigational history: on Client-Side all navigational history is available instead of being restricted to a single Web application. This information is really important to realize inter-application CSN when the user switches from an application to another (either by following a link or typing a new URL).
- Information Used: knowing which other Web applications the user has used or is using is really powerful to make adaptations, but it would be even more if we could also use information from these applications.

A second objective is to *analyze and design mechanisms to allow users make adaptations under demand in order to fulfil volatile requirements to adapt Web sites in a concern-sensitive or task-based way.*

Differently to other, more static, Web augmentation [1] approaches (e.g. those using GreaseMonkey [3]), we want to empower adaptation by allowing users to develop complex components that will be used in the adaptations (see section 3). Basically the main idea is to accomplish a deeper CSA approach by fully exploiting all Client-Side capabilities instead of limiting ourselves to attach restricted JavaScript code when the Web pages are loaded as when using GreaseMonkey. Then, we have a third objective, which is *to clearly determine what kind of software artefacts can be developed by users with programming skills*. As a consequence of the previously described objectives we have the followings new ones. First we want *to ease the development process of the artefacts found by giving users the guidelines to develop a particular kind of artefact*. On the other hand we have to *design a robust but flexible architecture to orchestrate the – crowdsourced – developed artefacts*.

Figure 1 shows an adaptation to depict the potential of our approach. Here a user is using IMDB. The image 1 shows the page of the movie "Black Swan" and from it the user navigates (with the link showed in image 2) to Amazon.com in order to buy the "Black Swan" DVD. When Amazon.com is loaded a menu is added (image 3) to offer searches about other movies which the user had visited before in IMDB (image 4).

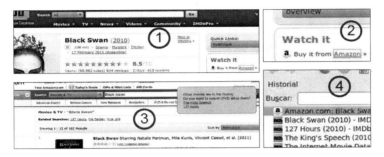

**Fig. 1.** Example of Client-Side adaptation based on navigational history

In the following section we propose a structure where the whole approach is modularized into components with specific responsibilities.

## 3   Solution Approach

Current solutions for CSA provide mechanisms to modify Web pages DOM in order change content or functionalities. Our goal is to provide a better support to the current user task or concern, but at the end we always need to change the pages' DOM to materialize the adaptation. We have to perform two different activities: 1) detect the current user concern/task, 2) change the Web pages DOM accordingly with the needs of the concern or task detected. Note that two different concerns could need similar DOM changes, for instance to remove some DOM elements, only changing the target DOM elements. As a consequence it is reasonable to reuse those software pieces which manipulate DOMs. We call these components: *augmenters* since they respond to classical definition of Web augmentation. Augmenters perform generic adaptations such as automatic form filling or text highlighting. Meanwhile, those artefacts which analyze concerns and apply *augmenters* are called *scenarios* since they realize scenario of Web applications usage. By combining augmenters, *scenarios* support customized adaptations for specific domains such as trip planning, house rental, etc. For example a scenario can use the form filling augmenter when the user is navigating among several Web sites for booking flights and hotels. The same augmenter can be used to fill forms related to a product search in e-commerce Web sites, for example by taking the department (e.g. *electronics*) and the keyword (e.g. *iphone4*) used in *amazon.com* to complete the form automatically in *fnac.fr*. Scenarios can use data collected by users to execute augmenters with different arguments.

A third kind of artefacts in our approach are *components*. These are auxiliary tools used to perform adaptations. From the point of view of *scenarios*, *components* perform critical functionality such as accessing the user navigational history, getting relevant information, etc. On the other hand, *components* are useful to empower augmenters by providing them more privileges that would not be available in simple JavaScript code, for example to get geo-location information. These three kinds of elements are developed and shared by users, then a crowdsourced development of three layers is achieved where: 1) *augmenters* are responsible of manipulating the DOMs, 2) *scenarios* are aware of the user activity and opportunely trigger some *augmenter* in order to adapt the Web pages, 3) *components* act as libraries used to get information or make operations allowing to reuse them by *augmenters* or *scenarios*.

Augmenters, Scenarios and Components are software artefacts that need to be coordinated. In the following section we introduce our framework for CSA which includes a set of tools which help to coordinate these user-developed artefacts.

### 3.1     A Framework for Client-Side Adaptation

Figure 2 shows the framework architecture based on the pyramid approach [4].

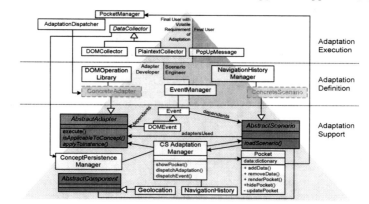

**Fig. 2.** Framework structure

Top levels are more abstract while lower ones are more detailed. At the top layer, final users can collect relevant information for their current task or concern by using *DataCollector* tools. When they navigate to other sites they are able to execute augmenters using this information; in this way they can satisfy volatile adaptation requirements (not foreseen by developers). At the middle layer, end users with programming skills can extend the framework by developing augmenters or scenarios as classes inheriting of *AbstractAdapter* and *AbstractScenario*, two outstanding framework hot-spots. The bottom layer shows the framework design in a more detailed view; a third hot-spot, *AbstractComponent* abstracts concrete components; for example we developed a component which offers geo-location information.

By conciseness reasons we outline only the main components:

- **Adaptation Support Layer**
  - ○ ClientSideAdaptationManager: is the Framework's core, whose functions are to coordinate others elements and to serve as communicator with the browser.
  - ○ ConceptPersistenceManager: is responsible for saving and restoring user data into the local files system.

o   AbstractAdapter and AbstractScenario: are abstract classes from which concrete augmenters and scenarios, correspondingly, developed by users must inherit.
o   AbstractCommponent: is an abstract class used for extending the framework by developing components to support new capabilities (e.g. geolocation).

- **Adaptation Definition Layer**
o   EventManager: is the responsible of adding and removing listeners (Adaptation Definition Layer) of events from the lower layer.
o   ConcreteAdapter and ConcreteScenarios: are scripts developed by users with programming skills. These classes are shown in Figure 3 in order to highlight their place in the hierarchy. Some concrete augmenters as HighlightAdapter, WikiLinkConverter, CopyIntoInputAdapter are included in our framework.

- **Adaptation Execution Layer**
o   DataCollector: is the tool to allow users collecting information while navigating. So far, two concrete DataCollectors have been implemented: one for selecting plaintext information, and another to handle DOM elements.
o   PocketManager: is our tool to allow users to move information among sites.
o   AdaptationDispatcher: is the responsible of executing an adaptation under user demand. It is useful to accomplish volatile requirements of adaptation.

# 4     Conclusions and Future Work

In this work we have presented a novel approach for CSA which proposes a flexible structure to support concern-sensitive and task-based adaptations. The framework allows three kinds of extensions to support and execute adaptations on Client-Side. The framework can be extended and/or used both by end-users or developers (e.g. by developing JavaScript code). In comparison with usual the CSA tools, we provide a flexible mechanism to integrate information while users navigate the web, instead of "just" providing tools to statically adapt Web sites.

We are working in two main directions to improve the approach. The first one is to improve the development process using the framework. The second one is to raise the abstraction level for developers by creating a domain specific language that will simplify the specification of both augmenters and scenarios; this will let users without JavaScript knowledge to develop adaptations easily.

# References

1.   Bouvin, N.O.: Unifying Strategies for Web Augmentation. In: Proc. of the 10th ACM Conference on Hypertext and Hypermedia (1999)
2.   Firmenich, S., Rossi, G., Urbieta, M., Gordillo, S., Challiol, C., Nanard, J., Nanard, M., Araujo, J.: Engineering Concern-Sensitive Navigation Structures. Concepts, tools and examples, JWE 2010, pp. 157–185 (2010)
3.   Greasemonkey, http://www.greasespot.net/ (last visit on April 11, 2011)
4.   Meusel, M., Czarnecki, K., Köpf, W.: A Model for Structuring User Documentation of Object-Oriented Frameworks Using Patterns and Hypertext. In: Aksit, M., Auletta, V. (eds.) ECOOP 1997. LNCS, vol. 1241, pp. 496–510. Springer, Heidelberg (1997)

# Applications of Mobile Application Interface Description Language MAIDL

Prach Chaisatien, Korawit Prutsachainimmit, and Takehiro Tokuda

Department of Computer Science, Tokyo Institute of Technology
Meguro, Tokyo 152-8552, Japan
{prach,korawit,tokuda}@tt.cs.titech.ac.jp

**Abstract.** Developments of mobile mashup applications have a rapid growth in the recent years. We present a development of Mobile Application Interface Description Language (MAIDL) and its applications. The language enables the development of mobile mashup applications with less programming efforts. Using our description language, composers are able to reuse existent mobile applications, Web services, and Web applications as the components to create a mashup mobile application or a Tethered Web service on a mobile device (TeWS). We demonstrate the further application of a TeWS to deliver a cooperative mashup via a functionality exchange between an Android and an iOS device.

**Keywords:** Mobile mashup application, description language, tethered Web service, mobile Web server.

## 1 Introduction

A composition of Web information and mobile devices unique features has recently become an important development trend. In this paper, we approach a development of an XML-based description language to compose mobile mashup applications and Tethered Web services on a mobile device (TeWS). Components in the mashup execution are derived from a combination of existent mobile applications, JavaScript-based Web automations and Restful Web service consumptions. The composition method applied a workflow model which later translated into a script in description language called Mobile Application Interface Description Language (MAIDL). Finally, a mobile application or a TeWS is generated from the MAIDL script as an output. Furthermore, a complex mashup example is provided to demonstrate applications of the generated TeWS between mobile devices.

To integrate various functionalities to a mashup component, developers are having no alternative but to study a very specific programming language API. Divided by its target platform, mobile applications are generally created as mobile Web pages and native language applications. The major drawback when creating a multiplatform mobile Web application is that it tends to employ fewer amounts of mobile devices useful features. Moreover, mobile software developments using the devices native programming language require more explicit

A. Harth and N. Koch (Eds.): ICWE 2011 Workshops, LNCS 7059, pp. 332–336, 2012.

knowledge. In the term of data flows and Web-enabled information reuses, current approaches do not allow applications be developed as rapid as the Web-based ones do.

Code, which is generated from MAIDL, is in a procedural paradigm rather than declarative [1], since the control part mainly consists of procedures that are passing parameters and synchronizing processes in the mashup runtime environment. For this reason, we proposed automatic code generation algorithms, which assist composers in creating mobile mashup applications. In this research, we applied partial information extraction [2] and the final output is not limited to mobile application as traditional methods are [3]. A TeWS can be generated and later consumed by other clients. Later in an example, we show how the TeWS is applied to a platform-independent communication between devices.

## 2  Overview

### 2.1  Objective

*Explore a mobile mashup model.* The topics discussed in section 1 show that a mashup model for the mobile mashup application is not concretely defined. We aim to find an optimal mashup model which leads to a better solution in creating mashup applications for mobile devices.

*Deliver reusability.* Our mashup components include existent mobile applications and Web information. Developing mashup applications with low-level API, such as creating an image recognition component with a new algorithm, is beyond our research scope.

*Enable fast prototyping.* Mashup applications can be created from a Web-based software generation tool. Composers are allowed to generate source code, compile, and test it immediately after the composition model is correctly prepared. Methods called *Mashup Output Context Transformation* and *Mashup Process Scheduling Algorithm* would assist composers by automatically managing foreground and background runtime behaviors of the mashup components.

*Demonstrate a Tethered Web service on mobile devices.* A mashup application in our approach can be created as a mobile application to run on a device or as a TeWS. Functionality exchanges and interactive collaborations between devices can be derived from our approach, and these are unique features and contributions which do not appear in other approaches. In order to run the most flexible configuration on mobile devices (such as third party mobile applications and embedded server modules), we use the Android open source platform [5] as our mashup runtime environment.

### 2.2  Overview of MAIDL and Its Abstract Model Composition

The general concept of MAIDL (shown in Fig. 1) is to provide data flows between mashup components for its execution and output. The components consist of:

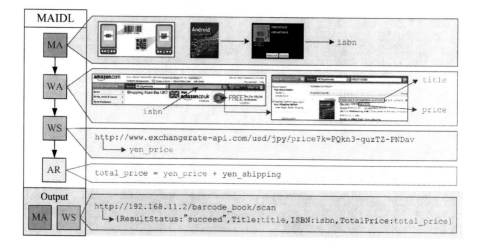

**Fig. 1.** Overview of MAIDL and its abstract model composition

1. Web Application Component (WA). A part of a Web page or a query through form in an HTML document can be reused through a WA component. Composers are provided with a tool to annotate tags and specify execution commands. JavaScript code will be generated according to the specification and execute automatically in the runtime environment on the mobile device.
2. Web Service Component (WS). Connections to REST Web services are applicable to our mashup composition. Composers specify a URL, a query path and a query expression (such as XPath or JSON dot notation) to access a part of the whole data.
3. Mobile Application Component (MA). A part of mashup execution can be derived from a mobile application. Our method allows an application which implemented Intent and Service [4] messaging protocol to be integrated.
4. Arithmetic Component (AR). A mathematical operation between parameters from one or more components can be performed through an Arithmatic Component. The operation includes addition, subtraction, division, multiplication, summation, comparison, array merge and GPS distance calculation from 2 pairs of GPS coordinates.

## 3   Cooperative Mashup

To demonstrate functionality exchanges and a cooperative mashup application, we created a mashup application using our approach. It requires interaction between 2 or more mobile devices. In this way, the application created in a TeWS output context can be deployed on an Android mobile phone. On the other hand, the iOS device [6] is manually programmed to consume the TeWS on the Android phone.

In this mashup application, geolocation of 2 devices are used as a data to find a list of restaurants located near the middle point between each devices GPS

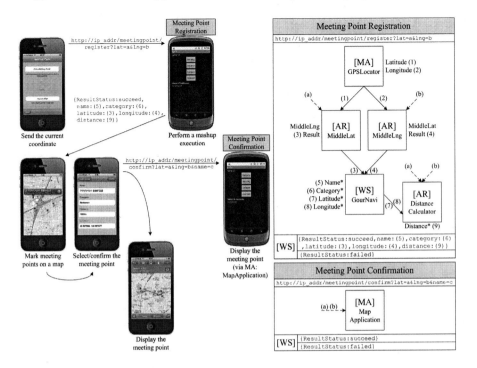

**Fig. 2.** Mashup models and screenshots of *Meeting Point*

coordinates (via the *GourNavi* Web service [7]). Fig. 2 shows 2 mashup models and mashup applications, *Meeting Point Registration* and *Meeting Point Confirmation*, which communicate between devices via TeWS in separated contexts.

For the internal runtime and the connection performance, the application on the iOS side was presumably lightweight. Since this is a cooperative mashup application for 2 devices with a handshaking-like protocol, multiple connections are not considered as a performance factor. Overall performance of this mashup application depends on the performance of *GourNavi* Web service. All other components work in native code. In usability and interaction test, if we assumed that 2 devices are connected using global IP addresses and are placed outdoors, the interactions between 2 devices might be interrupted by signal loss. Both sides must have a timeout configuration and a reconnection arrangement in the case of failure execution.

## 4    Evaluation

To deliver smooth interactions between devices of a mashup application in the context of TeWS, the behavior of running process, network latency and usage scenario has to be observed. Since MAIDL files contain information about each component and its runtime behavior, an alternative application of MAIDL for performance measurement can be considered. MAIDL files also contain a concrete description of the output message sent via TeWS. Applications on the client side might be generated or adapt themselves according to the description. A good example for the combination of a TeWS and a desktop-based Web application is to exchange multiple data from a mobile phone to automatically fill in personal information in an HTML form. The desktop Web application first observes the applicable TeWS on the device and connects to it. In addition, the result from our usability evaluation of MAIDL can be interpret that MAIDL might not perform well when mashup applications are composed by novice composers because of its complexity. Expert users are able to use MAIDL without confusion and may apply it to external libraries. However, both groups expectations are met. Composers in both groups rated that the approach delivered 75% subjective rating for creating mashup applications.

## 5   Conclusion

In this research, we proposed a fast-paced mashup development using MAIDL. The composition enables integration of annotated parts of Web pages, connections to Web services and the use of existent mobile applications. The output can be designated for a single device, as a normal mobile application, or for multiple devices, as a Tethered Web service. In the mashup example, we demonstrated how a mashup application works in a Tethered Web service context to deliver functionality exchange and cooperative application between devices. Our future work is to enable mobile mashups in the context of a Web application on a mobile device. To support a higher interactivity to run on desktop computers, the process control and the composition method might be different from the contexts we have observed.

## References

1. Gruhn, V., Schäfer, C.: An Architecture Description Language for Mobile Distributed Systems. In: Oquendo, F., Warboys, B.C., Morrison, R. (eds.) EWSA 2004. LNCS, vol. 3047, pp. 212–218. Springer, Heidelberg (2004)
2. Guo, J., Chaisatien, P., Han, H., Noro, T., Tokuda, T.: Partial Information Extraction Approach to Lightweight Integration on the Web. In: Daniel, F., Facca, F.M. (eds.) ICWE 2010. LNCS, vol. 6385, pp. 372–383. Springer, Heidelberg (2010)
3. Kaltofen, S., Milrad, M., Kurti, A.: A Cross-Platform Software System to Create and Deploy Mobile Mashups. In: Benatallah, B., Casati, F., Kappel, G., Rossi, G. (eds.) ICWE 2010. LNCS, vol. 6189, pp. 518–521. Springer, Heidelberg (2010)
4. Android Intents, http://developer.android.com/guide/topics/intents/
5. Android Developers, http://developer.android.com/index.html
6. iOS Technology Overview, http://developer.apple.com/technologies/ios/
7. Gourmet Navigator API, http://api.gnavi.co.jp/api/manual.htm

# A Domain-Specific Language for Do-It-Yourself Analytical Mashups

Julian Eberius, Maik Thiele, and Wolfgang Lehner

Technische Universität Dresden
Faculty of Computer Science, Database Technology Group
01062 Dresden, Germany
{julian.eberius,maik.thiele,wolfgang.lehner}@tu-dresden.de

**Abstract.** The increasing amount and variety of data available in the web leads to new possibilities in end-user focused data analysis. While the classic data base technologies for data integration and analysis (ETL and BI) are too complex for the needs of end users, newer technologies like web mashups are not optimal for data analysis. To make productive use of the data available on the web, end users need easy ways to find, join and visualize it.

We propose a domain specific language (DSL) for querying a repository of heterogeneous web data. In contrast to query languages such as SQL, this DSL describes the visualization of the queried data in addition to the selection, filtering and aggregation of the data. The resulting data mashup can be made interactive by leaving parts of the query variable. We also describe an abstraction layer above this DSL that uses a recommendation-driven natural language interface to reduce the difficulty of creating queries in this DSL.

**Keywords:** data analytics, data mashups, natural language queries.

## 1 Introduction

The increasing amount and variety of data available in the web leads to new possibilities in end-user focused data analysis. In the course of the *Open Data* trend, public agencies have started to make governmental data available using web services. In addition, there is a large amount of "crowdsourced" data from services such as Yelp (venue ratings) or Twitter (trending topics, sentiments).

To make productive use of this data, two elements are needed: first, a way to integrate the heterogenous data into a common representation, second, a way to analyze the integrated data to make it usable. cities The well-known solutions to these two problems are data integration through ETL processes into data warehouses, and the usage of BI (business intelligence) tools for analytics. These tools could basically be applied to these new forms of data as well, but for end-user data analysis they have two disadvantages: First, they are designed for skilled users. Second, ETL processes are constructed for static sets of input sources and are not suitable for on-demand joining of web data sources.

A. Harth and N. Koch (Eds.): ICWE 2011 Workshops, LNCS 7059, pp. 337–341, 2012.
© Springer-Verlag Berlin Heidelberg 2012

To make web data accessible to end users, new integration and analysis methods are necessary. They should accommodate to the skill levels of end-users, but also to their needs: compared with the business intelligence in enterprises, the skill level as well as the query complexity are much lower.

With regard to the vast amount tools for end-user driven mashup development that have been developed in recent years, we argue that there is room for improvement. Specifically, we argue that their scope, general mashup application development, and their user interface styles, for example data- and work flow graphs, are not optimal for the problem of end user data analytics.

We will discuss our view of the requirements of end-user data analytics in the next section (Section 2). We will then propose an approach to tackle the presented problems in Section 3 and finally discuss related work in Section 4.

## 2    Research Questions

Consider an exemplary use case for end-user business intelligence: a user plans to open a cafe, and needs to decide on its location. He requires to join data from multiple heterogenous sources. He needs statistical data about the districts of the city, such as average income, rent or age structure, data which is available from public agencies. In addition he needs data about the popularity of existing cafes in the various districts, available from services such as Yelp. When he has found the data, the user needs to to join, filter and aggregate it. For example, he needs to merge the statistical information about the cities districts with the average rating of existing venues in the district.

In a next step, a visualization the be preferable to a tabular display of the result data. The type and the properties of the visualization should be configurable by the user. In a last step, it would be beneficial if the user could easily vary the parameters of the mashup, e.g., aggregation or filter parameters, to enable an exploratory style of data analysis.

From this scenario, a number of requirements and research questions can be derived.

- How to deal with heterogenous data sources with varying degrees of structure when creating data mashups?
- How well-suited are the interfaces currently used (e.g. drag and drop data flow languages) for end-user mashup construction and are there alternatives?
- How to enable users to find the data sets that contain the information they are interested in?
- How can techniques such as (automatic) tagging and matching be used to recommend data sets that could fit into the user's data mashup?
- How to facilitate the selection of visualizations and interaction patterns that are appropriate for the data?

## 3    Approach

To support the outlined use cases we propose a declarative domain specific language (*DSL*), as well as a higher level natural language interface that supports the user in creating data mashups using this DSL. The language allows the user to query a repository of possibly heterogenous information that can have various degrees of structure, ranging from free text over CSV files and graph-structured data to relational databases.

It supports a set of operations such as joining of different data sets, filtering according to a given predicate or grouping. In contrast to the result of a query in a relational database system, executing a query in the proposed DSL results in a *data mashup*, which is a visualization of the selected data. The form of the visualization, e.g. a chart or map, can be specified in the query, or be automatically inferred from the data used in the mashup. In addition, it includes interaction features that can be specified in the query. Specifically, for each value in the query that is given as a variable, an interaction feature (slider, drop-down menu etc.) that allows to set this value will be present in the mashup.

To accommodate the language to the needs of end users while keeping it expressive enough for developers, the language can be used on two abstraction levels.

1. End-User Level: This level is suitable for end-user mashup creation. In contrast to previous mashup systems that mostly either use WYSIWYG application editing or a pipeline-style graphical connection of operators, we propose a iterative, recommendation-supported natural language interface, which will be described below.
2. DSL-Level: On this level, the actual domain specific language, i.e. the query language described above, resides. On this level, the language is similar to typical data flow languages, with the addition of the visualization operators, and variables which result in interaction features in the mashup. Input from the high-level interface are mapped to executable operators on this level to create executable mashups.

With the higher level interface, users can enter a query in natural language, which is then incrementally refined until a fitting data mashup can be created from the query. The first step would be very similar to systems like WolframAlpha[1] in which users enter entities and attributes which they want to compare, e.g., *"unemployment usa germany"*. In the proposed system, more complex cases including visualization directions or filter conditions are also possible, in the style of *"plot the unemployment rates in the usa and germany between 1990 and 2010."*

However, instead of presenting an answer on a best-effort basis, the platform would go through an incremental process of assisting the user in refining the query, as shown in Figure 1. In this process, the system will interpret the query using techniques from natural language processing to find the elements needed for the construction of the mashup: data sets, joins/filters/aggregates, visualization and interaction forms. These elements will be mapped to concrete operators on the DSL-level. For every missing element the user will be prompted to refine the query, giving recommendations based on the elements that have been recognized.

---

[1] http://www.wolframalpha.com/

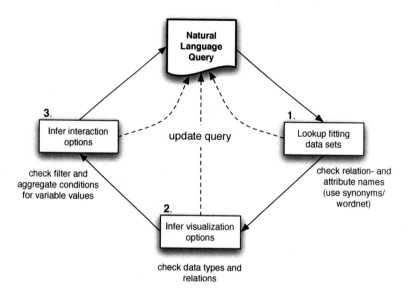

**Fig. 1.** Incremental Refinement of the Original Query Input

## 4    Related Work

An overview of available general end-user mashup development systems is given by Grammel et al [2]. Beyond these general systems, a number of data mash-up, analysis and visualization platforms have been proposed. Google Fusion Tables [1] provides tools for users to upload tabular data files, join, filter and aggregate the data and visualize the results. The interface is a standard, menu-based point and click interface, no steps of the process are assisted or automated. Similar tools are, for example, GeoCommons[2] and to some extend ManyEyes[3], which focus on the visualization and do not offer analytical functions.

One of the more successful platforms focusing on end-user data mashups is Yahoo Pipes[4]. It uses a visual data flow language to merge and filter feeds and to model user input. Executing a pipe (a data flow) results in a new feed, which can include parameters that the user specifies on execution. Resulting feed data can be displayed as a list, or on a map if the items contain spatial data. The system offers many operators and thus a high degree of flexibility, but lacks visualization or data other data exploration features, instead focusing on merging and processing of data. Furthermore, to use the system, the user has to understand the concept of data flow graphs, as well as many specific mashup problems, for example how web services are called with URL parameters, or that a geo-coding component has to be inserted into the pipe to display addresses on a map.

---

[2] geocommons.com

[3] manyeyes.alphaworks.ibm.com

[4] pipes.yahoo.com

There are many current systems that explore the application of natural language querying to semantic data bases. Kaufmann et al. propose a classification for these system that ranges from completely free form query entry to more structured or guided approaches with almost formal query languages [4]. They evaluate several systems and conclude that neither end of this spectrum is optimal for end-users. They argue that a guided free entry approach is preferable.

Recommending components to mashup creators has been explored for example by Greenshpan et al [3]. They developed a system that offers autocompletions based on previous mashups created by other users. Picozzi et al. on the other hand propose a system that recommends components to be added to a mashup using quality metrics that take both the new components as well as the already chosen components into account [5].

## 5    Conclusion and Planned Contributions

The increasing amount of publicly available data on the web raises the question how this data can be made usable for end-users. There is a need for simple tools for data joining, analyzing and visualizing web data from different sources.

The following specific contributions are planned:

- A DSL for data mashup construction, with query, visualization and interaction operators for working on heterogenous web data.
- A high-level natural language query interface and an iterative process for refining queries and mapping them to the concrete DSL.
- A recommendation engine for finding data sets, visualization and interaction forms fitting the given query.

The project is in the initial research phase. The next steps in the research plan include concretizing the operators of the DSL, exploring the capabilities of current NL-querying systems and experimenting with different ways of mapping natural language input to operators of the DSL and data sets in the repository.

## References

1. Gonzalez, H., Halevy, A.Y., Jensen, C.S., Langen, A., Madhavan, J., Shapley, R., Shen, W., Goldberg-Kidon, J.: Google fusion tables: web-centered data management and collaboration. In: SIGMOD 2010 (2010)
2. Grammel, L., Storey, M.-A.: A Survey of Mashup Development Environments. In: Chignell, M., Cordy, J., Ng, J., Yesha, Y. (eds.) The Smart Internet. LNCS, vol. 6400, pp. 137–151. Springer, Heidelberg (2010)
3. Greenshpan, O., Milo, T., Polyzotis, N.: Autocompletion for mashups. In: VLDB 2009 (2009)
4. Kaufmann, E., Bernstein, A.: Evaluating the usability of natural language query languages and interfaces to semantic web knowledge bases. In: Web Semantics: Science, Services and Agents on the World Wide Web (2010)
5. Picozzi, M., Rodolfi, M., Cappiello, C., Matera, M.: Quality-Based Recommendations for Mashup Composition. In: Daniel, F., Facca, F.M. (eds.) ICWE 2010. LNCS, vol. 6385, pp. 360–371. Springer, Heidelberg (2010)

# Information Extraction from Web Pages Based on Their Visual Representation

Ruslan R. Fayzrakhmanov*

Database and Artificial Intelligence Group
Institute of Information Systems, TU Vienna
Favoritenstrasse 9, A-1040 Vienna, Austria
fayzrakh@dbai.tuwien.ac.at

**Abstract.** This research is dedicated to enhancing the efficiency of web information extraction and web accessibility. The motivation behind the research, its aim and objectives are presented, and the performed work on developing web page model for information extraction is described. We also present work on making extracted information accessible to blind users, providing them with the means to navigate and access required information quickly. We also present our ongoing research on creating efficient methods and approaches for information extraction from the proposed model. There are two main approaches considered: 1) development of the library which provides required functionality to the programmer; 2) development of declarative Datalog-like language for information extraction.

**Keywords:** web information extraction, web page, wrapper, web accessibility.

## 1 Introduction

The Web is an enormous repository of information. It plays an important role in business, politics, science, and our everyday life. Web pages are the main components of the Web, presenting information in semi-structured and unstructured forms, using well-known standards, such as HTML and XHTML. These forms of representation and CSS are solely used for specifying visual formatting, and they are convenient forms for storing and transferring information through the Internet. But HTML, XHTML as well as DOM tree are not designed to present semantics and data types on a web page. As is generally known, most of the contemporary information extraction systems consider only source code or DOM tree, which, besides the characteristics mentioned, are exposed to frequent change. The semantics of a web page are hidden in its visual representation, where — beside textual and multimedia contents — colour, size, style (of text), and the relative position of elements play and important role. Regardless of the

---

* Supported by the Erasmus Mundus External Cooperation Window Programme of the European Union.

A. Harth and N. Koch (Eds.): ICWE 2011 Workshops, LNCS 7059, pp. 342–346, 2012.

template used for web page generation and its source code, humans are able to distinguish and identify different web objects on different web pages (e.g. news article, navigation menu) that allow us to put forward a hypothesis about existence of some permanent characteristics in web objects such as relative position and relative size.

The *idea* behind this research, which is a part of ongoing ABBA[1] porject, is based on utilizing positional information, spatial expansion of visual objects, and their visual characteristics for information extraction. In addition, in the research we solve the problem of accessibility of the extracted information for blind users. The *aim* of the research is the development of methods and tools to enhance the efficiency of information extraction for web pages based on their visual representation, and to present it in a form accessible for blind users. To achieve this goal, the following *objectives* were formulated:

1. Review and analysis of related work (100% completed).
2. Development of a web page model based on its visual representation (90% completed).
3. Development of methods for information extraction from the proposed web page model (10% completed).
4. Development of methodology for navigation through the extracted information for blind users (90% completed).
5. Development of the information extraction system on the basis of proposed methods (10% completed).
6. Development of a navigation system according to proposed methodology (90% completed).
7. Analysis of efficiency of proposed methods of information extraction and navigation (10% completed).

This research is carried out under the supervision of Prof. Reinhard Pichler, Dr. Robert Baumgartner (TU Vienna).

## 2  A Web Page Model

For the tasks of information extraction and web page understanding within the scope of the ABBA project, a web page model was developed, describing its visual characteristics and taking into account its DOM tree [6]. Continuing the research, we propose a *web page model* as a conjunction of its *geometrical* (GM) and *logical* (LM) models (cf. Fig. 1).

A **GM** is an ontological model and is formed as a result of the analysis of web page visual representation (its CSS model), generated by the browser's layout engine. A GM represents visual information in a form convenient for both information extraction and web page understanding. The *geometric object* (GO) of the GM has a rectangular shape and wraps some part of the web page canvas.

---
[1] The ABBA project (Advanced Barrier-free Browser Accessibility) is sponsored by the Austrian Forschungsförderungsgesellschaft FFG under grant 819563.

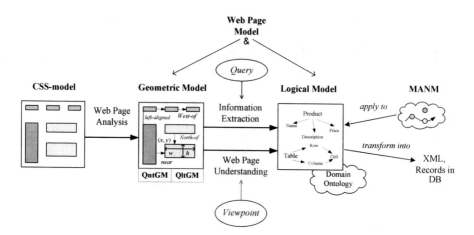

**Fig. 1.** Diagram represents the process of automatic creation of a web page model

It can correspond to some CSS box. The main attributes of a GO are features of a background (colour, background image), border (width, colour, style), contained text (colour, font size and style) as well as drawing order, which is used to define visibility of overlapped GOs. It can be calculated according to the painting order (W3C specification [1]).

Depending on the type of information representation, we define *quantitative* GM (QntGM) and *qualitative* GM (QltGM). Spatial relationships, such as distance and direction, are defined between GOs in the QntGM and expressed quantitatively (in pixels and angles respectively). In the QltGM, besides distance and direction, there are alignment and topological relationships (we use RCC8 [5]) expressed qualitatively via linguistic variables. These relationships are widely used both for graphical user interfaces [10] and positional information representation in GIS [4].

A **LM** is an ontological model and is formed as a result of the process of web page understanding or information extraction (cf. Fig. 1). In the first case, an LM represents a semantics of web objects on the web page with the required level of detail. In the second case, an LM describes the necessary part of the web page according to the request. An LM set a correspondence between GOs of the GM and concepts of the applied domain ontology. Thus, this solution contributes also to the Semantic Web development, providing us with necessary semantic metadata annotations [9].

An LM can be transformed to the XML format or stored in a database, but in this research we focus on accessibility of extracted information for blind users.

## 3   Development of Information Extraction Methods

Information extraction from the GM is represented as a gradual process of successive refinement of extracted information characteristics and its extraction [8].

For instance, to extract posts in a web forum, we need to indicate the location (in our case it is center) and occupied area of the object to be extracted. A post can be further described as a rectangular area which contains a textual message occupying a major part, and also contains an icon at the top-left corner, etc. When extracting items from the navigation menu, for instance, we first define its approximate area of occurrence and define the menu as a horizontally or vertically oriented list of textual elements. To specify extracted web object or its parts, one can use positional information, an HTML type of corresponding element in the source code, and its CSS style, provided by the GM of the web page.

We consider two solutions for information extraction. The **first** one involves developing the Java library, which provides necessary functionality for a programmer to create a wrapper. Algorithms implemented in the library should be efficient, giving a posibility to the programmer to utilize all potential of GM. The **second** solution involves developing declarative Datalog-like extraction language. Its predicates will not be evaluated over an extensional database of the facts representing the GM, but directly over the GM, represented as an ontological model. It will make the performance more efficient. This solution is similar to the Lixto solution, where ELog language is used and which predicates are evaluated over DOM tree [3]. This language is very efficient and useful for automatic wrapper generation according to the performed specifications of extracted information by the user, using only GUI. Thus, it does not require any programming skills from the end user.

## 4   Navigating Extracted Information

Within the scope of the ABBA project in which the author participate, multi-axial navigation model (MANM) along with the methodology of navigation were developed to make web pages more accessible to a blind user [7], [2]. In this research, the MANM is used for making extracted information (concepts in the LM) accessible.

The main component of the MANM is the axis (cf. Fig 2), which is a sequence of web page model elements to be read. The MANM is provided both with the possibility to navigate on the axis (e.g., news titles) and change axis. Moving from one to another axis can be performed by its selection from the

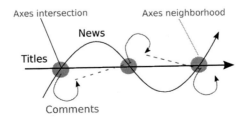

**Fig. 2.** Example of the quantitative geometrical model

set of all available axes, from the set of axes intersecting current element, from the spatial, or semantic neighbourhood of current element. For this reason, we consider semantic relationship between elements defined in the LM and their spatial relations defined in the GM.

## 5    Conclusion

This paper describes the current state of Ruslan R. Fayzrakhmanov's research. The work is dedicated to problems in information extraction from web page visual representation and web accessibility. The model of web pages for information extraction and the multi-axial navigation model are presented. Further work on the development of methods of information extraction is also described.

## References

1. Cascading Style Sheets Level 2 Revision 1 (CSS 2.1) Specification (2009), http://www.w3.org/TR/2009/CR-CSS2-20090908/
2. Baumgartner, R., Fayzrakhmanov, R.R., Holzinger, W., Krüpl, B., Göbel, M.C., Klein, D., Gattringer, R.: Web 2.0 vision for the blind. In: Proc. of Web Science Conference 2010 (WebSci 2010), Raleigh, USA, p. 8 (2010)
3. Baumgartner, R., Flesca, S., Gottlob, G.: The Elog Web Extraction Language. In: Nieuwenhuis, R., Voronkov, A. (eds.) LPAR 2001. LNCS (LNAI), vol. 2250, pp. 548–560. Springer, Heidelberg (2001)
4. Clementini, E., Di Felice, P., Hernández, D.: Qualitative representation of positional information. Artificial Intelligence 95(2), 317–356 (1997)
5. Cohn, A.G.: Qualitative spatial representation and reasoning techniques, pp. 1–30. Springer, Berlin (1997)
6. Fayzrakhmanov, R.R., Göbel, M.C., Holzinger, W., Krüpl, B., Baumgartner, R.: A Unified ontology-based web page model for improving accessibility. In: Proc. WWW 2010, pp. 1087–1088. ACM, New York (2010)
7. Fayzrakhmanov, R.R., Göbel, M.C., Holzinger, W., Krüpl, B., Mager, A., Baumgartner, R.: Modelling Web navigation with the user in mind. In: Proc. W4A 2010, Raleigh, USA, p. 4 (2010)
8. Gottlob, G., Koch, C., Baumgartner, R., Herzog, M., Flesca, S.: The Lixto data extraction project - back and forth between theory and practice. In: Transformation, pp. 1–12. ACM, Paris (2004)
9. Kashyap, V., Bussler, C., Moran, M.: The Semantic Web. Semantics for Data and Services on the Web. Springer, Berlin (2008)
10. Kong, J., Zhang, K., Zeng, X.: Spatial graph grammars for graphical user interfaces. ACM Transactions on Computer-Human Interaction 13(2), 268–307 (2006)

# End-User Programming for Web Mashups
## Open Research Challenges

Saeed Aghaee and Cesare Pautasso[*]

Faculty of Informatics, University of Lugano, Switzerland
firstname.familyname@usi.ch
http://www.pautasso.info/

**Abstract.** Mashup is defined as the practice of lightweight composition, serendipitous reuse, and user-centric development on the Web. In spite of the fact that the development of mashups is rather simple due to the reuse of all the required layers of a Web application (functionality, data, and user interface), it still requires programming experience. This is a significant hurdle for non-programmers (end-users with minimal or no programming experience), who constitute the majority of Web users. To cope with this, an End-User Programming (EUP) tool can be designed to reduce the barriers of mashup development, in a way that even non-programmers will be able to create innovative, feature-rich mashups. In this paper, we give an overview of the existing EUP approaches for mashup development, as well as a list of open research challenges.

## 1 Introduction

Facilitating software development from reusable components has always been one of the priorities in software engineering [1]. Recently, the proliferation of reusable Web resources, in the form of Web APIs, Web widgets, and Web data sources, has again brought up the notion of reuse within Web engineering with the advent of Web mashups.

The key characteristic of mashups, distinguishing them from other forms of service and software composition, lies in a development approach being carried out in a *lightweight* manner, in which simplicity and usability are more of a priority than quality and completeness [2]. This enables end-user composition activities, in which ordinary Web users are themselves the developers of creative mashups, which can fulfill their personal needs, and can be rapidly adapted as soon as their situational needs change [3]. However, developing mashups still requires significant technical skills. These range from knowing how to reuse components, to at least a basic understanding of programming and familiarity with Web technologies. Yet, such skills by definition are not mastered by non-programmers.

To address the above challenges, one solution is to reuse and adapt existing mashups that, thanks to directories such as ProgrammableWeb [4], can be easily discovered and shared. However, this should be complemented by leveraging

---

[*] PhD Supervisor.

A. Harth and N. Koch (Eds.): ICWE 2011 Workshops, LNCS 7059, pp. 347–351, 2012.

End-User Programming (EUP) [5] to reduce the complexity of mashup development as much as possible, to the extent that even non-programmers can develop and share their desired mashups. In doing so, mashups can reach their full potential to serve as user-centric situational applications on the Web, from which the vast majority of Web users can benefit.

Our research objective is to design, implement, and evaluate a EUP approach for mashups that satisfies the following two requirements. 1) supporting the needs and abilities of non-programmers. 2) enabling creation of any types of mashup that can be developed using manual approaches (i.e. programming and scripting languages). To this end, in the rest of the paper, we will provide a brief survey of existing EUP approaches for mashups, and further discuss a number of open challenges, which are not yet fully solved by the state of the art.

## 2   Overview of Existing EUP Approaches for Mashups

The research efforts behind the design of EUP approaches for mashups (so-called "mashup tools") have resulted in the growth of this field as an interesting research topic spanning areas including Model-Driven Development (MDD) [6], programming languages [7], software and service composition [8], and Human-Computer Interaction (HCI) [9]. Existing mashup tools can be classified according to the EUP technique [10] they utilize as follows:

− **Spreadsheets.** The advantage of using spreadsheets for creating mashups lies in its ease-of-use, intuitiveness, and expressive power to represent and manage complex data [11]. Mashroom [12] adapts the idea of spreadsheets and adds the nesting tables feature to support complex data formats such as XML and JSON. Husky [13] is also another spreadsheet-based tool aiming at streamlining service composition. However, the main shortcoming of such tools is the lack of support for designing the mashup User Interface (UI).

− **Programming by Demonstration (PbD).** PbD enables users to teach a system to do a task by demonstrating how the task is done [14]. Intel Mash Maker (IMM) [15] utilizes PbD to extract, store, manage, and integrate data from the Websites being browsed by the user. Vegemite [16] is another browser-based tool like IMM which adds scripting capabilities. The use of scripting allows users to augment and operate the extracted data. The focus of these tools are more on data extraction and visualization, and therefore, they do not provide support for service composition and orchestration.

− **Domain-Specific Language (DSL).** DSLs are small languages targeted for solving certain problems in a specific domain. DSLs can also be used as a EUP technique for reducing programming efforts [17]. The Enterprise Mashup Markup Language (EMML) [18] is a DSL based on XML for creating mashups. It supports variety of components as well as the use of scripting languages. Swashup [19] is also another DSL for mashups, based on Ruby-on-Rails. It simplifies invocation, and integration of Web APIs and data sources. Though these DSLs help to reduce programming efforts, they still can not be used by non-programmers due to the difficulty of learning their syntax and vocabulary [14].

- **Visual Programming.** Programming languages can also be expressed by visual symbols and graphical notations [20]. Visual programming is widely used by existing mashup tools in the form of wiring diagrams, in which users drag-and-drop mashup components (visualized as boxes) and connect them to form a mashup. Examples are Yahoo Pipes (YP) [21], IBM Mashup Center (IMC) [22], ServFace [23], and Presto Cloud [24]. The main problem of these tools, according to a recent study conducted by Namoun et. al., is the fact that the wiring paradigm is difficult to understand by non-programmers [25].
- **Model-based Automation.** This is concerned with automatically creating mashups based on knowledge about the user and the context in which she operates. Due to the fact that there is much more work on the tool side, this technique best serves the needs of non-programmers. The framework proposed by Carlson et. al. automatically creates mashups out of non-web service components [26]. Bakalov et. al., on the other hand, present an automatic mashup generation framework that is also capable of composing Web services (REST and SOAP) [27]. As described in [5], the problem of this technique lies in the high risk of generating irrelevant mashups with respect to the given requirements.

## 3   Open Research Challenges

- **Simplicity and Expressive Power Tradeoff.** When it comes to create complex mashups, the majority of existing mashup tools are not powerful enough. This can be witnessed by the fact that most of the registered mashups in the ProgrammableWeb are all developed using general-purpose Web scripting languages. If these are called *real* mashups, the majority of current EUP tools are limited to creating *toy* mashups that are not as feature-rich. On the other hand, increasing the expressive power of mashup tools (e.g., DSLs) can potentially result in a decrease in simplicity (gentle learning curve, and ease-of-use). Hence, the major challenge is to cope with this tradeoff.
- **Mashup Components Heterogeneity.** Mashup components are heterogeneous in terms of the technology through which they are made accessible. They can be classified into Web APIs, Web widgets, and Web data sources. Within enterprises, another class of mashup components may encompass legacy services such as databases, Plain Old Java Object (POJO), and Enterprise Java Beans (EJB). The challenge is how to abstract all these heterogeneous components in a way that facilitates their seamless composition.
- **Mashup Composition Techniques.** The development of mashups consists of Process Integration (PI), Data Integration (DI), and UI integration [28]. PI forms the logic of mashup by composing the functionality obtained from Web APIs. UI integration creates the visual front-end, by which users interact with the mashup. This is obtained through integration of various widgets [29]. The underlying data model of the mashup is obtained by the integration of two or more remote data sources [30]. A challenge for mashup tools is to fully support development within all of these three levels.
- **Mashup Evolution.** Mashup evolution can be caused by two reasons. The first is the change in the user requirements, which forces the mashup to be

reengineered to meet the new ones [31]. The other is the evolution of the building blocks of the mashup, that in case of Web services is very likely to happen. From the mashup EUP perspective, this has however remained a challenging matter.

– **Online Communities.** Empowering end-user communities is of value in the area of EUP [5]. With the growth of the Web 2.0, online communities and social networks can be used to promote sharing of mashups, technical discussion, and collaborative categorization [32]. Yet, only a few mashup tools, such as YP, offer online communities. Moreover, the potential of these communities to enable mashup development as a collaborative process has still to be fully exploited.

## 4   Conclusion and Future Work

This paper provides an overview and classification of existing approaches and open research challenges for enabling EUP for mashups. Our future research will be geared towards addressing these challenges by designing, implementing, and evaluating a novel mashup tool. To do so, we will utilize a User-Centered Design (UCD) methodology [33], in which the end-user needs and feedback affect every step of the design process. Getting closer to the mindset of the end-users can help with the design of a more *natural* and *powerful* EUP tool for mashups [34].

## References

1. McIlroy, D.: Mass-produced Software Components. In: Software Engineering Concepts and Techniques, NATO Science Committee, pp. 138–155 (1969)
2. Yu, J., Benatallah, B., Casati, F., Daniel, F.: Understanding Mashup Development. IEEE Internet Computing 12, 44–52 (2008)
3. Anderson, C.: The Long Tail: Why the Future of Business Is Selling Less of More. Hyperion (2006)
4. ProgrammableWeb, http://www.programmableweb.com/
5. Nardi, B.A.: A Small Matter of Programming: Perspectives on End User Computing. MIT Press (1993)
6. Bozzon, A., Brambilla, M., Facca, F.M., Carughu, G.T.: A Conceptual Modeling Approach to Business Service Mashup Development. In: Proc. of ICWS 2009 (2009)
7. Ennals, R., Gay, D.: User-Friendly Functional Programming for Web Mashups. In: Proc. of ICFP 2007 (2007)
8. López, J., Bellas, F., Pan, A., Montoto, P.: A Component-Based Approach for Engineering Enterprise Mashups. In: Gaedke, M., Grossniklaus, M., Díaz, O. (eds.) ICWE 2009. LNCS, vol. 5648, pp. 30–44. Springer, Heidelberg (2009)
9. Wong, J., Hong, J.: What do we "mashup" when we make mashups? In: Proc. of WEUSE 2008, pp. 35–39 (2008)
10. Myers, B.A., Ko, A.J., Burnett, M.M.: Invited Research Overview: End-User Programming. In: Proc. of CHI 2006 (2006)
11. Hoang, D.D., Paik, H.Y., Benatallah, B.: An Analysis of Spreadsheet-Based Services Mashup. In: Proc. of ADC 2010 (2010)
12. Wang, G., Yang, S., Han, Y.: Mashroom: End-User Mashup Programming Using Nested Tables. In: Proc. of WWW 2009 (2009)
13. Husky, http://www.husky.fer.hr/

14. Cypher, A., Halbert, D.C., Kurlander, D., Lieberman, H., Maulsby, D., Myers, B.A., Turransky, A. (eds.): Watch What I Do: Programming by Demonstration (1993)
15. Ennals, R., Brewer, E., Garofalakis, M., Shadle, M., Gandhi, P.: Intel Mash Maker: Join the Web. SIGMOD Rec. 36, 27–33 (2007)
16. Lin, J., Wong, J., Nichols, J., Cypher, A., Lau, T.A.: End-User Programming of Mashups With Vegemite. In: Proc. of IUI 2009 (2009)
17. Prähofer, H., Hurnaus, D., Mössenböck, H.: Building End-User Programming Systems Based on Domain-Specific Language (2006)
18. EMML, http://www.openmashup.org/)
19. Maximilien, E.M., Wilkinson, H., Desai, N., Tai, S.: A Domain-Specific Language for Web APIs and Services Mashups. In: Krämer, B.J., Lin, K.-J., Narasimhan, P. (eds.) ICSOC 2007. LNCS, vol. 4749, pp. 13–26. Springer, Heidelberg (2007)
20. Shu, N.C.: Visual Programming. Wiley (1992)
21. Yahoo Pipes, http://pipes.yahoo.com/pipes/)
22. IBM Mashup Center, http://www.ibm.com/software/info/mashup-center)
23. Nestler, T., Feldmann, M., Hübsch, G., Preußner, A., Jugel, U.: The ServFace Builder - A WYSIWYG Approach for Building Service-Based Applications. In: Benatallah, B., Casati, F., Kappel, G., Rossi, G. (eds.) ICWE 2010. LNCS, vol. 6189, pp. 498–501. Springer, Heidelberg (2010)
24. Presto Cloud, http://www.jackbe.com/enterprise-mashup/)
25. Namoun, A., Nestler, T., Angeli, A.D.: Service Composition for Non-programmers: Prospects, Problems, and Design Recommendations. In: ECOWS 2010 (2010)
26. Carlson, M.P., Ngu, A.H.H., Podorozhny, R., Zeng, L.: Automatic Mash Up of Composite Applications. In: Bouguettaya, A., Krueger, I., Margaria, T. (eds.) ICSOC 2008. LNCS, vol. 5364, pp. 317–330. Springer, Heidelberg (2008)
27. Bakalov, F., Konig-Ries, B., Nauerz, A., Welsch, M.: Ontology-Based Multidimensional Personalization Modeling for the Automatic Generation of Mashups in Next-Generation Portals. In: Proc. of ONTORACT 2008 (2008)
28. Hanson, J.J.: Mashups: Strategies for the Modern Enterprise. Addison-Wesley Professional (2009)
29. Daniel, F., Yu, J., Benatallah, B., Casati, F., Matera, M., Saint-Paul, R.: Understanding UI Integration: A Survey of Problems, Technologies, and Opportunities. IEEE Internet Computing 11, 59–66 (2007)
30. Di Lorenzo, G., Hacid, H., Paik, H.Y., Benatallah, B.: Data Integration in Mashups. SIGMOD Rec. 38, 59–66 (2009)
31. Dorn, C., Schall, D., Dustdar, S.: Context-aware adaptive service mashups. In: Proc. of APSCC 2009 (2009)
32. Grammel, L., Storey, M.A.: An End User Perspective on Mashup Makers. Technical report, University of Victoria (2008)
33. Vredenburg, K., Mao, J.Y., Smith, P.W., Carey, T.: A Survey of User-Centered Design Practice. In: Proc. of CHI 2002 (2002)
34. Myers, B.A., Pane, J.F., Ko, A.: Natural Programming Languages and Environments. Commun. ACM 47, 47–52 (2004)

# Multi-dimensional Context-Aware Adaptation
# for Web Applications

Vivian Genaro Motti and Jean Vanderdonckt

Louvain Interaction Laboratory – Louvain School of Management, Place des Doyens 1,
Université catholique de Louvain - 1348 Louvain la Neuve, Belgium
{vivian.genaromotti,jean.vanderdonckt}@uclouvain.be

**Abstract.** This tutorial presents the state-of-the-art of adaptation for web interfaces concerning multi-dimensionality and context-awareness. The specific goals include the presentation of: (i) fundamental concepts, as motivations, definitions and relevant context information; (ii) adaptation techniques for web applications, as methods, models, strategies and technologies; (iii) adaptable and adaptive web applications in scientific and commercial aspects.

**Keywords:** Web Interface Adaptation; Context-awareness; Multi-dimensions.

## 1   Context-aware Adaptation

A pre-defined context of use, of an able-bodied user, in a stable environment, with a conventional desktop PC, is often adopted for web applications currently developed. Though, actual web users are heterogeneous in their backgrounds, knowledge and goals; different devices, means and environments are used for interaction. Thus, considering a standard context of use may difficult or even prevent the interaction. Context concerns relevant information for the interaction, as: the user, the place, and available devices [1]. It can be mapped as a formal model by the triple (U,P,E) that characterizes the user, the platform and the environment [2]. The 'Future Internet' aims at providing users the right information, in the right time and in the right format, which requires high-level adaptation [3]. Since the early 90's, adaptation studies are being reported; in spite of the wide effort, the studies are widespread, and hard to be compiled to support the implementation of adaptation in web applications [4]. This tutorial presents an overview of the state of the art of Multi-Dimension Context-Aware Adaptation. It is organized in 3 parts:

**Fundamental Concepts.** Aiming to improve the users' interaction, adaptation transforms different levels and dimensions of systems. In this process context mainly involves user profiles, platforms and devices; and the dimensions are aspects, as modality or resources, subject to adaptation in different levels (e.g. at system level).

**Methods**. Many concepts support adaptation [5], [6] as: (i) The Context-Aware Design Space (CADS), a descriptive, exploratory and comparative, graphical representation for adaptation dimensions (means, UI component, deployment) [7];

A. Harth and N. Koch (Eds.): ICWE 2011 Workshops, LNCS 7059, pp. 352–354, 2012.
© Springer-Verlag Berlin Heidelberg 2012

(ii) The Context-Aware Reference Framework (CARF) lists context information, concerning: what, who, where, when, how, to what and why. A technique to adapt images can be initiated by the system, performed in the client, at run time, considering users and improve the accessibility; animation can be used to smoothly present it for users [8]; (iii) Technologies support the adaptation, but to accommodate varied scenarios, the system architecture must be organized in layers (content, presentation and processing), User-Interface Description Languages are recommended; (iv) Distinct adaptation levels are modeled in 3-layers, first-order rules define commands, as: R1='if it is a mobile device, then replace radio boxes by edit fields', a second-order and a third-order rule define priority strategies in richer ways 'if the user is an expert, then prefer R1 than R2' and 'if user is an expert and device is a tablet, then reverse the preference order of R1 and R2'. Evolutive models capture user feedbacks, analyzes dynamic context, adapting efficiently [9].

**Examples.** Many web applications exemplify adaptation, as (i) Rekimoto's pre-distributed pick and drop exemplifies static UI deployment [10]. Pick and drop extends the drag-and-drop paradigm, users select a resource icon, drag it to another device, copying and sharing it. (ii) Sedan-Bouillon is a plastic website, users specify platform screens for its workspaces that are re-molded and re-distributed at the workspace level (title, content, navigation bar) [11]. (iii) A toolkit distributes interfaces in different levels partitioning the GUI over the display processes and distributing over devices and users a complex application. An interface and a workspace can be decomposed and migrated, and atomic elements, as buttons, can be detached and distributed [12].

# References

1. Dey, A., Abowd, G.: CybreMinder: A Context-Aware System for Supporting Reminders. In: HUC 1999. LNCS, vol. 1707, pp. 172–186. Springer, Heidelberg (1999)
2. Calvary, G., et al.: A Unifying Reference Framework for Multi-Target User Interfaces. Interacting with Computers 15(3), 289–308 (2003)
3. Brusilovsky, P., Kobsa, A., Nejdl, W.: The Adaptive Web, Methods and Strategies of Web Personalization. Springer, Heidelberg (2007)
4. Motti, V.G.: A computational framework for multi-dimensional context-aware adaptation. In: Proceedings of the 3rd ACM SIGCHI Symposium on Engineering Interactive Computing Systems (EICS 2011), pp. 315–318. ACM, New York (2011), http://doi.acm.org/10.1145/1996461.1996545, doi:10.1145/1996461.1996545
5. de Koch, N.P.: Software Engineering for Adaptive Hypermedia Systems. Reference Model, Modeling Techniques and Development Process. Munich. Thesis (2000)
6. López-Jaquero, V., Vanderdonckt, J., Montero, F., González, P.: Towards an Extended Model of UI Adaptation: the ISATINE framework. In: Gulliksen, J., Harning, M.B., van der Veer, G.C., Wesson, J. (eds.) EIS 2007. LNCS, vol. 4940, pp. 374–392. Springer, Heidelberg (2008)

7. Vanderdonckt, J., Grolaux, D., Van Roy, P., Limbourg, Q., Macq, B., Michel, B.: A Design Space for Context-Sensitive User Interfaces. In: Proc. of ISCA - IASSE 2005, pp. 207–214 (2005)

8. Dessart, C.-E., Motti, V., Vanderdonckt, J.: Showing User Interface Adaptivity by Animated Transitions. In: Proc. EICS 2011, Pisa. ACM Press, New York (2011)

9. Vanderdonckt, J.: Model-Driven Engineering of User Interfaces: Promises, Successes, and Failures. In: Proc. of ROCHI 2008 (Iasi), pp. 1–10. Matrix ROM, Bucharest (2008)

10. Rekimoto, J.: Pick and Drop: A Direct Manipulation Technique for Multiple Computer Environments. In: Proc. of 10th UIST 1997, pp. 31–39. ACM Press, New York (1997)

11. Balme, L., Demeure, A., Calvary, G., Coutaz, J.: Sedan-Bouillon: A Plastic Web Site. In: PSMD 2005, INTERACT 2005 Workshop on Plastic Services for Mobile Devices (2005)

12. Melchior, J., Grolaux, D., Vanderdonckt, J., Van Roy, P.: A Toolkit for Peer-to-Peer DUI: Concepts, Implementation, and Applications. In: Proc. of EICS 2009, pp. 69–78. ACM Press (2009)

# Engineering the Personal Social Semantic Web

Fabian Abel and Geert-Jan Houben

Web Information Systems, Delft University of Technology
{f.abel,g.j.p.m.houben}@tudelft.nl

**Abstract.** In this tutorial, we discuss challenges and solutions for engineering the *Personal Social Semantic Web*, a Web where user modeling and personalization is featured across system boundaries. Therefore, we learn user modeling and personalization techniques for Social Web systems. We dive into engineering aspects of social tagging and microblogging services and examine appropriate modeling and mining techniques for these systems. We discuss Semantic Web and Linked Data principles that allow for linkage and alignment of distributed user data and show how system engineers can exploit the Social Semantic Web to personalize user experiences.

## 1  Summary

Social Web sites, such as Facebook, YouTube, Delicious, Flickr and Wikipedia, and numerous other Web applications, such as Google and Amazon, rely on implicitly or explicitly collected data about their users and their activities to provide personalized content and services. As these applications become more and more connected on the Web, a major challenge is to allow various applications to exchange, reuse, and integrate the user data from different sources. Such data comes in different flavors: user data such as user profiles, social networks, social tagging data, blogs, etc. as well as usage data like clickthrough data or query logs. The amount of user data available on the Web is tremendously growing so that sharing and mining these heterogeneous data corpora distributed on the Web is a non-trivial problem that poses several challenges to the Web engineering community.

A core challenge is to support people in overcoming the information overload on the Web. Here, adaptation and personalization are key strategies as people have individual demands and thus need individual support. However, understanding the personal demands of people is another non-trivial challenge. It requires appropriate solutions that allow for inferring and modeling the personal concerns, interests, preferences and other user characteristics. In this tutorial, we discuss user modeling and personalization within the context of today's Web sphere where Social Web systems foster user participation and where Semantic Web technologies provide means to engineer interoperable services.

This tutorial is composed of four modules: we give (i) an introduction into basic concepts and approaches for user modeling, adaptation and personalization (UMAP) on the Web and (ii) summarize methods and metrics that allow

A. Harth and N. Koch (Eds.): ICWE 2011 Workshops, LNCS 7059, pp. 355–356, 2012.

engineers and researchers to evaluate the quality of UMAP systems. We outline (iii) basic and advanced models and algorithms for implementing UMAP functionality in the context of Social Web systems and finally present (iv) strategies and techniques for engineering the personalized systems on the Social Web by leveraging Semantic Web technologies. In each module we give an overview of related work and recent trends, discuss selected models, algorithms and techniques in detail and provide hands-on examples.

**Introduction to UMAP.** We introduce basic user modeling techniques such as stereotyping or overlay user modeling, basic adaptation principles and personalization techniques. In particular, we summarize core principles of content-based and collaborative recommender systems and present Web mining methods.

**Evaluation of UMAP systems.** Evaluating the quality of user modeling and personalization often requires implicit or explicit user feedback which can be costly to obtain. We give an overview on evaluation strategies such as user studies and leave-n-out evaluation methods. Furthermore, we outline useful metrics, significance tests and present examples on evaluating UMAP functionality on the Web.

**UMAP on the Social Web.** Here, we discuss models and techniques for inferring user interests in Social Web systems and exploiting user profiles for personalization such as personalized search or social recommender systems. Moreover, we examine the challenges and opportunities of cross-system user modeling and personalization.

**Engineering the Personal Social Semantic Web.** Given techniques learnt before, we investigate principles for personalizing user experiences in the Social Semantic Web. We discuss Linked Data principles, techniques for connecting online accounts of users – including useful vocabularies, tools and services – and approaches for aligning user data originating from different sources. Based on these solutions, we explore architectures for cross-system user modeling and personalization, methods and protocols for ensuring trust and privacy and outline future perspectives for building a Personal Social Semantic Web.

Some parts of this tutorial are based on [2]. Supplemental material, slides and references for this tutorial are publicly available via the supporting website [1].

# References

1. Abel, F., Houben, G.J.: Engineering the Personal Social Semantic Web – Supporting Website (2011), http://wis.ewi.tudelft.nl/icwe2011/tutorial/
2. Abel, F., Herder, E., Houben, G.J., Henze, N., Krause, D.: Cross-system User Modeling and Personalization on the Social Web. In: User Modeling and User-Adapted Interaction (UMUAI), Special Issue on Personalization in Social Web Systems, vol. 22(3), pp. 1–42 (2011)

# Automating the Use of Web APIs through Lightweight Semantics

Maria Maleshkova[1], Carlos Pedrinaci[1], Dong Liu[1], and Guillermo Alvaro[2]

[1] Knowledge Media Institute (KMi)
The Open University, Milton Keynes, United Kingdom
{m.maleshkova,c.pedrinaci,d.liu}@open.ac.uk
[2] Intelligent Software Components (iSOCO). Madrid, Spain
{galvaro}@isoco.com

**Abstract.** Web services have already achieved a solid level of acceptance and play a major role for the rapid development of loosely-coupled component-based systems, overcoming heterogeneity within and between enterprises. Current developments in the world of services on the Web are marked by the proliferation of Web APIs and Web applications, commonly referred to as RESTful services, which show high potential and growing user acceptance. Still, despite the achieved progress, the wider adoption of Web APIs is hindered by the fact that their implementation and publication hardly follow any standard guidelines or formats. REST principles are indeed a good step in this direction but the vast majority of the APIs do not strictly adhere to these principles. As a consequence, in order to use them, developers are obliged to manually locate, retrieve, read and interpret heterogeneous documentation, and subsequently develop custom tailored software, which has a very low level of reusability. In summary, most tasks during the life-cycle of services require extensive manual effort and applications based on existing Web APIs suffer from a lack of automation.

This tutorial introduces an approach and a set of integrated methods and tools to address this drawback, making services more accessible to both experts and non-expert users, by increasing the level of automation provided during common service tasks, such as the discovery of Web APIs, their composition and their invocation. The tutorial covers i) the conceptual underpinnings, which integrate Web APIs with state of the art technologies from the Web of Data and Semantic Web Services; ii) the presentation of an integrated suite of Web-based tools supporting service users; iii) and hands-on examples illustrating how the tools and technologies can help users in finding and exploiting existing Web APIs.

## 1  Description

The tutorial is entirely driven by and supported by current developments on the Web, and will familiarise the participants with innovative yet applicable tools and technologies that could directly be integrated in Web developers daily activities. It provides both key background information as well as an approach for addressing some of the main challenges faced when using Web APIs. We introduce an integrated set of tools, which support the automated use of APIs:

A. Harth and N. Koch (Eds.): ICWE 2011 Workshops, LNCS 7059, pp. 357–358, 2012.

– Web API Annotation via SWEET [1] is a Web application that supports users in creating lightweight semantic descriptions of Web APIs by enabling the marking of service properties within HTML documentation and associating these with semantic annotations.

– Storage and discovery via iServe [2] is a public registry of semantic Web services, which unifies service publication and discovery on the Web through the use of semantics. iServe imports the semantic descriptions of Web services conforming to heterogeneous formalisms (hRESTS, MicroWSMO, SAWSDL, and OWL-S) and publishes them as RDF triples on the Web of Data using a lightweight service model.

– Consumption via the generic client of an invocation framework that provides a unique entry point for the invocation of most Web APIs that can be found on the Web. The framework relies on non-intrusive semantic annotations of HTML pages describing Web APIs, in order to capture both their semantics as well as information necessary to carry out their invocation.

## 2    Tutorial Modules

Introduction (morning session): This presentation provides required background information, short overview of the key issues and concepts related to the usage of Web services, best practices while dealing with Web APIs, and the support offered through applying lightweight semantics.

- Current trends and developments in the world of services on the Web
- Problems and challenges faced when using Web APIs
- Current approaches for discovering and invoking Web APIs
- Best practices with Web APIs and use of lightweight semantics

Hands-on session part I (afternoon session): Using the presented approach and tools to support Web API search and discovery.

- Performing service search without tools support
- Web service annotation
- Web service search and discovery

Hands-on session part II (afternoon session): Using the presented approach and tools to support service invocation.

- Invoking services
- Service monitoring
- Example applications and implementations

Slides from the training session can be viewed at http://www.slideshare.net/mmaleshkova/automating-the-use-of-web-apis-through-lightweight-semantics.

## References

1. SWEET, http://sweet.kmi.open.ac.uk
2. iServe, http://iserve.kmi.open.ac.uk

# Improving Quality in Use of Web Applications in a Systematic Way

Philip Lew[1] and Luis Olsina[2]

[1] School of Software, Beihang University, China
[2] GIDIS&Web, Engineering School, Universidad Nacional de La Pampa, Argentina
philiplew@gmail.com, olsina1@ing.unlpam.edu.ar

**Abstract.** A first step to evaluate quality is to define nonfunctional requirements usually through quality models. The ISO 25010 standard describes one such model for general usage in specifying and evaluating software quality requirements, but its concepts need to be adapted based on a specific information need and context, i.e. for evaluating WebApps in a real situation particularly when it comes to evaluating quality in use (QinU). WebApps and their quality evaluation have been proposed in research through many approaches, but mostly for the purpose of understanding, rather than improving. In this tutorial, we demonstrate employing a quality modeling framework and strategy to instantiate quality models with the specific purpose not only to understand the current situation of a WebApp, but also to improve it.

**Keywords:** Quality in use, Actual usability, Improvement, SIQinU strategy.

## 1  Tutorial Contents

Web applications (WebApps) have evolved considerably since the simple informational and ecommerce websites of the 90's. We start by giving an overview of the Web eras as well as the unique intrinsic features of WebApps. This characterization will help us identifying/mapping quality features. As background, the ISO 25010 [1] characteristics and the relationship among internal quality, external quality, and QinU models are discussed. We argue the need to model *information quality* and *learnability in use* dimensions for measuring and evaluating quality for WebApps which is absent in this standard.

Then, we illustrate how to instantiate quality models for the purpose of improvement assuming that understanding is the means and improvement is the ultimate goal. With evaluation as a step toward improvement, quality models must be instantiated with this in mind. So, by using the 2Q2U (*Quality, Quality in use, Usability and User experience*) modeling framework [2, 4], we show how to instantiate external quality (EQ) and QinU models with the goal of improving. These models are developed and used while executing a specific strategy for improving QinU for WebApps, namely SIQinU (*Strategy for Improving Quality in Use*) [3].

SIQinU has a six-phased process which starts with identifying problems in the QinU of a WebApp and then characterizing these problems using an instantiated QinU model. These problems come from evaluating a WebApp in a real context of

A. Harth and N. Koch (Eds.): ICWE 2011 Workshops, LNCS 7059, pp. 359–360, 2012.

use, collecting data directly from the application through the use of weblogs. Weblogs are not new, but this approach is novel in that our objective in data collection is not related to where users go and how long they stay on each page, but rather related to when executing planned real tasks. These problems in QinU are then mapped to potential problems in the WebApp's EQ, or intrinsic properties which lead to deriving a specific instantiated EQ model for the WebApp that is tied to the problems in QinU. This is followed by evaluating the WebApp using this EQ model resulting in an EQ benchmark. The EQ benchmark gives us indication of poorly performing EQ attributes and these poorly performing attributes give us the basis to make recommendations for improvements to the WebApp. After recommendations have been implemented, we evaluate EQ again to determine where and to what degree EQ was improved. Then finally, we use the same context of use as in the first phase, using real users executing a real task, and evaluate QinU again to determine the improvement gained as a result of the changes in EQ and improvements just made.

Ultimately, in the process of using SIQinU, we are able to gain insight regarding the *depends on* and *influences* relationships [1] for the particular 2Q2U instantiated models, and their characteristics and attributes driven by our purpose to improve. In addition, we can continue to iterate the SIQinU improvement cycle to gain further insight and granularity adding a temporal component for later study. Finally, in the tutorial, we illustrate SIQinU using JIRA (www.atlassian.com), a well-known defect tracking WebApp, by specifying a task designed to collect information at the sub-task level so that specific screens and their properties (EQ attributes) could be identified for potential problems leading to poor performance in QinU.

# References

1. ISO/IEC 25010:2011(E): Systems and software engineering. Systems and software Quality Requirements and Evaluation (SQuaRE). System and software quality models (2011)
2. Lew, P., Olsina, L., Zhang, L.: Quality, Quality in Use, Actual Usability and User Experience as Key Drivers for Web Application Evaluation. In: Benatallah, B., Casati, F., Kappel, G., Rossi, G. (eds.) ICWE 2010. LNCS, vol. 6189, pp. 218–232. Springer, Heidelberg (2010)
3. Lew, P., Olsina, L.: Instantiating Web Quality Models in a Purposeful Way. In: Auer, S., Díaz, O., Papadopoulos, G.A. (eds.) ICWE 2011. LNCS, vol. 6757, pp. 214–227. Springer, Heidelberg (2011)
4. Olsina, L., Papa, F., Molina, H.: How to Measure and Evaluate Web Applications in a Consistent Way. In: Modelling and Implementing Web Applications, ch. 13, pp. 385–420. Springer HCIS (2008)

# Author Index

Abel, Fabian 355
Abu Helou, Mamoun 135
Achilleos, Achilleas 181
Aghaee, Saeed 1, 347
Alarcon, Rosa 74
Alvaro, Guillermo 357

Bellido, Jesus 74
Biewald, Lukas 171
Blichmann, Gregor 25
Bolchini, Davide 289
Bozzon, Alessandro 109
Brambilla, Marco 109
Braunschweig, Katrin 302

Chaisatien, Prach 332
Chudnovskyy, Olexiy 37
Clemente, Pedro J. 236
Cohen, Marcelo 119
Conejero, José María 236

Daniel, Florian 49
Della Valle, Emanuele 109
Dolog, Peter 145
Domingue, John 13
Durao, Frederico 145

Eberius, Julian 337
Eickhoff, Christoph 196
Escalona, Maria Jose 278
Escott, Eban 223

Fayzrakhmanov, Ruslan R. 342
Firmenich, Sergio 327
Fraternali, Piero 109

Gaedke, Martin 37
Gebhardt, Hendrik 37
Geiger, Nina 196
Genaro Motti, Vivian 352
Gordillo, Silvia 327
Granić, Andrina 266

Hahn, Marcel 196
Hayes, Ian J. 223
Herbert, Matthias 99

Hölzl, Matthias 211
Houben, Geert-Jan 355

Jayakanthan, Ranganathan 177
Jugel, Uwe 49

Kalchgruber, Peter 307
Kapitsaki, Georgia M. 181
Katz, Philipp 312
Keller, Matthias 155
Kermek, Dragutin 266
King, Paul 223
Kmieciak, Miłosz 86
Ko, Han-Gyu 127
Ko, In-Young 127
Kochman, Sebastian 86
Kopecký, Jacek 13

Lage, Ricardo 145
Lautamäki, Janne 62
Leginus, Martin 145
Lehner, Wolfgang 302, 337
Lew, Philip 359
Li, Ning 13
Liu, Dong 13, 357

Mainetti, Luca 289
Maleshkova, Maria 13, 357
Malý, Jakub 317
Mather, Neil 322
Meißner, Klaus 25
Mikkonen, Tommi 62
Morales-Chaparro, Rober 159

Nebeling, Michael 167
Nečaský, Martin 317
Norrie, Moira C. 167
Nussbaumer, Martin 155

Olsina, Luis 359
Orehovački, Tihomir 266
Oussena, Samia 322

Paiano, Roberto 289
Pandurino, Andrea 289

Papadopoulos, George A.    181
Pasini, Chiara    109
Pautasso, Cesare    1, 347
Pedrinaci, Carlos    13, 357
Pietschmann, Stefan    25
Polillo, Roberto    251
Preciado, Juan C.    159, 236
Prutsachainimmit, Korawit    332

Robles Luna, Esteban    278
Rodríguez-Echeverría, Roberto    236
Rossi, Gustavo    278, 327
Roßnagel, Heiko    99

Sánchez-Figueroa, Fernando    159, 236
Schill, Alexander    312
Schwabe, Daniel    119
Sepulveda, Cristian    74
Soi, Stefano    49

Strooper, Paul    223
Sundararajan, Deepak    177

Thiele, Maik    302, 337
Thieme, Tobias    99
Tietz, Vincent    25
Tokuda, Takehiro    332

Urbieta, Matias    278

Vanderdonckt, Jean    352

Weinhold, Frank    37
Wilson, Scott    49
Winckler, Marco    327
Wojciechowski, Paweł T.    86

Zhang, Gefei    211
Zibuschka, Jan    99
Zündorf, Albert    196